How Asians View Democratic Legitimacy

T0396388

EDITED BY | YUN-HAN CHU
YU-TZUNG CHANG
MIN-HUA HUANG
KAI-PING HUANG

How Asians View Democratic Legitimacy

Edited by Yun-han Chu, Yu-tzung Chang, Min-hua Huang, and Kai-Ping Huang
© National Taiwan University Press 2023

ISBN 978-986-350-718-5
GPN 1011200265

This book has been peer-reviewed and accepted for publication
by National Taiwan University Press.

National Taiwan University Press
No. 1, Sec. 4, Roosevelt Rd., Taipei, Taiwan 106, R.O.C.
https://press.ntu.edu.tw
E-mail: ntuprs@ntu.edu.tw

In memory of
our colleague, mentor, and friend,
Professor Yun-han Chu

Acknowledgments

This volume was written to mark the 20th anniversary of the Asian Barometer Survey (ABS). The ABS was established in 2001 by Professor Yun-han Chu with the goal of studying the democratization of East and Southeast Asia, and the network has since grown to include most countries in the region. The ABS also serves as the secretariat of the Global Barometer Surveys (GBS), which coordinates regional surveys in Africa, the Arab region, Eurasia, and Latin America. The success of both the ABS and GBS would not have been possible without Professor Chu's leadership. Unfortunately, COVID-19 delayed the publication of this commemorative volume and as we prepared to finally launch the volume, our beloved Professor Chu sadly passed away on February 5, 2023. Professor Chu was a respected teacher and scholar, and he played a crucial role in promoting Taiwan's relationship with the international academic community. His absence will be profoundly mourned by both his peers and his students. This volume is a tribute to him and his devotion to research in the social sciences. Professor Chu inspired countless students and researchers, and his legacy will continue to live on in the lives of those who knew him.

本書總結亞洲民主動態調查二十年來的成就，以紀念亞洲民主動態調查對全球民主化研究的貢獻。亞洲民主動態調查由朱雲漢院士於 2001 年成立，目的在就東亞和東南亞地區民眾的態度做追蹤以理解其對民主體制的看法與支持。在朱院士多年的努力與帶領下，亞洲民主動態調查持續擴張並涵蓋區域內多數國家，且進一步成為全球民主動態調查的秘書處，負責協調非洲、阿拉伯地區、歐亞地區和拉丁美洲的調查。本書原訂於 2021 年出版，但因新冠肺炎疫情而延遲，當我們終於完成這本紀念集時，我們敬愛的朱院士於 2023 年 2 月 5 日與世長辭。朱院士是一位受人尊敬的老師與學者，他極力推動台灣與國際學術界的交流並增加台灣在全球民主化研究的能見度。朱院士的離世，是亞洲民主動態調查與國際社會科學領域的重大損失，悲痛之情溢於言表，全體師生同表沉痛悼念。本書致敬朱院士及其為學術界的奉獻，朱院士啟發了無數學生與學術同儕，他的精神與智慧將永存人間。

Table of Contents

Figures and Tables

Tables

Preface

This book celebrates the 20th anniversary of the Asian Barometer Survey (ABS). The ABS is an applied research program on public opinion toward political values, democracy and governance, and development across the region. This research project has four main objectives, including generating scientifically reliable and comparable data, strengthening intellectual capacity for democracy studies, disseminating survey results to the public, and advancing the research frontiers of the global study of democratization under the auspices of the Global Barometer Surveys (GBS).

In the last two decades, the ABS has conducted five rounds of surveys and published hundreds of articles and books exploring and explaining important intellectual puzzles. The ABS provided empirically grounded answers to the lingering authoritarian nostalgia among citizens in the region. It dispelled the myth that contextual factors in Asia, such as political culture and electoral politics, might mitigate the negative effects of corruption on political trust. Instead, it found a strong trust-eroding effect of political corruption in Asian democracies. There was also no evidence that contextual factors lessened the corruption-trust link in Asia. The ABS is also the pioneer in systematically analyzing the demand side dynamics in making sense of the growing popular disenchantment with democracy. Now, Covid-19 is creating a new kind of stress test. There is a demand—from policy actors, investors, journalists, researchers, and ordinary people themselves—for reliable information about popular political orientations and preferences as well as about how citizens evaluate the quality of democratic governance. The ABS's mission is to assist practitioners and policy makers in identifying areas of weakness in the existing political system, which have helped inform policy elites at many U.S.-based and international NGOs and donor organizations.

The ABS has built a solid academic foundation over the years, and there is no better way to celebrate the accomplishments than with a commemorative volume containing important findings uncovered by our colleagues in the region and around the world. We also include chapters focusing on individual countries in order to compare and contrast specific dynamics affecting the future of democracy in the region. In the past two decades, the ABS has been made possible by the contributors of this volume. Furthermore, the ABS is indebted to government agencies and international organizations for funding this ever-expanding endeavor. Among the organizations that contributed to this project are the Ministries of Education and Science and Technology in Taiwan, the Institute of Political Science at Academia Sinica, the Henry Luce Foundation, the World Bank, and the UNDP. As well as commemorating the long-term collective efforts of those involved in the ABS in various forms, this edited volume also marks an important moment that will hopefully inspire the future generations who will work together under the auspices of ABS and GBS.

Editors

Yun-han Chu was Distinguished Research Fellow in the Institute of Political Science at Academia Sinica and Professor of Political Science at National Taiwan University. He was the founder of the Asian Barometer Survey and specialized in the politics of Greater China, East Asian political economy, and democratization. He was the Coordinator of the Asian Barometer Survey, regional network of survey on democracy, governance, and development, covering more than eighteen Asian countries. He also served on the editorial board of the *Journal of Democracy*, *China Review*, *Journal of Contemporary China*, *International Studies Perspectives*, *Journal of Chinese Political Studies*, *China Perspective*, *China: An International Journal*, and *Journal of East Asian Studies*. He was the author, coauthor, editor, and coeditor of seventeen books.

Yu-tzung Chang is the Director of Fu Hu Center for Democratic Studies and Professor of Political Science at National Taiwan University. He is currently the co-principal investigator of the Asian Barometer Survey. He studies democratization, electoral politics, and the political economy of East Asia. His research has appeared in journals such as the *Journal of Democracy*, *Democratization*, *Electoral Studies*, *International Political Science Review*, *Journal of East Asian Studies*, *Journal of Contemporary China*, *International Journal of Public Opinion Research*, *Issues & Studies*, and *Taiwan Journal of Democracy*.

Min-hua Huang is Professor in the Department of Political Science at the College of Social Sciences in National Taiwan University and the Principal Investigator of the Asian Barometer Survey. He specializes in the politics of China, democratic legitimacy, methodology, and democratization. Before joining NTU, he worked at Shanghai Jiaotong University, Texas A&M University, and National Chengchi University. He was also a Visiting Fellow at the Brookings Institution's Center for East Asia Policy Studies (2014-2015). His recent writings include "The Anti-Corruption Campaign, Luxury Consumption, and Regime Trust in China: Changing Patterns of Perceived Political Risk and Their Consequences" with Chi-Hsien Kuo and Ching-I Huang, *Journal of Contemporary China* (2022); "Evaluation of COVID-19 Governance in China: The Effects of Media Use, Pandemic Severity, and Provincial Heterogeneity" with Ruixia Han and Jian Xu, *Journal of Asian Public Policy* (2022); and "Cognitive Explanations of Indian Perceptions of China" with Yongrong Cao and Hsin-Che Wu, *Asian Survey* (2021). His degrees are from the

University of Michigan (Ph.D.), the National Sun Yat-Sen University (M.A.), and National Taiwan University (B.A.).

Kai-Ping Huang is Associate Professor of Political Science at National Taiwan University. Her research interests include party systems, formal institutions, and democratization focusing on East and Southeast Asia. Her work has appeared in the *Journal of Democracy*, *Comparative Politics*, *Journal of Contemporary China*, *Journal of East Asian Studies*, and several edited volumes.

Contributors

Le Bao is a Postdoctoral Fellow in the Massive Data Institute (MDI) at the McCourt School of Public Policy, Georgetown University. He studies political methodology and comparative political behavior. He received his Ph.D. in Political Science from American University in 2022 and was a Visiting Fellow at the Institute for Quantitative Social Science, Harvard University.

Thawilwadee Bureekul is the Deputy Secretary-General of King Prajadhipok's Institute (KPI) where she is involved in the planning, management, implementation, and coordination of the Institute's research projects. In addition to her role at KPI, Dr. Bureekul is a professor at several universities in Thailand, including the Asian Institute of Technology, Thammasat University, Burapha University, Mahidol University, and Silpakorn University. She succeeded in proposing "Gender Responsive Budgeting" in the Thai Constitution, and she was granted the "Woman of the Year 2018" award and received the outstanding award on "Rights Projection and Strengthening Gender Equality" in the Year 2022 as a result.

Eric C. C. Chang is Associate Professor of Political Science at Michigan State University. His primary areas of interest are comparative political economy, comparative political institutions, and democratization.

Larry Diamond is a Senior Fellow at the Hoover Institution, the Mosbacher Senior Fellow in Global Democracy at the Freeman Spogli Institute for International Studies (FSI), and a Bass University Fellow in Undergraduate Education at Stanford University. He is also Professor by courtesy of Political Science and Sociology at Stanford and served for 32 years as founding co-editor of the *Journal of Democracy*. He leads the Hoover Institution's programs on China's Global Sharp Power and on Taiwan in the Indo-Pacific Region. His book, *Ill Winds: Saving Democracy from Russian Rage, Chinese Ambition*, and *American Complacency*, analyzes the challenges confronting liberal democracy in the United States and around the world at this potential "hinge in history" and offers an agenda for strengthening and defending democracy at home and abroad.

Damba Ganbat is a Chairman of the Board of the Academy of Political Education in Ulaanbaatar, Mongolia. The Academy of Political Education is a non-government institution which engages in research and training both in the city and countryside and has made key contributions in promoting democratic values such as human rights and freedoms, rule of law, role of an individual in the society and democratic election. From 1999 to 2010, he worked as an Executive Director of the Academy. Since 2009 to 2017, he had been an advisor to the President of Mongolia on research and a Director of the Institute for Strategic Studies of Mongolia. From September 2017 to 2021, he was an Ambassador of Mongolia to Federal Republic of Germany.

Jung-ah Gil is Research Professor at Korea University. She received her Ph.D. in Political Science from Seoul National University in 2019. Her primary areas of interest in research are political attitudes among citizens, especially voting behavior and recent mass polarization. Dr. Gil's work has been published in several English and Korean journals, such as *Social Science Research*, *Korean Political Science Review*, and *Korean Party Studies Review*.

Linda Luz Guerrero is President and CEO of Social Weather Stations (SWS) and Vice-President/President-elect of the World Association for Public Opinion Research (WAPOR) Asia and the Pacific. She directs all the cross-country projects of SWS, namely the World Values Survey, the Comparative Study of Electoral Systems, the International Social Survey Programme, and the Asian Barometer (formerly called Comparative Survey of Democratization and Value Changes in East Asia). She was a Fulbright scholar in 2002 and a Betty Go Belmonte awardee on Peace and Social Cohesion in 2010.

Ken'ichi Ikeda (Ph.D.) has been a professor in the Department of Media, Journalism and Communications at Doshisha University, Kyoto, Japan since April 2013, after 21 years of teaching at the University of Tokyo. He is interested in social/political participation, voting behavior, and the mediated effects of Internet use on political behavior. He published books such as *Political Discussion in Modern Democracies: A Comparative Perspective* in 2010 (co-editor, Routledge), *Social Networks and Japanese Democracy* in 2011 (with Sean Richey, Routledge), and *International Encyclopedia of Political Communication* in 2015 (3 Volumes, associate editor, Wiley-Blackwell), and *Contemporary Japanese Politics & Anxiety Over Governance* in 2023 (single authored, Routledge). In Japanese, he published more than 20 books in these 30 years.

Gillian Koh is the Deputy Director (Research) and Senior Research Fellow in the Governance and Economy Department at the Institute of Policy Studies, National

University of Singapore, and part of the Asian Barometer Survey (Singapore) team. Her research interests are in the areas of party and electoral politics, the development of civil society, state-society relations, and state governance and citizen engagement in Singapore. Among other things, Dr. Koh conducts surveys on Singaporeans' political attitudes, sense of identity, rootedness and resilience and also helmed several IPS scenario-planning projects. Dr. Koh has published and co-published articles on civil society and political development in Singapore. She was the co-editor of *Migration and Integration in Singapore: Policies and Practice* (2015) as well as *State-Society Relations in Singapore* (2000) and *Civil Society and the State in Singapore* (2017), and also the co-author of *Singapore Chronicles: Civil Society* (2016) as well as *Social Capital in Singapore: The Power of Network Diversity* (2021).

Iremae D. Labucay is a Fellow at Social Weather Stations. She has nearly 20 years of experience in survey research methodology, management, and analysis.

Wai-man Lam is Associate Professor cum Head of Social Sciences at School of Arts and Social Sciences, Hong Kong Metropolitan University. Her current research interests include comparative government and civil society, global governance, political culture and identity, and state-society relations. She has published widely, including book chapters and journal articles in *Citizenship Studies*, *The China Quarterly*, *Social Indicators Research*, *Journal of East Asian Studies* and elsewhere. She is the author and joint author of two books on Hong Kong's political culture and public policy making and the coeditor of three existing volumes on Hong Kong politics.

Xuchuan Lei is Professor and Associate Dean in the School of Public Administration of Southwest Jiaotong University. His main research fields are political culture, political behavior, and policy analysis.

Jie Lu, Associate Dean of International Affairs at the School of International Studies, is Ye Chenghai Chair Professor of Political Science at Renmin University of China. Before joining Renmin University of China in 2019, he taught at American University in Washington, DC, as Assistant Professor and tenured Associate Professor. His fields of research include local governance, the political economy of institutional change, public opinion, and political participation. His regional expertise focuses on the Greater China Region and East Asia. Dr. Lu is the co-author of *Understandings of Democracy: Origins and Consequences Beyond Western Democracies* (Oxford University Press, 2022) and the author of *Varieties of Governance in China: Migration and Institutional Change in Chinese Villages* (Oxford University Press,

2015). Dr. Lu obtained his Ph.D. in Political Science at Duke University. He received his M.A. in international relations and B.A. in environmental engineering from Tsinghua University, China.

Ngok Ma is currently Associate Professor at the Department of Government and Public Administration, Chinese University of Hong Kong. His research areas include party politics and elections, democratization, state-society relations, value changes and social movements in Hong Kong. He is the author of *Political Development in Hong Kong: State, Political Society and Civil Society* (University of Hong Kong Press, 2007). He has published nine books, more than 25 journal articles, and more than 30 book chapters on Hong Kong politics. His newest work is on the 2019 Anti-Extradition Movement: *The Resistant Community: the 2019 Anti-Extradition Movement in Hong Kong*（《反抗的共同體：二〇一九香港反送中運動》）.

Saiful Mujani is Professor of Political Science at the Universitas Islam Negeri Syarif Hidayatullah Jakarta in Jakarta, Indonesia. His publications appear in several scientific journals such as *American Journal of Political Science*, *Comparative Political Studies*, *Journal of Experimental Political Science*, and *Journal of Democracy*. His most recent books are *Voting Behavior in Indonesia since Democratization* (Cambridge University Press, 2018) and *Piety and Public Opinion: Understanding Indonesian Islam* (Oxford University Press, 2018).

Andrew J. Nathan is Class of 1919 Professor of Political Science at Columbia University. He studies the politics and foreign policy of China, political participation and political culture in Asia, and the international human rights regime. Nathan's books include *Chinese Democracy* (1985), *The Tiananmen Papers* (2001), *China's Search for Security* (2012), *Will China Democratize?* (2013), and *China's Influence and the Center-Periphery Tug of War in Hong Kong, Taiwan and Indo-Pacific* (2021). He has served at Columbia as Director of the Weatherhead East Asian Institute and as Chair of the Political Science Department. He is Chair of the Morningside Institutional Review Board (IRB). Off campus, he is a member of the Board of Human Rights in China and a former board member of the National Endowment for Democracy and of Freedom House. He is the regular Asia and Pacific book reviewer for Foreign Affairs.

Hyunjin Oh is Assistant Professor in the Department of Policy Studies at Hanyang University. She received her Ph.D. from the Department of Politics at the University of Virginia. She worked as a Research Professor at the Institute of

Governmental Studies and Research Fellow at the Varieties of Governance Center of Korea University. Her research interests include comparative political attitudes and behaviors, the quality of democracy, and democratic citizenship.

Chong-Min Park is Professor Emeritus of Public Administration and former Dean of the College of Political Science and Economics at Korea University. He has directed the Asian Barometer Survey in South Korea.

Steven Rood is the Fellow-in-Residence and Board Member of Social Weather Stations and Visiting Fellow at the Australian National University College of Asia and the Pacific.

Ratchawadee Sangmahamad is a senior academic of the Research and Development Office at King Prajadhipok's Institute. Her research focuses on gender, citizenship, election studies, and conducting the quantitative research. She has published books as a co-author, such as *Value Culture and Thermometer of Democracy*, *Thai Citizens: Democratic Civic Education*, *Thai Women and Elections: Opportunities for Equality*, and many articles.

Shreyas Sardesai is a survey researcher based in New Delhi. He spent over a decade working for the Lokniti programme of the Centre for the Study of Developing Societies, a well-known and highly cited survey research organization in India. He also has extensive news media experience having worked with some of India's leading TV news channels for eight years before entering the survey research domain in 2010. He studied History at St. Stephen's College, Delhi (B.A.) and Political Science at Jawaharlal Nehru University, Delhi (M.A.).

Paul Schuler is Associate Professor in the School of Government and Public Policy at the University of Arizona. He specializes in Southeast Asia and authoritarian regimes.

Sandeep Shastri is Professor of Political Science and Vice Chancellor of Jagran Lakecity University in Bhopal, India. He is the Coordinator of the South Asia Barometer which is a part of the Asia Barometer.

Jill Sheppard is a senior lecturer in the School of Politics and International Relations at the Australian National University. Her research interests are elections and voting, compulsory voting, political participation, and public opinion, particularly in Australia but also in a comparative context. She is an investigator on several major survey studies of Australian public opinion and behavior, including the Australian Election Study, World Values Survey, and Asian Barometer Survey.

Doh Chull Shin is a US-based social scientist conducting comparative research on democratic politics and human well-being. His books on the former include *Confucianism and Democratization in East Asia* and *Mass Politics and Culture in Democratizing Korea*, which Cambridge University Press published. The books on the latter include *The Quality of Life in Confucian Asia* and *The Quality of Life in Korea*, which Springer published. He has also published over 100 articles in a variety of professional journals. Of these articles, the one on avowed happiness has been citied more than 2,000 times in myriads of disciplinary and multidisciplinary journals published across the world.

Ern Ser Tan is Associate Professor of Department of Sociology, Academic Convener of Singapore Studies, Faculty of Arts and Social Sciences, and Academic Adviser of Social Lab, Institute of Policy Studies at the National University of Singapore. He received his Ph.D. from Cornell University, USA. He is the author of "Does Class Matter?" (2004, World Scientific), "Class and Social Orientations" (2015, IPS), and "Public Housing and Social Mixing" (2020, UN-Habitat) and a co-author of *Social Capital in Singapore: The Power of Network Diversity* (2021, Routledge). He is Chairman of the Research Advisory Panel, Housing and Development Board (HDB). He was appointed a Justice of the Peace in 2013.

Kay Key Teo is a Research Fellow at the Institute of Policy Studies, Social Lab, a research center at the National University of Singapore. Her research interests are in political and social attitudes, public opinion, voting behavior, and Singapore society. She is interested in examining these topics using a mix of quantitative and qualitative methods.

Mai Truong is Assistant Professor of Political Science at Mount St. Mary's University. She received her Ph.D. in Political Science from the University of Arizona. She studies contentious politics under authoritarian rule. Her regional focus is Southeast Asia.

Chris Weber is Professor in the School of Government and Public Policy at the University of Arizona. He specializes in political psychology and political behavior, with a focus on American political campaigns and ideology.

Stan Hok-wui Wong is a Visiting Associate Professor at the University of St. Thomas. His research interest centers on democratization, public opinions, social movement, and comparative authoritarianism with a focus on East Asia. He has published academic articles in peer-reviewed journals such as *British Journal of Political Science*, *China Quarterly*, *Journal of Peace Research*, and *Political Behavior*. He is the author of *Electoral Politics in Post-1997 Hong Kong*.

Chin-en Wu is an Associate Research Fellow at the Institute of Political Science at Academia Sinica, Taiwan. He received his Ph.D. from the University of Michigan. His main research interests include political economy of development, democratization, and party system.

Wen-chin Wu is an Associate Research Fellow of the Institute of Political Science at Academia Sinica (IPSAS), Taiwan. His research focuses on comparative and international political economy, comparative authoritarianism, and Chinese politics. He is particularly interested in the economic statecraft and media politics in dictatorships. Dr. Wu received his B.A. from National Chengchi University, M.A. from National Chengchi University and Katholieke Universiteit Leuven, and Ph.D. from Michigan State University. Before joining the IPSAS, Dr. Wu was a postdoctoral fellow of the Asian Barometer Survey co-hosted by the IPSAS and National Taiwan University. During the 2019-2020 academic year, he was a visiting scholar at the Harvard-Yenching Institute at Harvard University. Dr. Wu has published in *Democratization*, *International Studies Quarterly*, *Journal of Contemporary China*, *Political Communication*, among others.

Yang Zhang is Assistant Professor of Political Science at Renmin University of China. His research interests include public opinion, political participation, and social networks, with a focus on China.

1 Introduction to *How Asians View Democratic Legitimacy*

Yun-han Chu

Global Trend and Regional Context

For decades, liberal democracy has been extolled as the best system of governance to have emerged out of the long experience of history. Today, such a confident assertion is far from self-evident. Indeed, we are witnessing the end of "the-end-of-history" triumphalism. Instead, democracy is facing a global crisis. The long-expected democratic transitions in authoritarian regimes and consolidation of new democracies have come to a halt or even been reversed. In Western democracies, the rise of authoritarian populism poses critical challenges to the practices of liberal democracy. Many basic tenets that explain the resiliency of American democracy were called into question under Donald Trump, and the country is likely to be consumed by divisions for the foreseeable future despite Biden's victory in 2020. The European democracies have suffered two consecutive economic crises, the Great Recession of 2008-2009 and more recently the Great Lockdown of 2020, the latter of which caused the worst economic contraction since the Great Depression. On both occasions, their system of governance turned out to be not so well-equipped to mitigate the contagion of either the financial crisis or the Covid-19 pandemic.

The momentum of the Third-Wave democratization had lost its steam well before the 2008-2009 global financial crisis. As Larry Diamond astutely observed, the world slipped into a democratic recession at the turn of the century (Diamond 2008). In the first decade and a half of this new century, the rate of democratic breakdown has been substantially higher than the pace of the preceding fifteen-year period. A majority of young democracies that emerged during the third wave are unstable and illiberal, if they remain democratic at all (Diamond 2015). East Asia was not immune from the trend of democratic backsliding. Democratic backsliding in the region sometimes occurred suddenly and dramatically in the form of military coups, as in the case of Thailand in 2006 and 2014 and once again Myanmar in 2021. In other instances, backsliding has occurred through subtle and incremental degradations of democratic rights and procedures as in the cases of Cambodia under Hun Sen and the Philippines under Macapagal Arroyo and more recently Rodrigo Duterte, who vows to be a "dictator" against "evil."

Over the last decade, the allure of the Western-style liberal democracy has significantly declined in the eyes of Asian elites and citizens alike. The reality of contemporary democracies looks much less appealing than the end-of-history story might suggest. The incapacity of Western governments to come to necessary decisions and take actions in a timely manner poses significant questions for their effectiveness vis-à-vis Asian countries. Scholars have picked up many worrisome signs of democratic deconsolidation. Across Western societies, citizens place less and less trust in key democratic institutions. They are increasingly willing to jettison institutions and norms that have traditionally been regarded as central components of democracy and are increasingly attracted to alternative regime forms (Foa and Mounk 2016).

In many established democracies of the West, the return to the staggering scale of economic inequality which was last seen during the Gilded Age is produced by the vast amount of political power held by the wealthy, enabling them to control legislative and regulatory activity. In turn, the concentration of resources at the top of the distribution leads to an even more disproportionate influence of wealthy elites over public life, fueling further discontent at the gap between public policies and public preferences. Elected representatives are increasingly unable to represent the views of the people, and politics has become a game for the rich and powerful (Hacker and Pierson 2011).

At the same time, East Asian authoritarian and semi-democratic regimes remain fierce competitors to democracies. In particular, Singapore is the most economically developed authoritarian state in history, while China is also poised to join the list of developed countries with large middle classes and international corporations. The resiliency of the Chinese communist regime and the economic ascendance of China has made the region's overall environment much more hospitable for non-democratic regimes until the Sino-American trade war repercussions forced countries in the region to choose sides.

With the shift of economic gravity away from the United States and Japan to China, East Asia has become one of the few regions in the world where regime type poses no barrier to trade and investment and is becoming perhaps the only region in the world where newly democratized countries are economically integrated with and dependent on non-democratic regimes. China has rapidly emerged not only as the region's locomotive of economic growth but also as the principal architect of regional integration and new rules of economic engagement, most notably with the launch of the Belt and Road Initiative and the establishment of the Asian Infrastructure Investment Bank. In a nutshell, history no longer loads the dice in favor of Western-style liberal democracies.

Even at the height of the third-wave democratization, East Asia defied the global trend. Between 1986 and 2015, among the eighteen sovereign states and autonomous territories in the region, only five countries, namely the Philippines, South Korea, Taiwan, Mongolia, and Indonesia, successfully transitioned to democracy. Meanwhile, most of the region's authoritarian regimes survived the tidal wave of the global movement toward democracy, and much of East Asia today is still governed by non- and semi-democratic regimes which have displayed great resilience and are seemingly capable of coping with the multiple challenges brought about by complex economies, diverse interests, the internet revolution, and globalization. In the ideological arena, the sustained interest in "Asian values" as well as the "Chinese model of development" debate among elites suggests that liberal democracy is far from establishing itself as "the only game in town."

It is imperative to identify the structural, institutional, cultural, and ideological roots of the ongoing global democratic recession with the help of scientifically reliable empirical data and causal analyses. Much of the received wisdom about the superiority of liberal democracy can no longer be taken for granted. The neoliberal myth that liberal democracy, free markets, and economic globalization reinforce each other does not stand up to serious scrutiny. It is now necessary to reexamine the existing paradigms and refresh our analytical strategy to identify the structural, institutional, cultural, and ideological obstacles to democratic development in the region.

The Asian Barometer Survey

This edited volume sets out to address the ongoing debate over the future of democracy in Asia. It also showcases the width and depth of the collaborative intellectual enterprise that the network of the Asian Barometer Survey (ABS) has built up over the last two decades. Co-founded by Fu Hu and Yun-han Chu in 2000, the overarching concern of the ABS is the future of democracy in Asia. The project's intellectual agenda highlights the importance of the growth of mass belief in democratic legitimacy in the process of democratization and democratic consolidation. Between 2001 and 2020, the ABS completed five waves of region-wide comparative surveys. The ABS initially covered eight countries and territories and subsequently expanded to cover virtually all of East Asia, Southeast Asia, and South Asia, except for North Korea, Brunei, and Laos. In 2017, a team-based at Australia National University (ANU) led by Ian McAllister joined the ABS as its latest country member. Today, the ABS functions as the largest link in the global survey network for the study of democracy, covering twenty countries and territories, more than 50 percent of the world's population, and the bulk of the population living in the developing world. The project has also played a crucial role in deepening collaboration among five regional barometer surveys and forging long-term ties with important international organizations such as the World Bank, International IDEA, United Nations Development Programme, and the European Union.

Since its founding, the ABS has made giant strides on its four stated objectives. The first is to generate a region-wide base of scientifically reliable and comparable data on public opinion regarding political values, civic engagement, social trust, regime legitimacy, democracy, quality of governance, human security, economic reform, globalization vs. economic nationalism, and the region's international relations. The second objective is to strengthen intellectual and institutional capacity for democracy studies by surveying ordinary citizens in participating countries. The third objective is to disseminate survey results to the academic community, the general public, and policy elites to enhance the quality of public discourse over democracy and good governance throughout the region. The fourth objective is to advance the research frontiers of the global study of democratization by deepening collaboration with other regional comparative surveys under the auspices of the Global Barometer Surveys (GBS).

One of the project's most valuable outputs is a digital archive that makes both the survey data as well as related academic publications easily accessible and retrievable online for a large number of potential English-speaking users in the academic, media, government, and NGO sectors. Since the first release of ABS data in 2004, scholars, graduate students, and practitioners from all over the world have made more than 9,400 requests for free access to our survey data, making ABS the region's most sought-after cross-national survey. Growing numbers of studies using ABS data or citing the ABS project have appeared in leading journals, such as *American Political Science Review*, *Annual Review of Political Science*, *American Journal of Political Science*, *Journal of Politics*, *Journal of Democracy*, and *British Journal of Political Science*, gradually increasing academic visibility and influence of the ABS project in political science and related fields.

The ABS is headquartered in Taipei and co-hosted by the Institute of Political Science of Academia Sinica and the Hu Fu Center for East Asia Democratic Studies at National Taiwan University. The ABS is presently headed by Yun-han Chu as the Director and governed by the Steering Committee comprised of one representative from each country team plus some prominent political scientists (such as Andrew Nathan, Larry Diamond, Ken'ichi Ikeda, Ian McAllister, and Doh Chull Shin) acting as members of the steering committee. Currently, members of the ABS team from Taiwan include scholars from the Department of Political Science and Graduate Institute of National Development at National Taiwan University: Yun-han Chu, Yu-tzung Chang, Yeh-lih Wang, Ming-tong Chen, Min-hua Huang, Chen-Dong Tso, Hans H. Tung, Chelsea Chia-chen Chou, Kai-Ping Huang, and Jason Kuo. The team also includes Chin-en Wu, Alex C. H. Chang, and Wen-chin Wu from the Institute of Political Science at Academia Sinica. The history of the ABS can be traced back to Fu Hu's study of political participation in the Neihu district of Taipei in 1978, which was later expanded to research on political behavior and attitudes in the Greater China region (including Taiwan, Hong Kong, and mainland China) in the 1990s, and eventually developed into a regional and global democratization project after 2000. It is a genuinely Taiwan-based social science project that has now expanded on a regional and global scale thanks to ceaseless efforts over more than forty years.

Over the past decade, the ABS team has solved many important intellectual puzzles. For instance, we provided empirically grounded answers to the lingering authoritarian nostalgia among citizens in South Korea, Taiwan, Thailand, the Philippines, and Mongolia almost two decades after these East Asian third-wave democracies embarked on their transition to democracy (Chang, Chu, and Park 2007). We debunked the prevailing myth suggesting that contextual factors in Asia, such as political culture and electoral politics, might neutralize the negative impact of corruption on political trust. Utilizing data from the ABS, we found a strong trust-eroding effect of political corruption in Asian democracies. We also found no evidence that contextual factors lessen the corruption-trust link in Asia. Furthermore, the trust-eroding effect was robust even after taking into account the endogenous relationship between corruption and trust (Chang and Chu 2006).

We were the first research team to point out that it is problematic to rely on indicators that mention the word "democracy" (the "D-word") for measuring democratic legitimacy. Popular conceptions of the "D-word" have been contaminated by competing public discourses and socialization mechanisms, so the word "democracy" has lost much of its conceptual clarity and semantic consistency when it travels across borders. We introduced a more reliable tool to compare the cultural foundation for liberal democracy across countries, especially between democratic and non-democratic regimes. This new attitudinal scale enables researchers to probe further into the substance and depth of popular commitment to democracy. These items were intentionally designed to avoid the "D-word," while probing respondents' value orientations toward certain fundamental organizing principles of liberal democracy, such as political equality, political liberty, and popular accountability. A newly developed typological analysis, which has been applied in two waves of the ABS, enables us to differentiate the substance of democratic legitimacy from its appearance. With this new typology, we are able to resolve the puzzle of why citizens living in non-democratic countries, such as China and Vietnam, professed a much higher level of overt support for democracy while people in consolidated Asian democracies such as Japan and South Korea, registered a much lower level of overt support for democracy. In the former category, a large proportion of their citizens are not liberal democratically oriented and only give superficial support for the "D-word." Other regional barometer surveys subsequently adopted this new measurement strategy, as we have demonstrated its fruitfulness and great potential in advancing our understanding of how political scientists can compare the strength of democratic legitimacy across nations and how people's political predispositions shape the way they experience and view the political regime (Chu and Huang 2010, 2011).

In addition, political theory typically expects democratic regimes to be more legitimate than authoritarian regimes because democracy is built on the consent of the ruled and universal suffrage. Empirically, however, ample survey data have shown that the public's diffuse support for the regime varies considerably across democracies, and the observed level of regime legitimacy under non-democratic regimes may be substantially higher than that of emerging democracies. Our empirical work has provided solid answers to solve this major puzzle, lending strong support to the argument that the installation of regular and competitive elections in and by itself does not serve as the main pillar for creating and sustaining legitimacy for emerging democracies. Moreover, our empirical findings register an important qualification to the prevailing view that the resiliency of Southeast Asian non-democratic regimes are primarily due to their superior capability in delivering economic prosperity. In these countries, whether the government is perceived by the citizens as being responsive to their needs, effective in controlling corruption, and adhering to the expectation that ordinary people are treated fairly and equally were shown to be more important than economic performance in generating regime support. Furthermore, regime legitimacy in these political systems also turns out to have ideological and cultural origins. Southeast Asian non-democratic regimes gain support from cultivating nationalism and national identity. They also benefit from being embedded in a more hospitable cultural soil where traditional social and political values are still prevalent. While popular political convictions matter to all political systems in the region, they matter more to non-democratic polity when compared to democratic regimes (Chang, Chu, and Welsh 2013).

At the same time, the ABS team also pioneered the systematic analysis of demand-side dynamics in making sense of the growing popular disenchantment with democracy. We argue that to comprehensively address the question of why there has been a rise in authoritarian populism and a visible decline in popular confidence in democracy among citizens across both established and third-wave democracies, we need to examine both supply-side (i.e., evolving political practices and institutional engineering led by political elites) and demand-side (i.e., transformative opinions and behaviors among the masses) dynamics. The supply-side dynamics have received a lot of attention from students of democratization and democracy-promotion institutions. Meanwhile, in practical terms, advice and assistance have been offered to emerging democracies in areas such as constitutional design, choices of electoral systems, best practice for enhancing electoral integrity, the rule of law, transparency, protection of minorities' rights, and capacity building in legislative and judicial branches (Diamond and Morlino 2005; Carothers 2015). In contrast, the demand-side dynamics have been given scant attention so far. Therefore, we focus on some key micro-dynamics that have driven related mass attitudes and behaviors, all of which are centered on how people understand democracy in different ways. We systematically examined the 2010-2013 Global Barometer Surveys (GBS) data covering five regional barometers, including the ABS. The GBS offers large-scale comparative survey data with the appropriate instruments that capture the critical trade-off dynamics in how people conceptualize democracy. Thus, GBS data enables us to extend this line of research with a more extensive and also more focused geographical coverage. More specifically, we have empirically established that (1) people hold distinct understandings of democracy, (2) popular conceptions of democracy are significantly shaped by socioeconomic and political contexts, (3) such varying conceptions generate different baselines for people to assess democratic practices and to establish their views of democracy, and (4) such distinct conceptions also drive political participation in different ways. Overall, popular understandings of democracy have critically shaped how citizens respond to authoritarian or populist practices in contemporary politics (Lu and Chu 2021).

In view of the above research achievements, we invited ABS partners to contribute their intellectual findings to this edited volume and celebrate the twentieth anniversary of the ABS together. Except for the introduction, this volume contains twenty-seven chapters, which are grouped into two parts. Part I includes eleven chapters based on previously published studies and updated using the latest ABS data. Part II focuses on country-specific issues and contains sixteen chapters covering each country or autonomous territory in the ABS. Themes include potential threats to the third-wave democracies, evolving ideology in one-party states, cases of denied democracy, growing opposition under hybrid regimes, and peculiar challenges for long-term democracies. The contributors are the indispensable partners that have made the ABS possible over the past two decades. This edited volume not only celebrates the long-term collective efforts of those who participated in the ABS project but also marks an important milestone that will hopefully inspire those who will be working together under the auspices of ABS in the next twenty years.

Part One: Regional Trends

The ABS has devoted itself to the academic community by providing data to better our knowledge about how ordinary people perceive democracy. Since its inception in 2001, the ABS has accumulated individual-level data across fifteen countries and autonomous territories, with some countries having data covering more than twenty years. In every survey, the ABS asks people to evaluate their political systems and examines the reasons for regime support. Support for democracy is at the core of the ABS as we seek to understand how East Asians, with their distinct cultural heritage and political development, embrace a Western political institution. Since the late 1980s, the Philippines, South Korea, and Taiwan began to democratize, followed by Mongolia, Thailand, and Indonesia in the 1990s. Yet, while democracy in Mongolia, South Korea, and Taiwan gradually consolidated, democracy has struggled to take root in Southeast Asia, and (competitive) authoritarian regimes have been resilient enough to resist the trend of third-wave democratization. At the same time, China has slowly emerged as a regional power overshadowing Japan and the United States. The rise of China and its authoritarian exemplar provides an alternative to democracy in the context of the democratic recession in the mid-2000s. The ABS has closely followed political developments in the region and around the world and updated questionnaires to capture the sentiments of the time. This rich data has helped us understand the trends in support for democracy in the region, why democratic regimes have difficulty winning the hearts and minds of ordinary citizens, and how China's rise poses a further challenge to democracy. The first part of the edited volume highlights the research conducted by scholars over the ABS network in the past two decades. These chapters offer a glimpse into the future of democracy in the region.

As one of the regional survey projects focusing on democratization, how democracy is understood by ordinary people is a constant concern for comparative analysis. The ABS has tried different instruments to capture the meanings of democracy among ordinary people. These instruments are also compared with other surveys that also attempt to measure the same thing. Chapter 2 analyzes two different instruments used in the fifth wave of the ABS and found that no matter which instrument is in use to measure understandings of democracy, significant variations appear between Asian societies, with some leaning toward the liberal notions of democracy, while others lean toward the authoritarian notions. The findings indicate that the prevalence of different notions of democracy might be due to societies' socioeconomic, political, cultural, and historical characteristics, rather than the measuring instruments used. These findings serve as a basis for the chapters that follow when democratic legitimacy is the theme of this edited volume. In addressing the problem of different conceptions of democracy across countries, authors of the chapter suggested using certain regime types or values (political culture) as a common ground to solve the problem of different conceptions.

As democratic recession raised alarm in the West, Chapter 3 explores whether a similar trend can be seen in East Asian democracies. By tracing support for democracy across the five waves of surveys, the chapter finds two trends in the region. Among democratic regimes, Japan, Korea, and Taiwan appear consolidated as more and more citizens, young and old, are supporting democracy as the best form of government and rejecting alternatives. Yet, in Mongolia and the Philippines, support for authoritarian strongman leadership has gained traction, and people are increasingly holding authoritarian orientations. The author argues that these divergent paths can be explained by whether regimes deliver fairly distributed economic development that helps cultivate durable democratic values, which in turn consolidates democratic legitimacy.

Though democracy appears to be consolidated in Northeast Asia, concerns still remain. Chapter 4 examines system preferences among citizens living in liberal democracies. It is generally assumed that citizens living in democracies accept liberal democracy as the "only game in town" as a result of their political experiences. However, the author found that the most prevalent type in Northeast Asian liberal democracies are citizens who accept democracy but reject authoritarianism only partially. The so-called "authentic democrats" are still a minority among ordinary people. Based on the findings drawn from the fourth wave (2014-2016), the author casts doubt at the assumption that experiencing and learning about democratic politics will automatically lead to democratic consolidation. If democracy is still far from being the "only game in town" in democratic Northeast Asia, this does not bode well for Southeast Asia where the cultural and economic conditions lag still further behind.

Why is it so difficult for people in the region to embrace democracy wholeheartedly? Since its inception, the ABS has explored whether this Western political institution is compatible with values and cultures nurtured by a centuries-old authoritarian political order. Many of the studies coming out of the ABS are devoted to explaining regime support from a cultural perspective. Chapter 5 summarizes how cultural heritage sustains regime support. The authors find that people holding Confucian values are more likely to support the regime, regardless of type, indicating that such values serve as a ballast stone reinforcing regime legitimacy.

Chapter 6 extends the authors' 2010 article exploring the distributions of patterns of democratic orientations across sixteen countries. The chapter is expanded to include autocracies and utilizes data from all five waves of the ABS. The findings show that the majority of citizens in liberal democracies are Consistent and Critical Democrats, and thus, regime support is sustained by strong democratic values. Yet, the latest waves show that citizens in several countries are moving toward authoritarianism, indicating that the overall downward trend of democratic support in the region can be explained by a greater willingness of citizens to embrace authoritarianism.

Cultural explanations help us understand why people in authoritarian countries support a hierarchical power order. Although Chapter 7 confirms this relationship, it raises a caveat for authoritarian countries. The chapter examines the sources of diffuse regime support and finds that government performance and traditional social values generate political legitimacy. While authoritarian countries can rely on both to sustain support, they create trade-offs: government efficiency accelerates modernization, which in turn cultivates democratic values that gradually replace traditional values. In this regard, high political trust and diffuse support will not protect authoritarian regimes from challenges indefinitely.

Chapter 8 examines how values affect political participation in the region. The author found that traditional social values facilitate contact-type governmental political participation, whereas liberal democratic values facilitated active-type governmental political participation and interacted with trust in the national government. Distrust of the system drives active-type political participation among those holding liberal democratic values throughout the region. However, the author points out that active-type participation should not be viewed in a negative light since it offers an opportunity for the government to regain trust if it takes its message seriously.

Besides value orientations, government performance or the quality of governance is another important source of political legitimacy. Chapter 9 compares expert assessment and ordinary people's evaluations on the quality of democratic governance and finds significant divergence between experts and ordinary people. In countries with low expert assessment, people tend to give a high score of governance. This correlation is then reversed for affluent liberal democracies. The chapter argues that even in affluent liberal democracies, people deem their regimes to be weak on democratic accountability and the rule of law, indicating that democracies in the region remain short of standards of liberal democracy in the eyes of their publics.

The last three chapters of Part I discuss how perceptions of corruption, economic equality and performance impact regime legitimacy. While perceptions are still influenced by subjective attitudes, the government's performance plays a role to some degree. From different angles, these chapters explore the legitimacy issue, and the findings suggest that different regime types emphasize different aspects of economic problems. Collectively, economic governance is central to regime support, and when people perceive that the economic pie is not distributed equally, it will likely also affect their perception of political corruption.

Chapter 10 examines how perceived corruption undermines political trust. Based on the two authors' arguments in a 2006 article, this chapter updated the analysis using the fifth wave data (2018-2020) and found the same pattern that political corruption had a corrosive effect on political trust. As corruption violates the principle of political equality, bending the rules to serve personal interest instead of public interest, it undermines governmental performance and ability to respond to citizens' demands, ultimately undermining trust in the regime.

Following the 2008 financial crisis, concern about rising income inequality has grown. Since the fourth wave survey, the ABS has included an item measuring perceived income inequality. Chapter 11 explores how perceived income inequality affects regime support. Arguing that perceived inequality negatively affects political stability, the chapter finds that perceived inequality decreases support for the current regime and increases support for regime change. As a result, rising perceived inequality might contribute to regime change in autocracies and democratic backsliding in democracies, confirming that poor governance undermines regime legitimacy.

Though most of the chapters examine how poor governance erodes regime support, given that power relations between the state and the society are different under democracy and autocracy, different types of poor performance may have varying effects on regime support under democracy and autocracy. Chapter 12 finds that poor economic performance is more damaging to autocracies, but income inequality is more harmful to liberal democracies. Reasoning that autocracies depend on economic prosperity as a source of regime legitimacy and democracies on economic equality, the chapter portrays a more complex picture of the relationship between governance performance and regime support.

Part Two: Country Dynamics

In addition to the vast population and immense geographical area covered by the ABS, the wide heterogeneity in economic, political, and social development across the region poses a great challenge for the successful implementation of the fieldwork as well as for analysis of the distinct trajectory of each democratization process. In terms of economic development, the ABS covers advanced economies such as Japan and Singapore but also includes less developed countries like Cambodia and Myanmar. In terms of political development, the ABS countries range from established democracies such as Japan, India, and Australia to one-party states that have never experienced democracy like China and Vietnam. In fact, many ABS surveyed countries have experienced a certain level of democratization but evolved in divergent directions: some cases, such as South Korea and Taiwan, show a consolidated and stable democracy, some cases, such as Mongolia, Indonesia, and the Philippines, exhibit a general optimistic trend with an up-and-down development, and still others, particularly Hong Kong, Thailand, Cambodia, and Myanmar have evolved in a worrying direction. Finally, the growth of societal forces adds much uncertainty in hybrid regimes like Singapore and Malaysia. As to the social dimensions, the complexity of the ethnic, religious, class profile diverges from near-perfect homogeneous profiles like Japan and South Korea to extremely complex cases such as Myanmar and India. It is impossible to impose a universal framework to account for the democratization process of those countries. Therefore, the analytical strategy for the Part II chapters is to give discretion to the contributors in each chapter to tell a compelling story about an important issue in the country's political development using data from the ABS. The purpose is to present as much political diversity as possible and extend our empirical understanding to transcend diverging levels of economic, political, and social development.

While each of the chapters can be viewed as an independent case study, they are ordered by the following regime characteristics. The first group contains those long-term democracies which have been democracies since after World War II, namely, Japan, Australia, and India. The second group includes third-wave democracies which achieved democratization around the 1990s, namely, Taiwan, South Korea, Mongolia, Indonesia, and the Philippines. The third group covers cases of a recent denial of democracy by military coup or political repression, namely, Hong Kong, Thailand, Cambodia, and Myanmar. The fourth group consists of hybrid regimes where there is uncertainty related to the growing challenge posed by the opposition, namely, Singapore and Malaysia. Finally, the last group is composed of one-party states where authoritarian resilience has become a hot topic recently in political science, namely, mainland China and Vietnam.

Although countries are grouped according to their democratic development, it does not mean that mature democracies face less or no challenges in terms of democratic legitimacy. In fact, all types of countries have faced different kinds of legitimacy problems. Part Two contributors are all country experts, and we encourage them to identify the most challenging areas for the legitimacy of their country's regime. The decline of tolerance toward those holding opposing views is one of the challenges of long-term democracies. As elsewhere, political polarization undermines democracy in Asia as well. The three chapters on the state of democracy in long-term democracies examine how traditional Asian values can serve as a bulwark to support political tolerance. Their caveat is that such values make citizens more likely to trust their governments, but such an orientation could be conducive to populist leaders who gradually lead countries in an authoritarian direction.

From the five chapters in the category, two challenges are identified for the third-wave democracies. Due to fierce competition between political parties, supporters of opposing parties question the legitimacy of regimes, which cripples the deepening of democratic norms. Therefore, on the surface, there appears to be vibrant democracy, but underneath, the population is gradually doubting democracy and strengthening its conservative orientation. The second problem is that poor governance and mediocre economic performance have undermined citizens' support for democracy. In developing countries, economic improvement has become a source of democratic legitimacy. Citizens might tolerate corruption and authoritarian measures if the government can improve the economy. This attitude prevents countries from consolidating democracy. For countries where democracy was replaced by autocracy, there appears to be a surge in democratic orientations and support for democracy. Many countries in the region have experienced regime changes, either due to military takeovers or the consolidation of one-party rule. The citizens are struggling against authoritarian governments, yet their demand for democracy is for political freedom while most of them are not ready to accept pluralism for civil liberty to flourish.

Authoritarian countries in the region have posed a challenge to liberal democracy. Also, they question the theory of modernization that predicts economic development will eventually lead to political liberalization. Several hybrid regimes and one-party states in the region have resisted the trend of third-wave democratization. Although economic development has fostered democratic orientation among educated and young people, the performance of the government also sustains popular support for the regime. According to the findings of previous chapters, regime legitimacy is a function of how well the state lives up to the expectations of the people. For one-party states, economic growth sustains regime support but also ideologies and values (nationalism and Confucian values) fostered by authoritarian regimes.

Long-term Democracies

Chapter 13 examines political and social tolerance in the Japanese context. Although political tolerance is expected to be affected by the liberal democratic institutional context, the author found that certain Asian values can also promote political tolerance. In addition, although an emphasis on vertical hierarchies in social networks worked against social tolerance as expected, social network homogeneity was actually associated with greater social tolerance, contradicting theoretical expectations. The chapter concludes with a call to develop more standards and norms to better incorporate the diversity within Asian cultural traditions.

Australia first joined the ABS for the fifth wave in 2019, and the country has moved rapidly closer to Asia through migration, trade, and technological links in recent decades. Interestingly, Chapter 14 finds that despite being considered a "Western" country, Australians show many similarities with their Asian neighbors in terms of their traditional values, orientations toward the state, and satisfaction with political institutions. As the author argues, inclusion of Australia in the ABS provides a unique opportunity to probe how Australia compares with its neighbors and generate insights about the country's identity and democracy.

Chapter 15 finds that Indians tend to have higher levels of trust in non-elected institutions when compared to elected institutions. The gap in trust between elected and non-elected institutions may be because citizens are more "connected" to elected institutions and, therefore, more critical in their appraisals when compared to more distant non-elected institutions. In addition, the most recent survey in 2019 also found that citizens' overall trust in institutions was higher than their distrust. The authors attribute the high levels of institutional trust to pro-incumbency sentiment following the BJP's return to power under the leadership of Prime Minister Narendra Modi.

Third Wave Democracies

Chapter 16 explores whether there has been any difference in attitudes toward Taiwan's democracy between supporters of the winning and losing camps over the past twenty years. This question is important because "losers' consent" is essential for the consolidation of democracy. The findings show that election winners are more likely to be "Consistent Democrats" (high direct and indirect support for democracy) while election losers are more likely to be "Critical Democrats" (low direct support for democracy but high indirect support for democracy) or "Non-Democrats" (high direct and indirect support for democracy). Despite Taiwan's success in consolidating its democracy, the persistence of this gap between the winners and losers of elections warns us to guard against complacency.

Chapter 17 finds that although South Korea's democracy appears to be consolidated at the mass-level attitudinal dimension, citizens' attachment to liberal democratic norms is still shallow. Although citizens accept that democracy has become "the only game in town," their weak attachment to liberal democratic norms suggests that the country remains vulnerable to "the tyranny of the democratic but illiberal majority."

Chapter 18 points out that Mongolia was considered "one of the least likely cases" to have undergone democratic transition. Despite the apparently unlikely success of Mongolian democracy and support for democracy among its citizens, as in the case of South Korea, citizens' attachment to liberal democratic norms remains relatively weak. The author argues that Mongolia still faces many challenges to move beyond electoral democracy. In particular, he points out that legal procedures and practices to control corruption need to be strengthened, and horizontal accountability needs to be deepened.

Chapter 19 finds that Indonesians are generally positively oriented toward the political system and how democracy works in the country. Consistent with the findings in other countries in Southeast Asia on the importance of economic conditions in explaining system support, the author finds that the political economy model is more persuasive than the political culture perspective to explain system support.

In Chapter 20, the authors find growing satisfaction with democracy and trust in institutions among Filipino citizens, despite fears among many observers of an authoritarian turn in politics under the presidency of Rodrigo Duterte. Like their counterparts elsewhere in Southeast Asia, Filipinos place a high priority on economic development. The steady improvement in the country's economy in the years leading up to the fifth wave can explain Filipino's satisfaction with democracy, even in the face of Duterte's authoritarian tendencies.

Democracy Denied

Chapter 21 reveals the growing gap between the aspirations of Hong Kong citizens and the performance of the Hong Kong government, which fueled the recent protests. Younger and more educated Hong Kong citizens have weaker identification with China and are dissatisfied with the performance of the government in civil liberties (freedom) and responsiveness (democracy). Increasingly, the government finds its support base reduced to those who are older, have lower income, and are less educated. Despite Beijing's recent crackdown, the growing gap between citizens and government will lead to further challenges to the system in the future.

In Chapter 22, the authors examine factors that affect Thai citizens' support for democracy across the five waves of the ABS, a period marked by considerable political instability, including two successful military coups as well as mass protests and worsening political polarization. The authors show that satisfaction with the government and democracy has declined over the five survey waves. However, they also find that Thai citizens place a high priority on human security. Therefore, if people are satisfied with their own economic condition and the country's overall economy, they are more likely to be satisfied with the government and the way that democracy works.

Chapter 23 explores the growing opposition in Cambodia and its social basis before the Hun Sen regime outlawed the main opposition party to preempt its threat in the run-up to the 2018 general election. By highlighting trends in public opinion data, the author argues that the opposition was gaining momentum with increasing electoral efficacy, growing civil society, increasing demands for control of corruption, and belief in both horizontal and vertical accountability, even though constant political regression and the China factor worked against these trends. This chapter concludes that Hun Sen's crackdown on the opposition was a last-ditch effort to save his power in the face of growing political empowerment.

In Chapter 24, the authors explain the potential reasons behind Burma's failed democratization. While the direct factor leading to its democratic regression was the bargaining failure between political elites and the military, the conflicting attitudes, specifically the superficial support of democracy and the general inclination toward illiberalism and authoritarian values at the popular level, could have also undermined the nascent democracy. The authors conclude that the necessary condition for democracy to thrive in Burma (Myanmar) is not just the retreat of the military from politics but also to overcome the many difficult problems related to conservative political culture and politically inactive citizenry in the democratization process.

Hybrid Regimes

Chapter 25 seeks to explain Singaporeans' overall preference for democracy and orientations toward substantive or procedural understandings of democracy. Although, as the authors point out, Singapore has long been seen as "a counterfactual to modernization theory," analysis of three waves of survey data in Singapore suggests that modernization theory is salient in explaining the democratic attitudes of Singaporeans. In particular, more educated respondents also show a greater overall preference for democracy. At the same time, more educated respondents, respondents with higher political interest, and younger respondents are more likely to understand democracy in procedural terms rather than substantive terms.

In Chapter 26, the author discusses the political impact of the first power transition since Malaysia's independence in 1957. Despite the political crisis that broke out in February 2020 after Mahathir Mohamad's sudden resignation as prime minister, the author argues that there is an emerging consensus between supporters of the winning and losing camps on measures such as institutional trust, democratic evaluation, liberal democratic values, and regime support. According to the author, behind the seemingly troubled elite politics that failed to generate a governing alliance in parliament, ordinary citizens have already learned to view politics in a non-partisan fashion, and supporters of both camps are willing to accept the legitimacy of the democratic system and participate in politics. This emerging consensus among the general public offers a path forward for Malaysia to resolve the crisis in elite politics by making the voice of the people heard at the ballot box.

One Party States

Chapter 27 describes the evolution of social norms and political ideology in mainland China over three decades (1993-2019) using data from the ABS and an ongoing research project initiated by the late Dr. Tianjian Shi. As predicted by modernization theory, the authors find that significant socioeconomic transformations over the past decades have eroded the influence of Confucian social legacies, including a decline in hierarchical orientation toward authority (in particular parents and in-laws). However, the authors did not find a similar trend for orientations toward Confucian political legacies. In particular, many Chinese continue to identify with paternalistic leadership, believe that judges should accept the view of the executive branch when they decide important cases, and reject the necessity of legislative checks on the executive branch.

Chapter 28 explores the structure of ideology in Vietnam using data from the ABS. Focusing on four ideological dimensions (redistribution, nationalism, globalization, and authoritarian policies), the authors find that although Vietnam is a single-party regime, there is a significant grouping of ideological preferences. In particular, those who prefer distribution are more nationalistic and more likely to prefer authoritarian policies. Closeness to the party predicts authoritarian orientation, distribution, and nationalism. However, despite differences between north and south, and between ethnic minority groups and the Kinh, these factors did not have consistently significant relationships with the four dimensions of ideology.

By Way of Conclusion

The empirical findings presented above provide a mixed picture of the state of democracy in Asia today. While most of the region's democracies do not face any imminent existential crisis, they still suffer from a fragile foundation of legitimacy. The level of diffuse regime support in Japan, South Korea, Taiwan, Mongolia, and the Philippines are consistently lower than that of their neighboring hybrid and authoritarian regimes. Distrust of democratic institutions is also widespread. In all East Asian democracies except Indonesia, most citizens dismissed the trustworthiness of what are arguably the two key institutions of representative democracy, political parties and parliament. Compared with democracies in the region, non-democratic were also rated as more responsive by their citizens when compared to their democratic neighbors (Chu, Pan, and Wu 2015).

Democracies have failed to win over the hearts of many Asian citizens because political polarization, elite infighting, partisan gridlock, and corruption scandals have debilitated governments. Many citizens withdrew their support for the democratic form of government because it fails to deliver an acceptable level of good governance in terms of the rule of law, controlling corruption, impartiality and fair treatment, provision of social safety net, and being responsive to citizens' needs. Many non-democracies in East Asia enjoy a higher level of popular support also due to the fact that they become a vibrant force in driving regional development while democracies show signs of languishing. For three consecutive decades, Japan, the only established democracy in the region, has been trapped in the loss of vision and adaptability in an age of digital revolution and globalization. The Covid-19 pandemic crisis now is creating a new kind of stress test, bringing into question the very ability of its democratic system to cope with an existential challenge, i.e., protecting the citizens from a menacing public health crisis and the society from a devastating economic catastrophe.

One of the most corrosive forces that undermines the legitimacy of Asian democracies is the widening gap between the rich and the poor. While glaring income inequality is a source of popular discontent everywhere, this explosive issue has reached the boiling point primarily in Asian democracies. Many forces operating at the regional and global level have not been conducive to democratic consolidation and expansion in East Asia. First, the neoliberal economic reform that came with democratization and the permeation of its overarching guiding ideology have deprived the state bureaucracy in Asia's young democracies of the necessary policy instruments and the steering capability to facilitate industrial upgrading and arrest the trend of growing income inequality. At the same time, in virtually all Asian societies, globalization and economic integration have strengthened the position of the transnational economic elites and shifted the power balance in society at the expense of workers, farmers, the middle class, and local communities.

Much like their counterparts in other regions, Asian democracies have also suffered from a hollowing out of democratic sovereignty as the power of making the most important decisions and rules is either transferred to supra-national organizations and multilateral arrangements or subordinated to the interests of transnational corporate elites and the super-rich. In order to foster a more conducive environment to democratic development, it is imperative to harness the power of the transnational corporate elites and their allies through enacting regional as well as global conventions on foreign investment, capital movement, financial arbitrage, corporate income tax, capital gains tax and inheritance tax, and new international rules on labor, migration, environment, food safety, cyber security, equal access to digital resources, and so on. Obviously, none of the above is achievable through actions undertaken by any individual country. It can be accomplished only through concerted multilateral actions propelled by visionary leaders, vibrant regional and global social movements, and a strong global civil society pushing for democratic global governance.

Another potent transformative force to be reckoned with is the explosion of internet communication and social media. The breakthrough in digital technology is a double-edged sword when it comes to coping with the wrenching challenges that Asia's representative democracies are facing today. The internet revolution has the potential to empower resource-poor citizens to break up the political oligopoly of the entrenched elites as it facilitates information-sharing, promotes transparency, and substantially reduces the cost of coordinating collective action. It also might help the development of democratic citizenship through the enhancement of a sense of political empowerment and the expansion of online social networking and political engagement.

On the other hand, it might overburden representative democracies with its many unintended consequences: frequent and sudden outbursts of online activism, destroying social capital and burning down the bridges between contending groups with the rise of cyber tribalism, and drastically compressing the time span for democratic institutions to respond to the pressing demands or problems of the day. It also tends to amplify the corrosive effect of the hollowing out of democratic sovereignty and the political polarization over economic distribution on the legitimacy of democratic regimes, especially in the eyes of the citizens who lack the patience to wait until the next parliamentary session, much less the next election, for the slow and cumbersome democratic process to come up with a policy response.

In the final analysis, Asia's millennials will hold the key to the region's democratic future. While the baby boomer generation still possesses the economic and political clout in East Asia now, their children are a powerful transformative group that is destined to shape the region's political future. In some East Asian countries, young voters under the age of 30 have already become the critical force shaping the outcome of recent elections.

East Asia's current youth cohort, who were born between the early 1980s and the 2000s, is the generation of millennials. This generation knows very little about the People Power uprising in 1986, the Tiananmen Square protests and fall of the Berlin Wall in 1989, or even the Asian Financial Crisis in 1997. Their referent points are shaped by trends and events of the last fifteen years: a rising China and declining United States, mass commercialization of Asian pop culture, and broadly the experience of rapid social change and vibrant economic growth.

The Asian Barometer Survey has shown that Asian millennials are open to liberal democracy but are not committed to it. They value the outcomes of political systems more than their underlying normative principles. They are more inclined to conceive democracy in terms of good governance and social equity than as either the norms and procedures around electoral accountability and political competition or freedom and liberty. It is not enough for the region's young democracies to provide its citizens with freedom, open political competition, and free and fair elections; they have to deliver tangible outcomes in terms of social equity and good governance to win over the hearts of their younger-generation citizens (Chu and Welsh 2015). In particular, Asian political systems have to address the salient issue of inter-generational distributive justice in terms of upward social mobility and a level playing field.

Our empirical data also indicate that the normal channel of vertical accountability evolving around electoral cycles is no longer sufficient in addressing the expectations and demands of millennials. The traditional pattern of political mobilization, often through local political machines, patron-client networks, or trade unions is of diminishing utility in capturing Asia's millennials who are physically mobile, hooked up to the new medium of information flows, and embedded in social networks among peers. The prevalence of the internet has transformed East Asia's millennials' pattern of political engagement and fostered activism in areas such as blogging and virtual social networks. It will become imperative for all East Asian political systems, democratic or not, to address the growing popular demand for real-time interactive e-government at all levels of government and the provision of online deliberative and consultative mechanisms in all areas of public policy and governance. Without these necessary institutional innovations and adaptations, governance performance and regime legitimacy will suffer.

References

Carothers, Thomas. 2015. "Democracy Aid at 25: Time to Choose." *Journal of Democracy* 26 (1): 59-73. doi: 10.1353/jod.2015.0010.

Chang, Alex, Yun-han Chu, and Bridget Welsh. 2013. "Southeast Asia: Sources of Regime Support." *Journal of Democracy* 24 (2): 150-164. doi:10.1353/jod.2013.0025.

Chang, Eric C. C., and Yun-han Chu. 2006. "Corruption and Trust: Exceptionalism in Asian Democracies?" *The Journal of Politics* 68 (2): 259-271. doi:10.1111/j.1468-2508.2006.00404.x.

Chang, Yu-tzung, Yun-han Chu, and Chong-Min Park. 2007. "Authoritarian Nostalgia in Asia." *Journal of Democracy* 18 (3): 66-80. doi:10.1353/jod.2007.0043.

Chu, Yun-han, and Bridget Welsh. 2015. "Millennials and East Asia's Democratic Future." *Journal of Democracy* 26 (2): 151-164. doi:10.1353/jod.2015.0020.

Chu, Yun-han, and Min-hua Huang. 2010. "The Meanings of Democracy: Solving an Asian Puzzle." *Journal of Democracy* 21 (4): 114-122. doi:10.1353/jod.2010.0009.

—. 2011. "Typological Analysis of Democratic Legitimacy." Chap. 1 in *Reviving Legitimacy: Lessons for and from China*, edited by Deng Zhenglai and Sujian Guo, 15-26. Lanham, Maryland: Rowman & Littlefield-Lexington.

Chu, Yun-han, Hsin-hsin Pan, and Wen-chin Wu. 2015. "Regime Legitimacy in East Asia: Why Non-Democratic States Fare Better than Democracies." *Global Asia* 10 (3): 98-105.

Diamond, Larry. 2008. "The Democratic Rollback: The Resurgence of the Predatory State." *Foreign Affairs* 87 (2): 36-48.

—. 2015. "Facing Up to the Democratic Recession." *Journal of Democracy* 26 (1): 141-155. doi:10.1353/jod.2015.0009.

Diamond, Larry, and Leonardo Morlino. 2005. *Assessing the Quality of Democracy.* Edited by Larry Diamond and Leonardo Morlino. Baltimore: Johns Hopkins University Press.

Foa, Roberto Stefan, and Yascha Mounk. 2016. "The Danger of Deconsolidation: The Democratic Disconnect." *Journal of Democracy* 27 (3): 5-17. doi:10.1353/jod.2016.0049.

Hacker, Jacob S., and Paul Pierson. 2011. *Winner-Take-All Politics: How Washington Made the Rich Richer—and Turned Its Back on the Middle Class.* New York: Simon & Schuster.

Lu, Jie, and Yun-han Chu. 2021. *Understandings of Democracy: Origins and Consequences Beyond Western Democracies.* London and New York: Oxford University Press.

2 Revisiting Popular Understandings of Democracy in Asia: Evidence from New Survey Instruments in the Fifth Wave of the ABS

Jie Lu and Le Bao

It is nothing new to argue that people hold different views on many critical things, including democracy. For students of political science, this lack of consensus is highly expected, since they cannot even agree among themselves (i.e., the so-called experts on political issues) on what democracy means (Schmitter and Karl 1991) or on the effective measures of democracy for empirical analysis (Treier and Jackman 2008). For laymen, democracy is no different from other big but fuzzy words (including but not limited to the rule of law, transparency, accountability, etc.) frequently mentioned by politicians and pundits with varying or even opposing political views and policy proposals.

Thanks to the dominance of the liberal democracy discourse that has been successfully established since the Third Wave (Huntington 1991), "democracy" has become the only discursive game in town, if not the only political one (Dalton, Shin, and Jou 2007; Shin 2017). For whatever reasons, most people associate "Democracy" with many desirable things, although many may just throw up their hands when probed for the meaning of democracy (Cho 2014, 2015). Even those who can attach substantive meanings to the "D-word" do not necessarily share a similar understanding of the term. Likewise, most politicians rarely denounce democracy in public and have tried to present their behaviors, policy-making, and even power maneuvers as democratic, even though their blatant and outrageous violations of certain fundamental principles of democracy have been documented by journalists and scholars. In particular, for many authoritarian leaders, democracy is a necessary and convenient political fig leaf that can be stretched for and tailored to their political rule and survival. Moreover, such tailored discourses on democracy have been systematically cultivated and promoted, especially in non-democracies (Kirsch and Welzel 2019; Kruse, Ravlik, and Welzel 2019; Lu, Aldrich, and Shi 2014; Lu and Shi 2015).

It should not be difficult for students of political science to see through politicians' manipulation of discourses and related political campaigns. However, it would be a mistake to downplay the significance of such manipulation and campaigns or simply brush them aside as naïve political tricks or clumsy maneuvers. Existing scholarship on the influence of elite discourse on public opinion (Druckman 2004; Druckman, Peterson, and Slothuus 2013; Zaller 1992) strongly suggests that political leaders can obtain concrete benefits by engaging such campaigns and discourse manipulation (Geddes and Zaller 1989; Lu, Aldrich, and Shi 2014; Stockmann 2012), in particular, by shaping how their people understand democracy (besides securing a garb of democracy to ease their power maneuvers).

The Asian Barometer Survey (ABS) deeply believes that knowing how ordinary people define democracy and why they conceptualize democracy in specific ways provides a critical lens through which we can examine and answer many critical questions raised in the aforementioned debates and discussions on the prospect of democracy in today's world. Therefore, in the first wave of region-wide comparative survey, the ABS adopted an open-ended survey instrument to document how Asians conceptualize democracy, without providing any cues. Later, to ensure more theoretically focused comparison and build upon the information collected via open-ended survey instruments, the ABS developed other empirical strategies to measure popular understandings of democracy using closed-ended survey instruments. This essay will review the ABS's evolving empirical strategies to examine varying conceptions of democracy in Asia and revisit some of its early findings using the most recent information collected via new ranking and rating instruments in the fifth wave of the ABS.

Crafting Survey Instruments for Varying Conceptions of Democracy

Initially, when the ABS began its first round of region-wide comparative survey in the early 2000s, there was little information available in the literature on how to effectively capture different conceptions of democracy. Therefore, using an open-ended instrument asking people "What does democracy mean to you?" was the most reasonable and default choice (Schaffer 1998). Without cuing respondents in any direction, the open-ended instrument provides significant leeway for respondents and allows researchers to document whatever top-of-mind features people associate with democracy. Furthermore, to offer sufficient opportunities for respondents to voice their thoughts, all interviewees were instructed to probe each respondent three times for additional answers. With such information, ABS researchers have generated some thought-provoking findings (Dalton, Shin, and Jou 2007; Shi 2009, 2015; Shi and Lu 2010) and contributed greatly to the growing literature of popular understandings of democracy. Nevertheless, besides its high costs of data collection and processing, there also are significant challenges in identifying theoretically meaningful and comparable themes for comparative analysis from thousands of ambiguous words, fragmented sentences, or incomplete statements (Schaffer 2014).

To overcome the aforementioned deficiencies in using the open-ended survey instrument to measure popular understandings of democracy, the ABS has tried to develop some closed-ended survey instruments to more effectively capture various conceptions of democracy and to enable more theoretically focused examination since its third wave. Nevertheless, the specific form and included answer categories might have a noticeable impact on collected survey responses. To minimize possible artificial impact of the instrument format and wording, ABS researchers conducted extensive and independent content analyses of the data collected in the first and second waves of the ABS via the open-ended instruments. They further cross-validated their findings and coding schemes to identify some key components in popular responses to the open-ended instruments.

The qualitative analysis of data from the first and second waves shows that Asians have regularly and repeatedly mentioned the following four latent components: (1) social equity, (2) good government, (3) norms and procedures, and (4) freedom and liberty. To minimize the possible influence of measurement errors on post-survey inferences, the third and fourth waves intentionally included four sets of indicators for each component (i.e., trying to tap the same latent component from distinct perspectives) in the new survey instruments. The crafting of all indicators is also based on popular responses to the open-ended survey instrument in the first and second waves. For respondents' effective ranking of the distinct features of democracy, the third and fourth waves selected one indicator from each of the four sets, presented the four indicators collectively as a ranking set, and asked respondents to select one as the most essential characteristic of democracy with the following probe: "Many things may be desirable, but not all of them are essential characteristics of democracy. If you have to choose only one from each four sets of statements that I am going to read, which one would you choose as the most essential characteristic of a democracy?" To minimize possible question order effects, the third and fourth waves further rotated the order of the four components in each of the four sets.[1] Basically, closed-ended survey instruments asked respondents to identify the most essential characteristic of democracy when confronted with the trade-offs between (1) social equity, (2) good government, (3) norms and procedures, and (4) freedom and liberty. They were asked to do the ranking four times with distinct indicators for each of the four components. Moreover, each time, they were confronted with the trade-offs presented in a different order.

With such information, ABS researchers have systematically explored how Asians might be willing to engage in the aforementioned trade-offs in assessing democracy, the possible origins of such willingness, and its implications for critical political attitudes and behaviors (Huang, Chu, and Chang 2013; Lu 2013; Lu and Shi 2015). In collaboration with other teams of the Global Barometer Surveys network, ABS researchers have successfully expanded their examination of popular conceptions of democracy using the ranking instruments into Latin America, Africa, North America, and the Middle East for a much broader and richer comparison (Lu and Chu 2022).

Different from the ranking instruments adopted by the third and fourth waves of the ABS for popular understandings of democracy, the World Values Survey (WVS) has adopted a set of rating instruments to capture similar dynamics in today's world, which was first used in its European sub-survey. Methodologically, ranking and rating instruments have their respective merits and limitations. The ABS ranking instruments are more capable of assessing how people deal with potential trade-offs between distinct aspects of democracy, by asking respondents to select one out of four components. Nevertheless, such enforced comparisons and choices might make respondents anxious and uncomfortable, thus leading to more non-responses. The WVS rating instruments do not confront respondents with such enforced comparisons and choices, but simply ask them to rate different aspects of democracy independently. Although the lack of enforced comparisons and choices might reduce the anxiety among respondents, independent ratings might incur another problem that makes subsequent data analysis and theorization challenging. That is, some respondents might simply rate all specified aspects of democracy as equally critical and essential, thus, compromising the value of the collected information for assessing the relative salience of democracy's different aspects.

To enable an effective comparison with the WVS module of popular understandings of democracy, the fifth wave of the ABS adopted the same rating instruments to measure varying conceptions of democracy. Using a 10-point scale, the fifth wave asked respondents to assess the essentialness of seven aspects of politics for democracy: "Many things may be desirable, but not all of them are essential characteristics of democracy. On the scale of 1 to 10, 1 means not an essential characteristic of democracy and 10 means an essential characteristic of democracy, please choose the level for each statement." (RT1) "The court protects the ordinary people from the abuse of government power." (RT2) "Politics is clean and free of corruption." (RT3) "People have the freedom to take part in protests and demonstrations." (RT4) "When making laws, the government seeks advice from religious authorities." (RT5) "Political leaders rule by following their own wisdom rather than people's preferences to ensure a society's collective welfare." (RT6) "Rule by one party that represents the interests of all classes." (RT7) "Qualified candidates are pre-selected by religious leaders."

Furthermore, to ensure some continuity and valid comparison with the ranking instruments used in the third and fourth waves, the fifth wave kept one set of ranking instruments, asking respondents to choose the most essential characteristic of democracy among: (RK1) "People are free to express their political views openly." (RK2) "Basic necessities, like food, clothes and shelter, are provided for all." (RK3) "People choose the government leaders in free and fair elections." And (RK4) "Politics is clean and free of corruption."

New Evidence from the Fifth Wave of the ABS

ABS's evolving empirical strategies of measuring popular understandings of democracy have clearly indicated its consistent but growing ambition in using this bottom-up perspective to examine democracy's contemporary crisis and assess its prospect in different regions. The transition from the open-ended instrument to the closed-ended ranking instruments has enabled ABS researchers' more theoretically focused exploration and analysis. Hopefully, the most recent switch from ranking to rating instruments will allow ABS researchers to engage in a much broader and richer comparative examination on the same issue, by generating some interesting dialogues between ABS and WVS data. Here, we review the performance of the rating and ranking instruments of varying conceptions of democracy in the fifth wave of the ABS.

Using the only set of ranking instruments in the fifth wave of the ABS, we can revisit how Asians deal with potential trade-offs between key democratic principles and possible instrumental gains. We plotted the weighted percentages of prioritizing freedom and liberty (RK1), social equity (RK2), norms and procedures (RK3), and good government (RK4) in Figure 2.1. A fifth category of "DK" is also presented in Figure 2.1 for weighted percentages of non-response to the ranking instrument.

Figure 2.1 Responses to the PUD Ranking Instrument in the Fifth Wave of the ABS

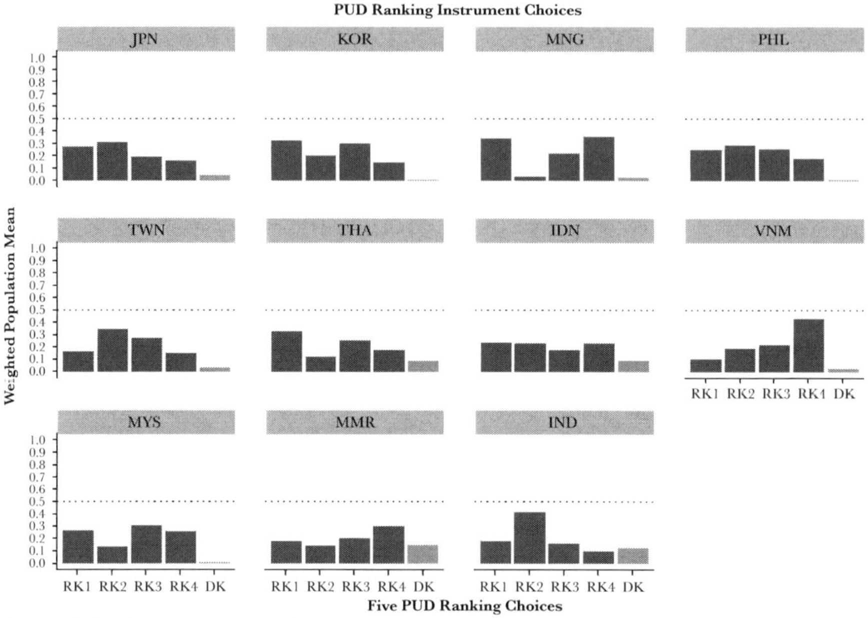

PUD Ranking Instrument Choices

Source: Asian Barometer Survey. Authors prepared.

As illustrated in Figure 2.1, when confronted with the trade-offs between key principles and instrumental gains of democracy, people in the eleven societies prioritize distinct aspects. The largest percentage of citizens in South Korea, Thailand, and Malaysia endorse democratic principles (e.g., freedom and liberty, or norms and procedures) as the most essential features of democracy. Meanwhile, the largest percentage of citizens in Japan, Mongolia, Philippines, Taiwan, Indonesia, Vietnam, Myanmar, and India endorse instrumental gains (e.g., social equity, or good government) as the most essential features of democracy. This is compatible with earlier findings on the prevalence of a substantive understanding of democracy in Asia (Huang, Chu, and Chang 2013; Lu 2013; Lu and Chu 2022; Lu and Shi 2015). Will the newly incorporated WVS module reveal a similar or different pattern of popular understandings of democracy in Asia? Figure 2.2 presents the weighted means of all seven rating instruments for each of the eleven societies.

Figure 2.2 Responses to the PUD Rating Instruments in the Fifth Wave of the ABS

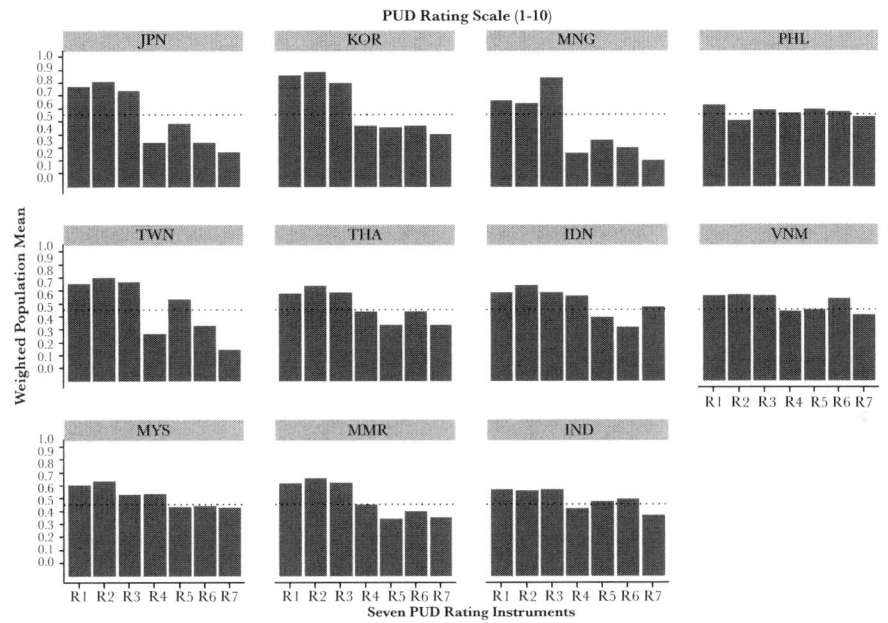

Source: Asian Barometer Survey. Authors prepared.

Instead of enforcing a choice between different aspects of democracy, the rating instruments ask respondents to assess distinct aspects of democracy independently. As shown in Figure 2.2, on average, the first three instruments (RT1 to RT3, namely, the rule of law, good government, and freedom of political participation) are consistently rated as highly essential for democracy in most of the societies. On the other hand, the importance of religious authority (RT4 and RT7), paternalistic meritocracy (RT5), and one-party rule (RT6) have received varying responses in these societies. However, in the Philippines, Indonesia, Vietnam, Malaysia, and India, some of the last four instruments are also rated as highly essential for democracy. Clearly, the trade-off dynamics displayed in Figure 2.1 are no longer obvious in Figure 2.2. This is partly driven by the distinct designs of ranking and rating instruments. What are the possible relations between the two instruments as documented in the fifth wave of the ABS?

To address such a concern, Figure 2.3 displays the weighted means of all seven rating instruments for each answer category of the ranking instrument in the fifth wave. Basically, we attempt to examine whether respondents prioritizing distinct aspects of democracy (as specified in the ranking instrument) might assess the selected aspects of democracy (as specified in the rating instruments) in different ways. As illustrated in Figure 2.3, regardless of whether Asian respondents prioritize social equity, good government, norms and procedures, or freedom and liberty as the defining feature of democracy, their respective ratings of the essentialness of the specified seven aspects of democracy do not show substantively significant differences. In other words, ranking and rating instruments appear to capture distinct cognitive and psychological dynamics in popular understandings of democracy. It is noteworthy that the pattern shown in Figure 2.3 is quite consistent with that in Figure 2.2. Basically, the first three instruments are rated much higher than the remaining four instruments by citizens in Asia, regardless of how they prioritize over democracy's democratic principles and instrumental gains.

Figure 2.3 Ranking-Rating Instruments in the Fifth Wave of the ABS

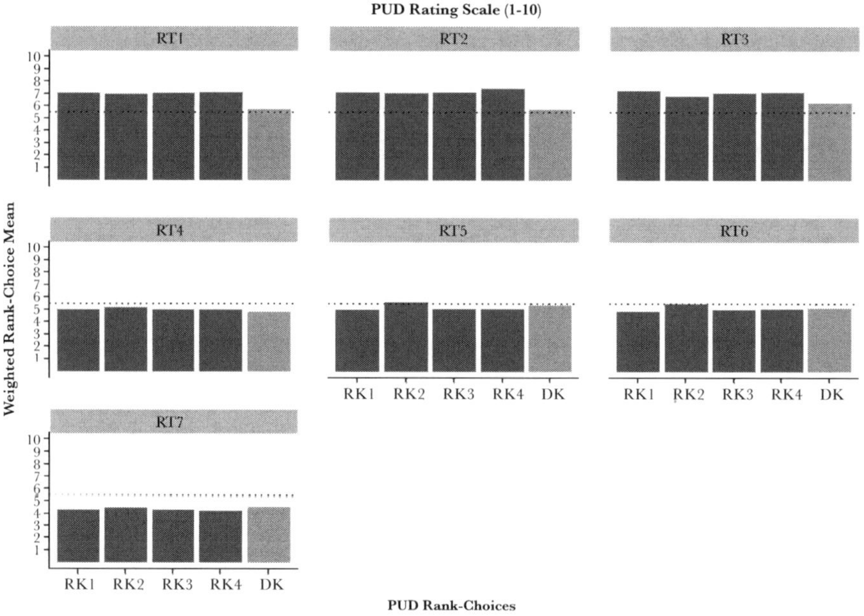

Source: Asian Barometer Survey. Authors prepared.

To more effectively summarize the findings based on the seven rating instruments in the fifth wave of the ABS, we use measurement models to explore the latent structure of the seven rating instruments. More specifically, we use both exploratory and confirmatory factor analysis to examine the performance of the rating instruments in capturing popular understandings of democracy as a latent construct. The analysis suggests that the seven instruments tap upon a two-dimensional latent construct: R1, R2, and R3 are loaded on one dimension;

while R4, R5, R6, and R7 are loaded on another dimension. Furthermore, the correlation between the two latent dimensions is -0.019 but statistically insignificant. In other words, the two dimensions of varying democratic conceptions (as captured by the seven rating instruments) are statistically independent. Basically, Asians who assess R1, R2, and R3 as highly essential for democracy are equally likely to value or discount the essentialness of R4, R5, R6, and R7 for democracy. In contrast to the trade-off dynamics highlighted by the ranking instrument, there is little tension between the varying aspects of democracy that the rating instruments focus on.

Figure 2.4 presents the results of the two-dimensional measurement models of the rating instruments, focusing on the distributions of two latent factor scores for each of the eleven societies. Similar to most recent findings of WVS scholars (Kirsch and Welzel 2019; Kruse, Ravlik, and Welzel 2019), we can differentiate between the so-called "authoritarian notions of democracy" and the "liberal notions" using the rating instruments. RT1, RT2, and RT3 are indicators of the latter, while RT4, RT5, RT6, and RT7 are the indicators of the former.

Figure 2.4 Latent Scores of PUD Rating Instruments in the Fifth Wave of the ABS

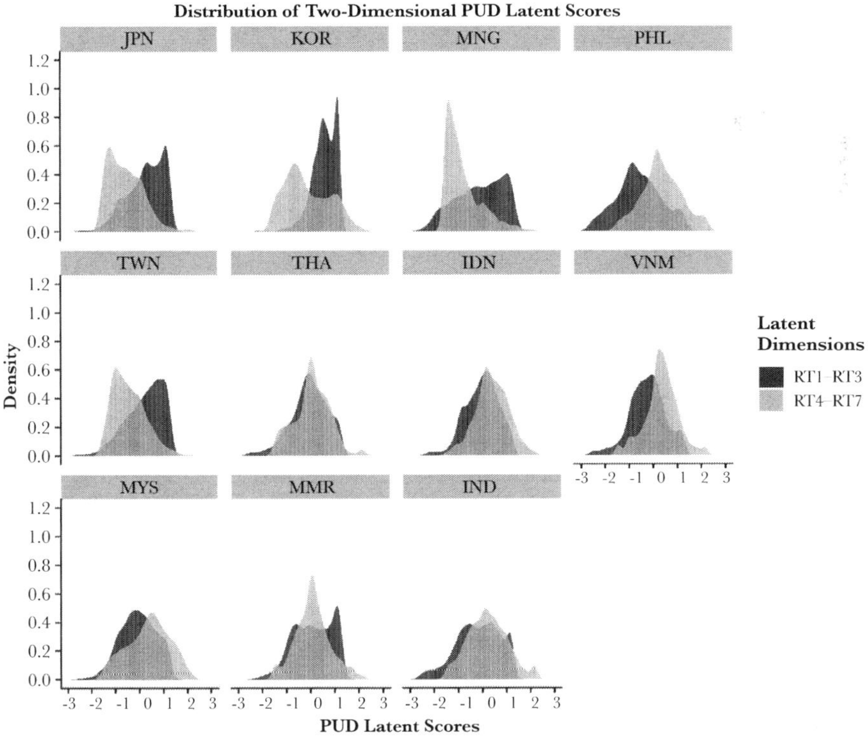

Distribution of Two-Dimensional PUD Latent Scores

Source: Asian Barometer Survey. Authors prepared.

Distributions of the two latent scores vary between Asian societies. In societies like Japan, South Korea, Mongolia, and Taiwan, the distribution of "authoritarian notions of democracy" is to the left of the distribution of "liberal notions." This suggests that, in these societies, people are more likely to rate the rule of law, good government, and freedom of political participation as highly essential features of democracy. Conversely, in societies like the Philippines, Vietnam, and Malaysia, the distribution of "authoritarian notions of democracy" is to the right of the distribution of "liberal notions." This indicates that people in these societies are more likely to rate the respect for religious authority, paternalistic meritocracy, and one-party rule as highly essential features of democracy. Meanwhile, in societies like Thailand, Indonesia, Myanmar, and India, the two distributions overlap to a significant level. This suggests that people in these societies do not significantly differentiate between the varying aspects when they consider the essential aspects of democracy.

Conclusions and Suggestions

Varying conceptions of democracy offer a critical and valuable lens through which scholars can examine contemporary democracy's crisis from a bottom-up perspective. As one of the most prominent comparative survey projects that explore critical political attitudes and behaviors, the ABS has incorporated instruments to examine how people understand democracy since its first survey wave. Over the past decades, the ABS has adapted its survey instruments to enable more theoretically-focused and richer comparative research on this topic. Besides the continuous use of the open-ended survey instruments, the ABS crafted new closed-ended ranking instruments (based on its findings using the open-ended instrument in ABS I and II) for its third and fourth waves to explore critical trade off dynamics in how people conceptualize democracy. In its most recent wave of comparative survey, the fifth wave of the ABS has adopted the WVS module for popular understandings of democracy to facilitate and enable much richer and more fruitful dialogues with related literature.

The new evidence from the fifth wave of the ABS has confirmed some of the key findings of both ABS and WVS scholars. In many Asian societies, when confronted with the trade-offs between democracy's key principles (e.g., related norms, values, procedures, and institutions) and instrumental gains, people are more inclined to prioritize the latter over the former. Basically, a substantive understanding of democracy still prevails in these Asian societies. Meanwhile, the differences between authoritarian and liberal notions of democracy also are notable in Asian societies, similar to what WVS scholars have found in other regions of the world. Systematic latent variable modeling suggests the lack of any robust relationship between the two notions of democracy in Asian societies, which is quite different from the documented salience of the trade-off dynamics captured by ABS's ranking instruments. No matter which instruments are under examination, significant variation is recorded between Asian societies. This suggests critical roles that might have been played by these societies' socioeconomic, political, cultural, and historical characteristics in shaping how their people conceptualize democracy.

Both ranking and rating instruments are valuable for our understanding and theorization of how popular conceptions of democracy might shape the prospect of democracy in today's world. They are likely to serve distinct theoretical goals. If possible, it might be interesting to see the incorporation of both instruments in future waves of ABS, GBS, or WVS surveys. Then students of democracy can further explore the respective values of these instruments in enriching the scholarship of democratic satisfaction, transition, consolidation, or even deconsolidation.

Note

1. Detailed information about the ranking instruments in the third and fourth waves can be found in Lu (2013).

References

Cho, Youngho. 2014. "To Know Democracy Is to Love It: A Cross-National Analysis of Democratic Understanding and Political Support for Democracy." *Political Research Quarterly* 67 (3): 478-488. doi:10.1177/1065912914532721.

—. 2015. "How Well Are Global Citizenries Informed about Democracy? Ascertaining the Breadth and Distribution of Their Democratic Enlightenment and Its Sources." *Political Studies* 63 (1): 240-258. doi:10.1111/1467-9248.12088.

Dalton, Russell J., Doh C. Shin, and Willy Jou. 2007. "Understanding Democracy: Data from Unlikely Places." *Journal of Democracy* 18 (4): 142-156. https://www.muse.jhu.edu/article/223229.

Druckman, James N. 2004. "Political Preference Formation: Competition, Deliberation, and the (Ir)relevance of Framing Effects." *American Political Science Review* 98 (4): 671-686. http://www.jstor.org/stable/4145331.

Druckman, James N., Erik Peterson, and Rune Slothuus. 2013. "How Elite Partisan Polarization Affects Public Opinion Formation." *American Political Science Review* 107 (1): 57-79. doi:10.1017/s0003055412000500.

Geddes, Barbara, and John Zaller. 1989. "Sources of Popular Support for Authoritarian Regimes." *American Journal of Political Science* 33 (2): 319-347. doi:10.2307/2111150.

Huang, Min-hua, Yun-han Chu, and Yu-tzung Chang. 2013. "Popular Understandings of Democracy and Regime Legitimacy in East Asia." *Taiwan Journal of Democracy* 9 (1): 147-171.

Huntington, Samuel P. 1991. *The Third Wave: Democratization in the Late Twentieth Century*. Norman: University of Oklahoma Press.

Kirsch, Helen, and Christian Welzel. 2019. "Democracy Misunderstood: Authoritarian Notions of Democracy around the Globe." *Social Forces* 98 (1): 59-92. doi:10.1093/sf/soy114.

Kruse, Stefan, Maria Ravlik, and Christian Welzel. 2019. "Democracy Confused: When People Mistake the Absence of Democracy for Its Presence." *Journal of Cross-Cultural Psychology* 50 (3): 315-335. doi:10.1177/0022022118821437.

Lu, Jie. 2013. "Democratic Conceptions in East Asian Societies: A Contextualized Analysis." *Taiwan Journal of Democracy* 9 (1): 117-145.

Lu, Jie, and Tianjian Shi. 2015. "The Battle of Ideas and Discourses Before Democratic Transition: Different Democratic Conceptions in Authoritarian China." *International Political Science Review* 36 (1): 20-41. doi:10.1177/0192512114551304.

Lu, Jie, and Yun-han Chu. 2022. *Understanding of Democracy: Origins and Consequences Beyond Western Democracies*. New York: Oxford University Press.

Lu, Jie, John Aldrich, and Tianjian Shi. 2014. "Revisiting Media Effects in Authoritarian Societies: Democratic Conceptions, Collectivistic Norms, and Media Access in Urban China." *Politics & Society* 42 (2): 253-283. doi:10.1177/0032329213519423.

Schaffer, Frederic Charles. 1998. *Democracy in Translation: Understanding Politics in an Unfamiliar Culture*. Ithaca: Cornell University Press.

—. 2014. "Thin Descriptions: The Limits of Survey Research on the Meaning of Democracy." *Polity* 46 (3): 303-330. doi:10.1057/pol.2014.14.

Schmitter, Philippe C., and Terry Lynn Karl. 1991. "What Democracy Is... and Is Not." *Journal of Democracy* 2 (3): 75-88. doi:10.1353/jod.1991.0033.

Shi, Tianjian. 2009. "Is There an Asian Value? Popular Understanding of Democracy in Asia." In *China's Reforms at 30: Challenges and Prospects*, edited by Dali L. Yang and Litao Zhao, 167-194. Singapore: World Scientific Publishing. doi:10.1142/9789812834256_0008.

—. 2015. *The Cultural Logic of Politics in Mainland China and Taiwan*. New York: Cambridge University Press.

Shi, Tianjian, and Jie Lu. 2010. "The Meanings of Democracy: The Shadow of Confucianism." *Journal of Democracy* 21 (4): 123-130. doi:10.1353/jod.2010.0012.

Shin, Doh Chull. 2017. "Popular Understanding of Democracy." In *Oxford Research Encyclopedia of Politics*. January 25. Accessed March 4, 2021. doi:10.1093/acrefore/9780190228637.013.80.

Stockmann, Daniela. 2012. *Media Commercialization and Authoritarian Rule in China*. New York: Cambridge University Press. doi:10.1017/cbo9781139087742.

Treier, Shawn, and Simon Jackman. 2008. "Democracy as a Latent Variable." *American Journal of Political Science* 52 (1): 201-217. doi:10.1111/j.1540-5907.2007.00308.x.

Zaller, John R. 1992. *The Nature and Origins of Mass Opinion*. New York: Cambridge University Press. doi:10.1017/cbo9780511818691.

3 Trends in Support for Democracy in East Asian Democracies

Larry Diamond

One of the most important developments in Asia in the past thirty years has been the emergence of a sizable group of democracies in a region that had been overwhelmingly authoritarian. Until the mid-1980s, Japan was the only stable democracy in East Asia. The Philippines had a rough, illiberal electoral democracy, but it yielded to the regional authoritarian trend in the 1970s. Thailand experimented with democracy in the 1970s but could not sustain it. Beginning with the "People Power" revolution in the Philippines in 1986, the region took a more decisive turn toward democracy. The electoral revolution that overthrew the Marcos dictatorship and brought Corazon Aquino to power in the Philippines that year was followed in 1987 by mass demonstrations and then a transition to democracy in South Korea through elections. That same year, a process of gradual transition to democracy was initiated in Taiwan, culminating in the first direct presidential election in 1996. Today, Taiwan is a liberal democracy with a vibrant two-party system and a vigorous civil society. As communism was crumbling in the Soviet empire, Mongolia made a transition to democracy in 1990, and following the 1997 financial crisis, the three-decade-old Suharto dictatorship fell from power in Indonesia in 1998, and the country made a transition to democracy the following year. In the early 1990s, Thailand shook off the constraints of a military-dominated semi-democracy and became a full electoral democracy. Unlike Japan, Korea, Taiwan, Mongolia, the Philippines, and Indonesia however, Thailand has since oscillated back and forth between democracy and military authoritarian rule. More recently, the Philippines has seen a return of illiberal and authoritarian practices.

These historical developments have given rise to a cohort of seven countries in East and Southeast Asia that have either been continuously democratic for more than two decades or at least have had substantial experience with (and demand for) democracy. To what extent do public attitudes and values in these countries support democratic evolution?

We can assess this question by examining the trends in attitudes and values toward democracy and authoritarianism in these seven countries over the roughly twenty-year period (2001-2018) encompassing the five waves of the Asian Barometer. The first wave was conducted in 2001 in Thailand and Taiwan, and in 2002 and/ or 2003 in Japan, Korea, and Mongolia, and Thailand (Indonesia was not surveyed until the second wave). The second wave was mostly conducted in 2006 (but in late 2005 in the Philippines and in early 2007 in Japan). The third wave was mostly administered in 2010 (but in 2011 in Japan). The fourth wave was done between 2014 and early 2016, and the fifth wave was conducted from mid-2018 to mid-2019.

To begin with, to what extent have citizens in these seven Asian democracies (or sometimes democracies) been satisfied with the way democracy is working in their country? As we see in Figure 3.1, most citizens of these seven democracies have consistently said that they are "very" or at least "fairly" satisfied with the way democracy works in their country. In fact, in striking contrast to Latin America, for example, (and to a lesser extent, Sub-Saharan Africa and even the Western democracies,) levels of satisfaction have been rising in the last decade and are now quite high (generally two-thirds and above) (Foa et al. 2020; Chu et al. 2020). Democratic satisfaction has increased from half to two-thirds of Japanese citizens, from 62 to 74 percent of Koreans, and from 53 to 69 percent of people in Taiwan. Thailand has seen a decline, but from an exceptionally high level (dropping from 90 to 74 percent in this period). Only Mongolia has seen a sharp and in fact steady drop, from 70 percent to 48 percent to 37 percent in the fifth wave survey (Figure 3.1).

Figure 3.1 Trends in Satisfaction with Democracy

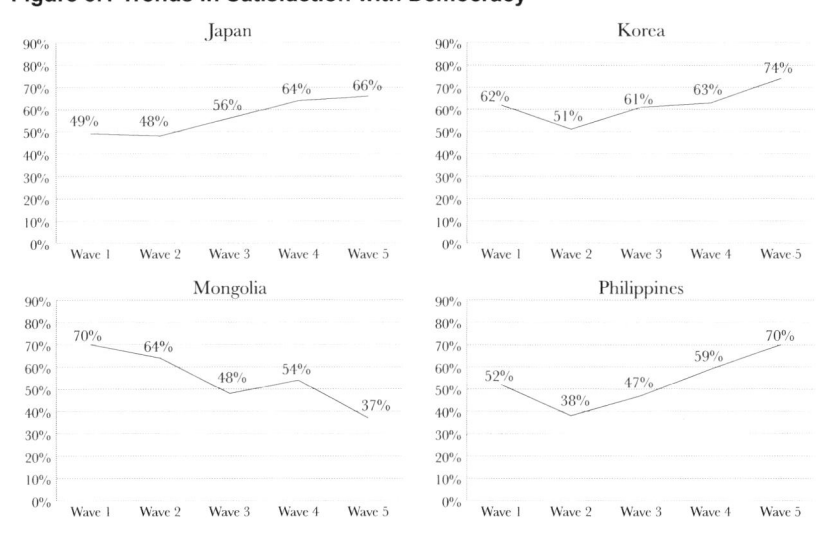

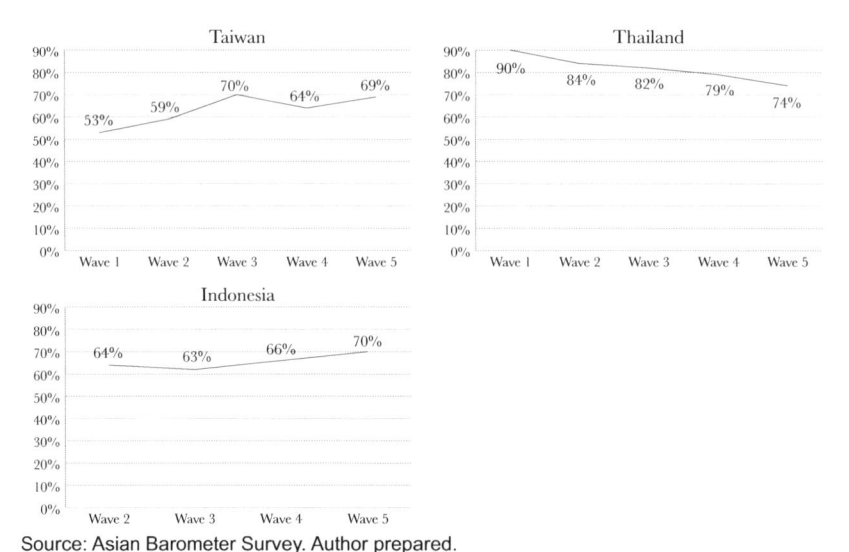

Source: Asian Barometer Survey. Author prepared.

What about support for democracy? Over the course of its five waves, the Asian Barometer has used a number of items to try to assess the extent to which Asians think democracy is the best form of government. The most direct measure, though not necessarily the most revealing, is simply to ask people whether they think that "democracy is always preferable" or that "sometimes an authoritarian government can be preferable," or that to someone like themselves, it doesn't matter. The percentage saying "democracy is always preferable" has varied across the seven countries and over time (Figure 3.2). Perhaps surprisingly, it has tended to be highest in Thailand, generally hovering around 80 percent, and it has been consistently 70 to 75 percent in Indonesia. The belief that "democracy is always preferable" has also been substantial in Japan, finishing at 68 percent in 2019 (down from 77 percent in the first survey in 2003). This measure of support for democracy has substantially increased in Korea, from half the public in 2003 to three-quarters in 2019. But across the five waves, it has only hovered around 50 percent in Taiwan. In two countries, this measure of support for democracy has substantially and steadily declined in the last two decades, from 58 to 37 percent in Mongolia and from 64 to 40 percent in the Philippines. This is one sign (and we will see others) of the deterioration of both democracy and public support for democracy in these two countries. In fact, it may help to explain the rapid slide toward autocracy, with seemingly little popular resistance, under current Philippine President Rodrigo Duterte.

Figure 3.2 Percent Saying Democracy Is Always Preferable

Source: Asian Barometer Survey. Author prepared.

While the most straightforward way to determine support for democracy is to simply ask people directly, it is not necessarily the most reliable. For one thing, Asian Barometer (and other research) shows that the "D-word"—democracy—has different meanings for different people, and the patterns of meaning vary within and across countries. Some people understand democracy more as the delivery of prosperity or order or other ends people want from the government. Others (correctly) understand democracy as a set of political procedures to ensure such things as freedom of speech or competitive elections, for example. The word may evoke negative images in some social or historical contexts, yet without triggering any concrete desire for an authoritarian type of system. In addition, when the "D-word" is used, support for democracy can vary significantly depending on how the question is asked. In addition to posing the "democratic preference" question above, with its three possible responses (including, "it doesn't matter to me"), the Asian Barometer asked people (in each of the last three surveys) whether they agree with the following statement: "Democracy may have its problems, but it's still the best form of government." This sounds similar to the first democracy question, but the recognition of imperfections ("Democracy may have its problems….") and the difference in response categories (a four-point Likert scale of strongly agree, agree, disagree, and strongly disagree) elicits significantly more positive responses in every single country. In fact, some of these differences are astonishing. In the fifth wave, when we compare responses on this item to those saying "democracy is always best," support for democracy jumps from 68 to 94 percent in Japan, from 47 to 89 support in Taiwan, from 37 to 75 percent in Mongolia, and from 40 to 86 percent in the Philippines (with smaller increases in the other three countries; Table 3.1). And when we asked whether "democracy is capable of solving the problems of our society," respondents in each country offered levels of support that fell somewhere in between the two above measures. We also asked people in these seven countries whether political leaders should be chosen in popular elections or on the basis of their "virtue." In five of the seven countries, 79 to 89 percent of the public say "elections," and 72 percent choose this option in Mongolia. Only in the Philippines is support for democratic elections more equivocal (50 percent).

Table 3.1 Preference for Democracy

Country	"Democracy is always preferable."	"Democracy may have its problems, but it's still the best form of government."	"Democracy is capable of solving the problems of our society."
Japan	68	94	73
Korea	75	83	79
Taiwan	47	89	55
Mongolia	37	75	66
Thailand	79	92	85
Philippines	40	86	73
Indonesia	76	94	89

Source: Asian Barometer Survey. Author prepared.

Given these significant—and in some cases, dramatic—differences in support for democracy depending on the survey item, survey researchers dating back to Richard Rose and his colleagues have found it meaningful to test the "Churchill hypothesis"—that democracy may have really serious problems, but it is in fact seen to be superior to all the other imaginable alternatives (Rose, Mishler, and Haerpfer 1998). As Rose and his colleagues did in their seminal work on Central and Eastern Europe in the late 1990s (and the Afrobarometer has also subsequently done), we tested support for three authoritarian alternatives: army rule, one-party rule, and one-man rule (getting "rid of parliament and elections" and having "a strong leader decide things").[1]

We gain important and distinctive insights into public regime preferences when we analyze the responses to these authoritarian regime alternatives. Consistently across the five waves of surveys, we find that the three advanced industrial democracies of the region—Japan, Korea, and Taiwan—exhibit generally the highest levels of rejection of authoritarianism (Figure 3.3). People in Taiwan may be cool to democracy when the "D-word" is mentioned, but they emphatically reject the available alternatives. Over time since the first wave in 2000, the percentage of people in Taiwan approving of a strong leader has declined from 21 to 16 percent, of a single party, from 18 to 7 percent, and of army rule, from 8 to 3 percent. Overall, the percentage of Taiwan's citizens rejecting all three alternatives has risen over the last two decades from 70 to 81 percent, and in Japan that proportion has risen from 68 to 86 percent. In Korea, it has declined slightly but remains above two-thirds (68 percent). Indonesia has oscillated between 51 and 68 percent (where it finished in the fifth wave), while rejection of all three authoritarian options has fallen in Mongolia (from 46 to 29 percent) and in the Philippines (from 40 to 31 percent).

Figure 3.3 Percent Rejecting All Three Authoritarian Options

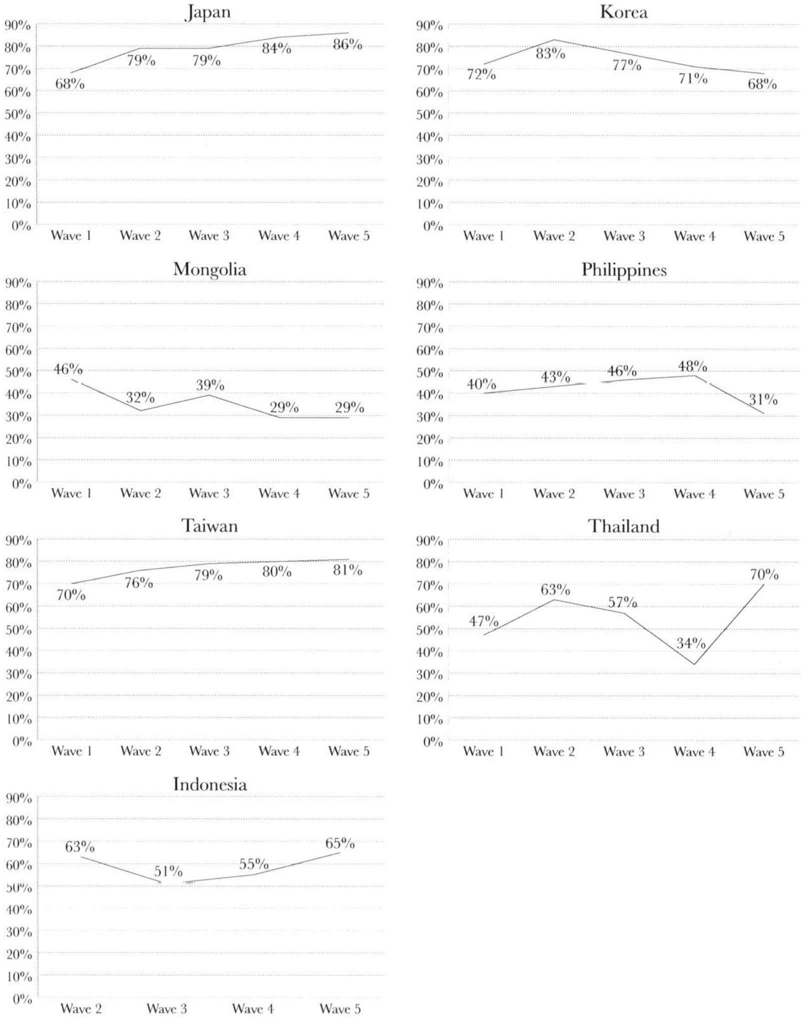

Japan

90%
80%
70% 68%   79%   79%   84%   86%
60%
50%
40%
30%
20%
10%
0%
Wave 1   Wave 2   Wave 3   Wave 4   Wave 5

Korea

90%
80%   83%
70% 72%   77%   71%
60%   68%
50%
40%
30%
20%
10%
0%
Wave 1   Wave 2   Wave 3   Wave 4   Wave 5

Mongolia

90%
80%
70%
60%
50% 46%
40%   32%   39%
30%   29%   29%
20%
10%
0%
Wave 1   Wave 2   Wave 3   Wave 4   Wave 5

Philippines

90%
80%
70%
60%
50%   43%   46%   48%
40% 40%
30%   31%
20%
10%
0%
Wave 1   Wave 2   Wave 3   Wave 4   Wave 5

Taiwan

90%
80%   79%   80%   81%
70% 70%   76%
60%
50%
40%
30%
20%
10%
0%
Wave 1   Wave 2   Wave 3   Wave 4   Wave 5

Thailand

90%
80%   70%
70%   63%
60%   57%
50% 47%
40%   34%
30%
20%
10%
0%
Wave 1   Wave 2   Wave 3   Wave 4   Wave 5

Indonesia

90%
80%
70% 63%   65%
60%
50%   51%   55%
50%
40%
30%
20%
10%
0%
Wave 2   Wave 3   Wave 4   Wave 5

Source: Asian Barometer Survey. Author prepared.

It is these attitudes toward authoritarian alternatives that generate the dramatic separation among the seven countries. By 2018-2019, five of the countries had decisive majorities (at least two-thirds of the public) rejecting all authoritarian options, while Mongolia and the Philippines revealed weak resistance to the authoritarian populism that was gaining momentum in their politics (Figure 3.4). Perhaps the most interesting pattern of variation over time is in Thailand, which saw support for army rule spike (to 54 percent) in the fourth wave, which was administered only a few months after the May 2014 military coup. However, by the time of the fifth wave (in late 2018 and early 2019), support for army rule had fallen to the lowest level ever recorded for Thailand in the Asian Barometer (13 percent), and the rejection of all three authoritarian options rose to a historic high (70 percent). See Table 3.2 for the complete trend data.

Figure 3.4 Trends in Support for Authoritarian Strong Leader

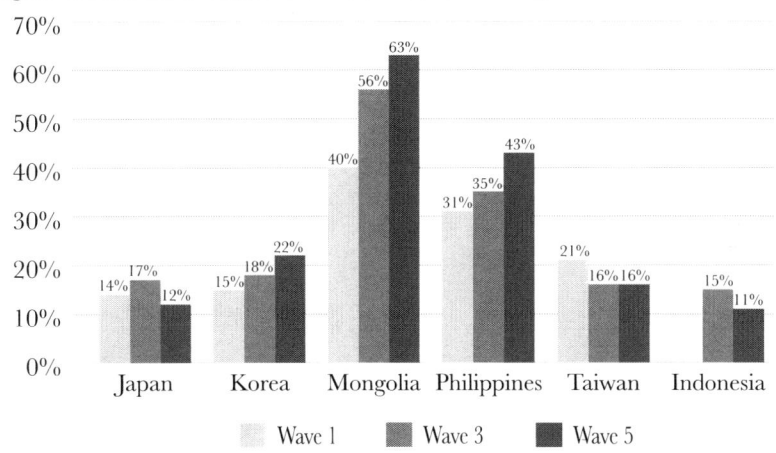

Source: Asian Barometer Survey. Author prepared.

Table 3.2 Trends in Support for Authoritarian Alternatives

Question	Country	Wave 1	Wave 2	Wave 3	Wave 4	Wave 5
Get rid of parliament and elections and have a strong leader decide things (% of strongly agree and agree, weighted, excl. invalid answers)	Japan	14%	17%	17%	13%	12%
	Korea	15%	12%	18%	21%	22%
	Mongolia	40%	63%	56%	65%	63%
	Philippines	31%	38%	35%	33%	43%
	Taiwan	21%	18%	16%	16%	16%
	Thailand	23%	24%	26%	38%	16%
	Indonesia	/	10%	15%	16%	11%
Only one political party should be allowed to stand for election and hold office	Japan	24%	10%	8%	8%	7%
	Korea	13%	7%	10%	14%	16%
	Mongolia	26%	28%	25%	31%	29%
	Philippines	30%	33%	32%	30%	43%
	Taiwan	18%	12%	10%	9%	7%
	Thailand	38%	19%	20%	35%	17%
	Indonesia	/	9%	17%	12%	8%
The army should come in to govern the country	Japan	1%	4%	4%	3%	2%
	Korea	10%	5%	7%	9%	14%
	Mongolia	11%	12%	12%	20%	14%
	Philippines	37%	25%	24%	29%	45%
	Taiwan	8%	7%	5%	4%	3%
	Thailand	18%	21%	20%	54%	13%
	Indonesia	/	32%	43%	38%	30%
Rejection of all three alternatives	Japan	68%	79%	79%	84%	86%
	Korea	72%	83%	77%	71%	68%
	Mongolia	46%	32%	39%	29%	29%
	Philippines	40%	43%	46%	48%	31%
	Taiwan	70%	76%	79%	80%	81%
	Thailand	47%	63%	57%	34%	70%
	Indonesia	/	63%	51%	55%	65%

Source: Asian Barometer Survey. Author prepared.

Democratic Values

A different way of measuring democratic culture is to look not at attitudes toward regime types—democratic or authoritarian—but rather at underlying values with regard to democratic principles and practices. For many years predating the Asian Barometer, Taiwan political culture researchers Hu Fu and Yun-han Chu (who would later found and direct the Asian Barometer) tested levels of support for presumed traditional Asian illiberal or authoritarian values such as communitarianism, deference to executive authority, and preference for order over freedom (Fu and Chu 1996). To the extent societies support statements like the seven listed in Table 3.3, they can be said to have authoritarian or illiberal value orientations. For example, do respondents agree that "Government leaders are like the head of a family; we should all follow their decisions"? Are they fearful of too much political pluralism of ideas and organization? Do they think the executive should be unchecked by the judiciary and the legislature?

The data in Table 3.3 and Figure 3.5 tell a powerful story, somewhat consistent with the modernization thesis. As Japan, Korea, and Taiwan have become richer and more "post-industrial" over the past two decades, and as younger generations socialized in an era of affluence have replaced older ones who grew up in harder times, values have clearly changed. The average level of agreement with authoritarian political values has fallen steadily in each of these three countries, from 36 to 29 percent in Japan, from 44 to 30 percent in Korea, and from 49 to 36 percent in Taiwan (Figure 3.5 and Table 3.3). These three countries are now predominantly not only democratic systems but in important political respects, liberal societies that manifest the "emancipative" values of human autonomy and empowerment that Ronald Inglehart and Christian Welzel have documented in their trailblazing work (Inglehart 1997; Inglehart and Welzel 2005; Welzel and Inglehart 2008, 2019). However, about three in five citizens in the other four democracies or sometime-democracies of East Asia still cling predominantly to illiberal political values. Support for these authoritarian values has declined only modestly in Mongolia and Thailand, and it has even increased in the Philippines and Indonesia. Notable in particular have been the sharp increases over time in the percentage of Indonesians who think the government should decide whether certain ideas can be discussed in society (from 50 to 65 percent) and the percentage of Filipinos who think the same (increasing from 54 percent in 2010 to 69 percent in 2018). The Philippines has also experienced significant decline in support for judicial independence and for legislative oversight of the executive, again consistent with the objective trend of rising authoritarian populism under President Duterte.

Figure 3.5 Trends in Average Percentages of Authoritarian Values

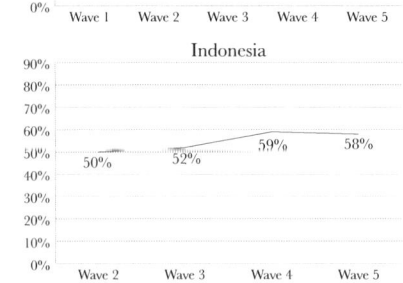

Source: Asian Barometer Survey. Author prepared.

Table 3.3 Trends in Support for Authoritarian Values

Question	Country	Wave 1	Wave 2	Wave 3	Wave 4	Wave 5
"Government leaders are like the head of a family; we should all follow their decisions." (% of strongly agree and agree, weighted, excl. invalid answers)	Japan	14%	25%	15%	15%	13%
	Korea	47%	37%	38%	36%	27%
	Mongolia	66%	73%	57%	58%	60%
	Philippines	52%	56%	40%	47%	56%
	Taiwan	34%	26%	22%	18%	18%
	Thailand	58%	58%	44%	45%	45%
	Indonesia	/	76%	72%	76%	78%
"The government should decide whether certain ideas should be allowed to be discussed in society." (% of strongly agree and agree, weighted, excl. invalid answers)	Japan	30%	19%	16%	14%	14%
	Korea	40%	38%	41%	42%	30%
	Mongolia	77%	85%	76%	71%	77%
	Philippines	60%	59%	54%	61%	69%
	Taiwan	28%	23%	24%	18%	16%
	Thailand	53%	49%	67%	55%	62%
	Indonesia	/	50%	54%	61%	65%
"Harmony of the community will be disrupted if people organize lots of groups." (% of strongly agree and agree, weighted, excl. invalid answers)	Japan	58%	47%	42%	42%	39%
	Korea	35%	39%	38%	36%	31%
	Mongolia	68%	83%	72%	76%	68%
	Philippines	54%	57%	55%	50%	52%
	Taiwan	62%	61%	55%	54%	49%
	Thailand	84%	87%	68%	88%	87%
	Indonesia	/	45%	52%	63%	58%
"When judges decide important cases, they should accept the view of the executive branch." (% of strongly agree and agree, weighted, excl. invalid answers)	Japan	24%	30%	24%	24%	19%
	Korea	31%	22%	30%	30%	25%
	Mongolia	26%	54%	43%	48%	33%
	Philippines	61%	66%	67%	65%	72%
	Taiwan	33%	37%	36%	37%	36%
	Thailand	60%	67%	31%	60%	51%
	Indonesia	/	38%	49%	55%	49%
"If the government is constantly checked by the legislature, it cannot possibly accomplish great things." (% of strongly agree and agree, weighted, excl. invalid answers)	Japan	38%	36%	38%	35%	39%
	Korea	46%	38%	36%	42%	32%
	Mongolia	59%	60%	54%	51%	51%
	Philippines	50%	54%	66%	58%	65%
	Taiwan	70%	62%	59%	58%	52%
	Thailand	52%	52%	45%	53%	39%
	Indonesia	/	38%	40%	45%	43%
"If we have political leaders who are morally upright, we can let them decide everything." (% of strongly agree and agree, weighted, excl. invalid answers)	Japan	32%	36%	42%	35%	29%
	Korea	63%	65%	58%	57%	34%
	Mongolia	69%	82%	76%	75%	74%
	Philippines	53%	59%	60%	63%	69%
	Taiwan	38%	34%	24%	20%	21%
	Thailand	75%	71%	78%	73%	56%
	Indonesia	/	46%	44%	47%	50%

(Continuing on the next page)

Table 3.3 Cont.

Question	Country	Wave 1	Wave 2	Wave 3	Wave 4	Wave 5
"If people have too many different ways of thinking, society will be chaotic." (% of strongly agree and agree, weighted, excl. invalid answers)	Japan	56%	55%	54%	51%	50%
	Korea	47%	44%	42%	42%	34%
	Mongolia	80%	76%	65%	71%	57%
	Philippines	57%	63%	70%	66%	64%
	Taiwan	75%	68%	68%	64%	63%
	Thailand	76%	81%	80%	85%	81%
	Indonesia	/	56%	55%	68%	62%
Average of percentages of authoritarian values	Japan	36%	35%	33%	31%	29%
	Korea	44%	40%	40%	41%	30%
	Mongolia	64%	73%	63%	64%	60%
	Philippines	55%	59%	59%	59%	64%
	Taiwan	49%	45%	41%	38%	36%
	Thailand	65%	66%	59%	66%	60%
	Indonesia	/	50%	52%	59%	58%

Source: Asian Barometer Survey. Author prepared.

The Effect of Age

Modernization theory, particularly as developed in recent decades by Ronald Inglehart and Christian Welzel and their collaborators, asserts that liberal democratic (or "empancipative") values are substantially the product of economic development, which generates greater "action resources," such as higher incomes and living standards, greater knowledge and information, and wider access to travel and communication. Moreover, "people's values take shape during their adolescence" (Welzel and Inglehart 2019, 142), and are the product of generally prevailing levels of development in society. Hence, generations socialized in more prosperous conditions should have more democratic values than prior generations who grew up in national circumstances with lower incomes, less education, and less access to information. If this assertion of modernization theory is correct, we would expect younger age cohorts to manifest more democratic values and to be more inclined to reject authoritarian rule. The age effect might be less apparent in relation to superficial support for democracy, and weaker or nonexistent in Japan, which has enjoyed a high level of prosperity for many decades now. But if the argument holds, it suggests a hopeful scenario for East Asia, as younger, more democratic generations gradually replace older ones more inclined to defer to authority and to be wary of social pluralism.

Where economic development has been most robust and sustained over the past four decades, in Korea and Taiwan, the expected age pattern does hold. However, the comparative picture is more complex—and in the case of the Philippines, unsettling. Over the five waves of the Asian Barometer, the average scores on the index of authoritarian values (indicating the average number of statements each age group agreed with) were consistently positively related to age in three countries: Korea, Mongolia, and Taiwan. The relationship has been particularly striking in Korea and Taiwan (and somewhat less so in Mongolia). With each step up the age ladder—from young people (17-29) to maturing adults (30-45), to middle aged (45-65) and elderly (65 and older)—the propensity to agree with authoritarian value statements increased, and this pattern held in virtually every survey. Noteworthy also has been the huge difference between the elderly and other age groups in Korea and Taiwan, and the general movement over time away from authoritarian values among all age groups, and especially the elderly—as we would expect with generational replacement. Figures 3.6 and 3.7 show the trends among age groups in Taiwan and Korea. In every survey in Taiwan since 2001, the elderly have had more authoritarian values, and people under 45 less authoritarian values. But by the fifth wave survey in 2018, the difference had shrunk dramatically—mainly because the average agreement with authoritarian values dropped sharply among the over-65 age group, from 4.19 to 2.67. Young people in Korea are also somewhat more inclined to say they support democracy and oppose authoritarian regime options than those over 65, but in Taiwan, where a majority do not say democracy is always preferable, reservations about "democracy" are stronger among the young.

Figure 3.6 Average Scores on the Seven-item Scale of Authoritarian Values in Taiwan

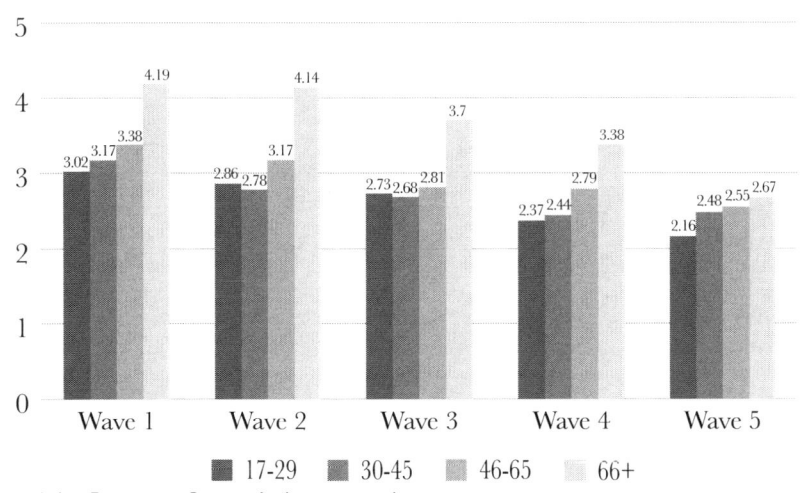

Source: Asian Barometer Survey. Author prepared.

Figure 3.7 Average Scores on the Seven-item Scale of Authoritarian Values in Korea

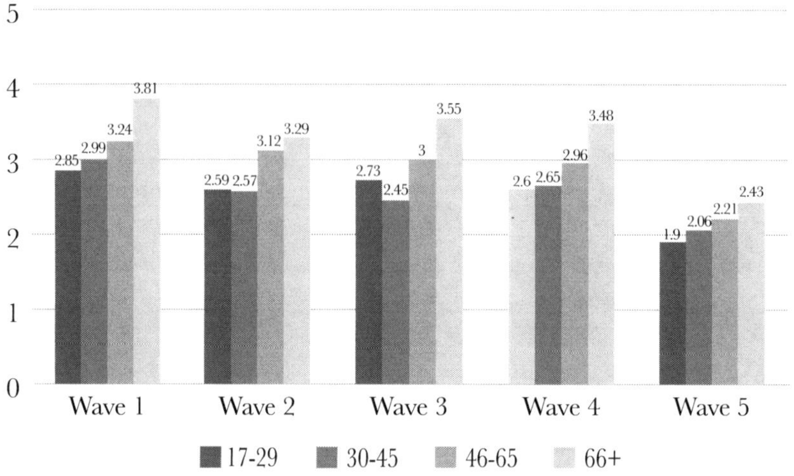

Source: Asian Barometer Survey. Author prepared.

Because Japan had long since achieved a high level of economic development when it was first surveyed in 2003, there was little clear effect of age then or since. Thailand has also shown a more mixed pattern, but with some decline in authoritarian values over time (save among the oldest age group). By contrast, Indonesia and especially the Philippines have displayed a worrying trend, reflective of the illiberal drift in each country. Values in Indonesia have become somewhat more authoritarian since the country was first surveyed in 2006 (during Wave 2). And young people are either more authoritarian than their elders or show no difference. The one striking difference in the Philippines (in Wave 5) is that those 65 and younger are at least half a point higher on the authoritarian values index than those over 65, and non-elderly Filipinos have recently increased by half a point (to around 4.6) in their average agreement with the seven authoritarian value statements. Filipinos over age 65 are also more likely to say (in Wave 5) that democracy is always preferable (51 percent) than the younger age groups (which range from 36 to 42 percent), and they are also somewhat more likely to reject all authoritarian options (but still only 38 percent of them do so). Thus, the downward trajectory of Philippine democracy is hardly just an elite phenomenon. From a political culture perspective, the country's democracy is not in good health. One reason why may be that levels of corruption and economic inequality in the Philippines have remained much worse than they were in Korea and Taiwan during their decades of emergence from poverty, and the Philippines has not achieved the sustained and broadly distributed economic development that these two countries (and a generation before, Japan) did. Indonesia has done somewhat better in terms of growth and distribution, but it confronts recurrent pressures of identity politics to a degree that Korea and Taiwan did not. And neither the Philippines nor Indonesia is yet near the middle-class level of economic development that appears to have ignited transformative value change in Korea and Taiwan.

Conclusion

There is good news and bad news in these two decades of public opinion surveys in the seven most pluralistic polities of East Asia. At the level of public opinion, Japan, Korea, and Taiwan appear to be consolidated and increasingly liberal democracies. Their citizens show high levels of satisfaction with the way democracy is working in their countries, and while people in Taiwan equivocate somewhat on items that include the word "democracy," they think that with all its problems, democracy "is still the best form of government" (89 percent) and that political leaders should be chosen by elections (86 percent). More emphatically, strong majorities in each of these societies reject all conceivable authoritarian options and have consistently done so across five surveys over the last two decades (and in steadily increasing proportions in Japan and Taiwan). Finally, in these three countries, authoritarian political values no longer attract the support of more than about a third of the public, on average.

The other four societies exhibit more fragile, fleeting, or conflicted attitudes toward democracy. In Indonesia and Thailand, overwhelming majorities of the public express support for democracy (however the question is worded), and about two-thirds of the public in each country now reject all authoritarian options. Thus, except for the brief post-coup surge in support for military rule in Thailand, both countries seem to be in a steady trend away from sympathy for authoritarian rule. But the pro-democratic leanings of these two societies still manifest a decidedly illiberal twist, co-existing with a considerable willingness to condone restrictions on freedom of expression and concentration of power in the executive branch.

The public opinion data in the Philippines and Mongolia tell a more troubling story. In these two countries, support for an authoritarian strong leader has recently surged at the same time that the political systems have been trending in an authoritarian populist direction (clearly in the Philippines, less starkly but still worrisomely in Mongolia). Overall (as measured most recently in 2018), only three in ten citizens in either country reject all three authoritarian options. Over the five surveys, the Philippines has become a steadily more illiberal country, with average levels of support for authoritarian values increasing from 55 to 64 percent in the fifth wave (the highest of the seven countries). Looking at the trends across a variety of measures, democracy in the Philippines appears to be in real and serious trouble. Even on an item as simple and straightforward as preferring leaders to be elected by the people, rather than being anointed on the basis of virtue, the percentage of Filipinos preferring elections has fallen from 68 to 50 percent between 2010 and 2018.

While the current presidential administration in Korea has been trending in an illiberal direction (Shin 2020), the continuing strong rejection by the public of authoritarian options and values suggests that this trend will not be sustainable. Japan and Taiwan rank as the most liberal democracies in Asia, and the trends in rejection of authoritarian values and options bear this out. Thailand and Indonesia back somewhat illiberal visions of democracy, which is to some extent what they have (or in the case of Thailand, had). Strong public support for democracy in principle suggests that the current military-dominated pseudo-democracy in Thailand rests on dubious public legitimacy. Its people want at least electoral democracy. That is what the Philippines had for most of the three decades between 1986 and 2016, but it is now steadily withering under a populist authoritarian president whose tough-guy demeanor has elicited shockingly high levels of public support (Reuters 2020).

All of this suggests that democracy will remain a contested ideal in East Asia for some time to come, and that the surest way to build a durable base of support for liberal and democratic values is through sustained and fairly distributed economic development.

Note

1. We have also asked about a fourth alternative, rule by experts, but it is not clear that people understand this as an authoritarian alternative in clear contrast to democracy, and so I do not consider it here.

References

Chu, Yun-han, Kai-Ping Huang, Marta Lagos, and Robert Mattes. 2020. "A Lost Decade for Third-wave Democracies?" *Journal of Democracy* 31 (2): 166-181.

Foa, Roberto Stefano, A. Claystone, M. Slade, A. Rand, and R. Williams. 2020. *The Global Satisfaction with Democracy Report 2020*. Cambridge: Bennett Institute for Public Policy, University of Cambridge. https://www.cam.ac.uk/system/files/report2020_003.pdf.

Fu, Hu, and Yun-han Chu. 1996. "Neo-authoritarianism, Polarized Conflict and Populism in a Newly Democratizing Regime: Taiwan's Emerging Mass Politics." *Journal of Contemporary China* 5 (11): 23-41.

Inglehart, Ronald. 1997. *Modernization and Postmodernization*. Princeton: Princeton University Press.

Inglehart, Ronald, and Christian Welzel. 2005. *Modernization, Cultural Change, and Democracy*. New York: Cambridge University Press.

Reuters. 2020. *Philippines' Duterte Scores Record High Rating, Despite Virus Crisis*. October 5. Accessed March 4, 2021. https://www.reuters.com/article/us-philippines-duterte/philippines-duterte-scores-record-high-rating-despite-virus-crisis-idUSKBN26Q0YK.

Rose, Richard, William Mishler, and Christian Haerpfer. 1998. *Democracy and Its Alternatives: Understanding Post-communist Societies*. Oxford: Polity Press.

Shin, Gi-wook. 2020. "South Korea's Democracy Decay." *Journal of Democracy* 31 (3): 100-114.

Welzel, Christian, and Ronald Inglehart. 2008. "The Role of Ordinary People in Democratization." *Journal of Democracy* 19 (1): 126-140.

—. 2019. "Political Culture, Mass Beliefs, and Value Change." In *Democratization*, edited by Christian W. Haerpfer, Patrick Bernhagen, Christian Welzel, and Ronald Inglehart, 127-144. Oxford: Oxford University Press.

4 Have East Asians Embraced Their Democratic Political System as "the Only Game in Town"? Ascertaining a Variety of Their System Preferences

Doh Chull Shin

"What I learned during the war is that food and culture are equal."
Jasmila Zbanic (qtd. in Higgins 2022)

Over the past four decades, more than 80 countries have made significant progress toward democracy by holding free elections and expanding competition among multiple political parties. These institutions, however, have failed to transform most of those countries into fully functioning democracies. To properly operate their institutional hardware, nascent democracies require the "software" that is congruent with the various hardware components (Almond and Verba 1963). A key component of such political software is what ordinary citizens think about democracy and its alternatives.

In both the scholarly community and policy circles, citizens are widely known to play a crucial role in the process of transforming authoritarian political systems into consolidated democracies (Dalton and Welzel 2014). Yet little is known about how they participate in this process of democratic consolidation. In what different ways or patterns do ordinary citizens engage in this process that requires the realignment of their system preferences? The present study attempts to address this completely ignored question in the context of democratic East Asia.

This study is presented in five parts. In the section that follows immediately, I briefly offer a critical review of previous research on citizen support for democracy. Based on this review, I explicate the notion of system preferences and ascertain its five distinct patterns. The third section discusses how these patterns are discovered with the data culled from the fourth wave of the Asian Barometer Survey (ABS hereafter) in five East Asian democracies. The fourth section compares proportions of those engaged in these patterns to highlight the most and least prevalent in each country and throughout democratic East Asia. The final section summarizes key findings and discusses their implications for further democratization in East Asia.

Prior Research

Over the past two decades, the Asian Barometer Survey has conducted five waves of multinational surveys and thereby enabled a large number of researchers to monitor and compare how East Asians engage in the process of democratization (Chu et al. 2008; Chu and Huang 2010; Shin and Wells 2005). To date, the studies based on these surveys were concerned mostly with the *level* or *quantity* of pro-democratic and anti-authoritarian regime orientations. Many of them compared the percentages upholding those orientations across time and space. Others constructed composite indices tapping favorable orientations to democracy and autocracy and thereby determined the prevalence of democrats who favor democracy more than autocracy.

These percentages and indices are summary statistics, which merely refer to the properties of a collective unit to which individual citizens belong. As such aggregate statistics, they are not capable of unraveling the process in which individual citizens compare democracy and autocracy and prefer one of these systems to the other. Nor are they capable of ascertaining the different paths which people take to become citizens of a democratic state.

Moreover, previous research endeavors relied on responses to a series of survey questions containing the word "democracy," which refers to a political phenomenon highly desired throughout the world (Sen 1999). They defined and measured support for democracy *inclusively* in terms of the extent to which favorable orientations toward democracy prevail over those toward autocracy. In measuring democratic support, they also mistakenly equated rejections of illiberal norms and practices with acceptances of liberal norms and practices.

In previous analyses of the ABS, East Asians who did not truly favor democracy or even favored autocracy to some extent were regarded as exclusive or unqualified supporters of a democratic system. As a result, the extant literature portrays highly inaccurate and inflated accounts of the extent to which they prefer democracy. It also offers little information about how they have altered their system preferences in the wake of experiencing democratic politics.

Conceptualization

As citizens of post-authoritarian societies, people in democratic East Asia remain socialized into authoritarian politics. As democratic novices, they are also poorly informed about the virtues of democracy (Shin and Kim 2018). To many of these people, therefore, democracy does not represent the best solution to the problems facing their societies (Rose, Mishler, and Haerpfer 1998). As a result, they are not likely to reject autocracy. Nor are they likely to embrace democracy *unconditionally* as the best system of government.

Between the old system of autocracy and the new system of democracy, do citizens of East Asian democracies accept just one or both types as a newly preferred system of government? If they accept democracy as such a system, do they accept it fully or partially? If they reject autocracy as such a system, do they do it fully or partially? Responses to these questions all of which were never explored before are considered together to ascertain five patterns of system preferences.

Table 4.1 shows these patterns; they are: (1) *autocrats* rejecting democracy fully and accepting autocracy either partially or fully; (2) *hybrids* accepting democracy partially and also accepting autocracy either partially or fully; (3) *antiauthoritarians* rejecting autocracy fully and yet refusing to accept democracy fully; (4) *proto-democrats* accepting democracy fully and also accepting autocracy either partially or fully; and (5) *authentic democrats* accepting democracy fully and rejecting autocracy fully. Of these five patterns, the fifth represents the unconditional or exclusive embrace of democracy, accepting democracy as "the only game in town."

Table 4.1 Five Patterns of System Preferences

		Accepting Democracy		
		Not at all	Partially	Fully
Rejecting Autocracy	Not at all	*Autocrat*	*Hybrid*	*Proto-democrat*
	Partially	*Autocrat*	*Hybrid*	*Proto-democrat*
	Fully	*Antiauthoritarian*	*Antiauthoritarian*	*Authentic Democrat*

Source: Author prepared.

Measurement

To ascertain these five diverse patterns of system preferences, I chose two sets of four items from the fourth wave of the ABS in the three liberal democracies (Japan, Korea, and Taiwan) and two electoral democracies (Indonesia and Mongolia) during the 2014-16 period. The first set comprised four separate questions each of which deals with one of the four essential practices of democratic governance without referring to the word "democracy." They include (1) choosing political leaders through open and competitive elections (Q82); (2) allowing news media to publish news and ideas without government control (Q81); (3) allowing the people to participate in the political process and express what they want (Q80); and (4) having government leaders implement voters' interests and preferences (Q79). Responses affirming these democratic practices are considered together to determine whether democracy is not preferred at all, partially preferred, or fully preferred.

The second set of four questions deals with four different alternatives to democratic government. They are: (1) to get rid of parliament and elections and have a strong leader decide things (Q130); (2) to allow only one political party to stand for election and hold office (Q131); (3) to have the military to govern the country (Q132); and (4) to get rid of elections and parliaments and have experts make decisions on behalf of the people (Q133). As with the first set, responses affirming each mode of autocratic governance are considered together to determine whether autocracy is not preferred at all, partially preferred, or fully preferred.

Finally, these three categories—none, partial, and full—of autocratic and democratic responses are considered together to identify those who engage in each of the five patterns of system preferences. Those who failed to answer most or all four questions in each set are placed into the separate category of missing cases. Within each country, proportions of those engaged in each of the five patterns are compared to determine the extent to which their system preferences are concentrated or dispersed. Proportions engaged in each pattern are also compared across the five countries to identify the most and least popular patterns of system preferences among the citizenries of democratic East Asia as a whole.

Rejecting Autocracy

Five democracies in East Asia have allowed their citizenries to participate and compete in the electoral and non-electoral processes over several decades. Has such a long period of democratic political life enabled them to fully de-align themselves from the various modes of autocratic governance, some of which were once practiced in their own country or are currently practiced in other nondemocratic countries in the region? If not, to what extent are they detached or undetached from the legacies of the autocratic past? Table 4.2 presents the relevant data to these questions concerning the breadth and depth of authoritarian detachment. The first column in the table shows for each country the proportion of its citizenry *fully detached* from all four types of autocratic government, including civilian dictatorship, military dictatorship, one-party rule, and meritocracy. The second and third columns show, respectively, the proportions of the *partially detached* from some modes of autocratic government and the *undetached* from any type. In all five countries, those undetached from autocracy, who remain fully attached to it, are least numerous and form small minorities of less than 10 percent. The fully detached, who are unattached to autocracy, are most numerous in all countries except Mongolia. Yet, they form majorities only in three liberal democracies, ranging 65 percent in Korea to 76 percent in Japan. In Mongolia, the fully detached from the legacies of communist one-party rule account for only one quarter (25 percent) of its citizens.

Table 4.2 Proportions of the Detached and Undetached from the Legacies of Autocracy

	Fully Detached	Partly Detached	Undetached	Missing
Japan	76%	19%	1%	4%
Korea	65	31	3	2
Mongolia	25	66	8	1
Taiwan	72	24	1	4
Indonesia	47	38	4	12
(pooled)	57	36	3	5

Source: Asian Barometer Survey, fourth wave. Author prepared.

The undetached and partially detached are considered together to identify those who remain attached to autocracy. Their proportions range from a small minority of one-fifth (20 percent) in Japan to a large majority of three quarters (74 percent) in Mongolia. When all five countries are considered together, nearly two out of five (39 percent) people in democratic East Asia remain attached to autocracy to some extent. Even after decades of democratic rule, the legacies of the authoritarian past persist in every democratic country and remain a potent force to contend with its further democratization. Evidently, autocracy has not disappeared as a preferred system of government in democratic East Asia.

Has any of the four different modes of autocratic government become a *passe* in any of five democratic countries? If not, which mode remains the most resilient or unyielding to the forces of democratization? Does this type vary across the five countries? I explore these questions by examining whether people in every country remain attached to each mode of autocratic government. Table 4.3 shows that in all five countries, 3 to 64 percent of the citizenries remain attached to one mode or another. In the entire democratic region, 14 to 25 percent are attached to each mode. This finding indicates that none of the four modes of authoritarian government considered in this study has become a *passe* in democratic East Asia.

Table 4.3 Proportions of the Attached to Autocratic Regimes

	Civilian Dictatorship	Military Dictatorship	One-party Dictatorship	Meritocracy
Japan	12%	7%	3%	8%
Korea	20	14	9	20
Mongolia	64	31	20	42
Taiwan	15	8	4	12
Indonesia	14	10	33	13
(pooled)	25	14	14	19

Source: Asian Barometer Survey, fourth wave. Author prepared.

Which mode of autocratic government are East Asians most reluctant to abandon even when they have lived under decades of democratic rule? Civilian dictatorship, which replaces the democratic institutions of elections and parliament with a powerful leader, remains the most impervious or unyielding to decades of democratic politics. In all five countries, more than 10 percent remain attached to it. In Mongolia, those attached to this mode comprise a large majority of nearly two-thirds (64 percent). When considered together, one-quarter (25 percent) of those in all five countries refuses to give up on it. Of the four modes of autocratic governance, civilian dictatorship comprises the most resilient to the forces of democratization.

In which of the five countries do the autocratic legacies of the past prevail the most? In which country do they prevail the least? To address these questions, I calculated the average number of autocratic legacies favored by citizens of each country. Figure 4.1 shows that Japan, the oldest democracy in the region, registers the lowest number of 0.3, followed by Taiwan (0.4), Korea (0.6), Indonesia (0.8), and Mongolia (1.6). When these numbers are compared across the countries, two notable cross-national differences emerge. First, people who once lived under communist autocracy are the least reluctant to abandon autocracy. Second, citizens of electoral democracies are less reluctant to do so than their peers in liberal democracies.

Figure 4.1 Overall Levels of Citizen Attachment to Autocracy and Democracy (on a 5-point Index)

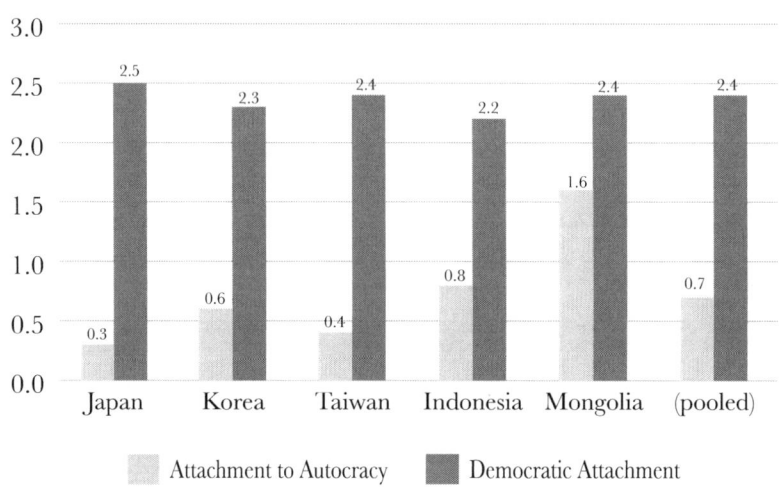

Source: Asian Barometer Survey, fourth wave. Author prepared.

Accepting Democracy

Like motherhood and patriotism, democracy has become a socially desirable phenomenon. Besides, it often means different things to different people. To minimize biased responses to the questions containing the word "democracy," the ABS excluded this word and asked a new set of four questions each of which queried one of the four essential practices. Have the citizenries of five East Asian democracies embraced all, some, or none of the practices? For each country, Table 4.4 shows the proportions of the unattached, partially attached, and fully attached.

In every country, the unattached are least numerous while the partially attached are most numerous. Like the undetached from autocracy, the unattached to democratic governance form small minorities of less than 10 percent in all five countries. Like the partially detached from autocracy, the partially attached to democracy are most numerous, forming large majorities of over 70 percent in each country. Those people who engage in either of these two categories vary relatively little across five countries. The unattached, for example, vary by 4 percentage points from 3 percent in Indonesia to 7 percent in Korea. The partially attached vary by 6 percentage points from 71 percent in Japan and Mongolia to 76 percent in Indonesia.

Table 4.4 Proportions of the Attached and Unattached to Democratic Government

	Unattached	Partly Attached	Fully Attached	Missing
Japan	4%	71%	19%	6%
Korea	7	74	18	2
Mongolia	6	72	21	1
Taiwan	4	75	18	2
Indonesia	3	76	10	11
(pooled)	5	74	17	4

Source: Asian Barometer Survey, fourth wave. Author prepared.

In contrast, the fully attached to democracy, unlike the fully detached from autocracy, constitute small minorities of less than one quarter in all five countries. And their proportions vary considerably across the countries from 10 percent in Indonesia to 21 percent in Mongolia. More surprising is that they are most numerous in Mongolia where the undetached from autocracy is most numerous and the fully detached from it is least numerous. This finding indicates that among East Asians, a high level of affinity for democracy coexists with a high level of affinity for autocracy. It also indicates that many East Asians simultaneously uphold both democracy and autocracy as a preferred system of government. Contrary to what is known in a large body of the literature, favorable orientations to autocracy are not always inversely related to affinity for democracy among East Asians.

Is there any essential practice of democratic governance East Asians have accepted unanimously? If not, which practices are the most and least approved among them? According to Table 4.5, none of them is approved either unanimously or overwhelmingly in any of the five countries. Even in Japan where elections have been conducted regularly since November 1946, less than four-fifths (76 percent) endorse electing political leaders. In all other countries, merely substantial majorities, which range from 74 percent in Mongolia and 81 percent in Taiwan, endorse this practice. In democratic East Asia today, there is neither a unanimous nor overwhelming endorsement of popular elections, the most fundamental and oldest practice of democratic government. In all five countries, nonetheless, this is the most approved practice of the four democratic practices considered.

Table 4.5 Proportions of the Attached to Four Essential Practices of Democracy

	Popular Elections	Media Freedom	Political Participation	Responsive Government
Japan	76%	66%	59%	38%
Korea	76	64	39	50
Mongolia	74	55	64	47
Taiwan	81	56	64	34
Indonesia	80	26	43	51
(pooled)	77	53	54	44

Source: Asian Barometer Survey, fourth wave. Author prepared.

The least approved is the practice of holding political leaders responsive to the electorate by implementing their voters' preferences. Only in Indonesia, a bare majority of 51 percent approved of this practice. In two liberal democracies, Japan (36 percent) and Taiwan (34 percent), the smallest minorities of less than two fifths approve it. In democratic East Asia as a whole, a minority of two-fifths (44 percent) endorse implementing responsive government. Of four democratic practices, this is the only one a majority (56 percent) refuse to endorse. In East Asian democracies, people are least eager to accept the democratic practice of holding government leaders responsive to the electorate while they are most reluctant to do away with the legacy of civilian dictatorship.

Figure 4.1 shows the number of democratic practices the citizenry of each country accepted on average from a total of four. The national means of the accepted practices vary little from 2.2 in Indonesia to 2.4 in Japan. Scoring lower than 3.0, these means indicate that people in all five countries failed to accept most of the essential democratic practices considered. They also indicate that the acceptance of democratic practices, unlike the rejection of autocratic rules, has little to do with the type of autocratic system in which East Asians once lived in the past and the type of democratic system in which they currently live.

Patterns of System Preferences

Separate analyses of orientations to autocracy and democracy have revealed that most people in democratic East Asia are neither fully rejecting the former nor fully accepting the latter. These analyses have also revealed that rejecting the former does not often lead to accepting the latter. These findings make it necessary to examine how autocracy and democracy interact with each other in the minds of individual citizens and to ascertain distinct patterns of system preferences that emerge from the interactions of those two systems.

For each country, Table 4.6 shows the proportions of its citizenry engaged in the five patterns discussed earlier. The most noticeable feature of the table is that in all five countries, people engage in every pattern, although those engaged in each pattern vary a great deal from a low of one percent to a high of 57 percent. It also shows that out of 25 cells in the table, only three register bare majorities from 53 to 57 percent. This indicates that citizenries are not heavily concentrated into one pattern in any of those countries. Instead, they are distributed into all five patterns. Evidently, system preferences among the citizenries of East Asian democracies vary a great deal in kind.

The autocratic pattern, showing those who reject democracy fully and accept autocracy either partially or fully, is the least prevalent in all five countries; they form small minorities of less than five percent. When the five democratic countries are considered together, only three percent of their entire citizenries remain attached exclusively to the autocratic system of the past. In every country, moreover, they are also overwhelmed by *antiauthoritarians*, who fully reject autocracy without accepting democracy fully. In every democratic East Asian country, a large majority of its citizenry have de-aligned from autocracy either partly or fully.

Table 4.6 Proportions of the Engaged in Five Patterns of System Preferences

	Autocrats	Anti-authoritarians	Hybrids	Proto-democrats	Authentic Democrats	(missing)
Japan	1%	57%	14%	4%	14%	10%
Korea	3	47	25	5	13	6
Mongolia	4	15	56	14	8	4
Taiwan	2	53	20	3	15	7
Indonesia	2	39	32	4	5	18
(pooled)	3	42	29	6	11	9

Source: Asian Barometer Survey, fourth wave. Author prepared.

Have those de-aligned from autocracy realigned themselves with democracy? Table 4.6 shows that the democratic pattern of rejecting autocracy fully and accepting democracy fully is not the most popular pattern in any East Asian country. What prevails most throughout democratic East Asia is the *antiauthoritarian* pattern of rejecting autocracy fully but accepting democracy partially. Four countries, including all three liberal democracies, engage in this pattern with 39 percent in Indonesia to 57 percent in Japan. Only Mongolia shows a small minority for this type of 15 percent. In Mongolia, adherents to this *antiauthoritarian* pattern are outnumbered by the pattern of hybridizing autocracy with democracy (56 percent).

In all five countries, the exclusively and fully committed to democracy constitute small minorities of much less than one-fifth of their citizenries. In three liberal democracies, they range from 13 percent in Korea to 15 percent in Taiwan. In two electoral democracies, they range from five percent in Indonesia to eight percent in Mongolia. There are twice as many *authentic democrats* in liberal democracies as in electoral democracies. Between the old and new liberal democracies, however, there is little difference (14 percent in Japan vs. 13 percent in Korea and 15 percent in Taiwan).

When all these five countries are considered together, only one in ten people (11 percent) has embraced democracy as the *exclusively* or unconditionally preferred system of government. In every country, moreover, they are outnumbered by *antiauthoritarians* or *hybrids*. In Mongolia, they are outnumbered even by *proto-democrats* who embrace democratic practices fully without rejecting autocracy fully. All these figures confirm the paucity of authentic or fully committed democrats throughout democratic East Asia.

Most notably, proportions of *authentic democrats* account for small fractions of what is known in the democratization literature as a minimum threshold of democratic consolidation. According to Larry Diamond (1999, 68), for example, a political system becomes a consolidated democracy when a supermajority—70-75 percent—of its citizenry embrace democracy as "the best form of government." By this standard, East Asian democracies are all far from consolidated. Nor has any of them traveled more than one-fifth of the necessary journey to its consolidation.

Summary and Conclusion

In East Asia today, only five of 17 independent states are recognized as democracies and none of these democracies is rated as a full democracy (Economist Intelligence Unit 2020). Has any of these five democracies become a consolidated democracy? To explore this question, the present study chose the popular notion that a political system becomes such a system when an overwhelming majority of its citizenry embrace democracy as the only game in town and thereby analyzed the ABS fourth wave conducted in five East Asian democracies.

The analyses of the ABS reveal that most people in these countries neither reject autocracy fully nor accept democracy fully. As a result, they refuse to embrace democracy with the full exclusion of autocracy and engage in one of four other patterns of system preferences. As majorities or pluralities in all five countries engage in either *antiauthoritarian* or *hybrid* pattern, the results indicate that democracy is yet to become the most preferred system of government in democratic East Asia.

All three liberal democracies in this region have incessantly implemented democratic politics over four to seven decades. And yet only 13 to 15 percent of their citizenries embrace democracy as the only game in town, which is widely regarded as the hallmark of democratic consolidation (Di Palma 1990, 113; Linz and Stepan 1996, 5). This indicates that even in liberal democratic East Asia, *authentic democrats* have grown at the meager rate of less than four percent per ten years. At this rate, none of the five countries is likely to become a consolidated democracy before the end of this century.

In every democratic country, moreover, democracy is not the most preferred system of government even among the most affluent and college-educated segments of its population. Nor is it the most preferred system among the young in their 20s and 30s who have lived all their lives under democratic rule. Evidently, neither socioeconomic resources or democratic political experiences, both of which are widely touted as promoters of democratization, have de-aligned East Asians from autocracy and realigned them with democracy.

These findings from East Asia directly challenge the Western theories linking democratic consolidation to the experiencing and learning of democratic politics and the modernizing of the traditional economy and social life (Inglehart and Welzel 2005; Rose 2007; Sen 1999; Welzel 2013). They also run counter to the popular claim that East Asia will become a region of democracies within a generation (Diamond 2012).

References

Almond, Gabriel A., and Sidney Verba. 1963. *The Civic Culture: Political Attitudes and Democracy in Five Nations*. Princeton: Princeton University Press. http://www.jstor.org/stable/j.ctt183pnr2.

Chu, Yun-han, and Min-hua Huang. 2010. "Solving an Asian Puzzle." *Journal of Democracy* 21 (4): 114-122. doi:10.1353/jod.2010.0009.

Chu, Yun-han, Larry Diamond, Andrew Nathan, and Doh Chull Shin. 2008. *How East Asians View Democracy*. New York: Columbia University Press. doi:10.7312/chu-14534.

Dalton, Russell J., and Christian Welzel. 2014. *The Civic Culture Transformed: From Allegiant to Assertive Citizens*. New York: Cambridge University Press. doi:10.1017/cbo9781139600002.

Di Palma, Giuseppe. 1990. *To Craft Democracies: An Essay on Democratic Transitions.* Berkeley: University of California Press. http://ark.cdlib.org/ark:/13030/ft467nb2sk/.

Diamond, Larry. 2012. "Why East Asia—including China—Will Turn Democratic within a Generation." January 24. https://www.theatlantic.com/international/archive/2012/01/why-east-asia-including-china-will-turn-democratic-within-a-generation/251824/.

—. 1999. *Developing Democracy: Toward Consolidation.* Baltimore: Johns Hopkins University Press.

Economist Intelligence Unit. 2020. "Global Democracy in Retreat." https://www.eiu.com/n/global-democracy-in-retreat. Accessed August 20, 2020.

Higinns, Andrew. 2022. "Filmmaker Shows Humanity of Warring Sides." In *New York Times* (January 15, A4).

Inglehart, Ronald, and Christian Welzel. 2005. *Modernization, Cultural Change, and Democracy.* New York: Cambridge University Press. doi:10.1017/cbo9780511790881.

Linz, Juan J., and Alfred Stepan. 1996. *Problems of Democratic Transition and Consolidation.* Baltimore: Johns Hopkins University.

Rose, Richard. 2007. "The Democracy Barometers (Part I): Learning to Support New Regimes in Europe." *Journal of Democracy* 18 (3): 111-125.

Rose, Richard, William Mishler, and Christian Haerpfer. 1998. *Democracy and its Alternatives: Understanding Post-Communist Societies.* Baltimore: Johns Hopkins University Press.

Sen, Amartya Kumar. 1999. "Democracy as a Universal Value." *Journal of Democracy* 10 (3): 3-17. doi:10.1353/jod.1999.0055.

Shin, Doh Chull, and Hannah Kim. 2018. "How Global Citizenries Think about Democracy: An Evaluation and Synthesis of Recent Public Opinion Research." *Japanese Journal of Political Science* 19 (2): 222-249.

Shin, Doh Chull, and Jason Wells. 2005. "Challenge and Change in East Asia: Is Democracy the Only Game in Town?" *Journal of Democracy* 16 (2): 88-101. doi:10.1353/jod.2005.0036.

Welzel, Christian. 2013. *Freedom Rising: Human Empowerment and the Quest for Emancipation.* New York: Cambridge University Press.

5 Sources of Regime Legitimacy in Asian Societies: Evidence from the Fifth Wave of the Asian Barometer Survey

Yun-han Chu and Wen-chin Wu

Any political regime needs to acquire legitimacy among its citizens to survive. A regime is legitimate if its citizens consciously recognize and accept its political power. A regime with inadequate legitimacy needs to devote more resources to maintaining its rule via coercion, which may further reduce popular support and make it more vulnerable and more likely to collapse (Gilley 2006). As elections are used as a tool for political leaders to get a mandate from citizens, democratic regimes are usually regarded as more legitimate than non-democracies regimes where elections are absent or unfair. However, there is an enduring puzzle in the literature of comparative democratization: Why do some non-democratic countries maintain higher regime legitimacy among their citizens than their democratic counterparts? (Chang, Chu, and Welsh 2013; Chu, Pan, and Wu 2015; Nathan 2020)

To address this puzzle, in this chapter, we investigate how values emphasized by different political thoughts, the Confucian tradition and the Western liberal tradition in particular, are related to citizens' support for their political regimes in Asia. We examine the divergent claims about the underpinnings of regime legitimacy with the data from the fifth wave of the Asian Barometer Survey. Specifically, we compare the empirical relevance of two traditions to a systematic understanding of the sources of regime legitimacy in thirteen Asian countries, where there are various political regimes, including established and emerging democratic regimes, hybrid regimes, and authoritarian regimes. We find that values of both Confucian and Western liberal traditions can explain citizens' regime support in Asia. Yet, the Confucian tradition seems to be more relevant in explaining citizens' regime support than the Western liberal tradition does, especially in countries where there are historical and cultural legacies of the Confucian traditions (i.e., China, Japan, Korea, Taiwan, and Vietnam). In other words, the Confucian tradition plays a crucial role in shaping citizens' political attitudes and providing legitimacy across different regimes in Asia.

The rest of this chapter is organized as follows. The next section reviews theoretical perspectives on regime legitimacy. The third section introduces the research design of this chapter. The final section concludes.

Theoretical Perspective

Legitimacy is vital for the stability of any regime type. A regime is legitimate when citizens consciously accept their government has the right to exercise authority over themselves. Lipset (1959, 86) argues that regime stability depends on both "the *effectiveness* and *legitimacy* of the political system" (emphasis in original). While effectiveness refers to "the actual performance of a political system," system legitimacy "involves the capacity of a political system to engender and maintain the belief that existing political institutions are the most appropriate or proper ones for the society." As a result, citizens would regard a political system as legitimate or not based on "the way in which its values fit in with their primary values" (Lipset 1959, 86-87). It has to be noted that elections, or any other political institutions, are not an essential part when Lipset (1959) defines legitimacy. Instead, it is citizens' acceptance and support for a political system that is capable of responding to their values.

Easton (1975) further points out that regime legitimacy stems from citizens' "diffuse support," a concept that refers to "evaluation of what an object is or represents" and "a reservoir of favorable attitudes or goodwill that helps members to accept or tolerate outputs to which they are opposed or the effects of which they see as damaging to their wants" (Easton 1975, 444). Accordingly, diffuse support is expressed in two forms: trust and belief in legitimacy.

As citizens' diffuse support is critical in sustaining a political system, subsequent studies have investigated the variation of it across different regime types. According to the Western liberal political tradition, a government needs to get citizens' consent to exercise its political power. Holding regular elections is a way to get citizens' consent and mandate. Politicians or political parties need to step down if they are unable to get approval from their citizens in elections. As a result, political regimes with free and fair elections are regarded as democracies and assumed to be "more legitimate" than those non-democratic regimes without free and fair elections. However, studies on comparative public opinion find a puzzle of regime support across different regimes. That is, some non-democratic regimes, while denying democratic rights to their citizens, still enjoy a higher level of support from their citizens than their democratic counterparts (Chang, Chu, and Welsh 2013; Chu, Pan, and Wu 2015; Nathan 2020).

To address this puzzle, scholars have developed three lines of research. The first school of thought suggests that some democracies have a lower level of regime support than other democratic and non-democratic regimes because of the presence of critical citizens (Norris 1999). People who believe in democratic values and principles would be more critical in evaluating their political regimes, resulting in a low level of regime support. Yet, what this perspective cannot explain is why some non-democratic regimes still have high support even though they threaten their citizens with violence and suppression.

The second school of thought suggests that regime legitimacy is created and sustained less at the "input" but more at the "output" side of a political system (Chu, Pan, and Wu 2015). Although non-democratic regimes do not provide their citizens a choice through free and fair elections, they can still establish a higher level of political support if they can successfully deliver economic well-being and good governance to their citizens. Meanwhile, institutional settings that uphold popular accountability and democratic representation do not immunize democracies from poor economic performance and bad governance, which would lead to a lower level of support among citizens.

The third line of research focuses on the role of culture and suggests that the observed level of regime legitimacy is buttressed by the functioning of the political system as well as the prevailing political predispositions of its citizens. This culturalist approach challenges previous studies that apply Western concepts of legitimacy to the politics of East Asia (Chu 2013). According to this culturalist perspective, some political regimes have higher support because of their endowment of a large portion of deferential and compliant citizens. The discourse on the "Asian values" represents an important extension of this culturalist approach. According to Lucian Pye (1985, 1999), East Asia has vivid paternalistic power and superior-inferior relations that will never disappear with the modernization of the social economy. In addition, rapid social and economic changes will not only result in an individual sense of insecurity but also create a new form of power-dependency. Huntington (1997) further claims that Confucianism values group interests greater than individual interests, political authority more than individual freedoms, and social responsibility over individual rights. In addition, Confucianism encourages social harmony and cooperation, avoids conflict, values the attainment of social order, and maintains hierarchical social structures. As a result, Huntington (1997) maintains that characteristics of the Confucian tradition will not assist the development of democracy in the region. Nevertheless, the political development in Taiwan, a country that emphasized Confucianism during its authoritarian period, demonstrates that Confucianism may coexist with Western democratic values in shaping citizens' regime support.

Studies on the relationship between Confucianism and ordinary citizens' political values suggest that Confucian values may explain citizens' regime support in Asia, a region where many countries experienced economic modernization during the Cold War. According to Tu (1996), "the Confucian scholar-official still functions in the psycho-cultural construct of East Asian societies." Shin (2011) reports that citizens in East Asian countries with a Confucian legacy tend to be attached to paternalistic meritocracy, prioritize economic well-being over freedom, and define democracy in substantive (rather than procedural) terms. Shi and Lu (2010) find that the popular understanding of the concept of "democracy" among Chinese citizens does not match the meaning defined in the liberal democratic political thoughts but the guardianship discourse with intellectual relevance to the Confucian values. In particular, many ordinary Chinese citizens think that "democracy" means government for the people and government by elites, rather than government by the people. Accordingly, the current Chinese government is democratic and legitimate in the eyes of ordinary citizens as long as it meets the people's needs (Lu and Shi 2014). Together, these studies in the culturalist tradition suggest the substantive legitimacy of a regime is rooted in traditional values held by ordinary citizens. As many Asian countries have been influenced by Confucian values, in this chapter, we argue that Confucian values play a key role in explaining citizens' regime support.

Key Elements of Confucian Political Thoughts

In this chapter, we identify the following four key elements underscored by traditional Confucian political thought (Chu 2016): (1) The delivery of material well-being to the people, including delivering economic prosperity, provision of basic necessities, access to public service, and protection of human safety; (2) A responsive government that addresses the people's needs and wins over their hearts; (3) A trustworthy public authority that commands the trust and respect of the people; (4) A government mandated by people that is capable and virtuous, protects the public interest, abides by the law, refrains from abusing the power of the office, and treats people from different social strata and backgrounds in a fair and equal manner.

What distinguishes the Confucian tradition from the Western liberal tradition is whether these four elements are sufficient to explain regime support. While these elements emphasized by Confucian political theory are relevant and important in sustaining regime legitimacy, one would argue that they are not essential to regime legitimacy. In particular, the Western liberal political theory maintains that the installment and application of democratic rules and procedures, such as competitive election and the separation of powers, are essential and arguably more important than the four elements ordained by the Confucian political theory. Yet, it is important to note that we are not arguing that Confucian tradition and the Western liberal tradition are always mutually exclusive in shaping citizens' regime support. It also has to be noted that the elements of Confucian political thoughts proposed in this chapter are not limited to Confucianism only. Other countries in the world, especially those Scandinavians, also emphasize on substantive policy outcomes, quality of governance, and collective welfare. While our goal in this chapter is to highlight the role of the Confucian tradition in shaping citizens' political values and regime support in Asia where many countries are predominated by Confucianism, the elements upheld by the Confucianism may be upheld in other countries influenced by non-Confucian traditions as well. As a result, both Confucian and Western liberal traditions overlap with each other and simultaneously influence citizens' political and cultural values as well as their regime support. For instance, both traditions uphold the importance of controlling corruption, law-abiding government, and equal and fair treatment. We tackle this issue in our empirical analysis.

In the next section we examine the on-going debate over regime legitimacy in Asia by analyzing the latest wave of the ABS data from thirteen countries. We focus on attitudes and values of ordinary citizens in Asia when investigating their regime support, because political legitimacy flows out of the heart of the people. In other words, ordinary citizens are the final judge on the extent to which their political system is legitimate or not.

Empirical Analysis

To test our theory on Confucianism and regime support, we use the data of the fifth wave of the ABS covering thirteen countries: Australia, China, India, Indonesia, Japan, South Korea, Malaysia, Mongolia, Myanmar, the Philippines, Taiwan, Thailand, and Vietnam.

Our measurement of regime support has been constructed from four questions that ask about respondents' preference, pride, and confidence in their own system of government. Specifically, we use the following four questions to measure respondents' supportive attitude toward their political regimes: 1) *Over the long run, our system of government is capable of solving the problems our country faces*; 2) *Thinking in general, I am proud of our system of government*; 3) *A system like ours, even if it runs into problems, deserves the people's support;* 4) *I would rather live under the system of government than any other that I can think of.* In each question, respondents may choose one among the following four options: "strongly agree," "somewhat agree," "somewhat disagree," and "strongly disagree."

With respondents' answers to the battery of questions on regime legitimacy, we calculate the percentage of citizens in each country who "strongly agree" or "agree" with each statement. Figure 5.1 illustrates the distribution of respondents who express their support for the political regimes of their countries. A general pattern, as shown in Figure 5.1, is that citizens in the four fully democratized East Asian countries, Japan, Korea, Taiwan, and Mongolia have lower support for their regimes. By contrast, citizens in Australia have higher regime support than those of four countries. Notably, citizens in other authoritarian or hybrid regimes also have higher regime support. In particular, citizens in China, the Philippines, and Vietnam have the highest regime support.

Figure 5.1 Regime Support in Asian Countries

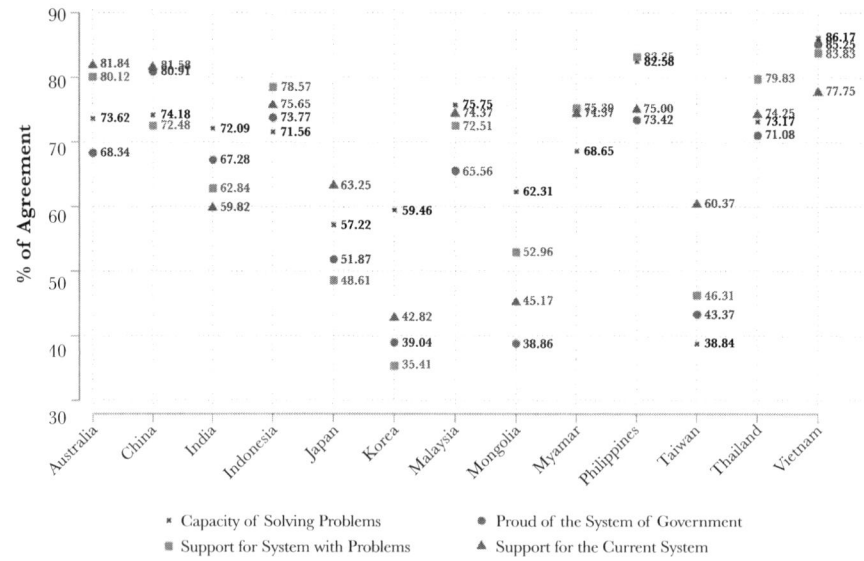

Source: Asian Barometer Survey. Authors prepared.

Based on respondents' answers to those four questions on regime support, we create a composite index of regime support with exploratory factor analysis (EFA). The Cronbach's alpha statistic of these four questions is 0.81, suggesting that they are jointly reliable in terms of measuring regime support. Figure 5.2 illustrates the mean score of each country. The index of regime support, as illustrated in

Figure 5.2, is negative in South Korea, Taiwan, Mongolia, Japan, and Malaysia. Meanwhile, the remaining eight countries have positive values on the index of regime support. This contrasting result highlights the puzzle that this essay aims to answer: Why do citizens have high regime support in authoritarian countries like China, Singapore, and Vietnam?

Based on our discussions in the previous section, our answer to this puzzle is that Confucian values may help explain high regime support in Asia. In the rest of this section, we explore the relationship between regime support and regime characteristics or performance criterion emphasized by either Confucian or Western liberal tradition in thirteen countries in the fifth wave of the ABS. First, we divide the thirteen countries into two groups based on the legacies of Confucianism in these countries. In particular, we regard Japan, Korea, Taiwan, China, and Vietnam as Confucian societies. The other eight countries are coded as "Others/ Non-Confucian." Second, we classify the questions asked by the ABS into three categories based on whether they are valued by the Confucian or the Western liberal traditions (or both). Table 5.1 summarizes the values upheld by either tradition analyzed in this chapter.

Figure 5.2 Regime Support in Asian Countries (the Mean Score)

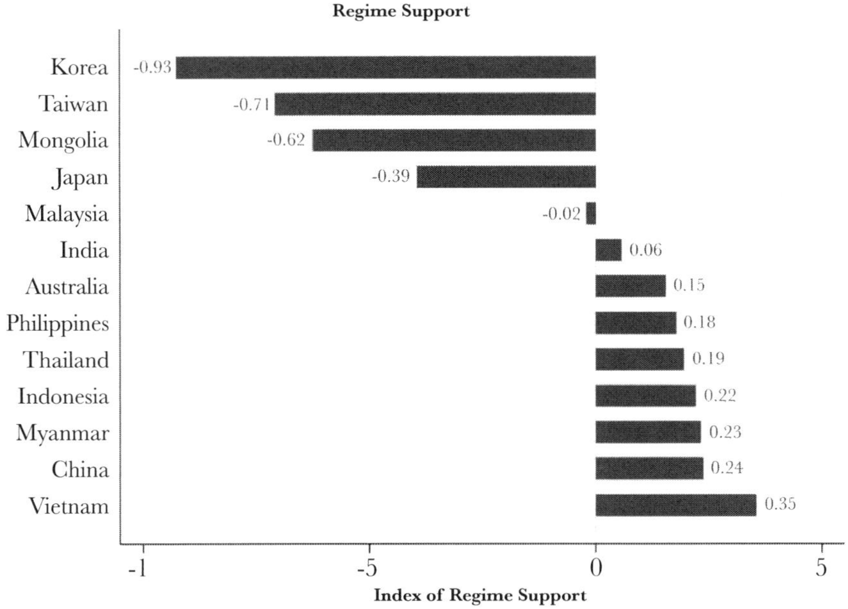

Regime Support

Country	Value
Korea	-0.93
Taiwan	-0.71
Mongolia	-0.62
Japan	-0.39
Malaysia	-0.02
India	0.06
Australia	0.15
Philippines	0.18
Thailand	0.19
Indonesia	0.22
Myanmar	0.23
China	0.24
Vietnam	0.35

Index of Regime Support

Source: Asian Barometer Survey. Authors prepared.

Table 5.1 Values Emphasized by the Confucian and/or the Western Liberal Traditions

Confucian Tradition	Western Liberal Tradition	Both
• Economic prosperity	• Popular accountability	• Clean politics
• Provision of public service	• Horizontal accountability	• Law-abiding officials
• Provision of basic necessity	• Transparency	• Fair treatment of citizens
• Human safety	• Civil liberties	
• Trust in institutions	• Political competition	
• Trust in officials	• Citizen empowerment	
• Government responsiveness		

Source: Authors prepared.

We recode respondents' answers to the questions on different political and cultural values with a [-2, +2] interval with five discrete numbers. A higher number indicates more agreement on the value. We also use 0 to indicate a neutral attitude, including answers like "don't know." Figures 5.3 to 5.4 illustrate the country averages for respondents' answers to the questions on their values emphasized by the Confucian and Western liberal traditions, respectively. In particular, Figure 5.3 shows that countries with Confucian legacies emphasize more on values upheld by Confucianism, such as human safety, provision of public services and basic necessity, and trust in institutions than countries less influenced by Confucianism. By contrast, Figure 5.4 shows that countries with more Confucian legacies emphasize less on some values of the Western liberal tradition than other countries with less Confucian legacies, such as civil liberties, popular accountability, political competition, and citizen empowerment. These findings suggest that our classifications of Confucian/Non-Confucian societies and Confucian/Western liberal values are valid not only at face values but internal consistency.

We regress the index of regime support on the three sets of values indicated in Table 5.1. We run the same regression model for two different samples of Confucian and non-Confucian countries, respectively. We also include other variables on respondents' demographic characteristics and their cultural beliefs, such as traditional political values, collectivist orientations, deference to authority, conflict avoidance, and loyalty to the national community.

Figure 5.3 Values Emphasized by the Confucian Tradition in Asian Societies

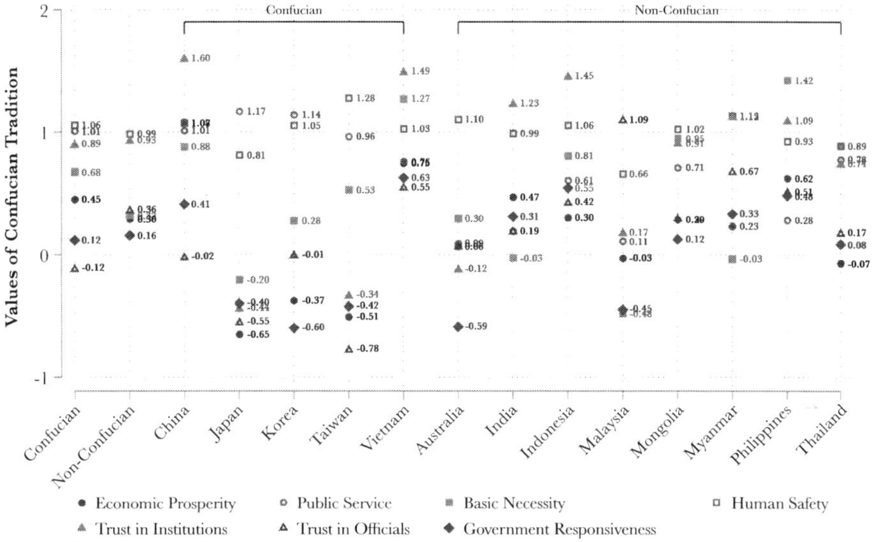

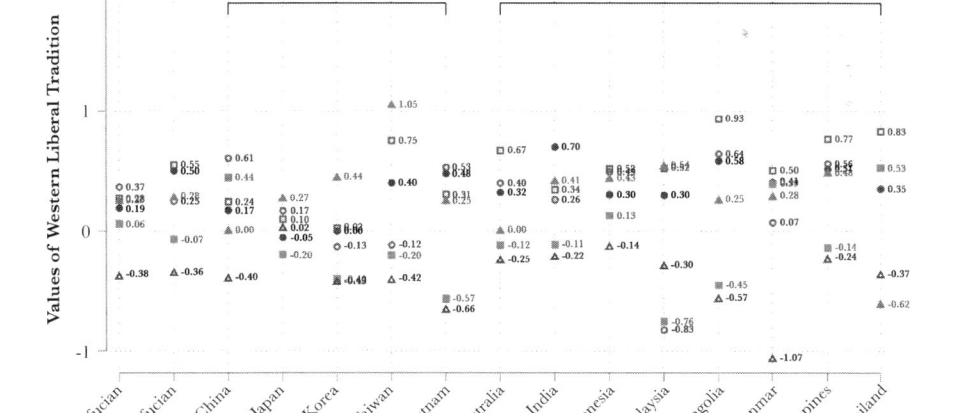

Source: Asian Barometer Survey. Authors prepared.

Figure 5.4 Values Emphasized by the Western Liberal Tradition in Asian Societies

Source: Asian Barometer Survey. Authors prepared.

We report the estimation results in Models 1 and 2 in Table 5.2. The results show that values emphasized by Confucian tradition are positively correlated with regime support in both Confucian and non-Confucian societies. In addition, some values are more emphasized in Confucian societies, including provision of public services, provision of basic necessities, and trust in institutions. More importantly, the explanatory power of the values emphasized by the Western liberal tradition, including horizontal accountability, transparency, freedom protection, political competition, citizen empowerment, are insignificant in Confucian countries (Model 1). By contrast, horizontal accountability and freedom protection are statistically significant in non-Confucian countries (Model 2). These results have two implications. First, Confucian values are essential to regime legitimacy in both Confucian and non-Confucian societies in Asia. Second, values emphasized by Western liberal tradition are less correlated with citizens' regime support in Confucian societies.

We further investigate the relationships between citizens' regime support and Confucian values for each Confucian society analyzed in this chapter. Models 3 to 7 report the estimation results. Specifically, the results of Models 3 and 7 suggest that Confucian values have the strongest explanatory power to account for regime support in China, because all of the values emphasized by Confucian tradition are statistically significant. Meanwhile, all of the five Confucian societies emphasize trust in institutions and government responsiveness. It is also noteworthy that most values emphasized by Western liberal tradition are not statistically related to regime support in those Confucian countries.

To summarize, we find that the values emphasized by the Confucian tradition, such as political trust and government responsiveness, are more crucial than values underscored by the Western liberal tradition over shaping citizens' support for the regime in Confucian countries in Asia.

Table 5.2 Sources of Regime Support, Pooled Sample (Fifth Wave of the ABS)

	Model 1 (Confucian)		Model 2 (Non-Confucian)		Model 3 (China)		Model 4 (Japan)		Model 5 (Korea)		Model 6 (Taiwan)		Model 7 (Vietnam)	
Democratic Traits														
Male	0.034	[0.030]	0.004	[0.021]	0.074***	[0.016]	0.010	[0.058]	0.002	[0.053]	-0.030	[0.049]	-0.031	[0.039]
Age	0.003	[0.002]	0.004	[0.002]	0.002**	[0.001]	0.011***	[0.002]	0.004	[0.002]	0.005*	[0.002]	0.003	[0.002]
Education	0.028	[0.031]	0.063	[0.031]	0.096***	[0.014]	-0.053	[0.052]	0.062	[0.062]	0.014	[0.042]	-0.136***	[0.039]
Characteristics of the Regime														
Characteristics Emphasized by the Confucian Tradition														
Economic Prosperity	0.108**	[0.022]	0.158***	[0.016]	0.038**	[0.014]	0.198***	[0.055]	-0.013	[0.049]	0.102**	[0.038]	0.166***	[0.039]
Provision of Public Services	0.071*	[0.021]	0.064*	[0.026]	0.048**	[0.017]	0.079	[0.042]	0.166***	[0.043]	0.101*	[0.042]	0.031	[0.035]
Provision of Basic Necessities	0.059*	[0.017]	0.035***	[0.006]	0.057***	[0.013]	0.016	[0.031]	0.053*	[0.024]	-0.006	[0.025]	0.008	[0.031]
Human Safety	0.016	[0.010]	0.063***	[0.010]	0.029*	[0.014]	-0.025	[0.036]	0.015	[0.042]	0.038	[0.041]	0.045	[0.031]
Trust in Institutions	0.194**	[0.029]	0.101**	[0.020]	0.087***	[0.014]	0.235***	[0.041]	0.060*	[0.031]	0.222***	[0.030]	0.244***	[0.036]
Trust in Officials	0.068	[0.038]	0.062*	[0.023]	0.018*	[0.008]	0.112***	[0.030]	0.029	[0.027]	0.114***	[0.032]	0.112***	[0.025]
Responsiveness	0.106*	[0.023]	0.123**	[0.029]	0.045**	[0.016]	0.153***	[0.043]	0.177***	[0.040]	0.086*	[0.036]	0.162***	[0.041]
Characteristics Emphasized by the Western Liberal Tradition														
Popular Accountability	0.089**	[0.017]	0.128**	[0.027]	0.147***	[0.033]	0.024	[0.045]	0.099*	[0.046]	0.105**	[0.039]	0.068*	[0.034]
Horizontal Accountability	0.019	[0.031]	0.098*	[0.039]	0.056***	[0.015]	-0.007	[0.036]	-0.008	[0.034]	0.066*	[0.030]	0.062*	[0.027]
Transparency	-0.002	[0.017]	0.008	[0.017]	0.005	[0.010]	0.036	[0.028]	0.126***	[0.031]	0.011	[0.024]	-0.017	[0.017]
Freedom Protection	0.005	[0.005]	0.067**	[0.016]	0.010	[0.010]	0.021	[0.031]	0.043	[0.030]	0.080*	[0.032]	0.006	[0.019]
Political Competition	0.011	[0.029]	0.015	[0.013]	0.000	[.]	0.012	[0.028]	0.047*	[0.022]	-0.047	[0.038]	0.003	[0.018]
Citizen Empowerment	0.012	[0.008]	-0.025	[0.022]	0.004	[0.011]	-0.008	[0.025]	0.032	[0.028]	0.026	[0.030]	0.017	[0.022]

(Continuing on the next page)

Table 5.2 Cont.

	Model 1 (Confucian)		Model 2 (Non-Confucian)		Model 3 (China)		Model 4 (Japan)		Model 5 (Korea)		Model 6 (Taiwan)		Model 7 (Vietnam)	
Characteristics Emphasized by Both Traditions														
Corruption	-0.021	[0.017]	-0.050	[0.048]	0.013	[0.018]	0.071	[0.052]	0.010	[0.049]	-0.034	[0.042]	-0.003	[0.031]
Law-abiding Officials	0.070***	[0.007]	0.070**	[0.015]	0.048***	[0.012]	0.013	[0.031]	0.016	[0.032]	0.065**	[0.025]	0.054**	[0.020]
Fair Treatment	0.039	[0.053]	0.024	[0.024]	-0.024*	[0.011]	0.033	[0.037]	0.191***	[0.031]	0.068*	[0.029]	0.067*	[0.033]
Political Culture														
Traditional Political Values	0.042	[0.054]	0.005	[0.086]	0.126***	[0.020]	0.064	[0.051]	-0.091	[0.051]	-0.016	[0.054]	0.127**	[0.045]
Collectivist Orientations	0.032	[0.018]	0.078*	[0.026]	0.069***	[0.015]	0.099*	[0.045]	0.004	[0.038]	0.036	[0.034]	-0.045	[0.038]
Deference to Authority	0.018	[0.010]	0.040	[0.025]	0.003	[0.012]	0.018	[0.040]	0.036	[0.035]	0.018	[0.034]	0.022	[0.024]
Conflict Avoidance	0.023	[0.013]	0.014	[0.022]	0.031	[0.017]	0.035	[0.035]	0.011	[0.029]	0.029	[0.032]	-0.013	[0.036]
Loyalty to National Community	0.090	[0.039]	0.050**	[0.012]	0.153***	[0.014]	0.045	[0.029]	0.104***	[0.027]	0.066**	[0.024]	0.056*	[0.024]
Constant	-0.791***	[0.076]	-0.805***	[0.106]	-0.672***	[0.050]	-0.664***	[0.200]	-1.199***	[0.239]	-0.929***	[0.177]	-0.377**	[0.140]
Observations	9506		14542		4928		873		1268		1237		1200	
Adjusted R-squared	0.457		0.313		0.226		0.410		0.200		0.345		0.536	

Note: Clustered standard errors are reported in Models 1 and 2. Robust standard errors are reported in Models 3 to 7. *p<0.05, **p<0.01 and ***p<0.001.

Conclusion

A political regime is legitimate if its citizens would like to support instead of overthrowing it. In this chapter, we argue that citizens with more emphasis on values upheld by the Confucian teaching would be more supportive for their political regimes. This relationship is stronger in countries with legacies of Confucianism, such as China, Japan, Korea, Taiwan, and Vietnam. More specifically, values emphasized by the Confucian tradition, including trust in institutions and government responsiveness, can better explain citizens' regime support that those emphasized by the Western liberal tradition, such as accountability, political competition, and freedom protection. These findings suggest that the social and historical relevance of Confucian political theory is not limited to Confucian societies but also to non-Confucian societies in Asia.

Nevertheless, it should be clarified that we do not intend to argue that the Western liberal tradition is unfit to account for citizens' regime support in Asia. Neither do we argue that the Confucian tradition can replace the Western tradition in explaining Asians' political attitudes and regime support. Instead, we argue both traditions complement each other in explaining citizens' political values and attitudes. The Western liberal tradition upholds the "input" and "procedure" aspects of a political system, whereas the Confucian tradition prioritizes the "output" and "substantive" aspects of it (Chu, Pan, and Wu 2015). Yet, we would like to note that Confucian values examined in this chapter, especially those on collective well-being of citizens, are not limited to Confucianism but also upheld in other regions in the Western world. For instance, Scandinavian countries emphasize on substantive quality of governance and democracy. Therefore, the findings of this chapter not only advance our understanding of cultural origins of regime legitimacy across Asian countries but can be applied to investigate other societies that share similar values of collective welfare over individual welfare with the Confucian tradition.

Acknowledgments

This chapter is revised based on Chu, Yun-han. "Sources of Regime Legitimacy in Confucian Societies." *Journal of Chinese Governance* 1, no. 2 (2016): 195-213. The authors updated the empirical section with the data from the fifth wave of the Asian Barometer Survey.

References

Chang, Alex, Yun-han Chu, and Bridget Welsh. 2013. "Southeast Asia: Sources of Regime Support." *Journal of Democracy* 24 (2): 150-164.

Chu, Yun-han. 2013. "Sources of Regime Legitimacy and the Debate over the Chinese Model." *China Review* 13 (1): 1-42.

—. 2016. "Sources of Regime Legitimacy in Confucian Societies." *Journal of Chinese Governance* 1 (2): 195-213. doi:10.1080/23812346.2016.1172402.

Chu, Yun-han, Hsin-hsin Pan, and Wen-chin Wu. 2015. "Regime Legitimacy in East Asia: Why Non-democratic States Fare Better Than Democracies." *Global Asia* 10 (3): 98-105.

Easton, David. 1975. "A Re-assessment of the Concept of Political Support." *British Journal of Political Science* 5 (4): 435-457.

Gilley, Bruce. 2006. "The Meaning and Measure of State Legitimacy: Results for 72 Countries." *European Journal of Political Research* 45 (3): 499-525. doi:10.1111/j.1475-6765.2006.00307.x.

Huntington, Samuel P. 1997. "After Twenty Years: The Future of the Third Wave." *Journal of Democracy* 8 (4): 3-12.

Lipset, Seymour Martin. 1959. "Some Social Requisites of Democracy: Economic Development and Political Legitimacy." *American Political Science Review* 53 (1): 69-105. doi:10.2307/1951731.

Lu, Jie, and Tianjian Shi. 2014. "The Battle of Ideas and Discourses Before Democratic Transition: Different Democratic Conceptions in Authoritarian China." *International Political Science Review* 36 (1): 20-41. doi:10.1177/0192512114551304.

Nathan, Andrew J. 2020. "The Puzzle of Authoritarian Legitimacy." *Journal of Democracy* 31 (1): 158-168.

Norris, Pippa. 1999. *Critical Citizens: Global Support for Democratic Government*. New York: Oxford University Press.

Pye, Lucian W. 1985. *Asian Power and Politics: The Cultural Dimensions of Authority*. Cambridge, Massachusetts: Harvard University Press.

—. 1999. "Civility, Social Capital, and Civil Society: Three Powerful Concepts for Explaining Asia." *Journal of Interdisciplinary History* 29 (4): 763-782.

Shi, Tianjian, and Jie Lu. 2010. "The Meanings of Democracy: The Shadow of Confucianism." *Journal of Democracy* 21 (4): 123-130.

Shin, Doh Chull. 2011. *Confucianism and Democratization in East Asia*. New York: Cambridge University Press.

Tu, Weiming, ed. 1996. *Confucian Traditions in East Asian Modernity: Moral Education and Economic Culture in Japan and the Four Mini-Dragons*. Cambridge, Massachusetts: Harvard University Press.

6 The Evolution of Democratic Legitimacy: Empirical Examination of Asian Societies in the Past Two Decades

Yun-han Chu and Min-hua Huang

Chu and Huang's article "Solving an Asian Puzzle" published in the *Journal of Democracy* (2010) proposed a four-category typology for analyzing democratic orientation, explaining why Taiwan and South Korea, which are more democratic than other countries in the region on objective measures, show lower support for democracy in subjective surveys. The main finding was that because Taiwan and South Korea have only recently undergone the process of authoritarian transition and democratization, domestic political competition is intense. Therefore, although the democratic system has stabilized, the public remained critical of the government's performance. This critical attitude was reflected in more negative responses to questions with the so-called "D-word." However, adherence to liberal-democratic values was found to be more deeply rooted than in other societies that show a higher level of support for democracy (anchored on the "D-word"). In other words, it was not that the people in Taiwan and South Korea did not support democratic institutions, but that they were more demanding about how democracy works in practice. This produced the type of "critical citizen" identified by Pippa Norris (1999). Aside from Taiwan and South Korea, a similar trend was also observed in Hong Kong.

A decade later, the two survey waves analyzed in the 2010 article have grown to five waves. At the same time, the political situation in countries across the region has changed dramatically. Since Thailand's coup in 2014, the military government led by Prayut Chan-o-cha has been reluctant to return to democracy. In recent years, anti-military and even anti-royalist protest movements that are distinct from the Yellow Shirt and Red Shirt protests of the past have emerged (Strangio 2020). Since the start of Hong Kong's Occupy Central Movement in 2011, the anti-CCP democracy movement has become increasingly radicalized. In particular, since the start of the Umbrella Movement in 2014, there has been worsening violence between police and protesters. In response, the Chinese government passed the Hong Kong national security law in 2020, imposing mandatory arrest and imprisonment on those involved in the pro-democracy movement (Davidson 2020). In Cambodia, the Hun Sen regime has a historically poor record on civil liberties and political rights, and has used the judiciary to repress opposition parties and limit political competition. In late 2017, the main opposition leader was arrested, and the main opposition party was subsequently dissolved, eliminating any real challenge to the ruling Cambodian People's Party (CPP). This resulted in the absence of the main opposition party, which won 44 percent of the seats in 2013, in the July 2018 election, allowing the CPP to win all of the seats (Morgenbesser 2019). In the context of these developments, and many others across the region, this chapter analyzes changes in democratic legitimacy across the region using all five waves of the ABS and applying the same typology of democratic orientation as Chu and Huang's 2010 article.

Recap of Typology, Measurement, and Empirical Patterns

Chu and Huang's (2010) typology of democratic orientation is based on the measurement of two attitudes toward democracy, namely overt support for democracy (mentioning the "D-word") and liberal-democratic values (without mentioning the "D-word"). In terms of operationalization, the two scales are composite measures. The support for democracy scale has five items: desirability, suitability, preferability, efficacy, and priority. The liberal-democratic values scale has seven items measuring authoritarian orientation. Rejection of these orientations indicates adherence to liberal-democratic values such as political equality, popular accountability, political liberalism, political pluralism, and separation of power. We used categorical factor analysis to construct the scales. We also adjusted the sample size so that each country is weighted evenly. The 61 country surveys across five waves were combined to form a unified factor score. The overall mean was then used to divide respondents' scores into high/low categories on support for democracy and liberal-democratic values. This produced a two-by-two typology of democratic orientations as follows:

1. Consistent Democrat: high support for democracy, high liberal-democratic values.
2. Critical Democrat: low support for democracy, high liberal-democratic values.
3. Non-democrat: low support for democracy, low liberal-democratic values.
4. Superficial Democrat: high support for democracy, low liberal-democratic values.

In the Consistent Democrat and Non-democrat categories, the results for the two scales are consistent, indicating a consistently high or low level of democratic legitimacy in the minds of citizens. The other two categories show inconsistent results. Critical Democrats are "critical" because, despite their intrinsic identification with liberal-democratic values, they are relatively harsh in their evaluations of the political system. Superficial Democrats are "superficial" because despite their apparently high level of support for democracy, once there is no "D-word" prompt, they show a lower orientation toward liberal-democratic values.

Chu and Huang (2010) identified five patterns of democratic orientation. These five patterns are also the basic unit for analysis in this chapter. The evolution of democratic orientations in each country is described in terms of the shifts between these five patterns. The patterns are defined as follows:
• Pattern I: predominant Consistent Democrats with substantial Critical Democrats.
• Pattern II: predominant Critical Democrats with substantial Consistent Democrats.
• Pattern III: no predominant category, all types are more or less evenly distributed.
• Pattern IV: high concentration of Superficial Democrats.
• Pattern V: Superficial and Non-democrats constitute three-quarters.

Predominant means around 50 percent, or at least more than 40 percent of respondents, while substantial means over one-quarter. Since this chapter combines the five waves of data to perform factor analysis, the results will be slightly different from the findings in Chu and Huang (2010).

Trajectory of Evolving Democratic Legitimacy

As of September 2020, the data availability for each of the 16 countries included in the ABS is as follows: Australia only has one wave of data; Myanmar has two waves of data; Cambodia and Singapore have three waves of data; Vietnam, Malaysia, and Hong Kong have four waves of data; Japan, South Korea, China, Mongolia, the Philippines, Taiwan, and Thailand have five waves of data. Therefore, the statistical findings are presented in Table 6.1 as distributional patterns. However, when discussing developments at the country level, analysis is carried out on a country-by-country basis.

Trajectory 1: Oscillation between Pattern I and II—Japan and South Korea

In the five waves of the survey, Japan and South Korea's distribution of the four types of democratic orientation oscillated between Pattern I and Pattern II. The difference between the two countries is in the direction of the trajectory over time. In the case of Japan, the first two waves clearly showed Pattern I, with a majority of respondents classified as Consistent Democrats (50 percent). However, in the last three waves, Japan shifted to Pattern II with a majority of Critical Democrats, with the proportion ranging from 51 percent to 56 percent. The trajectory in Japan is an evolution from Pattern I to Pattern II, with Japanese now openly expressing dissatisfaction with their democratic system. However, there was no clear direction in the trajectory of South Korea. The first wave, second wave, and the fourth wave show Pattern II, while the third wave and fifth wave show Pattern I. We can essentially view South Korea as a hybrid of Pattern I/Pattern II, with the specific context of each wave determining whether its democratic orientation oscillates closer to Pattern I or Pattern II.

Trajectory 2: Stable Pattern II—Taiwan and Hong Kong

Although the fifth wave data for Hong Kong are yet to be released, based on all five waves in Taiwan and the first four waves in Hong Kong, we can find a stable Pattern II in the distribution of democratic orientations. A closer look at the findings for Taiwan shows a steady increase in Critical Democrats. When combined with Consistent Democrats, we find that the ratio increased from 64 percent in 2001 to 84 percent in 2018. This shows a deep-rooted adherence to freedom and democracy in Taiwan, providing clear evidence for the deepening of democracy. In Hong Kong, although the third wave survey showed some fluctuation, in particular, a significant fall in the proportion of Critical Democrats and an increase in the proportion of Superficial Democrats, the first wave, second wave, and fourth wave showed a stable Pattern II, with Critical Democrats accounting for the highest proportion, and the combined proportion of Critical Democrats and Consistent Democrats at nearly 70 percent. If we look at the deviation in the third wave, we can find that the timing of the survey coincided with the beginning of the democratic movement in Hong Kong in 2010. Given that the controversy over "the 2012 election reforms" in 2010 were a starting point for pro-democracy protest movement in Hong Kong, we can see how many people in Hong Kong were cognitively mobilized to maintain a critical orientation when facing the dilemma of choosing between democratic reform and not angering the CCP. In this time of crisis, the nearly 10 percentage point drop in the proportion of Critical Democrats indicates that in terms of political mobilization, not all citizens chose a position that was critical of the existing system, and a significant proportion reverted to supporting the system. Whether the findings of the 2016 survey represent a return to normal (similar to the findings of the first and second wave), or a process of finding a new balance will have to wait for the results of the fifth wave survey in order to make an informed judgment.

Table 6.1 A Typological Analysis of Democratic Orientation in Asia (Frequency Distribution in Percent)

Country and Survey Year	Consistent Democrats	Critical Democrats	Non-Democrats	Superficial Democrats	Pattern
Australia_2018	51	34	9	6	I
Japan_2003	50	30	9	11	I
Japan_2007	50	29	12	9	I
S. Korea_2019	44	40	7	9	I
S. Korea_2011	44	30	10	16	I
S. Korea_2003	25	46	18	11	II
S. Korea_2006	36	37	15	12	II
S. Korea_2015	34	37	14	15	II
Japan_2019	31	56	8	5	II
Japan_2011	30	55	11	4	II
Japan_2016	35	51	10	5	II
Taiwan_2018	37	47	10	6	II
Taiwan_2014	37	43	13	7	II
Taiwan_2006	32	42	16	10	II
Taiwan_2010	37	40	14	8	II
Taiwan_2001	25	39	24	12	II
Hong Kong_2016	34	36	15	14	II
Hong Kong_2012	34	25	17	24	III
Hong Kong_2007	32	34	18	17	II
Hong Kong_2001	31	38	16	15	II
Indonesia_2019	27	20	23	30	III/V
Indonesia_2016	20	24	30	26	III/V
Indonesia_2011	30	26	20	23	III
Indonesia_2006	40	20	17	24	III
Philippines_2018	11	23	43	23	III/V
Philippines_2014	9	36	42	13	III/V
Philippines_2010	15	31	36	18	III/V
Philippines_2005	12	30	39	20	III/V
Philippines_2002	23	26	24	26	III
Singapore_2014	18	23	35	24	III/V
Singapore_2010	18	27	18	37	III/IV
Singapore_2006	23	28	27	23	III

(Continuing on the next page)

Table 6.1 Cont.

Country and Survey Year	Consistent Democrats	Critical Democrats	Non-Democrats	Superficial Democrats	Pattern
Malaysia_2019	21	25	30	25	III
Malaysia_2014	12	25	38	**26**	III/V
Malaysia_2011	21	17	20	**42**	III/IV
Malaysia_2007	24	14	22	**40**	III/IV
China_2019	24	25	23	28	III
China_2015	18	32	27	24	III
China_2011	29	21	17	**34**	III/IV
China_2007	27	11	18	**44**	IV
China_2002	**32**	13	13	**42**	IV
India_2019	16	29	33	22	III
Thailand_2018	29	14	23	**34**	III/V
Thailand_2014	26	14	28	**32**	III/V
Thailand_2010	**33**	12	15	**40**	III/IV
Thailand_2006	23	10	15	**53**	IV
Thailand_2001	27	6	9	**58**	IV
Vietnam_2018	13	11	28	**48**	IV/V
Vietnam_2015	10	3	22	**65**	IV/V
Vietnam_2010	20	7	10	**64**	IV
Vietnam_2005	**30**	4	4	**62**	IV
Mongolia_2018	19	24	33	24	III/V
Mongolia_2014	14	20	40	**27**	III/V
Mongolia_2010	28	8	17	**48**	IV
Mongolia_2006	13	3	22	**62**	IV/V
Mongolia_2002	24	10	20	**46**	III/IV
Cambodia_2015	8	24	36	**32**	III/V
Cambodia_2012	14	13	27	**46**	IV/V
Cambodia_2008	13	7	21	**59**	IV
Myanmar_2019	13	19	**37**	31	V
Myanmar_2015	15	14	**36**	35	V

Source: Asian Barometer Survey. Authors prepared.

Trajectory 3: Transition (Pattern III) toward Authoritarianism (Pattern V)—Indonesia, the Philippines, and Singapore

In Chu and Huang (2010), Pattern III represented a transition pattern, where the democratic orientations of respondents are roughly evenly distributed among the four categories, with no salient findings that can be identified. In the first ABS surveys carried out in Indonesia (2006), the Philippines (2002), and Singapore (2006), this pattern indicates a transitional state between authoritarianism and democracy. However, with the passage of time, we can see that the proportion of Consistent Democrats in Indonesia has continued to decline (from 40 percent in 2006 to 20 percent and 27 percent in 2016 and 2019 respectively). At the same time, there has been a corresponding increase in the combined proportion of Non-Democrats and Superficial Democrats (from 41 percent in 2006 to 56 percent and 53 percent in 2016 and 2019 respectively), producing a hybrid of Pattern III and Pattern V and a trend toward greater authoritarianism. As Figure 19.1 in Chapter 19 shows, the recent surge of ethno-nationalism in Indonesia has become a prominent phenomenon. Together with the rising Islamism, such as the blasphemy conviction of Jakarta Governor Basuki Tjahaja Purnama, the rise of religious fundamentalism is the key factor that might explain why the liberal democratic environment had become cloudier. The similar trend can also be seen in the five waves of the Filipino survey. In fact, starting from the second wave, the Philippines has developed from an even distribution between the four categories of democratic orientation to a concentration in the Critical Democrats and Non-Democrats. The proportion of Non-Democrats has also increased, from 24 percent in 2001 to 43 percent in 2018, an increase of 19 percent. The proportion of Critical Democrats rose from 26 percent in 2001 to 36 percent in 2014 but fell back to 23 percent in 2018, lower than the level in 2001. As a result, the combined proportion of Non-Democrats and Superficial Democrats has continued to rise from 50 percent in 2001 to 66 percent in 2018. This is a clear indication that the Philippines is moving in a more authoritarian direction, with the temporal coincidence of Duterte's controversial leadership style. In the three waves of data for Singapore (the second wave to the fourth wave), although the distribution between the four orientations is relatively even, the combined proportion of Non-Democrats and Superficial Democrats is also gradually expanding, growing from 50 percent in the second wave to 55 percent and 59 percent in the third and fourth waves respectively. To some extent, this reflects a political environment in which opposition parties continue to grow (the opposition party won four more seats in 2020). Political mobilization in the face of intensifying competition between the ruling party and opposition parties might have led to changes in democratic orientation in a more authoritarian direction, for instance, the appeal for "paternalistic meritocracy" as discussed in Chapter 25.

Trajectory 4: Transition Away from Authoritarianism (Pattern IV to Pattern III)—Malaysia and China

Although the political systems in Malaysia and China are very different, in terms of the democratic orientations of citizens, until the third wave, the two countries both showed an authoritarian tendency with Superficial Democrats as the largest category (in excess of 30 percent). However, in two recent waves of surveys, both Malaysia and China have shifted toward a more even distribution. This is closely related to the rapid economic and social development of both countries during this period. In terms of per capita income, Malaysia and China are ranked at the top of the economic latecomers in East Asia. China's per capita income in 2019 was US$8,254, while Malaysia's was US$12,120. In both countries, the per capita income is around US$10,000, which is considered by scholars to be an income level with a high likelihood of democratic transition. However, there are some subtle differences between the two countries. In Malaysia, due to the rapid rise of the opposition camp after 2013, Barisan Nasional lost power for the first time in 2018. At the same time, religious and ethnic mobilization has intensified. As a result, on the authoritarian side we can see a shift from Superficial Democrats to Non-Democrats. In contrast, following Xi Jinping's rise to power, China has seen a shift from Consistent Democrats moving to Critical Democrats. However, whether such a shift reflects public criticism of the regime's performance, or whether support for democratic institutions has declined under the political atmosphere of Xi Jinping's monopoly of power can only be determined by a covariate analysis with other variables.

Trajectory 5: Becoming More Authoritarian (Moving from Pattern IV to V)—Thailand, Vietnam, Mongolia, and Cambodia

The fifth trajectory is a strengthening of authoritarianism. The common feature of Thailand, Vietnam, Mongolia, and Cambodia is that in the first two or three waves of available data, the dominance of Superficial Democrats (Pattern IV) was observed (before 2010 in Thailand, before 2015 in Vietnam, before 2010 in Mongolia, and before 2012 in Cambodia). However, in recent surveys there has been a trend of Superficial Democrats moving toward Non-Democrats (becoming Pattern V), despite the fact that the percentage of Superficial Democrats and Non-Democrats together might not reach three-quarters, but at least shows predominance above 55 percent. The difference is that in Thailand, Mongolia, and Cambodia which hold elections, we can see that a significant proportion of the population are still Consistent Democrats (five waves in Thailand; the first and third waves in Mongolia), and Critical Democrats (the fourth wave in Cambodia). And in some of these cases, there is an incremental increase of Critical Democrats over the years, especially in Mongolia and Cambodia, where electoral competition became fierce and eventually led to the 2019 constitutional amendment in the former case (shifting toward more parliamentarism) and legal coup in the later one (preempt any challenge from the opposition). Therefore, the trajectory is from Pattern IV to a hybrid distribution of Pattern III/V. In contrast, in Vietnam, there has been a steady increase in the proportion of Non-Democrats from 4 percent in 2005 to 28 percent in 2018. The proportion of Consistent Democrats, which was significant in 2005, fell to 10 percent and 13 percent in 2015 and 2018, respectively. This shows that although the political situation in Thailand and Mongolia is moving in the direction of greater authoritarianism, as long as formal elections are held, there will still be a proportion of citizens who are Consistent Democrats or Critical Democrats to serve as a check and balance on the regime. However, this challenge led Cambodian strongman Hun Sen to carry out a judicial coup d'état in response to the substantial growth in opposition forces, reversing the country's democratic progress. In Vietnam, the intra-party democracy of competition between factions within the ruling party has been replaced with an increasing concentration of power in the hands of the de facto top leader of Vietnam, Nguyễn Phú Trọng, who is concurrently the head of the General Secretary of the Communist Party, the Secretary of the Central Military Commission, and the head of state. The concentration of power under Nguyễn Phú Trọng not only reflects the outcome of factional struggles within the party, but also the influence of the concentration of power in China under Xi Jinping.

Trajectory 6: Staying at Authoritarianism (Pattern V)—Myanmar

Myanmar has finished its first power transition to the long-term opposition party led by Aung San Suu Kyi. Despite great expectations from the international community, Aung San's leadership has become increasingly mired in controversy, not just in handling the Rohingya crisis, but also exhibited in her leadership style. From the most recent two waves of the ABS survey we can find that over the period from before Aung San Suu Kyi took office (2015) to four years after she took office (2019), there has been no significant shift in the distribution of democratic orientations among Burmese people. This largely reflects the outside world's evaluation of Aung San Suu Kyi's administration, whose political calculations have far outweighed the considerations of democracy, freedom, and human rights. As a result, the administration has failed to substantially advance democratization in Myanmar and has in fact shown striking similarities with the previous military dictatorship.

In addition to the trajectories between the six categories of democratic orientation, Australia and India were included for the first time in the fifth wave. As expected, Australia shows the strongest liberal-democratic orientation of any national sample, with not only the highest proportion of Consistent Democrats (51 percent), but also the second-highest proportion of both Consistent Democrats and Critical Democrats combined, at 85 percent, only behind Japan (87 percent). India shows a relatively even distribution between the categories, although the balance tilts slightly in the direction of authoritarianism, reflected in the slightly higher proportion of Non-Democrats (33 percent). This is consistent with the significant popular support within the country for Modi's blend of Hindu nationalism and authoritarianism.

Conclusion

The classic modernization theory literature makes two main theoretical assumptions. First, sustained economic growth will drive social, cultural, and political development. One of the main manifestations of this trend is that the growth of social mobilization will accelerate the development of social values toward a more pluralistic and liberal orientation (Deutsch 1961). Second, after a country has completed its democratic transformation, the sustainability of the democratic system requires a high degree of democratic legitimacy in society. The five waves of the Asian Barometer Survey lend some support to both hypotheses, but which need to be understood within the unique political contexts of each country. For Japan, Taiwan, and South Korea, which follow the first and second trajectory, the stability of the democratic system can be demonstrated by the fact that Consistent Democrats and Critical Democrats are in the majority. However, the relative shares of these two types of democratic orientation are influenced by the recent fluctuations in the performance of the government in Japan and South Korea, whereas in Taiwan there is long-term steady growth in the proportion of Critical Democrats. Hong Kong in the second trajectory as well as Indonesia, the Philippines, and Singapore in the third trajectory and Malaysia on the fourth trajectory are to a large extent influenced by the culture and political systems of their former colonial rulers (British, American, and Dutch). In these societies, subjective democratic orientations are more evenly distributed between the four categories. In particular, the combined ratio of Consistent Democrats and Critical Democrats is close to or exceeds 40 percent of the population. This shows that regardless of whether the countries are more authoritarian (Indonesia, the Philippines, Singapore), or moving toward greater democracy (Malaysia), there is still a significant base of support for democratic legitimacy.

The trajectory of China largely can be explained by the growing orientation toward democracy and freedom in the context of economic modernization. This can also explain the dramatic growth of the opposition and its subsequent rise to power in Malaysia in recent years. However, in the domestic politics of both China and Malaysia, rapid economic and social development has also led to growing nationalism. Those in power often manipulate these ideas to achieve their internal and external political goals. So while democratic legitimacy in both countries is moving in a positive direction, there remains the possibility that they may reverse course in the future and revert to greater authoritarianism. Finally, countries that have become more authoritarian or continue to show an authoritarian trajectory include Thailand, Vietnam, Mongolia, Cambodia, and Myanmar. Thailand is an example of a country in the midst of dramatic social change that has yet to regain its normal equilibrium. The period since 2006, when Yellow Shirt and Red Shirt protests were sparked by the military coup against Thaksin's Pheu Thai Party to the student protests over the past two years demanding curbs on the power of the military and royal family shows that Thailand does not lack the conditions for democratic transition but continues to be held in a state of authoritarian rule under the suppression of the military. In response to similar developments in Cambodia, the regime has effectively carried out a judicial coup against the opposition to prevent any meaningful challenge to its rule. Following the example of China, Vietnam has also regressed from a relatively pluralistic intra-party democracy to strongman rule. Finally, in Mongolia and Myanmar, nationalist political mobilization and authoritarian strongman rule remain in place. From the distribution of the categories of democratic orientation, we can see that democratic values in both countries remain relatively weak.

References

Chu, Yun-han, and Min-hua Huang. 2010. "Solving an Asian Puzzle." *Journal of Democracy* 21 (4): 114-122. doi:10.1353/jod.2010.0009.

Davidson, Helen. 2020. "Hong Kong Security Law 'May Break International Laws.'" *The Guardian*. September 04. Accessed March 4, 2021. https://www.theguardian.com/world/2020/sep/04/hong-kong-security-law-may-break-international-laws-china-human-rights-un.

Deutsch, Karl W. 1961. "Social Mobilization and Political Development." *American Political Science Review* 55 (3): 493-514. doi:10.2307/1952679.

Morgenbesser, Lee. 2019. "Cambodia's Transition to Hegemonic Authoritarianism." *Journal of Democracy* 30 (1): 158-171. doi:10.1353/jod.2019.0012.

Norris, Pippa. 1999. *Critical Citizens: Global Support for Democratic Government.* Oxford: Oxford University Press.

Strangio, Sebastian. 2020. "Defying State of Emergency, Thailand Student Protests Roll Onward." *The Diplomat*. October 19. Accessed March 4, 2021. https://thediplomat.com/2020/10/defying-state-of-emergency-thailand-student-protests-roll-onward/.

7 The Puzzle of Authoritarian Legitimacy
Andrew J. Nathan

Studies of Asians' attitudes toward democracy contain a puzzle. Since the Asian Barometer Survey (ABS) began in 2001, it has consistently found that the region's autocracies outscore its democracies in terms of "institutional trust." In each of the four survey waves from 2001 to 2016, the public's average expressed level of trust in six governmental institutions was higher, for example, in China and Vietnam than it was in Japan and Taiwan. Many studies focused on China confirm the high level of public support for China's authoritarian regime (Shi 2015; Dickson 2016; Tang 2016; Chen 2004).

Why should authoritarian regimes enjoy more trust than democratic regimes, in which governments hold power by consent of the governed? Part of the answer may be that democracies include many "critical citizens"—people who are so strongly attached to democratic principles that they hold democratic institutions to stringent standards (Norris 1999). The presence of high levels of institutional trust under authoritarian regimes, however, challenges the common assumption that such regimes are sustained only by repression, censorship, corruption, and an ample flow of public goods, with citizens' unforced preference for nondemocratic rule playing no role.

In hopes of making progress toward solving this puzzle, the ABS began measuring regime legitimacy separately from institutional trust in its third wave survey in 2010. Although institutional trust is often used as a measure of regime legitimacy, the two concepts are not the same. One of the most influential attempts to conceptualize regime legitimacy was that of political scientist David Easton, who renamed the concept "diffuse regime support" and defined it as a "reservoir of favorable attitudes or good will that helps members to accept or tolerate [regime] outputs to which they are opposed or the effects of which they see as damaging to their wants" (Easton 1975, 444). Easton acknowledged that diffuse regime support would be difficult to measure, partly because the attitude is a complex one with at least two dimensions (which he labeled "trust" and "legitimacy") and partly because its referent, the regime, is difficult for respondents to distinguish from institutions, incumbents, and policies.

The third and fourth waves of the ABS nonetheless sought to measure Eastonian diffuse regime support (DRS) with a battery of questions that sought to set aside people's attitudes toward particular governmental institutions, incumbents, and policies in favor of a focus on how respondents feel about their country's type of political system—the regime, in Easton's sense of the term. The battery contains four questions: Does the respondent think that "over the long run, our system of government is capable of solving the problems our country faces"; is the respondent "proud of our system of government"; does the respondent believe that "a system like ours, even if it runs into problems, deserves the people's support"; and would the respondent "rather live under our system of government than any other that I can think of." There are four available responses, ranging from "strongly agree" through "agree" and "disagree" to "strongly disagree." For this study, nonresponses, including "don't know" and "no answer," are coded as neutral.

In the combined third and fourth waves dataset,[1] comprising surveys fielded in different countries at different times from 2010 to 2016, the new DRS measure confirms previous authors' findings that East and Southeast Asia's authoritarian regimes enjoy higher levels of popular support than the region's democratic regimes receive. Figure 7.1 shows that, in general, the more authoritarian the regime, the stronger is its DRS.[2]

Figure 7.1 Mean DRS by Country (Factor Score)

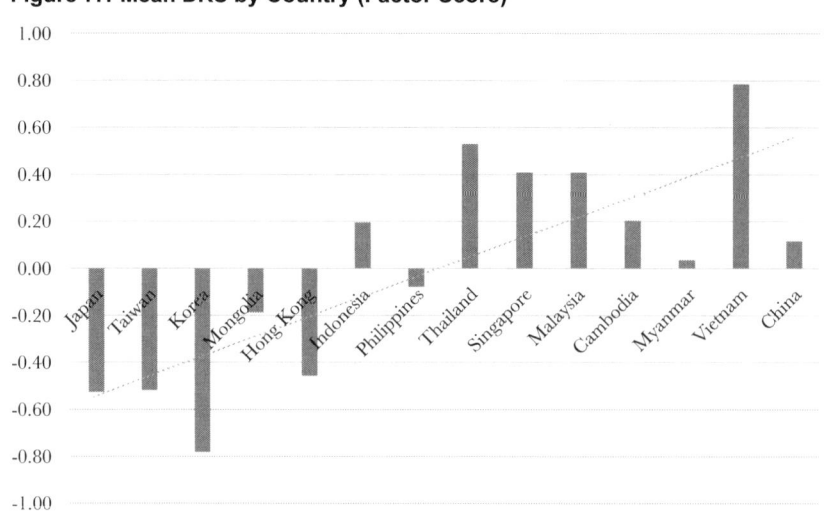

Source: Asian Barometer Survey. Author prepared.

Explaining Authoritarian Legitimacy

There are four explanations commonly suggested for why some authoritarian regimes enjoy high levels of legitimacy: government economic and political performance, propaganda, nationalism, and culture (Gilley 2009; Zhong and Chen 2013; Wong, Wan, and Hsiao 2011).

The ABS survey includes four separate measures of government performance. First, it asks respondents to rate the country's current economic condition, to state the overall trend they see over recent years, and to say how they think the national economy will be doing a few years hence. The model did not include a measure of actual economic performance in the model, since a country's overall economic performance would have different impacts on and be differently evaluated by different individuals. Second, the state of the respondent's "family economy" is probed via the same three questions: How is your family doing today, was it doing better or worse a few years ago, and how do you think it will be doing a few years from now? Next, opinions regarding the government's political performance are collected via questions about both the effectiveness and the fairness of governance. With regard to effectiveness, respondents are asked to rate how good a job the government is doing at fighting corruption, at administering rule of law, at being accountable to the public, at solving what the respondents see as the most important problem facing the country, and so on. Finally, seven other questions probe respondents' views of how fairly the government behaves: For example, does it treat rich and poor alike, safeguard the freedoms of speech and association, and guarantee access to basic necessities such as food, clothing, and shelter?

The impact of propaganda is gauged by two variables. "Media use" gets at how often respondents follow domestic and world news, and use the internet. "Media trust" scores respondents on how much they trust newspapers and television as news sources. Because the ABS was implemented in 14 countries, the questionnaire did not have enough space for country-specific questions that might have identified propaganda sources more specifically.

Nationalism is measured by a variable that I label "national pride." This is calculated as the respondent's average score on two questions: "How proud are you to be a citizen of [country]?" and "Given the chance, how willing would you be to go and live in another country?" (The two questions are of course scaled inversely, such that people with high scores on the first and low scores on the second are the most nationalistic.)

Finally, culture is measured with two batteries, one that assesses Traditional Social Values (TSV) and another that assesses Liberal Democratic Values (LDV).

The nine TSV items were formulated on the basis of a wide range of literature which argues that conflict avoidance, deference to authority, and an inclination to favor the group over the individual are values widely held in traditional societies (Inkeles and Smith 1974). The questionnaire items refer to general preferences and do not mention politics. The seven LDV items are designed to discern support for core liberal-democratic principles such as the freedoms of speech and association, judicial independence, and the separation of powers. These items present statements that contravene liberal-democratic values, so that disagreement signals LDV adherence.

When other variables are controlled in the regression equation shown in Table 7.1, the correlation between government performance and DRS is strong. Among the four performance variables, however, some aspects outweigh others in contributing to DRS. Contrary to conventional wisdom, respondents give no statistically measurable weight to the impact of government policies on their families' economic welfare, apparently crediting or blaming themselves rather than the government for however well or poorly their families are doing. What respondents do take into account on the economic front is the perceived health of the economy as a whole. But in nine of the fourteen countries, including both democracies and autocracies, citizens give even more weight to government fairness than they do to economic performance: Even in authoritarian regimes, people care more about whether the government treats them evenhandedly than they care about economic affairs. And the variable of government effectiveness is yet more important, having the strongest effect on DRS among the four performance variables across ten countries.

The authoritarian regimes of East and Southeast Asia tend to score higher on the two governance variables (effectiveness and fairness) than their democratic neighbors do, and this contributes to the robust DRS found in the authoritarian polities. To the extent, however, that authoritarian regimes are more susceptible than democracies to corruption and abuses of power, this finding points to a long-term threat to authoritarian legitimacy. Authoritarian regimes, like democracies, are being watched and evaluated by their citizens, who still expect—even if they cannot act on the expectation by freely voting—that the governments in their countries will perform effectively and fairly.

As for propaganda, regression analysis reveals that the intensity of citizens' media use has almost no influence on DRS (there is a statistically significant relationship only in Cambodia and China, and it is small). The more influential variable is media trust, which exerts a statistically significant positive (but again small) influence on DRS in all but three of the countries. This probably reflects

Table 7.1 Regression on DRS

	Japan	Taiwan	Korea	Mongolia	Hong Kong	Indonesia	Philippines	Thailand	Singapore	Malaysia	Cambodia	Myanmar	Vietnam	China
COUNTRY ECONOMY	0.170***	0.130***	0.066*	0.270***	NS	0.166***	0.168***	NS	0.081**	0.199***	0.171***	0.218***	0.121***	0.070***
FAMILY ECONOMY	NS	NS	NS	NS	NS	NS	NS	NS	0.075*	NS	NS	NS	NS	NS
GOVERNANCE EFFECTIVENESS	0.531***	0.533***	0.554***	0.335***	0.303***	0.414***	0.554***	0.322***	0.361***	0.526***	0.654***	0.741***	0.568***	0.257***
GOVERNANCE FAIRNESS	0.295***	0.284***	0.402***	0.138**	0.487***	0.223***	0.233***	0.362***	0.131**	0.473***	0.343***	0.233***	0.146***	0.157***
MEDIA USE	NS	NS	NS	NS	NS	NS	NS	NS	NS	NS	-0.091***	NS	NS	0.044***
MEDIA TRUST	NS	0.037*	0.075***	NS	0.072*	0.068**	0.045*	NS	0.060**	0.072***	0.104***	0.075*	0.074***	0.041***
NATIONAL PRIDE	0.105***	0.196***	0.141***	0.125***	0.110**	0.114**	NS	0.267***	0.217***	0.148***	NS	0.240***	0.162***	0.156***
TSV	0.287***	NS	0.194***	0.347***	0.282***	0.316***	0.379***	0.270***	0.108*	0.310***	0.305***	NS	0.427***	0.341***
LDV	-0.128***	-0.145***	-0.167***	-0.210***	-0.298***	-0.283***	-0.231***	NS	-0.264***	-0.250***	-0.328***	-0.549***	-0.171***	-0.261***
constant	-1.153***	-0.929***	-0.865***	-0.833***	-1.049***	-0.219	-0.474**	-1.104***	-0.419**	-0.733***	-0.583***	-1.454***	-0.448**	-0.776***
adjusted r squared	.338	.343	.284	.208	.293	.250	.238	.243	.284	.460	.473	.477	.331	.336
N	2655	2708	2243	1938	1724	2111	2052	1662	1495	2116	2166	1031	1604	4618
Out of	2961	3249	2407	2438	2424	3100	2400	2712	2039	2421	2400	1620	2391	7541
Missing %	10.33%	16.65%	6.81%	20.51%	28.88%	31.90%	14.50%	38.72%	26.68%	12.60%	9.75%	36.36%	32.92%	38.76%

NOTES: ABS Waves 3 and 4 combined. Data are weighted within each country. *p = .05, **p = .01, ***p = .001. OLS regression. Control variables not shown: male, age, urban residence, education level, religiosity, political efficacy, social capital, social trust, and a dummy variable to measure the difference between survey waves. NS = not statistically significant. "Urban" measures whether the subject's place of residence is urban or rural. Religiosity codes whether the subject describes himself as very, moderately, or slightly religious or not religious at all. Social capital is a factor scale of how many people the subject has contact with during an average week, how many people he thinks would help him in case of need and how many people he would help. Social trust is the mean of answers to questions on whether you can trust most people, trust people to be fair, think most people are trustworthy.

different dynamics in democracies and authoritarian systems. In the democracies, where media are diverse and often carry criticisms of the government, trust in media may help citizens to feel that they understand better why the government does what it does. In authoritarian systems, where the media are government-run or at least heavily government-influenced, the influence of media trust signifies that citizens who believe government propaganda are more likely to offer diffuse support to the regime.

Nationalism, or national pride, has a substantial positive influence on DRS in all countries except for Cambodia and the Philippines. In both democratic and authoritarian systems, citizens who express pride in their country and say that they are unwilling to move elsewhere are more likely than others to express support for the regime.

The final possible explanation for higher DRS under authoritarianism is culture. Both TSV and LDV have strong impacts on DRS in most countries, but their effects are opposed. In all countries except Myanmar and Taiwan, regardless of regime type, persons who affirm traditional values tend to accord greater legitimacy to the regime under which they live. The attitudes that are expressed through the TSV question battery, such as acceptance of hierarchy and deference to authority, incline citizens who hold these attitudes to support the existing political system regardless of what type it is, how it performs, how effective its propaganda is, or how proud these citizens feel of the nation. The LDV impact is the opposite. In all countries except Thailand, there is a statistically significant relationship between affirming liberal-democratic values and being more critical of one's government than fellow citizens who do not score as highly on LDV measures. This is true whether the regime is democratic or authoritarian, and holding all other variables constant. But the impact of LDV is not uniform across regime types. On average, a given quantum of LDV among the populace has a stronger downward pull on DRS in authoritarian regimes than in democracies.

To be sure, the LDV attitude cluster is more widely distributed in democratic as opposed to authoritarian countries. For example, the average per-item agreement with the seven LDV items is 63.4 percent of all respondents in Japan compared to 24.2 percent in Myanmar and 34.4 percent in China. But because persons who adhere to LDV are more likely to be alienated from the government if they live under an authoritarian regime than if they live in a democratic system, the spread of liberal-democratic values presents more of a threat to authoritarian regimes than it does to democracies.

The Authoritarian Dilemma

In drawing upon both performance and culture to generate legitimacy, Asian authoritarian regimes face a dilemma. To achieve high marks for performance, both democratic and authoritarian regimes implement policies that promote the modernization of their societies—measured in our survey by higher levels of education and urbanization. But these policies cause cultural values to change. In all countries except the Philippines and Vietnam there is a significant positive correlation between LDV and level of education, and with urban residence in eight of the twelve countries where the urban variable was measured (the ABS considers all Hong Kong and Singapore residents as urban, so there is no urban variable in our data from those societies). These shifts are more marked among the youth: in nine of the societies, LDV is associated with being younger. As LDV rises, TSV declines, and with this cultural shift comes a decline in diffuse regime support.

But the implications of this finding are different for the two types of regime. Only in authoritarian systems, not in democracies, is high LDV adherence associated with a desire for an alternative kind of regime. This is shown by two measures. The ABS assesses Detachment from Authoritarianism (DA) by scoring whether respondents disapprove of three forms of authoritarian rule: "We should get rid of parliament and elections and have a strong leader decide things," "Only one political party should be allowed to stand for election and hold office," and "The army should come in to govern the country."[3] Under all types of regimes, LDV is positively correlated with DA: That is, liberal citizens in both authoritarian and democratic regimes are unattracted to authoritarian alternatives. In effect, neither group sees an authoritarian alternative to what they already have.

But LDV adherents living in authoritarian systems do see an alternative. The ABS measures Democratic Regime Preference by asking respondents four questions about the attributes they prefer in government: for example, does the respondent believe that "Government is our employee, the people should tell government what needs to be done," or does she believe that "The government is like a parent, it should decide what is good for us"? In all types of political systems, adherents to LDV display a preference for regime characteristics associated with liberal democracy. This is not surprising in itself, as the LDV and regime characteristics batteries are quite similar. But the implications are encouraging for the stability of democratic systems and discouraging for that of authoritarian systems. In democracies, citizens may be dissatisfied with what they have but do not prefer an alternative. In authoritarian regimes, as LDV spread, so does a preference for democratic regime characteristics.

Authoritarian regimes may try to slow the erosion of deferential values, as China has done with its campaigns to revive Confucianism and promote nationalism. These efforts promote a kind of double-mindedness, with younger and more educated citizens feeling proud of their country's traditions and accomplishments and keen to contribute to their country's success, yet determined to assert their individuality in their private lives, to protect their personal and property rights, and to learn about the outside world. Yet at the same time, the shift away from TSV and toward LDV continues, and the better the regime performs in modernizing the society, the more rapidly the shift occurs. The high trust and DRS scores enjoyed by authoritarian regimes in East and Southeast Asia will not protect them indefinitely from challenges to their survival.

Acknowledgements

This article is an abridged version of "The Puzzle of Authoritarian Legitimacy," in *Journal of Democracy* 31(1) (January 2020), pp. 158-168, doi: 10.1353/jod.2020.0013.

Notes

1. The third wave (2010-12) surveyed thirteen countries, and the fourth wave (2014-16) covered fourteen. For this study, I combined the data from these two waves to create larger country samples capable of dampening the random measurement errors always found in survey research. Combining the two waves is acceptable for the present investigation because, even if DRS levels shift, their determinants are unlikely to have changed much in the handful of years between the two waves. The combined dataset has 40,103 respondents.
2. Countries are arranged from left to right according to their 2013 Freedom House scores. DRS is a factor score ranging from -2.89 to +1.92. A score below zero in Figure 7.1 does not necessarily indicate a legitimacy crisis. It is best to interpret the scores as simply comparative; a higher score indicates stronger average DRS than a lower score. More details can be found in the online Appendix of the published article.
3. Only two of the four questions were asked in China in the third wave; Myanmar was not surveyed in the third wave; the battery was not used in Vietnam in the fourth wave.

References

Chen, Jie. 2004. *Popular Political Support in Urban China*. Washington, D.C.: Woodrow Wilson Center Press. http://www.sup.org/books/title/?id=6944.

Dickson, Bruce J. 2016. *The Dictator's Dilemma: The Chinese Communist Party's Strategy for Survival*. Chap. 5, 214-262. New York: Oxford University Press.

Easton, David. 1975. "A Re-Assessment of the Concept of Political Support." *British Journal of Political Science* 5(4): 435-457. http://www.jstor.org/stable/193437.

Gilley, Bruce. 2009. *The Right to Rule: How States Win and Lose Legitimacy*. Chap. 2, 29-57. New York: Columbia University Press.

Inkeles, Alex, and David Horton Smith. 1974. *Becoming Modern: Individual Change in Six Developing Countries*. Cambridge: Harvard University Press.

Norris, Pippa. 1999. *Critical Citizens: Global Support for Democratic Government*. Oxford: Oxford University Press.

Shi, Tianjian. 2015. *The Cultural Logic of Politics in Mainland China and Taiwan*. Chap. 5, 107-146. New York: Cambridge University Press. doi:10.1017/CBO9780511996474.

Tang, Wenfang. 2016. *Populist Authoritarianism: Chinese Political Culture and Regime Sustainability*. New York: Oxford University Press. https://oxford.universitypressscholarship.com/view/10.1093/acprof:oso/9780190205782.001.0001/acprof-9780190205782.

Wong, Timothy Ka-ying, Po-san Wan, and Hsin-Huang Michael Hsiao. 2011. "The Bases of Political Trust in Six Asian Societies: Institutional and Cultural Explanations Compared." *International Political Science Review* 32 (3): 263-281. doi:10.1177/0192512110378657.

Zhong, Yang, and Yongguo Chen. 2013. "Regime Support in Urban China." *Asian Survey* 53 (2): 369-392. doi:10.1525/as.2013.53.2.369.

8 Do Liberal Democratic Values and Asian Traditional Values Have Differential Impacts on Political Participation in East and Southeast Asia?

Ken'ichi Ikeda

There have been hundreds of discussions on whether so-called "Asian values" and liberal democratic ideas are compatible in our flourishing Asian societies. This question has been discussed not only in academic fields such as political science but also in diverse forms of public discourse. A Google search for the words "Asian Values" in August 2020 returned more than 30 million hits (using the Japanese version of Google, we had 1.7 million hits). However, no one has won the debate, even with the focus limited to political participation, satisfaction with and stability of democracy, or economic prosperity. The basic goal of this article is to advance this discussion by considering the following aspects: (1) whether traditional "Asian values" (which we label Traditional Social Values (TSV)) and Liberal Democratic Values (LDV) determine political participation and (2) how the effects of these values are influenced by the perceived institutional constraints of a society, namely institutional trust, especially in the national government. In this investigation, we seek to elucidate some of the complexity in values, institutional trust, and political participation in East and Southeast Asia.

Values, Institutional Trust, and Political Participation

The traditional social values examined here emphasize paternalistic attitudes, aversion to heterogeneity among the people, and "harmony." In other words, they emphasize the importance of hierarchical social relations and of superiors holding dominance over their subordinates and not tolerating dissent, while also taking into account the welfare of their subordinates. This paternalistic value system, in which subordinates are expected to accept the decisions of their superiors and build harmonious social relations with others, is thought to be ubiquitous in everyday social situations. The Asian Barometer Survey (ABS) has measured such values in terms of deference to authority, conflict avoidance, and collectivism (subordination of the individual to the group) (Chu and Huang Unpublished). Although these values are not directly related to politics, as shown by the label traditional "social" values, this value orientation has an aspect of being at odds with liberal democratic values.

Liberal democratic values underpin a system of reciprocity among citizens and cross-checking between political institutions that aims for equal and transpartisan discussion and consensus-building among heterogeneous participants. To capture these values, the ABS uses an inverted scale of the following ideas: paternalism in the political world, purposeful harmony, and opposition to checks and balances, which represent the denial of liberal values. The ABS does not measure liberal democratic values directly to avoid responses being inflated by the social desirability of "democratic values" (Chu and Huang Unpublished). Therefore, the items are worded in an illiberal direction; thus, to be classified as a liberal democrat, the respondent must disagree with the items. Attitudes toward this liberal democratic values system serve as a code of conduct in discussing public affairs and social issues. In other words, these values are more directly related to politics than to social values.

In this chapter, we set political participation as the dependent variable and traditional social values, liberal democratic values, and institutional trust as independent variables. The interaction effects between these two categories of values and institutional trust will also be examined. "Institutional trust" here refers to the general level of trust in various institutions that support society, such as the cabinet, political parties, parliament, and the executive branch. Institutional trust is the part of social capital that underpins a flourishing society through trust, reciprocity, and networks of citizens.

Institutional trust interacts (and resonates) with values that affect political participation. Under traditional social values, where trust in institutions is required in a paternalistic manner and disagreement with policies and procedures emanating from institutions is discouraged, political participation is likely to differ from that in a liberal democracy. In other words, "As normative practices, paternalistic value emphasizes ethical dependence on rulers, and harmony orientation value inhibits disobedience against them." (Ikeda 2013, 21) Therefore, traditional social values discourage forms of political participation such as protests. Conversely, among those with liberal democratic values, are protests in response to distrust in institutions perceived as normatively acceptable and more common than when these values are weak?

To examine this issue, it is first necessary to make a distinction in political participation. Rosenstone et al. (1993) distinguished between electoral political participation and governmental political participation. In this chapter, we focus on governmental political participation. This is because the meaning of participation in electoral politics can be very different between countries and regions in East and Southeast Asia.

We use two subscales of governmental political participation that have been used since an epoch-making study by Almond & Verba (1963) and can have different behavioral meanings. Political participation can take the form of contact with politically powerful people (contact-type political participation) or involve the behavioral expression of political opinions and positions, sometimes with protest implications (active-type political participation).

Hypothesis Formation

First, let us see whether the relationship between institutional trust and values varies in relation to the two types of political participation. Let us consider a scatterplot of aggregate data based on each wave of the ABS in each country or region.

Figure 8.1 shows that the overall trend in traditional social values increases as trust in the national government increases.[1] In contrast, Figure 8.2 shows that liberal democratic values increase as trust in the national government decreases.

On the other hand, institutional trust is also correlated with participation. As Figures 8.3 and 8.4 show, contact-type political participation is positively correlated with trust in the national government, while active-type political participation is negatively correlated.

From these figures, we can infer that contact-type governmental political participation reflects traditional social values, while active-type political participation is consistent with a liberal democratic values perspective. In other words, contact-type political participation is more compatible with contact with political influencers; it is supported by traditional values and can imply hierarchical relationships between citizens (those with and without power). In contrast, it appears that active-type political participation seeks to sway untrustworthy governments through actions pushed by liberal democratic values.

This conjecture is based on a scatterplot of average scores from surveys in each country or region, and it is theoretically important to clarify whether those patterns occur consistently at the individual citizen level, i.e. psychologically consistent with the logics of values.

Figure 8.1 Scatterplot of the Relationship between Trust in the National Government and Traditional Social Values

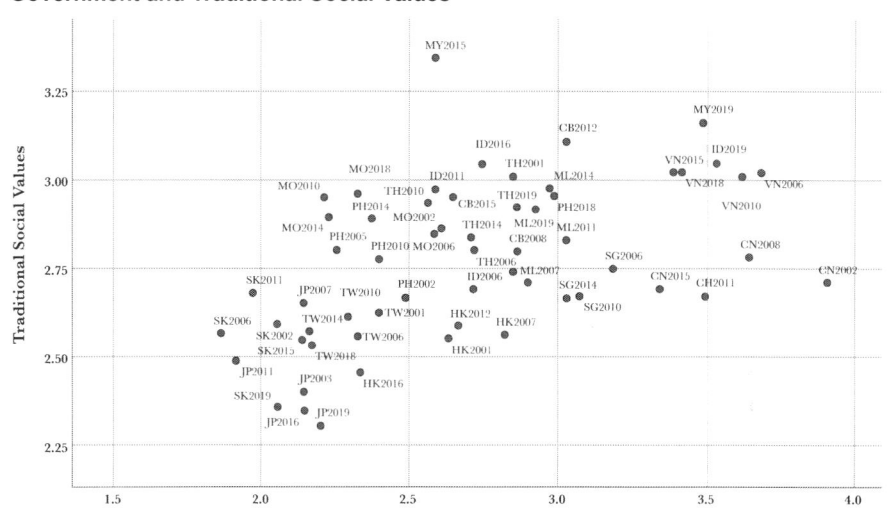

Source: Asian Barometer Survey. Author prepared.

Figure 8.2 Scatterplot of the Relationship between Trust in the National Government and Liberal Democratic Values

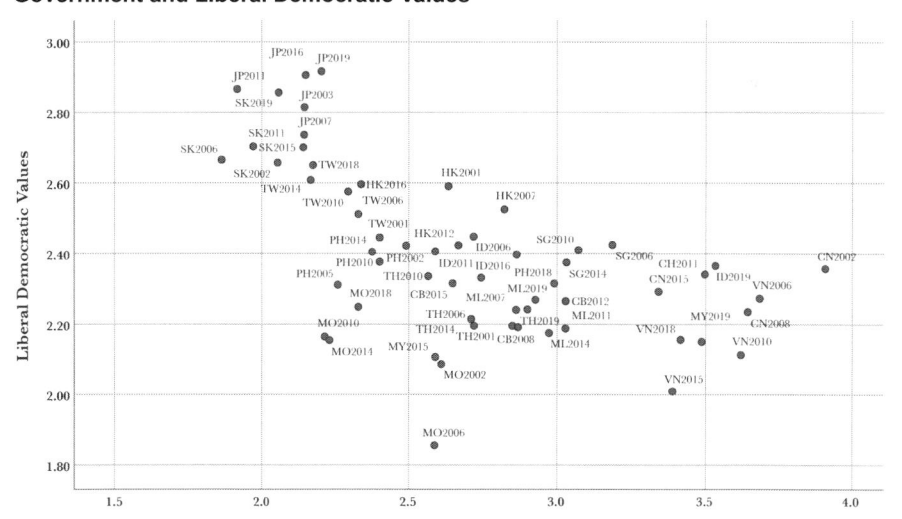

Source: Asian Barometer Survey. Author prepared.

Figure 8.3 Scatterplot between Trust in the National Government and Contact-type Political Participation

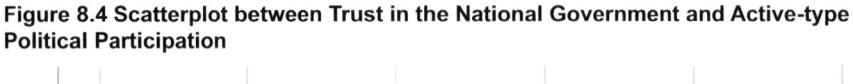

Source: Asian Barometer Survey. Author prepared.

Figure 8.4 Scatterplot between Trust in the National Government and Active-type Political Participation

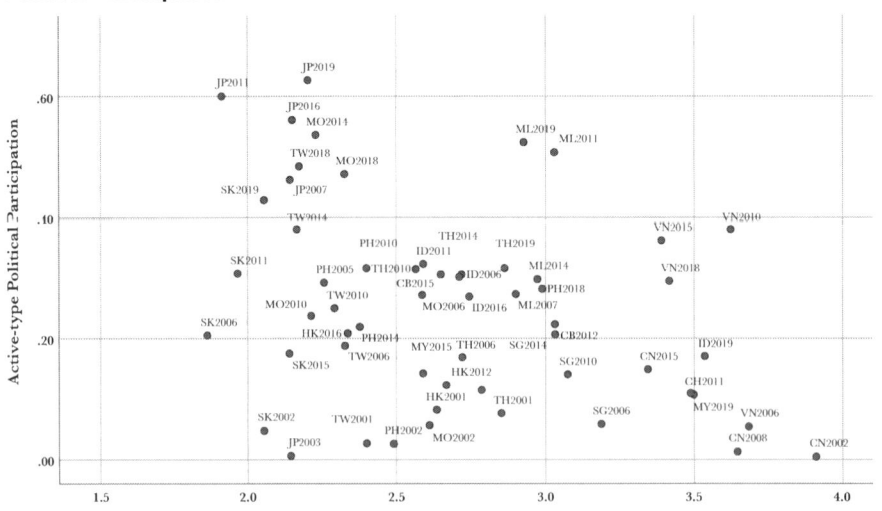

Source: Asian Barometer Survey. Author prepared.

Institutional Trust and Political Participation

First, let us examine the relationship between institutional trust and political participation. Institutional trust may exhibit two possible paths to political participation. The first possibility is that under conditions of high institutional trust in government, working on or approaching trustworthy institutions is perceived to be effective, thus promoting political participation that in turn leads to more trustworthy governments. The second is the opposite possibility: under conditions of low institutional trust in government, political participation can promote contesting demands or agitation outside the system against governments that cannot be trusted.

Although the links between trust and participation extend in opposite directions, the forms of participation may be compatible. To elaborate in more detail, the first pathway seems more compatible with conditions of high institutional trust, reflected in activities such as contacting political influencers, i.e., reaching out to political actors within the system to obtain desired political or nonpolitical outcomes. Norris identified this route with respect to institutional trust in her analysis of data from 44 World Values Survey countries in the mid-1990s (Norris 1999). This possibility is indeed suggested by the scatterplot in Figure 8.1. Although not addressed in this chapter, this pathway for action can also occur in electoral political participation, such as by supporting the ruling party and seeking a voice within it.

The second route is political participation in opposition to untrustworthy governments, primarily through non-institutional routes. This has a sense of political participation to restore institutional trust. In other words, it is political participation with confrontational logic and orientation to produce change from outside the government. It seems more likely to occur with the seizure of power at the ballot box (electoral political participation), through demands in forms such as petitions (external institutional participation other than through politicians), direct expressions of distrust, and more radical forms of political participation. In a previous study, Norris found a negative relationship between institutional trust and a type of specific governmental political participation that have "protest potential" (Norris 1999). A similar perspective is reflected in the argument of Chu and Huang (Unpublished) for "critical democrats." The widespread presence of such citizens in East and Southeast Asia can be seen in the scatterplot in Figure 8.2; the greater the participation of this type of citizen, the less trust they have in the national government. Similarly, using data from the fourth wave of the World Values Survey (conducted around 2000), Qi and Shin (2011) found high levels of active-type political participation (petitions, boycotts, and demonstrations) among critical democrats in 43 countries (excluding Japan, South Korea, and other developed countries).

Interaction with Values

The relevance of the above two directions depends on the values held by citizens, who may be assumed to behave in a manner consistent with their own values.

From the theoretical perspective of social capital, liberal democratic values are considered to promote political participation in general (Hypothesis 1, H1). According to Putnam's (1993, 2000) theory, social capital—consisting of trust in others and institutions, mutual reciprocity, and social networks among citizens—makes democracy work. However, it requires citizens' involvement; that is, it needs social and political participation, which enriches the community and society.

Next, we hypothesize that these forms of participation under liberal democratic values promote contact-type political participation when individuals trust the government (H2) and active-type political participation when they do not (H3). That is, there will be an interaction between contact-type participation and high or low levels of trust in the national government. As we see in H1, liberal democratic values generally encourage political participation, but higher trust and stronger (rather than weaker) liberal democratic values will increase the likelihood that contact-type participation will be attempted. At the same time, low trust in the government is associated with active type participation. While actions against governments may not always succeed, values push action.

What should we believe about traditional social values? Traditional social values have a direct link to political participation in the form of contacting authoritative government incumbents/powerful leaders (H4), and higher levels of trust in the national government will lead to further contact-type political participation (H5). This is because it is more consistent with the values that we expect will evoke paternalism. Conversely, traditional values will not be associated with active-type participation, or will suppress it (H6), as this type of participation may involve a high degree of extra-institutional actions, which connotes the divergence from traditional values that normatively assume ethical dependence on rulers.

Data

All survey data from waves 1-5 of the ABS will be included in the analysis, except that surveys missing the variables used in this study are excluded.[2] A total of 55 national surveys were used in the analysis, including seven in the first wave, 11 surveys in the second wave, 13 surveys in the third wave, 14 surveys in the fourth wave, and 10 surveys in the fifth wave. The total number of respondents was 61,953.

Details of the Main Variables

Political participation: Two subscales of governmental political participation are used. In order to construct the scale, the variables basically common to all the five waves of the ABS were adopted.

Contact-type political participation (the CONTACTPA scale) is measured by asking respondents whether they have had the following experiences in the past three years: "Contacted elected officials or legislative representatives at any level," "Contacted officials at higher level," and "Contacted other influential people outside the government." Active-type political participation (the ACTIVEPA scale) consisted of the following items: "Got together with others to raise an issue or sign a petition," "Attended a demonstration or protest march," and "Used force or violence for a political cause." The data were unified to "once," "more than once," and "never," respectively, and the former two were counted as positive responses.[3]

Institutional trust in the national government: In the ABS, institutional trust items were measured on a four-point scale and multiple institutions were listed. Because the purpose of this chapter is to focus on participation in governmental politics, we narrow the focus to one item and use institutional trust in the central government as a single measure.

Liberal democratic values and traditional social values: The Liberal Democratic Values (LDV) used an inverted four-point scale for each of the following five items: "Leaders are like the head of a family; we should all follow their decisions," "The government should decide whether certain ideas should be allowed to be discussed in society," "Harmony of the community will be disrupted if people organize lots of groups," "If the government is constantly checked by the legislature, it cannot possibly accomplish great things," and "If people have too many different ways of thinking, society will be chaotic."[4]

On the other hand, Traditional Social Values (TSV) are a group of items that relate to Asian values in everyday social situations, using a four-point scale for each of the following five items: "If parents' demands are unreasonable, children still should do what they ask," "Being a student, one should not question the authority of one's teacher," "For the sake of the family, the individual should put personal interests second," "A person should not insist on his own opinion if his co-workers disagree with him," and "For the sake of the national interest, individual interests could be sacrificed."

The correlation coefficient between the liberal democratic values scale and the traditional social values scale was not very high at -0.37 (the correlation coefficient for the entire sample).

Other variables

Internal political efficacy (EFFIC): It is well known that internal political efficacy facilitates political participation. The perception of one's own competence in politics is linked to the perceived meaningfulness and effectiveness of participation (Niemi, Craig, and Mattei 1991). Internal efficacy is measured by two items: "I think I have the ability to participate in politics" and "Sometimes politics and government seem so complicated that a person like me can't really understand what is going on" (a reverse-scored item).

Political interest (PINTERES): Needless to say, interest in politics is a driver of political participation. This variable is used to test whether the hypotheses about values and trust in government still hold even after controlling for the degree of political interest.

General trust in others (WVSTRUST): General trust is one of the important factors for increasing social engagement and making democracy work. Without the possibility of trusting not only others in one's social network, but also unknown others, political participation as a collective action will not be promoted. ABS, like the World Values Survey, measures this using the following items: "Generally speaking, would you say that 'most people can be trusted' or 'that you must be very careful in dealing with people'?"

Demographic factors: gender, age, education, employment status, and urban residence (nonurban vs. urban) are used as control factors.

Level 2 variables in each survey (survey year and country/region): We used Freedom House Index and GDP/capita (controlling for political, institutional, and economic factors). Moreover, the averages of liberal democratic values and traditional social values were introduced into the Level 2 equation. This aggregate level of values in each survey not only shows the relative impact of country/wave (i.e., each survey) means of values on political participation, but also controls for the mean differences of the values among surveys to provide more exact values for Level 1 effects.

Analysis

A hierarchical linear model (Raudenbush and Bryk 2002) was used, with Level 1 being the responses of individuals and Level 2 being the survey by year and country or region, which allows the differences in responses at the national and individual levels to be examined in isolation. The focus is on the relationship between values and trust in the government and political participation by individuals. The two dependent variables of political participation have a Poisson distribution, and the corresponding analysis was conducted.[5]

Result

The results for contact-type political participation are shown in Table 8.1 and in Figure 8.5. The figures show post hoc simulation analyses based on the results in the table and illustrate the effects, including the interaction effect.

From Table 8.1, we see that interest in politics and internal political efficacy increased contact-type governmental political participation by individuals at Level 1, as expected. The effect of demographic factors was higher for nonurban dwellers, employed people, males, older people, and those with higher levels of education. Generally, this is mostly consistent with existing findings in political participation research.

At Level 2, there was no discernible effect of GDP/capita. The same is true for the effect of the Freedom House Index. There were no effects of aggregate-level values.[6]

In relation to the hypothesis with interactions included, liberal democratic values do not reach statistical significance (and are not significant in relation to the effect alone), while the effect of traditional social values is significantly facilitative. There was no single effect of trust in the national government. The interaction effect of trust in the national government*liberal democratic values showed a slightly negative trend. Figure 8.5 (left panel) shows that the association between liberal democratic values and trust in the national government fell somewhat short of significance (p = .18), although as expected liberal democratic values moved in the direction of facilitating contact.

Table 8.1 HLM Model for Contact-type Political Participation

	Coefficient	t-ratio
Level 1		
Liberal democratic values (LDV)	0.11	1.43
Traditional social values (TSV)	0.16	2.09*
Trust in the national government	0.07	0.63
General trust	0.00	-0.17
Interest in politics	030	14.71***
Internal political efficacy	0.11	10.42***
Trust in the national government*LDV	-0.04	-1.36
Trust in the national government*TSV	-0.01	-0.44
Living in urban area	-0.08	-2.26*
Employed	0.17	8.45***
Gender (1 = male, 2 = female)	-0.21	-8.73***
Age	0.01	7.02***
Education	0.07	9.83***
Level 2		
ABS wave	0.23	3.53***
LDV survey average	-0.75	-1.25
TSV survey average	-0.02	-0.03
GDP per capita	0.00	-0.42
Freedom House score	0.01	0.13
Intercept	-0.45	-4.28***
No. of observations		61953
No. of (survey) countries		55

Note: Significance level p<0.05*, p<0.01**, p<0.001***

Figure 8.5 Post-hoc Simulation Analyses Based on Table 8.1

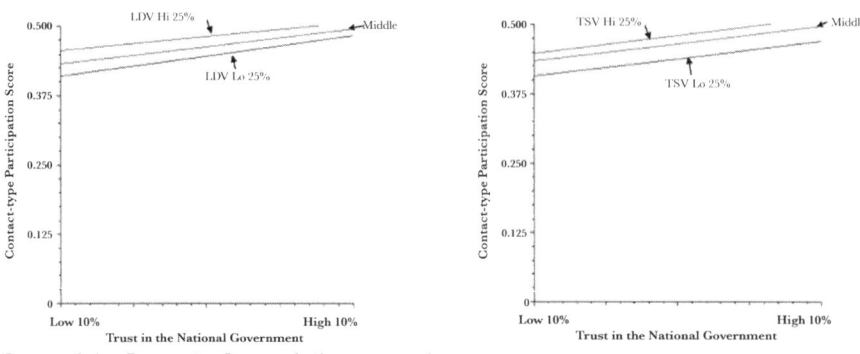

Source: Asian Barometer Survey. Author prepared.

On the other hand, as shown in Figure 8.5 (right panel), higher traditional values on their own significantly increased contact-type political participation, although without an interaction effect with trust in the national government.

In terms of the success or failure of the hypotheses, H1, H2, and H5 were not supported, and only H4, or the effect of traditional social values alone, was detected. As can be seen in Figure 8.6, while not a large difference, it is clear that there is a consistent difference between the top 25 percent of TSVs and the bottom 25 percent of TSVs, with the lower TSVs having about 5 percentage points less contact-type participation.

Table 8.2 HLM Model for Active-type Political Participation

	Coefficient	t-ratio
Level 1		
Liberal democratic values (LDV)	0.35	3.88***
Traditional social values (TSV)	-0.02	-0.16
Trust in the national government	-0.05	-0.35
General trust	0.04	0.92
Interest in politics	0.36	12.01***
Internal political efficacy	0.15	8.50***
Trust in the national government*LDV	-0.07	-2.30*
Trust in the national government*TSV	0.02	0.68
Living in urban area	-0.01	-0.17
Employed	0.09	2.71**
Gender (1 = male, 2 = female)	-0.12	-2.73**
Age	0.00	-0.59
Education	0.06	5.66***
Level 2		
ABS wave	0.41	5.48***
LDV survey average	-0.50	-0.95
TSV survey average	0.85	1.39
GDP per capita	0.00	1.90*
Freedom House score	-0.19	-3.27**
Intercept	-1.64	-9.52**
No. of observations	61953	
No. of (survey) countries	55	

Note: Significance level p<0.05*, p<0.01**, p<0.001***

Figure 8.6 Post-hoc Simulation Analyses Based on Table 8.2

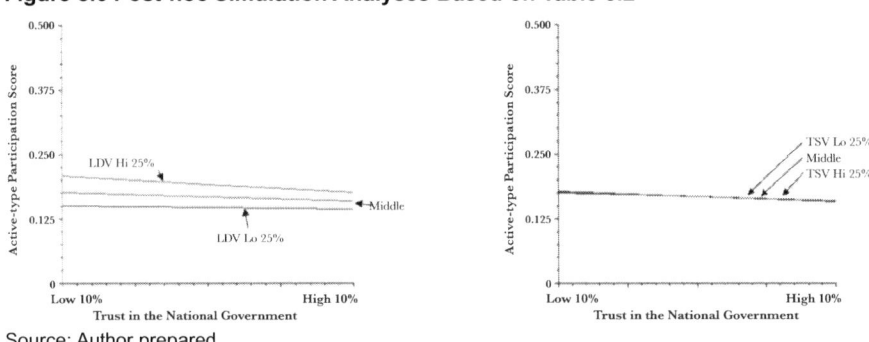

Source: Author prepared.

Next, the results for active-type political participation are presented in Table 8.2 and Figure 8.6. The graphs illustrate the results through post hoc simulations with interactions.

In terms of general results not related to our hypotheses, interest in politics and internal political efficacy increased active-type political participation at Level 1, which is in line with expectations for contact-type governmental political participation. The effects of demographic factors were more likely to influence active-type political participation for employed people, males, and educated people.

At Level 2, the effect of GDP/capita was weakly positive, with more affluent respondents increasing their active-type political participation. The effect of the Freedom House Index was significant and negative. Because a lower value implies a higher degree of political rights and freedom, this indicates that the more liberal the system is, the more it promotes active-type political participation. None of these results are unexpected. Although there is an alternative way to analyze with the discrete variable "regime type" instead of the Freedom House score, we used the latter because we decided that a continuous variable indexing both of political rights and civil liberties is more appropriate as an independent variable to explain political participation, rather than examining differences among regimes as a discrete variable.

Finally, no effects of values at the aggregate level were found.[7]

In relation to the hypotheses, liberal democratic values were highly significant and facilitated active-type political participation. In contrast, no effect was found for traditional social values. There was no single effect of trust in the national government, but it was significant and negative when the interaction variables were excluded. In other words, lower levels of trust promoted active-type political participation.

As for the interaction effect, the effect of trust in the national government*liberal democratic values was negative and significant. Figure 8.6 (left panel) shows that, as expected, the association between liberal democratic values and trust in the national government—i.e., lower trust in the national government and stronger liberal democratic values—promoted active-type political participation. In contrast, political participation remained low when liberal democratic values were low, regardless of the level of trust in the national government. In addition, there was no effect of traditional social values alone or in interaction with the trust in the national government (right panel of Figure 8.6).

Of the hypotheses, H1 and H3 were strongly supported. H6, the negation of traditional social values (predicting no significant difference), was also supported.

Discussion and Implications

Thanks to their 20-year longitudinal data as well as wide coverage of countries and regions in East and Southeast Asia, the five waves of the ABS provide us with an invaluable opportunity to examine the meaning of liberal democratic values and traditional social values and their impact on political participation.

We found a single facilitating effect of traditional social values on contact-type governmental political participation, while liberal democratic values facilitated active-type governmental political participation and interacted with trust in the national government. Distrust of the system drives active-type political participation among those holding liberal democratic values throughout East and Southeast Asia.

Although we have shown that values and trust in the government make a difference in political participation, it is also important to note that the magnitudes of their effect do not necessarily change the overall participation ratio in a powerful way. As we saw in Figures 8.5 and 8.6, the differences in values are not very large in the overall picture. Also, we need to be cautious in interpreting the results as the statistical significance detected here may have become significant because of the large sample size.

Despite this, what are the implications of this chapter? The important one is that in East and Southeast Asia—a diverse region with vastly different political systems, cultures, and religious backgrounds—common effects of values on political participation have been found. While this was not necessarily a powerful finding, it can be considered one with universal implications for democratic practices. One objective of the ABS study was to find commonalities in the political life of citizens despite the diversity and heterogeneity within Asia. The results of this study are one small step toward that objective.

Notes

1. Legend: JP: Japan, HK: Hong Kong, SK: South Korea, CH: Mainland China, MO: Mongolia, PH: Philippines, TW: Taiwan, TH: Thailand, ID: Indonesia, SG: Singapore, VN: Vietnam, CB: Cambodia, ML: Malaysia, MY: Myanmar. Numbers are the year when the survey was conducted.

2. The surveys with missing variable(s) are in the first wave for Mongolia (age data) and the second wave for Cambodia and Hong Kong (active participation), which are excluded from the analysis. In the fifth wave, India and Australia are excluded from the analysis because they are the first ABS wave to be conducted in these countries, and for the sake of consistency in the analysis. Therefore, the countries analyzed in the fifth wave are Japan, South Korea, Mongolia, Philippines, Taiwan, Thailand, Indonesia, Vietnam, Malaysia, and Myanmar.

3. The political participation variable in the fifth wave of ABS is a more differentiated measure of participation frequency, but it was aggregated to match the scale with the first four waves.

4. Because there is a 10 percentage increase in the size of the target sample if we use average values for this LDV scale as well as the next TSV scale (i.e., if there are missing answers, we calculate the average without them), instead of using the full variable set (i.e., no missing answers for relevant variables), we used the average values.

5. The analytic mode is shown below (dependent variables are CONTACTPA or ACTIVEPA).

Level-1 Model

$E(DEPENDENT_{ij} | \beta_j) = \lambda_{ij}$

$\log[\lambda_{ij}] = \eta_{ij}$

$\eta_{ij} = \beta_{0j} + \beta_{1j}*(LDV_{ij}) + \beta_{2j}*(TSV_{ij}) + \beta_{3j}*(GOVTRUST_{ij}) + \beta_{4j}*(WVSTRUST_{ij}) + \beta_{5j}*(PINTERES_{ij}) + \beta_{6j}*(EFFIC_{ij}) + \beta_{7j}*(GOV\_LDV_{ij}) + \beta_{8j}*(GOV\_TSV_{ij}) + \beta_{9j}*(URBAN_{ij}) + \beta_{10j}*(EMPLOYED_{ij}) + \beta_{11j}*(GENDER_{ij}) + \beta_{12j}*(AGE_{ij}) + \beta_{13j}*(EDUCATIO_{ij})$

Level-2 Model

$\beta_{0j} = \gamma_{00} + \gamma_{01}*(WAVE_j) + \gamma_{02}*(LDV_j) + \gamma_{03}*(TSV_j) + \gamma_{04}*(GDP\_CAP_j) + \gamma_{05}*(FREEDOM_j) + u_{0j}$

$\beta_{1j} = \gamma_{10} + u_{1j}$

$\beta_{2j} = \gamma_{20} + u_{2j}$

$\beta_{3j} = \gamma_{30} + u_{3j}$

$\beta_{4j} = \gamma_{40}$

$\beta_{5j} = \gamma_{50}$

$\beta_{6j} = \gamma_{60}$

$\beta_{7j} = \gamma_{70} + u_{7j}$

$\beta_{8j} = \gamma_{80} + u_{8j}$

$\beta_{9j} = \gamma_{90}$

$\beta_{10j} = \gamma_{100}$

$$\beta_{11j} = \gamma_{110}$$
$$\beta_{12j} = \gamma_{120}$$
$$\beta_{13j} = \gamma_{130}$$

LDV, TSV, GOVTRUST, WVSTRUST, PINTERES, EFFIC, GOV_LDV, GOV_TSV, AGE, and EDUCATIO were centered around the group mean. WAVE, LDV, TSV, GDP_CAP, and FREEDOM were centered around the grand mean. Table 8.1 and Table 8.2 show only fixed effects. However, though not shown, in both of the HLM analysis, we entered random effects for the intercept, LDV, TSV, trust in national government, as well as interaction terms for trust and two values. All the effects are significant at 0.001 level.

6. Though we see an increase in contact-type political participation in the most recent ABS wave, this seems an artifact due to some lack of the variables that compose the dependent variable in the earlier wave.

7. As for the effect of survey wave, the same significance appeared as in the analysis of contact-type political participation due to the same reason.

References

Almond, Gabriel A., and Sidney Verba. 1963. *The Civic Culture: Political Attitudes and Democracy in Five Nations*. Princeton: Princeton University Press. http://www.jstor.org/stable/j.ctt183pnr2.

Chu, Yun-han, and Min-hua Huang. Unpublished. "Four Orientations to Democracy." (2011)

Ikeda, Ken'ichi. 2013. "Social and Institutional Trust in East and Southeast Asia." *Taiwan Journal of Democracy* 9 (1): 13-45. http://www.tfd.org.tw/export/sites/tfd/files/publication/journal/dj0901/002.pdf.

Niemi, Richard G., Stephen C. Craig, and Franco Mattei. 1991. "Measuring Internal Political Efficacy in the 1988 National Election Study." *American Political Science Review* 85 (4): 1407-1413. doi:10.2307/1963953.

Norris, Pippa. 1999. *Critical Citizens: Global Support for Democratic Government*. Oxford: Oxford University Press.

Putnam, Robert D. 2000. *Bowling Alone: The Collapse and Revival of American Community*. New York: Simon & Schuster. https://scholar.harvard.edu/robertputnam/publications/bowling-alone-collapse-and-revival-american-community.

Putnam, Robert D., Robert Leonardi, and Raffaella Nanetti. 1993. *Making Democracy Work: Civic Traditions in Modern Italy*. Princeton: Princeton University Press. http://press.princeton.edu/titles/5105.html.

Qi, Lingling, and Doh Chull Shin. 2011. "How Mass Political Attitudes Affect Democratization: Exploring the Facilitating Role Critical Democrats Play in the Process." *International Political Science Review* 32 (3): 245-262. doi:10.1177/0192512110382029.

Raudenbush, Stephen W., and Anthony S. Bryk. 2002. *Hierarchical Linear Models: Applications and Data Analysis Methods (Second Edition)*. Thousand Oaks, CA.: Sage Publications. https://us.sagepub.com/en-us/nam/hierarchical-linear-models/book9230.

Rosenstone, Steven J., and John Mark Hansen. 1993. *Mobilization, Participation, and Democracy in America*. New York: Macmillan Publishing Company.

9 Quality of Democracy in East Asia
Hyunjin Oh and Chong-Min Park

Democratic decay or erosion has become a major concern across the globe (Graber, Levinson, and Tushnet 2018; Ginsburg and Huq 2018; Lührmann and Lindberg 2019). Many democracies, old and new alike, fail to fully embody the principles and mechanisms of liberal democracy. Democracies in East Asia are no exceptions (Shin 2018; Croissant and Diamond 2020; Chu et al. 2020). If citizens disapprove of their regime's democratic quality, they may lose faith in the prevailing system of government, which ultimately leads to regime instability (Park 2017). In this short essay, we examine public perceptions of the quality of democratic regimes in East Asia by utilizing cross-national public opinion data drawn from the last three waves of the Asian Barometer Survey (hereafter ABS).[1]

Any meaningful assessment of the quality of democracy requires that a country be a democracy (Roberts 2010). For that reason, our analysis includes six East Asian cases which Freedom House rates as "electoral democracies," namely Indonesia, Japan, Mongolia, the Philippines, South Korea, and Taiwan. We consider ordinary citizens to be the final, if not best, arbiters of democracy's quality. By using public opinion survey data, we examine how ordinary citizens view the general and dimensional quality of democracy in their country. In doing so, we seek to identify the weaknesses of East Asian democracies and their institutional challenges from the perspective of ordinary citizens. Before presenting the findings, it should be noted that the standards used by ordinary citizens from different countries may not be the same when they are asked to evaluate democratic quality in their own country. Yet, it should also be emphasized that "[a] basic understanding of democracy has diffused widely around the globe" (Dalton, Shin, and Jou 2008).

Expert-Based Assessments

Before presenting public perceptions of democratic quality, we present two well-known expert-based assessments as indicators of the actual level of democracy: Freedom House's ratings of political rights and civil liberties and V-Dem Institute's measures of democracy.

Table 9.1 Freedom House's Ratings on Freedom

	2010		2015		2019	
	Political Rights	Civil Liberties	Political Rights	Civil Liberties	Political Rights	Civil Liberties
Indonesia	2	3	2	4	2	4
Japan	1	2	1	1	1	1
Mongolia	2	2	1	2	1	2
Philippines	3	3	3	3	3	4
South Korea	1	2	2	2	2	2
Taiwan	1	2	1	2	1	1

Source: Freedom House. Authors prepared.

Freedom House annually reports a country's current situation regarding political rights and civil liberties on a scale from 1 (most free) to 7 (least free). As presented in Table 9.1, in 2019 Japan and Taiwan, each received an average score of 1, while Mongolia and South Korea, received average scores of 1.5 and 2, respectively. They all were classified as "free." Indonesia received an average score of 3 and the Philippines, 3.5. Both of them were rated as "partly free." Freedom House designates these six countries as "electoral democracies," indicating that they possess properties of minimalist democracy such as a competitive multiparty system, universal suffrage, regularly contested elections, and equal access of major political parties to the electorate. As shown in Table 9.1, the average ratings increased in Japan, Taiwan, and Mongolia over the last decade, but they decreased in South Korea, Indonesia, and the Philippines. In particular, Indonesia was downgraded from "free" to "partly free" status.

Distinguishing different conceptions of democracy, the V-Dem Institute has developed five democracy indices. The Electoral Democracy Index (EDI) emphasizes properties of "thin" democracy such as universal suffrage, free and fair elections, and multiparty competition (Dahl 1971). The electoral principle of democracy is treated as an essential element of any other conception of representative democracy. Thus, the Liberal Democracy Index (LDI) adds to the measure of electoral democracy the protection of liberal rights, strong rule of law, an independent judiciary, and effective checks and balances that limit the exercise of executive power. As shown in Table 9.2, in 2019 South Korea displayed the highest EDI and LDI scores, closely followed by Japan and Taiwan, while the Philippines displayed the lowest EDI and LDI scores. Over the past decade, South Korea and Taiwan improved on both indices. By contrast, Japan's democracy declined on both indices and Mongolia's democracy was stagnant on both indices. Democracy in the Philippines deteriorated on the LDI, but not on the EDI. Finally, Indonesia's democracy deteriorated on both indices.

Table 9.2 V-Dem Institute's Assessment of Democracy

	2010		2015		2019	
	Electoral Democracy Index	Liberal Democracy Index	Electoral Democracy Index	Liberal Democracy Index	Electoral Democracy Index	Liberal Democracy Index
Indonesia	0.71	0.57	0.68	0.53	0.64	0.49
Japan	0.87	0.79	0.82	0.73	0.82	0.74
Mongolia	0.69	0.54	0.66	0.51	0.68	0.52
Philippines	0.54	0.41	0.59	0.47	0.48	0.29
South Korea	0.77	0.65	0.71	0.61	0.84	0.78
Taiwan	0.76	0.62	0.84	0.70	0.81	0.70

Source: V-Dem Institute. Authors prepared.

Overall, the expert-based assessments, revealed by both Freedom House ratings and V-Dem indices, indicate that Japan, South Korea, and Taiwan are liberal democracies, whereas Mongolia and Indonesia, mere electoral democracies. The Philippines is, at best, an electoral democracy, as Freedom House indicates, or an electoral autocracy, as V-Dem democracy indices suggest. In view of the expert-based assessments and the World Bank's classification of income groups, we consider Japan, South Korea, and Taiwan affluent liberal democracies while Mongolia, Indonesia, and the Philippines less affluent electoral democracies.

General Quality

How do the ordinary people in our sample countries evaluate the quality of their prevailing system of government? The quality of democracy is a multidimensional and multilayered concept (Diamond and Morlino 2004; Bühlmann et al. 2012). Before presenting the disaggregated dimensional quality of democracy, we begin with aggregated general quality.

Extent of Democracy

When asked how much of a democracy their country was, in the early-2010s those who rated their prevailing system of government as either a full or slightly flawed democracy accounted for a majority of respondents (ranging from 54 percent for the Philippines to 67 percent for South Korea) in most sample countries, except for

Indonesia; in the mid-2010s they accounted for a majority (ranging from 54 percent for Indonesia to 68 percent for Japan) in all sample countries including Indonesia; in the late-2010s they accounted for a majority (ranging from 58 percent for Indonesia and Taiwan to 68 percent for South Korea) in most sample countries except for Mongolia. Over the decade surveyed, public approval surged in the Philippines (from 54 percent to 71 percent) and increased in Indonesia (from 47 percent to 58 percent). By contrast, public approval significantly declined in Mongolia (from 56 percent to 40 percent). In the 2010s, on average, in five of six countries (with the exception of Mongolia) a majority of the general public (ranging from 53 percent for Indonesia to 68 percent for South Korea) believed that their system was either a full or nearly full democracy. In comparison with expert-based assessments, ordinary people in the Philippines appear to overrate the level of democracy while their counterparts in Taiwan underrate it. See the details in Table 9.3.

Table 9.3 Evaluation of General Quality of Democracy

	Wave	Japan	Korea	Taiwan	Mongolia	Indonesia	Philippines
Level of Democracy[1]	Third wave	62	67	61	50	47	54
	Fourth wave	68	67	58	57	54	64
	Fifth wave	64	71	58	40	58	71
	Average	**65**	**68**	**59**	**49**	**53**	**63**
Satisfaction with Democracy[2]	Third wave	33	33	38	50	67	28
	Fourth wave	46	48	24	40	67	65
	Fifth wave	47	41	31	46	72	80
	Average	**42**	**41**	**31**	**45**	**67**	**58**

Note: 1. The percentage of respondents who replied "a full democracy" or "a democracy, with minor problems."
2. The percentage of respondents who replied "very satisfied" or "somewhat satisfied."
Source: Asian Barometer Survey. Authors prepared.

Satisfaction with Democracy

When asked how satisfied or dissatisfied they were with the way democracy worked in their country, in the early-2010s those who answered affirmatively represented a majority of respondents in Indonesia (67 percent) and Mongolia (50 percent), but only a minority in the remaining countries (ranging from 28 percent for the Philippines to 38 percent for Taiwan); in the mid-2010s they represented a majority in Indonesia (67 percent) and the Philippines (65 percent), but only a minority in the remaining countries (ranging from 24 percent for Taiwan to 48 percent for South Korea); in the late-2010s they represented a majority in the Philippines (80 percent) and Indonesia (72 percent), but only a minority in the remaining sample countries (ranging from 31 percent for Taiwan to 47 percent for Japan). During the decade surveyed, public satisfaction surged in the Philippines (from 28 percent to 80 percent) and rose in Japan (from 33 percent to 47 percent). In the 2010s, on average, only in Indonesia (67 percent) and the Philippines (58 percent) did a majority of the general public express some degree of satisfaction. By contrast, in the other countries, only a minority (ranging from 31 percent for Taiwan to 45 percent for Mongolia) remained satisfied. Notable is that affluent liberal democracies tend to display lower satisfaction than less affluent electoral democracies. Over the last decade, none of the liberal democracies enjoyed majority satisfaction while some electoral democracies enjoyed majority satisfaction. The finding suggests that ordinary people in affluent liberal democracies may hold higher benchmarks of satisfactory performance than their counterparts in less affluent electoral democracies.

Dimensional Quality

Our approach to the quality of democracy is multidimensional and disaggregated. Considering data availability, we choose five dimensions associated with liberal democracy, namely popular control, electoral competition, checks and balances, the rule of law, and freedom. Popular control and electoral competition are largely related to the electoral principle of democracy, while checks and balances and the rule of law are largely related to the liberal principle of democracy. To the extent that freedom facilitates political competition, it is related to the electoral principle. Yet, since freedom prevents the tyranny of the state or the majority, it is also related to the liberal principle (Coppedge et al. 2011). These five dimensions constitute standards of evaluation against which ordinary people assess the multifaceted quality of democracy.

Popular Control

Emphasizing accountability running from citizens to elected representatives, the dimension of democratic quality reflects the principle of popular sovereignty. Popular control requires more than electoral accountability. It extends beyond elections to encompass a range of popular control over the government in between elections. To assess the public's evaluation of popular control, we select two questions: one asks whether respondents agree or disagree with the statement "People have the power to change a government they don't like" (for the fifth wave: "Citizens are able to remove a government they don't like through elections") and the other "Between elections, the people have no way of holding the government responsible for its actions."

In all three surveys conducted in the 2010s, those who agreed with both statements accounted for a minority of respondents in all sample countries (ranging from 17 percent for South Korea to 34 percent for the Philippines in the early 2010s; from 12 percent for South Korea to 28 percent for the Philippines in the mid-2010s; and from 17 percent for Japan to 41 percent for Taiwan in the late-2010s). During the decade surveyed, positive perceptions rose significantly in Taiwan (from 26 percent to 41 percent) and increased in South Korea (from 17 percent to 27 percent), but decreased in the Philippines (from 34 percent to 25 percent). In the 2010s, on average, those who agreed with the statements on popular control represented only a small minority in all sample countries (ranging from 19 percent for Japan and South Korea to 31 percent for Taiwan). There is not much difference in agreement with the statements on popular control between liberal democracies (ranging from 19 percent to 31 percent) and electoral democracies (ranging from 21 percent to 29 percent). East Asian democracies, liberal or electoral alike, remain far short of public expectations of popular sovereignty.

Electoral Competition

Free and fair elections and multiparty competition constitute core properties of minimalist democracy. This aspect of democratic quality concerns the extent to which political parties or candidates fairly compete in elections. To assess the public's evaluation of electoral competition, we select two questions: one asks "How often do you think our elections offer the voters a real choice between different parties/candidates?" and the other asks whether respondents agree or disagree with the statement "Political parties or candidates have equal access to the mass media during the elections" (for the fifth wave: "In our country, parties or candidates not in power have opportunities to be elected into government").

In the first two surveys in the 2010s, those who gave affirmative responses to both questions constituted a minority of respondents in all sample countries (ranging from 31 percent for Mongolia to 47 percent for Indonesia in the early-2010s and from 28 percent for South Korea to 46 percent for Indonesia in the mid-2010s); in the late-2010s they constituted a majority only in Taiwan (55 percent) and were only a minority in the remaining countries (ranging from 21 percent for South Korea to 39 percent for the Philippines). During the decade surveyed, public approval substantially increased in Taiwan (from 43 percent to 55 percent), while it declined in Indonesia (from 47 percent to 29 percent) and South Korea (from 33 percent to 21 percent). In the 2010s, on average, those who had positive perceptions of electoral competition accounted for a minority in all sample countries (ranging from 28 percent for South Korea to 45 percent for Taiwan). In the eyes of ordinary

Table 9.4 Evaluation of Dimensional Quality of Democracy

	Wave	Japan	Korea	Taiwan	Mongolia	Indonesia	Philippines
Popular Control[1]	Third wave	19	17	26	18	26	34
	Fourth wave	21	12	25	22	23	28
	Fifth wave	17	27	41	24	20	25
	Average	**19**	**19**	**31**	**21**	**23**	**29**
Electoral Competition[2]	Third wave	34	35	43	31	47	42
	Fourth wave	34	28	36	36	46	37
	Fifth wave	37	21	55	24	29	39
	Average	**35**	**28**	**45**	**30**	**41**	**39**
Freedom[3]	Third wave	50	47	68	53	74	63
	Fourth wave	44	42	68	54	64	58
	Fifth wave	40	41	73	50	57	63
	Average	**45**	**43**	**70**	**52**	**65**	**61**
Horizontal Accountability[4]	Third wave	14	22	31	4	41	42
	Fourth wave	18	30	25	10	40	43
	Fifth wave	15	32	26	8	44	49
	Average	**16**	**28**	**27**	**11**	**42**	**45**
Rule of Law[5]	Third wave	49	19	22	6	17	15
	Fourth wave	46	21	17	12	14	16
	Fifth wave	37	35	24	6	17	27
	Average	**44**	**25**	**21**	**8**	**16**	**19**

Note: 1. The percentage of those giving affirmative responses to the following questions: "People have the power to change a government they don't like" (for the fifth wave: "Citizens are able to remove a government they don't like through elections") and "Between elections, the people have no way of holding the government responsible for its actions."
2. The percentage of those giving affirmative responses to the following questions: "How often do you think our elections offer the voters a real choice between different parties/ candidates?" and "Political parties or candidates have equal access to the mass media during the elections" (for the fifth wave: "Parties or candidates not in power have opportunities to be elected into government").
3. The percentage of those giving affirmative responses to the following questions: "People are free to speak what they think without fear" and "People can join any organization they like without fear."
4. The percentage of those giving affirmative responses to the following questions: "When government leaders break the laws, there is nothing the court can do" and "To what extent is the legislature capable of keeping government leaders in check?"
5. The percentage of those giving affirmative responses to the following questions: "How often do you think government leaders break the law or abuse their power?" and "How widespread do you think corruption and bribe-taking are in the national government?"
Source: Asian Barometer Survey. Authors prepared.

people, the electoral institutions of minimalist democracy remain deficient even in liberal democracies. There is little difference in public approval between liberal democracies (ranging from 28 percent to 45 percent) and electoral democracies (30 percent to 41 percent). Not only liberal but also electoral democracies in the region fall short of public expectations with respect to democratic public contestation for power.

Freedom

This dimension of democratic quality concerns the extent to which political rights and civil liberties are guaranteed. For the present analysis, we focus on the liberal rights of free speech and association. Since these liberal rights facilitate political competition, they are associated with the electoral principle of democracy. Yet, to the extent that these rights limit the exercise of executive power, they are also associated with the liberal principle. To assess public perceptions of freedom, we select two questions: one asks whether respondents agree or disagree with the statement "People are free to speak what they think without fear" and the other "People can join any organization they like without fear."

In the early-2010s those who agreed with both statements accounted for a majority of respondents in most of the sample countries (ranging from 50 percent for Japan to 74 percent for Indonesia) except for South Korea. In the last two surveys, they represented a majority in most of the sample countries (ranging from 54 percent for Mongolia to 68 percent for Taiwan in the mid-2010s and from 50 percent for Mongolia to 73 percent for Taiwan in the late-2010s), with the exceptions of Japan and South Korea. Over the decade surveyed, public approval significantly declined in Indonesia (from 74 percent to 57 percent) and Japan (from 50 percent to 40 percent). In the 2010s, on average, those with positive perceptions of freedom accounted for a majority (ranging from 52 percent for Mongolia to 70 percent for Taiwan) in most sample countries, with the exceptions of South Korea and Japan. Notable is that "free" liberal democracies such as Japan and South Korea display lower levels of public approval than "partly free" electoral democracies such as Indonesia and the Philippines.

Checks and Balances

This dimension of democratic quality pertains to judicial and legislative checks on executive power. The functioning of horizontal accountability primarily depends upon mutual constraints of constitutional powers. This inter-institutional accountability is accomplished through the separation of powers and checks and balances. To assess the public's evaluation of checks and balances, we select two questions: one asks "To what extent is the legislature capable of keeping government leaders in check?" and the other asks whether respondents agree or disagree with the statement "When government leaders break the laws, there is nothing the court can do."

In all three surveys conducted in the 2010s, those who gave affirmative responses to both questions accounted for a minority of respondents in all sample countries (ranging from 4 percent for Mongolia to 42 percent for the Philippines in the early-2010s; from 10 percent for Mongolia to 43 percent for the Philippines in the mid-2010s; and from 8 percent for Mongolia to 49 percent for the Philippines in the late-2010s). Over the decade surveyed, positive perceptions of horizontal accountability significantly increased in South Korea (from 22 percent to 32 percent). In the 2010s, on average, in all sample countries, only a small or large minority of the general public (ranging from 11 percent for Mongolia to 45 percent for the Philippines) held positive perceptions of horizontal accountability. Notable is that the affluent liberal democracies, Japan, South Korea, and Taiwan have less positive perceptions than the Philippines and Indonesia, which are mere electoral democracies.

Rule of Law

This dimension of democratic quality concerns legal institutions constraining the exercise of government power. Government bound by law is the sine qua non of the rule of law (Kleinfeld 2006). The "thick" notion of the rule of law includes control of corruption, both political and bureaucratic. To assess the public's evaluations of the rule of law, we select two questions: one asks "How often do you think government leaders break the law or abuse their power?" and the other "How widespread do you think corruption and bribe-taking are in the national government?"

In all three surveys conducted in the 2010s, those who gave affirmative responses to both questions represented a minority of respondents in all sample countries (ranging from 6 percent for Mongolia to 49 percent for Japan in the early-2010s; from 12 percent for Mongolia to 46 percent for Japan in the mid-2010s; and 8 percent for Mongolia to 37 percent for Japan in the late-2010s). Notable is that Japan consistently displayed the highest level of affirmative responses while Mongolia consistently displayed the lowest level. Over the decade surveyed, public approval increased significantly in South Korea (from 19 percent to 35 percent) and the Philippines (from 15 percent to 27 percent), yet declined in Japan (from 49 percent to 37 percent). In the 2010s, on average, only minorities of the general public in all sample countries (ranging from 8 percent for Mongolia to 44 percent for Japan) held positive views, indicating that the region's democracies, liberal and electoral alike, remain short of pubic expectations with respect to the rule of law.

Summary

In the eyes of their citizens, the political regimes in our sample countries have their own weaknesses. The political regime in Japan remains weak on democratic accountability. The political regimes in Taiwan and the Philippines remain weak on the rule of law. The political regimes in South Korea, Indonesia, and Mongolia remain weak on democratic accountability and the rule of law. Public approval of electoral institutions turns out to be higher than that of liberal institutions, suggesting that the political regimes meet the requirements of minimalist democracy in the eyes of ordinary people. Yet, judging from public views of democratic accountability and the rule of law, even liberal democracies in the region remain short of standards of liberal democracy.

Conclusion

The analysis shows that East Asian democracies have yet to develop beyond minimalist electoral democracy to embody principles and mechanisms of liberal democracy such as the checks and balances and the rule of law (Park 2017). It is also found that public evaluations of democratic quality often diverge from expert-based assessments (Ferrin and Kriesi 2016). Contrary to expert-based assessments, Japan, South Korea, and Taiwan have yet to establish themselves as high-quality liberal democracies in the eyes of their publics. The findings suggest that the more democratic a country is, the more likely its citizens are to be critical of the democratic quality of their prevailing system of government. Ordinary people in affluent liberal democracies may be better informed about politics and government than their counterparts in less affluent electoral democracies. Moreover, the former may hold higher benchmarks of good performance or "thicker" standards of democracy than the latter (Kruse, Ravlik, and Welzel 2019; Mauk 2020). Whatever the reasons, the findings suggest that public pressure for democratic reform is greater in affluent liberal democracies than in less affluent electoral democracies. In the eyes of ordinary people, the region's democracies, liberal and electoral alike, remain largely weak in democratic accountability and the rule of law, two mechanisms for limiting the tyranny of the state or the majority. The pressing institutional challenges facing East Asian democracies include strengthening the formal institutions of democratic accountability and the rule of law.

Acknowledgements

This work was supported by the Ministry of Education of the Republic of Korea and the National Research Foundation of Korea (NRF-2018S1A3A2075609).

Note

1. The data for the present analysis are drawn from the third wave (2010-2012), fourth wave (2014-2016), and fifth wave (2018-2020) of the ABS.

References

Bühlmann, Marc, Wolfgang Merkel, Lisa Müller, and Bernhard Weßels. 2012. "The Democracy Barometer: A New Instrument to Measure the Quality of Democracy and its Potential for Comparative Research." *European Political Science* 11 (4): 519-536. doi:10.1057/eps.2011.46.

Chu, Yun-han, Kai-Ping Huang, Marta Lagos, and Robert Mattes. 2020. "A Lost Decade for Third-Wave Democracies?" *Journal of Democracy* 31 (2): 166-181. doi:10.1353/jod.2020.0029.

Coppedge, Michael, John Gerring, David Altman, Michael Bernhard, Steven Fish, Allen Hicken, Matthew Kroenig et al. 2011. "Conceptualizing and Measuring Democracy: A New Approach." *Perspectives on Politics* 9 (2): 247-267. http://www.jstor.org/stable/41479651.

Croissant, Aurel, and Larry Diamond. 2020. "Introduction: Reflections on Democratic Backsliding in Asia." *Global Asia* 15 (1): 8-13.

Dahl, Robert A. 1971. *Polyarchy: Participation and Opposition*. New Haven: Yale University Press.

Dalton, Russell J., Doh C. Shin, and Willy Jou. 2008. "How People Understand Democracy." In *How People View Democracy*, edited by Larry Diamond and Marc F. Plattner, 1-15. Baltimore: Johns Hopkins University Press.

Diamond, Larry, and Leonardo Morlino. 2004. "The Quality of Democracy: An Overview." *Journal of Democracy* 15 (4): 20-31. doi:10.1353/jod.2004.0060.

Ferrin, Monica, and Hanspeter Kriesi. 2016. *How Europeans View and Evaluate Democracy*. Oxford: Oxford University Press.

Ginsburg, Tom, and Aziz Z. Huq. 2018. *How to Save a Constitutional Democracy*. Chicago: The University of Chicago Press.

Graber, Mark A., Sanford Levinson, and Mark Tushnet. 2018. *Constitutional Democracy in Crisis?* New York: Oxford University Press.

Kleinfeld, Rachel. 2006. "Competing Definitions of the Rule of Law." In *Promoting the Rule of Law Abroad: In Search of Knowledge*, edited by Thomas Carothers, 31-74. Washington, D.C.: Carnegie Endowment for International Peace. http://www.jstor.org/stable/resrep12779.

Kruse, Stefan, Maria Ravlik, and Christian Welzel. 2019. "Democracy Confused: When People Mistake the Absence of Democracy for Its Presence." *Journal of Cross-Cultural Psychology* 50 (3): 315-335. doi:10.1177/0022022118821437.

Lührmann, Anna, and Staffan I. Lindberg. 2019. "A Third Wave of Autocratization Is Here: What Is New about it?" *Democratization* 26 (7): 1095-1113. doi:10.1080 /13510347.2019.1582029.

Mauk, Marlene. 2020. "Disentangling an Elusive Relationship: How Democratic Value Orientations Affect Political Trust in Different Regimes." *Political Research Quarterly* 73 (2): 366-380. doi:10.1177/1065912919829832.

Park, Chong-Min. 2017. "Quality of Governance and Regime Support: Evidence from East Asia." *Asian Journal of Comparative Politics* 2 (2): 154-175. doi:10.1177/2057891116675769.

Roberts, Andrew. 2010. *The Quality of Democracy in Eastern Europe: Public Preferences and Policy Reforms*. Cambridge: Cambridge University Press.

Shin, Doh Chull. 2018. "The Deconsolidation of Liberal Democracy in Korea: Exploring Its Cultural Roots." *Korea Observer* 49 (1): 107-136. Seoul: Institute of Korean Studies. doi:10.29152/koiks.2018.49.1.107.

10 The Corruption and Trust Nexus Revisited
Eric C. C. Chang and Yun-han Chu

Corruption is considered one of the most harmful yet unresolved problems around the world, and due to its grave consequences, it has ignited much debate across different fields.[1] The importance of understanding corruption in Asia is even more pressing, since the post-war histories of most Asian countries, including China, Japan, South Korea, Taiwan, and the Philippines, have all been marked by numerous corruption scandals.

Chang and Chu (2006) represents one of the first empirical efforts to examine the relationship between citizens' perceptions of political corruption and their institutional trust in Asian democracies. Using the first wave of the Asian Barometer Survey (ABS henceforth) data, Chang and Chu find that political corruption strongly undermines institutional trust. They also refute the conventional view on political culture and electoral politics, showing that these contextual factors have little bearing on the corruption-trust nexus. Importantly, their findings also hold against the reciprocal relationship between corruption and trust.

The purpose of this short essay is to re-visit the study by Chang and Chu (2006) on the relationship between political corruption and institutional trust in Asian democracies. We will first briefly review how we conceptualize and define political corruption in the literature. Then we will discuss how the ABS taps citizens' perception of corruption, and compare the dynamic change of corruption perception in Asian democracies between the first wave and the most current wave (fifth wave) of the ABS. Finally, we will recap the findings from the previous study by Chang and Chu (2006) and update it with the most current data from the ABS.

Defining Corruption

Corruption, according to Transparency International (TI), is commonly defined as "the abuse of an entrusted power for private gain" and is widely seen as a cancer in a society.[2] Underneath this simple definition, however, lies a long and lengthy scholarly debate on the essence of political corruption that can be traced back more than 2,000 years. Importantly, scholarly conceptualization of corruption has changed from moral degeneration of whole societies to deviant behaviors by self-serving rulers (Gardiner 2002; Warren 2004). Equally important, Johnston (1991, 2001) suggests that the historical process in which the conception of corruption evolved is highly conflictual and characterized by the clash of multiple political forces and interests.

Through these dynamic and conflictual processes, contemporary wisdom now views corruption as a political pathology that lies at the heart of the relationship between wealth and power (Friedrich 1966; Johnston 2001), and many scholars have attempted to define corruption from different perspectives (Gardiner 2002). These definitions include: the public office definition that focuses on public officials and their political authority; the legal definition that relies on formal laws as an objective benchmark for public duties, the public interest definition that considers an act corrupt if it inflicts damage to the public and its interest; and the public opinion definition that tasks the public with determining whether a particular act is corrupt. However, the debate on how to best define political corruption remains anything but settled. For instance, while in general, most scholars agree that corruption involves the abuse of public powers for private gain, by what criteria we decide a particular act should be viewed as abuse is much less clear. Equally controversial are what counts as public duties and private gain (Johnston 2001; Kurer 2005). In short, no one unfortunately has been able to fully clarify these ambiguities. We are thus left with several partial and controversial definitions of corruption that are neither conceptually precise nor empirically operationalizable (Johnston 1991). Philp (1997, 446) goes as far as concluding that "one line definitions of political corruption are inherently misleading."[3]

Acknowledging these issues, we suggest that political corruption involves the following key characteristics. First, at the most fundamental level, political corruption involves the exercise of political authority by public officials. As Acton's famous remark—all power tends to corrupt and absolute power corrupts absolutely—indicates, political power lies at the heart of political corruption. Embezzlement, as illustrated by the case of Suharto in Indonesia, is the typical example. The emphasis on political power enables us to differentiate corruption from other unethical or even illegal behaviors that occur in the private domain, such as corporate fraud and business theft. Depending on the level of public authority involved, we can also differentiate corruption into national-level corruption and local-level corruption. The former refers to the behind-the-scene collusion between big businesses and high-ranking officials (such as presidents or prime ministers, members of government cabinets, and legislators) whereas the latter involves malfeasances by local bureaucratic workers and civil servants.[4]

More precisely, it is not the political power *per se* but the asymmetry or the monopoly of power that leads to political corruption. In fact, the public choice school rightfully argues that it is the government monopoly over the allocation of public resources that creates the market for political corruption.[5] Essentially, from a briber's standpoint, he is willing to engage in bribery to acquire his desired goods since no one, but the official is able to deliver the service (Gambetta 2002).

Extending the point above, we suggest that the second key characteristic of corruption is that corruption involves an illicit exchange of material benefits and political favors between private actors who desire access to resources and political officials who control access to those resources. A typical form of corruption transaction is bribery, where a briber (say, a restaurant owner) offers illegal payments (bribes) to allure public officials (a health inspector) to bend the rules (turning a blind eye to code violations). In fact, Johnston (2005) argues that bribery may be the predominant form of corruption in many countries. He even terms bribery as the "*de facto* synonym for corruption." Similarly, Porta and Vannucci (1999) treat political corruption as a type of hidden and illegal exchange in the market for political rents, where bribers and public officials collude in order to distort the legal structure of property rights and misallocate state resources for their own benefit. Extortion is another common form of corruption, and it shares the exact same transactional nature as bribery, except that officials are the ones that initiate the transaction and demand the illegal payment. Van Klaveren (2002) resonates the seriousness of extortion and considers corruption "in terms of a civil servant who regards his office as a business, the income of which he will seek to maximize."

Despite the conceptual similarities between corruption exchange and market exchange, there exists one critical difference between the two: while market exchange can potentially lead to Pareto efficiency, corruption only results in negative externalities that are substantially harmful to ordinary citizens. Importantly, ordinary citizens are not just innocent third-party bystanders; rather, they are the source of legitimate political authority. As Gambetta (2002) puts simply, a standard case of corruption occurs when a briber wants something that a public official is not supposed to deliver given his entrusted relation to the citizen. In other words, the third key characteristic of political corruption is that public officials knowingly betray citizens' mandate by committing wrongdoings.

In layman's terms, corruption takes place when the briber and the official work together to cheat the citizen. Particularly, if we use the standard principle-agent relationship to model the relationship between voters (principles) and elected officials (agents), then corruption can be seen as a deliberate opportunism and a moral hazard problem where egoistical politicians abuse their entrusted power for private gain instead of acting in the best interests of their constituencies. Essentially, political corruption is a form of intentional collusion between public officials and bribers to benefit each other at the expense of ordinary citizens.

In short, while no single definition can fully capture the complexity and nuance of corruption, we can nevertheless identify some major characteristics of political corruption, such as the manifestation of power asymmetry, an illicit exchange between material benefits and political favors, and the willful betrayal of the trust placed by the public.[6] Extending the existing studies, this essay also views corruption in behavior and relational terms, and as discussed previously, it considers embezzlement, bribery, and extortion to be major forms of corruption. Other types of corruption include nepotism (the appointment of government jobs based on kinship or social ties as opposed to professional qualifications), legislative or administrative conflict of interest (having a personal stake in the outcomes of the policies one enacts), and electoral fraud (manipulating electoral results through vote buying or intimidation).[7]

Measuring Corruption in ABS

Due to its illegal and secretive nature, corruption is extremely difficult to observe. As Fisman and Golden (2017) discuss, participants in corruption transactions always go the extra mile in hiding evidence; they prefer cash and leave no paper trail of transaction details, or even use shell companies and offshore accounts when necessary. Consequently, for decades, how to effectively measure political corruption has become extremely challenging for scholars. Early studies relied on anecdotal materials, such as press reports or judicial records, as proxies for corruption. These anecdotal materials, however, are at best partial and incomplete sources of corruption information. For instance, press reports can be based on speculation or misinformation and hence lack accuracy. They might also be biased due to certain hidden political or commercial agendas. Judicial records can also be narrow and problematic since they typically focus on convictions and do not include cases tried by prosecutors. They might also suffer from many confounding factors, such as prosecutorial zeal and resources, judicial integrity and efficiency, the government's judicial priorities, and even the partisan bias of the judicial branch (Chang and Golden 2007; Dincer and Johnston 2017). Most critically, freedom of the press and the level of judicial independence—the perquisite for the validity of these measurements—can be quite limited in less developed or authoritarian countries that are known to be associated with more corruption. In other words, these measurements can be less reliable in countries that need reliable measurements the most.

Given the limitations of these traditional approaches, most current studies turn to use surveys to measure corruption, and the ABS provides powerful empirical leverage to capture our conceptual understanding of political corruption in Asian countries. Specifically, it offers several items that allow researchers to directly tap into the various forms of political corruption discussed above. For instance, to operationalize citizens' perception of grand corruption at the national level, the ABS asks respondents how widespread they think corruption and bribe-taking are in the national government. Meanwhile, to measure citizens' perception of petty corruption at the local level, the ABS asks respondents how widespread they think corruption and bribe-taking are in their local/municipal government. Each item scores on a metric of 1-4, where 1 represents "almost everyone is involved" and 4 indicates "hardly anyone is involved." Finally, in addition to the perception of corruption, the ABS also probes citizens' experiences with corruption by asking: "Have you or anyone you know personally witnessed an act of corruption or bribe-taking by a politician or government official in the past year?" The binary response is coded as 1 if the respondent said yes.

Following Chang and Chu (2006), we focus on citizens' perception of corruption. Table 10.1 tabulates the percentage of respondents who believe most officials or almost every official in their national governments is corrupt across ten Asian democracies. Several interesting observations are in order. First, on first glance, there appears to be wide variation in citizens' perception of grand corruption in these ten Asian democracies: while only less than one-fifth of Australian citizens consider their national government corrupt, more than 80 percent of citizens in Mongolia think so. Second, citizens' corruption perceptions seem to well correspond to the expert opinions. Row two of Table 10.1 shows that the 2019 Corruption Perception Index published by the Transparency International, and the corruption perceptions from the ABS and the CPI are correlated to a greater extent, except for the cases of Taiwan and Thailand.[8] How to account for these two seemingly anomalies requires further analysis. However, one can only speculate that the rise of populism in Thailand and the strong partisan divide in Taiwan can at least shed some light into the gap between citizens' perception and experts' evaluation of corruption in these two countries. Finally, if we compare citizens' corruption perceptions of the fifth wave of the ABS compared to that of the first wave, we can see that while citizens in Japan and the Philippines perceive an improvement in corruption in their national government, citizens in other Asian democracies (South Korea, Thailand, and Taiwan) see little, if any, improvement in corruption. In fact, Taiwanese citizens even consider political corruption in their national government worsened. Turning our attention to the local-level corruption, Table 10.2 echoes similar patterns of local-level corruption as the national-level one.

Table 10.1 The National-level Political Corruption in Asian Democracies

	Japan	Philippines	South Korea	Thailand	Taiwan
Wave 5	34	47.5	44.7	33.8	58.6
2019 CPI	73	34	59	36	65
Wave 1	52.2	65.5	47.2	33.9	47.5
	Australia	India	Indonesia	Malaysia	Mongolia
Wave 5	19.4	37.8	45	37.4	83.2
2019 CPI	77	41	40	53	35
Wave 1	NA	NA	NA	NA	NA

Note: The number in the cell represents the percentage of survey respondents who consider most officials or almost every official is corrupt in their national governments.

Source: Asian Barometer Survey. Authors prepared.

Table 10.2 The Local-level Political Corruption in Asian Democracies

	Japan	Philippines	South Korea	Thailand	Taiwan
Wave 5	29.6	37.7	42.9	20.4	55.2
Wave 1	37.1	51.6	44.1	19.1	56.5
	Australia	India	Indonesia	Malaysia	Mongolia
Wave 5	18.8	40.6	29.7	33.1	49.0
Wave 1	NA	NA	NA	NA	NA

Note: The number in the cell represents the percentage of survey respondents who consider most officials or almost every official is corrupt in their local governments.

Source: Asian Barometer Survey. Authors prepared.

Political Corruption and Institutional Trust in Asian Democracies

Corruption acts as an infringement of trust. Rose-Ackerman and Palifka (2016) echo this point and argue that the key term in TI's definition of corruption is entrusted power. And when public officials purposely abuse the entrusted power and fail to perform the governing tasks they are expected to undertake, the mandate is broken and the trust relationship is undermined. More interestingly, Gambetta (2002) argues it is the trust relationship between voters and public officials that gives the latter the power to allocate resources that bribers desire. If this trust relationship were not to exist in the first place, public officials would not have the authority nor the opportunity to engage in corrupt behavior. Yet, by committing malfeasance, public officials betray the citizens' trust. The 2006 and 2014 coups in Thailand and the mass demonstrations in Taiwan and South Korea not too long ago have provided striking examples of the extent to which citizens can lose their faith in their corrupt politicians.

More generally, Chang and Chu argue that political corruption reduces citizens' institutional trust and undermines democratic consolidation in young

Asian democracies at three interrelated levels. First, at the attitudinal level, corruption violates the fundamental principle of democracy and thus reduces citizens' trust in political institutions. For instance, corruption compromises the notions of political equality since only citizens who pay through corrupt means can receive the government services. Second, at the institutional level, corruption hinders the development of political institutions because rent availability turns political institutions into electoral machines that focus on rent-seeking instead of preference-integrating. As a result, ordinary citizens are alienated from the policy-making process and lose their commitment to democratic principles. Finally, at the policy outcome level, corruption worsens governmental performance and reduces the government's ability to address popular demands. Consequently, citizens end up paying more for inefficient public works and lose their confidence in democratic governments in the process.

This essay replicates the key finding of Chang and Chu (2006) with the fifth wave of the ABS data. In comparison to the first wave of the ABS that only covers five East Asian democracies (Japan, the Philippines, South Korea, Thailand, and Taiwan), the fifth wave of the ABS covers five additional democracies in Asia (Australia, India, Indonesia, Malaysia, and Mongolia). Essentially, the fifth wave of the ABS has effectively expanded the scope of coverage beyond East Asia to both South Asia and Oceania. It is also noteworthy that the first wave of ABS was conducted between 2001-2003, whereas the fifth wave of the ABS was just recently surveyed. Therefore, it would be interesting to see if the dynamic relationship between political corruption and institutional trust has changed after nearly 20 years.

Following Chang and Chu, the dependent variable in this essay is citizens' institutional trust. The first wave of the ABS asks respondents how much trust they have in a set of political institutions, including the presidency (or the premiership in parliamentary systems), the courts, the national government, political parties, parliament, civil service, the military, the police, and local government. Each item scores on a metric of 1-6, where 1 represents "distrust fully" and 6 "trust fully" after reversing the scale. We take the mean across the individual scores and construct a composite variable of institutional trust.

The main independent variable, as previously discussed, is citizens' perception of corruption. We again take the average between citizens' perceptions of both national and local level corruption to generate a composite variable of corruption perception. Additionally, to be fully compatible with Chang and Chu, we also control the same covariates used in Chang and Chu's study to account for institutional trust. These covariates include citizens' economic evaluations, their satisfaction with democracy, their perceived fairness, their perceived influence, and their perceived freedom. We also include the same demographics variables to account for the heterogeneity among individuals (gender, age, subjective SES, and education).

Table 10.3 reports the estimated results. Again, replicating Table 10.1, Table 10.2 in Chang and Chu, Model 1 shows the results from the pooled sample with country fixed effects and clustered standard errors. Additionally, Model 2 to Model 11 present estimated results by each country. As we can see, the coefficients of corruption perceptions are negative and significant throughout the models. The magnitude of the coefficients also indicates a substantial and sizable association between corruption and institutional trust. The preliminary exploratory analysis also suggests that perceived corruption, together with present economic evaluation and satisfaction with democracy, are the most important driving factors influencing citizens' institutional trust. In short, the finding here corroborates the study by Chang and Chu, and it also further reiterates the corrosive effect of political corruption on institutional trust.

Before concluding, it is important to note that perception-based measurements ultimately reflect only the perception of corruption rather than its actual occurrence. As Seligson (2006) forcefully notes, there is no evidence whatsoever that perceptions of corruption accurately reflect the reality of corruption. Similarly, Treisman (2007) suggests that the widely used perception-based measurements are built on the basis of survey respondents' understandings of corruption's causes instead of corruption itself. Worse yet, the subjective nature of perception-based measurements inevitably invites the possibility of systematic errors and bias, casting doubt on the degree to which we can actually attribute the political or economic outcomes to corruption per se as opposed to other potentially confounding factors. Chang and Kerr (2017) further identify the sources of bias in perception-based corruption measurements. They propose an insider-outsider framework and argue that the way in which respondents form their perceptions of corruption depends critically upon their insider or outsider status. They draw the distinction between insiders and outsiders along two dimensions: cost-benefit instrumentality and affective identity. Importantly, they show that citizens' perceptions of corruption are likely to be shaped by whether they belong to the clientelist network of the elected officials and whether they share either partisan or ethnic affiliation with the incumbent. In other words, Chang and Kerr show that perception-based corruption measurements are likely to be driven by respondents' instrumental or identity biases. With these issues in mind, we need to remain cautious in interpreting the findings in a definitive and causal manner.

Table 10.3 Estimated Results

	Model 1 Pooled	Model 2 Japan	Model 3 S. Korea	Model 4 Mongolia	Model 5 Philippines	Model 6 Taiwan	Model 7 Thailand	Model 8 Indonesia	Model 9 Malaysia	Model 10 Australia	Model 11 India
Perceived Corruption	-0.168***	-0.141**	-0.393***	-0.117***	-0.138***	-0.157***	-0.200***	-0.0789**	-0.165***	-0.316***	-0.109***
	(0.0311)	(0.0461)	(0.0323)	(0.0332)	(0.0262)	(0.0324)	(0.0360)	(0.0273)	(0.0312)	(0.0449)	(0.0199)
Present Economic Evaluation	0.131***	0.0823**	0.125***	0.201***	0.182***	0.170***	0.136***	0.170***	0.152***	0.0472	0.0942***
	(0.0170)	(0.0315)	(0.0342)	(0.0309)	(0.0259)	(0.0224)	(0.0355)	(0.0273)	(0.0246)	(0.0329)	(0.0168)
Prospective Economic Evaluation	0.0433**	0.0292	0.106**	0.0723**	0.102***	0.0483**	0.0554	0.0372	0.0250	0.0372	0.0225
	(0.0098)	(0.0291)	(0.0337)	(0.0256)	(0.0211)	(0.0182)	(0.0340)	(0.0261)	(0.0195)	(0.0272)	(0.0190)
Retrospective Economic Evaluation	0.121***	0.118***	0.0290	0.149***	0.0948***	0.130***	0.249***	0.0761**	0.115***	0.102***	0.152***
	(0.0117)	(0.0253)	(0.0262)	(0.0292)	(0.0208)	(0.0199)	(0.0360)	(0.0266)	(0.0202)	(0.0249)	(0.0176)
Satisfaction with Democracy	0.173***	0.265***	0.203***	0.141***	0.180***	0.193***	0.311***	0.171***	0.185***	0.216***	0.0885***
	(0.0332)	(0.0364)	(0.0350)	(0.0336)	(0.0262)	(0.0312)	(0.0366)	(0.0342)	(0.0311)	(0.0376)	(0.0204)
Perceived Fairness	0.0393**	0.129***	-0.0077	0.0482*	0.0716***	0.102***	0.0580	0.0570*	0.0059	0.0489	0.0251
	(0.0107)	(0.0337)	(0.0235)	(0.0236)	(0.0193)	(0.0257)	(0.0326)	(0.0290)	(0.0196)	(0.0252)	(0.0156)
Perceived Increased Influence	0.159***	0.256***	0.0510	0.0878*	0.100***	0.160***	0.0814*	0.122***	0.206***	0.395***	0.148***
	(0.0216)	(0.0385)	(0.0324)	(0.0349)	(0.0224)	(0.0303)	(0.0395)	(0.0323)	(0.0315)	(0.0407)	(0.0184)
Perceived Increased Freedom	0.0518*	0.0020	-0.0243	0.0341	0.0564*	-0.0057	-0.0123	0.0048	0.0704**	0.0378	0.108***
	(0.0199)	(0.0291)	(0.0262)	(0.0222)	(0.0219)	(0.0310)	(0.0359)	(0.0312)	(0.0241)	(0.0274)	(0.0163)

(Continuing on the next page)

Table 10.3 Cont.

	Model 1 Pooled	Model 2 Japan	Model 3 S. Korea	Model 4 Mongolia	Model 5 Philippines	Model 6 Taiwan	Model 7 Thailand	Model 8 Indonesia	Model 9 Malaysia	Model 10 Australia	Model 11 India
Gender	0.0106	-0.0191	0.0826*	0.0304	-0.0020	-0.0788*	-0.0290	0.0913*	0.0433	-0.0096	0.0141
	(0.0126)	(0.0418)	(0.0365)	(0.0445)	(0.0378)	(0.0372)	(0.0456)	(0.0378)	(0.0382)	(0.0432)	(0.0295)
Age	-0.0006	-0.0020	0.0022	-0.0059***	-0.0019	-0.0001	0.0032	0.0017	-0.0005	-0.0042**	0.0008
	(0.0008)	(0.0013)	(0.0014)	(0.0015)	(0.0012)	(0.0013)	(0.0020)	(0.0014)	(0.0013)	(0.0013)	(0.0010)
Subjective SES	0.0092	0.0152	-0.0226	0.0405**	0.0001	0.0237	0.0023	0.0093	0.0179	0.0174	0.0032
	(0.0056)	(0.0141)	(0.0130)	(0.0138)	(0.0091)	(0.0139)	(0.0192)	(0.0118)	(0.0127)	(0.0140)	(0.0075)
Education	-0.0066	-0.0086	0.0096	-0.0291***	-0.0117	-0.0034	-0.0051	-0.0278***	-0.0121	-0.0022	-0.0009
	(0.0036)	(0.0092)	(0.0078)	(0.0066)	(0.0061)	(0.0057)	(0.0064)	(0.0051)	(0.0063)	(0.0052)	(0.0026)
Constant	2.186***	1.834***	2.794***	2.329***	2.276***	1.691***	1.771***	2.903***	2.362***	1.907***	2.559***
	(0.0861)	(0.256)	(0.232)	(0.228)	(0.185)	(0.213)	(0.274)	(0.200)	(0.208)	(0.227)	(0.123)
N	12508	705	1207	1073	1095	973	720	825	1064	1395	3451
Adjusted R2	.45	.40	.24	.25	.34	.40	.45	.28	.31	.30	.19

Notes: Clustered errors in Model 1; * p < 0.05, ** p < 0.01, *** p < 0.001
  Coefficients for fixed effects are not reported in the interest of space.

Notes

1. Mounting evidence has now suggested that political corruption can reduce economic growth, widen economic inequality, induce social unrest, and cause legitimacy crisis (Mauro 1995; Rose-Ackerman 1999).
2. See https://www.transparency.org/en/what-is-corruption.
3. Warren (2004, 329) also suggests the standard definition of corruption "has been outgrown by contemporary democracies." He further argues that the current definition of corruption suffers from several analytical weaknesses, such as being normatively static, individualistic, state-centric, focusing on behavior instead of morality, and failing to encompass democratic capacities.
4. The national-level corruption sometimes is termed as the grand corruption since it typically involves large sums of money, and the local-level corruption is often called the petty corruption since the size of monetary transaction is much smaller.
5. As evidenced by the Lockheed scandal in Japan or the Hanbo scandal in South Korea, the governmental monopoly of power and intervention in the market are the political roots of corruption in many Asian democracies.
6. Philp (2002) also highlights several basic components of corruption: it involves a public authority, it violates the public trust, it harms the public interest, and it benefits a third party by providing access to a good or service the third party could not otherwise obtain.
7. See Box 1.1 in Rose-Ackerman and Palifka (2016) for a more detailed discussion.
8. If we exclude both Taiwan and Thailand, the correlation between the 2019 CPI and the fifth wave of the ABS Wave is -.69 (note that higher values in the CPI represent lower levels of corruption).

References

Chang, Eric C. C., and Miriam A. Golden. 2007. "Electoral Systems, District Magnitude and Corruption." *British Journal of Political Science* 37 (1): 115-137. http://www.jstor.org/stable/4497282.

Chang, Eric C. C., and Nicholas N. Kerr. 2017. "An Insider-Outsider Theory of Popular Tolerance for Corrupt Politicians." *Governance* 30 (1): 67-84. doi:10.1111/gove.12193.

Chang, Eric C. C., and Yun-han Chu. 2006. "Corruption and Trust: Exceptionalism in Asian Democracies?" *The Journal of Politics* 68 (2): 259-271. doi:10.1111/j.1468-2508.2006.00404.x.

Dincer, Oguzhan, and Michael Johnston. 2017. "Political Culture and Corruption Issues in State Politics: A New Measure of Corruption Issues and a Test of Relationships to Political Culture." *Publius: The Journal of Federalism* 47 (1): 131-148. doi:10.1093/publius/pjw026.

Fisman, Raymond, and Miriam A. Golden. 2017. *Corruption: What Everyone Needs to Know*. New York: Oxford University Press.

Friedrich, Carl J. 1966. "Political Pathology." *The Political Quarterly* 37 (1): 70-85. doi:10.1111/j.1467-923x.1966.tb00184.x.

Gambetta, Diego. 2002. "Corruption: An Analytical Map." In *Political Corruption in Transition: A Skeptic's Handbook*, edited by Stephen Kotkin and András Sajó, 33-56. Budapest: Central European University Press.

Gardiner, John. 2002. "Defining Corruption." Chap. 2 in *Political Corruption: Concepts and Contexts*, edited by Arnold J. Heidenheimer and Michael Johnston, 25-40. Piscataway, NJ: Transaction Publishers.

Johnston, Michael. 1991. "Historical Conflict and the Rise of Standards." *Journal of Democracy* 2 (4): 48-60. doi:10.1353/jod.1991.0052.

—. 2001. "The Definitions Debate: Old Conflicts in New Guises." Chap. 2 in *The Political Economy of Corruption*, edited by Arvind K. Jain, 11-32. New York: Routledge.

—. 2005. *Syndromes of Corruption: Wealth, Power, and Democracy*. New York: Cambridge University Press. doi:10.1017/CBO9780511490965.

Van Klaveren, Jacob. 2002. "Corruption as a Historical Phenomenon." Chap. 5 in *Political Corruption: Concepts and Contexts*, by Arnold J. Heidenheimer and Michael Johnston, 83-94. Piscataway, NJ: Transaction Publishers.

Kurer, Oskar. 2005. "Corruption: An Alternative Approach to Its Definition and Measurement." *Political Studies* 53 (1): 222-239. doi:10.1111/j.1467-9248.2005.00525.x.

Mauro, Paolo. 1995. "Corruption and Growth." *The Quarterly Journal of Economics* 110 (3): 681-712. doi:10.2307/2946696.

Philp, Mark. 1997. "Defining Political Corruption." *Political Studies*, 436-462. https://journals.sagepub.com/doi/pdf/10.1111/1467-9248.00090.

—. 2002. "Conceptualizing Political Corruption." Chap. 3 in *Political Corruption: Concepts and Contexts*, by Arnold J. Heidenheimer and Michael Johnston, 41-58. Piscataway, NJ: Transaction Publishers.

Porta, Donatella Della, and Alberto Vannucci. 1999. *Corrupt Exchanges: Actors, Resources, and Mechanisms of Political Corruption*. Piscataway, NJ: Transaction Publishers.

Rose-Ackerman, Susan. 1999. *Corruption and Government: Causes, Consequences, and Reform*. New York: Cambridge University Press. doi:10.1017/cbo9781139175098.

Rose-Ackerman, Susan, and Bonnie J. Palifka. 2016. *Corruption and Government: Causes, Consequences, and Reform*. 2nd. New York: Cambridge University Press. doi:10.1017/cbo9781139962933.

Seligson, Mitchell A. 2006. "The Measurement and Impact of Corruption Victimization: Survey Evidence from Latin America." *World Development* 34 (2): 381-404. doi:10.1016/j.worlddev.2005.03.012.

Treisman, Daniel. 2007. "What Have We Learned About the Causes of Corruption from Ten Years of Cross-National Empirical Research?" *Annual Review of Political Science* 10 (1): 211-244. doi:10.1146/annurev.polisci.10.081205.095418.

Warren, Mark E. 2004. "What Does Corruption Mean in a Democracy?" *American Journal of Political Science* 48 (2): 328-343. doi:10.1111/j.0092-5853.2004.00073.x.

11 Inequality and Regime Support: Evidence from East Asia

Wen-chin Wu, Yun-han Chu, and Eric C. C. Chang

Economic inequality has become one of the most important challenges for almost every country in the world. Numerous studies point out that rising economic inequality has fomented political and economic problems, including corruption, popular uprisings, and civil wars. At the extreme, the French revolution in the late 18th century exemplifies how inequality can first intensify conflicts between the rich and the poor and then eventually collapse political regimes. Yet, most studies in this line of research are based on macro-level data, and it remains unclear how income distribution matters for ordinary citizens' political support. With this concern in mind, this chapter explores how income distribution is correlated with citizens' regime support, and whether the relationship varies across regime types. Our analysis from the fourth wave of the Asian Barometer Survey (ABS) data shows that unfair income distribution dampens ordinary citizens' political support and sows the seeds of regime instability, and this finding is robust in both democracies and autocracies.

This chapter contributes to the existing literature in two ways. First, it uses individual-level data to investigate the relationship between income distribution and regime support in both democratic and autocratic countries. It offers clear empirical evidence that ordinary citizens' regime support is driven by their perceptions of the unfairness of income distribution. Hence, this finding advances current studies on the political consequences of inequality.

Secondly, this chapter contributes to ongoing discussions of regime change and consolidation. Recently, scholars have raised concerns about democratic backsliding, which is partly caused by rising inequality. Similarly, inequality also destabilizes autocratic regimes since it intensifies distributive conflicts among ruling elites and ordinary citizens. Our finding that inequality undermines ordinary citizens' regime support in both democratic and autocratic countries enriches our understanding of inequality-induced regime instability.

The rest of this chapter is structured as follows. In the next section, we discuss previous studies on the relationship between income inequality and political stability. Based on these works, in the third section we argue that citizens' regime support decreases with their perceived distributive unfairness in both democracies and autocracies. We introduce the research design and test our hypothesis in the empirical section. The final section concludes.

Inequality, Transition to Democracy, and Democratic Consolidation

Income inequality refers to the unequal distribution of income among individuals or households. Studies have demonstrated that inequality leads to political instability because it intensifies the conflicts on distributive issues between the rich and poor citizens. When inequality is higher, the poor would be more tempted to use violence to force wealth redistribution. Accordingly, a higher level of inequality causes more crime, civil unrest, and even civil wars (Blau and Blau 1982; Cederman, Gleditsch, and Buhaug 2013; Nepal, Bohara, and Gawande 2011).

As well as the relationship between income inequality and conflict, scholars further investigate the role of income inequality in facilitating democratic transitions. Specifically, the availability of free and fair elections makes poor citizens in democracies more likely to successfully demand redistribution from political leaders than their counterparts in autocracies (Przeworski et al. 2000). In other words, a higher level of income inequality would make it easier for the poor to demand greater redistribution in democracies (Meltzer and Richard 1981). It follows that poor citizens living in autocracies would have an incentive to change their political regime to a democratic one. Therefore, scholars have argued that the level of inequality is correlated with the probability of democratic transition. Most notably, Acemoglu and Robinson (2005) contend that inequality and democratization form an inverted U-shaped relationship. They argue that democratization is most likely to happen when the inequality is at the middle level. This is because when inequality is high, the rich have a strong incentive to resist redistribution after democratization. And when inequality is low, the poor have a weak incentive to support democratic transitions because they will not benefit much from the post-revolution redistribution.

Meanwhile, Boix (2003) posits a negative relationship between inequality and democratization. On the one hand, poor citizens have a strong incentive to tax their rich citizens when inequality is high. On the other hand, rich citizens have an equally strong incentive to protect their wealth from being taxed. Thus, the rich would desire to repress the poor's demand for redistribution. Accordingly, democratic transition can only occur when inequality is so low that the rich would not oppose democratization.

Finally, recent studies have challenged the Boix-Acemoglu-Robinson thesis regarding the effects of inequality on democratic transitions. Houle (2009), for instance, argues that inequality has no effect on democratization. Haggard and Kaufman (2012) echo this argument and conclude that studies on inequality and regime change are "highly inconclusive at best" for third-wave democracies.

Despite the mixed empirical evidence on the relationship between inequality and democratization, we suggest that inequality destabilizes political regimes. In autocracies, the distributive conflict between the rich and the poor prevails since there are no institutional channels to address inequality. The poor may use violence to seize the rich's wealth, whereas the rich would also counteract the poor with violent means. A similar confrontation exists in democracies as well. According to Houle (2009), inequality impedes democratic consolidation in young democracies because it increases rich citizens' cost of redistribution. In other words, if a country cannot properly address the issue of redistribution after democratization, it is less likely to consolidate and faces the risk of democratic breakdown (Houle 2009).

As inequality facilitates political conflicts in both democracies and autocracies, scholars have also investigated the relationship between inequality and citizens' political attitudes. Anderson and Singer (2008) find that income inequality shapes citizens' lack of trust in political institutions and dissatisfaction with democracy in European countries, especially among those who support a leftist ideology. Similarly, Kuhn et al. (2016) report that rising inequalities in European countries have led to an increase in citizens' skepticism about the process of European integration, especially among those with a low level of education. Han and Chang (2016) demonstrate that inequality enlarges the democratic satisfaction gap between electoral winners and losers. Similarly, Wu and Chang (2019) find that citizens' satisfaction with democracy decreases with perceived unfairness of income distribution in East Asian and Latin American democracies. Together, those studies suggest that unequal income distribution causes citizens to become politically discontent.

Perceived Unfairness of Income Distribution and Regime Support

Based on the above literature, this section elaborates on how individuals' perceptions of income inequality affect their regime support. We suggest that when a citizen thinks that income distribution in her country is more unfair, she will be less satisfied with the current regime and become more supportive of changes, regardless of the current regime type of her country. We base our argument on recent developments in the literature of comparative democratization. As indicated in the previous section, democracy is conceptualized as a game of redistribution between rich and poor. When inequality increases, citizens in an authoritarian regime will become more supportive of a democratic alternative because they expect that the current unfair income distribution would be addressed in a new democratic regime.

Meanwhile, citizens in democracies may be unsatisfied with and less supportive of democracy if democracy cannot address the issue of redistribution. Importantly, inequality reduces poor citizens' political engagement in democracies because democracy is supposed to be an institution that can improve ordinary citizens' well-being (Solt 2008; Krieckhaus et al. 2014). Levitsky and Ziblatt (2018, 3) even claim that "the very health of our democracy hinges on" how the regime addresses inequality.

As inequality is a critical source of regime instability in both democracies and autocracies, we expect that citizens who perceive income distribution to be unfair would be less supportive of their countries' political system because they believe they deserve more from the system. To be sure, our analytical focus is the extent to which citizens consider the income distribution to be fair, not the level of income inequality per se. Although the concept of inequality differs from that of perceived unfairness, previous studies have argued that the individual perception of distributive unfairness is more important for predicting citizens' political attitudes than the actual, or even perceived, level of inequality (Gimpelson and Treisman 2018; Kaufman 2009; Wu and Chang 2019). According to Gimpelson and Treisman (2018), citizens may misperceive the true level of inequality because they may have limited access to information. Even if inequality is high, poorer citizens may not form hostile attitudes toward the rich if they perceive the level of inequality to be fair. Meanwhile, citizens may base their knowledge on their own experiences in order to get a rough idea of the unfairness of income distribution in their country. According to Kaufman (2009, 366), perception of unfairness is "a reasonable first approximation of beliefs [on] the distribution of wealth." In sum, we suggest that if a political system does not distribute wealth fairly in the eyes of ordinary citizens, it will have less popular support.

Based on the above discussion, the rest of this chapter tests the following hypothesis on distributive unfairness and regime support: *People who perceive a higher level of unfairness of income distribution have lower support for the regimes.*

Data

To test our hypothesis, we use the data from the fourth wave of the Asian Barometer Survey (ABS). The fourth wave of the ABS conducted face-to-face interviews with nationally representative samples in fourteen East Asian countries and territories between 2013 and 2015. It offers us an ideal dataset to empirically test our hypothesis because it covers both democratic and autocratic regimes. Specifically, it includes one established democracy (Japan), three third-wave democracies (Taiwan, Mongolia, and South Korea), three unconsolidated democracies (Malaysia, Indonesia, and the Philippines), one military dictatorship (Thailand), four autocracies (Cambodia, China, Singapore, and Vietnam), one nascent democracy (Myanmar), and one hybrid regime (Hong Kong). The variety of political regimes surveyed by the fourth wave of the ABS enables us to investigate how perceived unfairness of income distribution affects regime support across different political contexts.

Operationalization of Variables

The dependent variable in our empirical analysis is citizens' support for the current regime. Generally speaking, citizens' regime support results from their evaluation of the balance between that system's inputs and outputs (Easton 1965). In this article, we measure citizens' regime support with the following question from the fourth wave of the ABS: "a system like ours, even if it runs into problems, deserves the people's support." Respondents are asked to choose one response on a four-point scale, including strongly disagree (1), disagree (2), agree (3), and strongly agree (4). Figure 11.1 summarizes the distribution of respondents' answers to this question. As illustrated in Figure 11.1, citizens' regime support is lowest in South Korea and highest in Vietnam.

The key explanatory variable is ordinary citizens' evaluation of the fairness of income distribution in their countries. We use the following question: "How fair do you think income distribution is in your country?" Respondents are asked to choose one of the following four answers: (1) very fair, (2) fair, (3) unfair, or (4) very unfair. We expect regime support to be low if citizens perceive income distribution to be unfair.

Figure 11.2 presents respondents' answers to the question on perceived distributive unfairness in their countries. In only 4 of the 14 countries did a majority of respondents perceive their country's income distribution to be fair (i.e., Thailand, Malaysia, Vietnam, and Singapore). Essentially, distributive unfairness is a salient issue in the eyes of citizens in East Asia.

Figure 11.1 Regime Support in East Asia

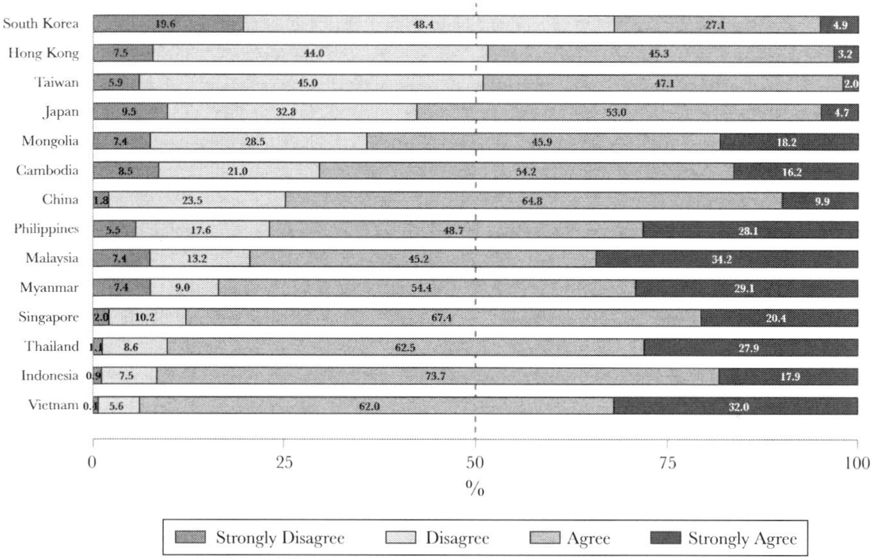

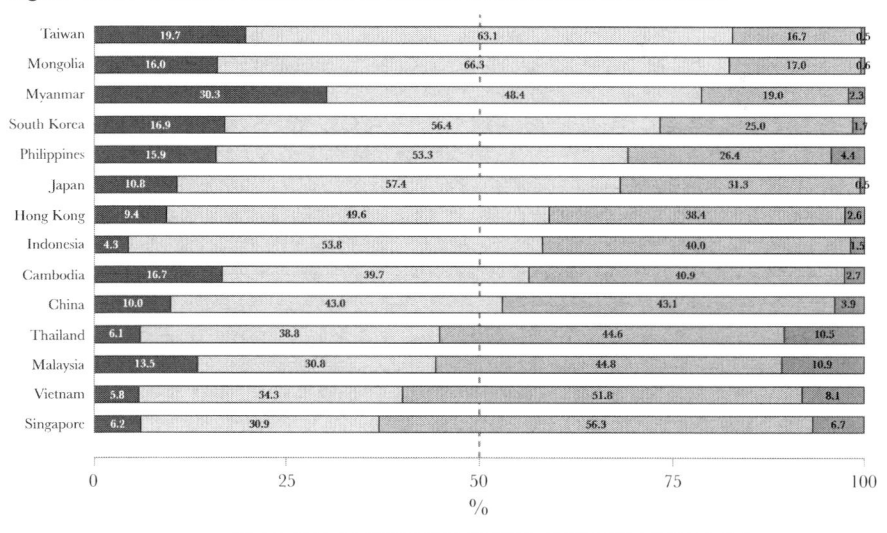

Source: Asian Barometer Survey. Authors prepared.

Figure 11.2 Perceived Unfairness of Income Distribution in East Asia

Source: Asian Barometer Survey. Authors prepared.

Figure 11.3 illustrates the bivariate relationship between the perception of unfairness of income distribution and regime support in East Asian countries. We calculated the percentages of respondents who perceived income distribution to be unfair and very unfair as well as the percentages of citizens who support and strongly support their countries' regimes. As demonstrated in Figure 11.3, countries with a higher proportion of citizens who perceive distributive unfairness are more likely to have a lower level of regime support. More importantly, the correlation between the two variables is substantial (-0.60). This result supports our hypothesis on income distribution and regime support. It further suggests that the perception of distributive unfairness is a more effective measure to explain regime support in East Asia than the objective measure of the Gini coefficient.

To comprehensively investigate the relationship between perception of income unfairness and regime support in East Asia, we estimate regression models with additional variables. Specifically, we are fully aware that our empirical finding in Figure 11.3 may be correlational rather than causal. In addition, the relationship between regime support and perceived distributive unfairness may be spurious and simultaneously determined by other variables. Therefore, we include three sets of variables that may be confounding with the relationship between respondents' regime support and perceived unfairness. First, we control for respondents' demographic factors, including gender, age, and level of education. Second, we incorporate respondents' economic situation by including their income sufficiency and self-evaluation of their families' present economic situation. As both the dependent and key independent variables in this chapter measure respondents' attitudes, their relationship may be correlated with respondents' attitudes on other issues. Accordingly, we include the third set of variables that focus on respondents' political attitudes, such as their perceived level of democracy, political efficacy, political interest, and social trust.

Figure 11.3 Regime Support in East Asia, by Level of Perceived Distributive Unfairness

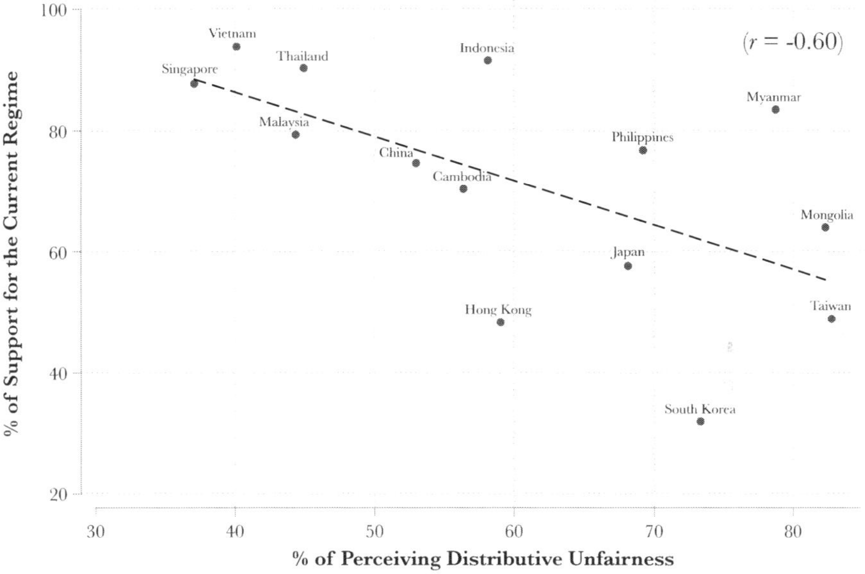

Source: Asian Barometer Survey. Authors prepared.

As our key explanatory variable, perceived distributive unfairness, is measured at the individual level, we estimate a multilevel random intercept model. Model 1 in Table 11.1 reports our estimation results and suggests that respondents who perceive income distribution to be more unfair are more likely to have lower support for the regime. Substantively, a change in a respondent's perception of income distribution from "very fair" to "very unfair," all else being equal, results in a reduction in the regime support probability by 21 percent (0.83 to 0.62). This finding remains unchanged in Model 2, where we adopt a stricter definition of regime support by coding those who "strongly support" the regime as 1 and other responses as 0 when constructing the dependent variable.

Table 11.1 Determinants of Regime Support in East Asia

	Model 1	Model 2	Model 3	Model 4
	Support for Current Regime		Support for Regime Change	
Male	0.007	0.019	0.019	0.157*
	[0.038]	[0.046]	[0.052]	[0.064]
Age	0.011***	0.010*	-0.012**	-0.006+
	[0.003]	[0.004]	[0.004]	[0.004]
Education	-0.134***	-0.080	0.295***	-0.173*
	[0.040]	[0.056]	[0.066]	[0.071]
Perceived Unfairness	-0.435***	-0.351***	0.602***	0.365***
	[0.052]	[0.053]	[0.085]	[0.103]
Income Sufficiency	-0.020	0.028	-0.007	0.023
	[0.049]	[0.053]	[0.042]	[0.056]
Economic Evaluation	0.113***	0.100*	-0.062	-0.211***
	[0.052]	[0.053]	[0.085]	[0.103]
Income Sufficiency	-0.020	0.028	-0.007	0.023
	[0.049]	[0.053]	[0.042]	[0.056]
Economic Evaluation	0.113***	0.100*	-0.062	-0.211***
	[0.027]	[0.040]	[0.051]	[0.051]
Democratic Evaluation	0.192***	0.131***	-0.279***	-0.202***
	[0.030]	[0.027]	[0.030]	[0.040]
Social Trust	0.165***	0.033	-0.335***	-0.455**
	[0.037]	[0.057]	[0.067]	[0.166]
Political Efficacy	-0.216*	-0.176*	0.006	0.359***
	[0.087]	[0.084]	[0.051]	[0.104]
Political Interest	0.046	0.248***	-0.022	0.009
	[0.044]	[0.035]	[0.055]	[0.081]
Constant	0.614+	-2.953***	2.391***	-1.423**
	[0.349]	[0.406]	[0.561]	[0.435]
Variance Component	·			
Country-level Intercept	0.894**	1.108***	0.244*	0.526***
	[0.272]	[0.319]	[0.114]	[0.142]
Log pseudo Likelihood	-8788	-6899	-5501	-3896
No. of Countries	14	14	14	14
No. of Observations	15891	15891	15766	15766

Note: The dependent variable in Models 1 and 2 is support for the current regime. The dependent variable in Models 3 and 4 is support for changing the current regime. Robust standard errors clustered by country are reported in brackets.
+ p<0.1, * p<0.05, **p<0.05, *** p<0.001.

Figure 11.4 Perceived Distributive Unfairness and Regime Support, by Country

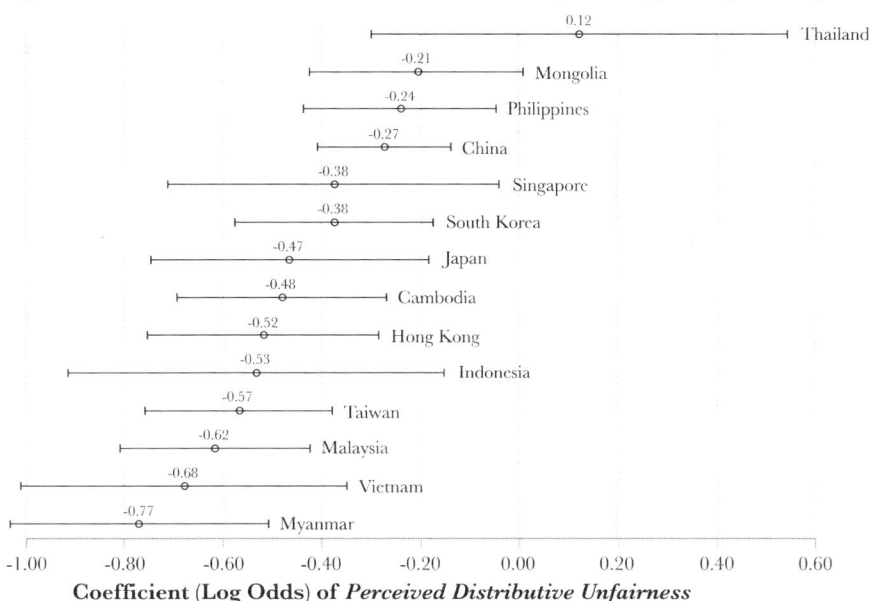

Coefficient (Log Odds) of *Perceived Distributive Unfairness*

Note: Solid lines are 95% confidence intervals.
Source: Author prepared.

The dependent variable in Models 1 and 2 is respondents' support for their countries' current regimes. Respondents may think of social desirability when answering this question. In addition, they may give "lip service" by answering strongly agree or agree to the question on regime support. To address this issue further, we use an alternative variable that measures citizens' regime support. The ABS asks respondents the following question: "Compared with other systems in the world, would you say our system of government works fine as it is, needs minor change, needs major change, or should be replaced?" Based on respondents' answers to this question, we construct two additional dependent variables. The first variable is a binary one that codes the answer "[i]t works fine, no need to change" as 1 and the other three answers as 0. The second variable codes "[s]hould be replaced as 0" and the other three answers as 1. Thus, both operationalizations indicate a loose and strict way to measure regime support, respectively. Models 3 and 4 report the additional results, suggesting that when an individual perceived income distribution to be more unfair, they are more likely to support changes to or replacement of the current regime.

In addition to pooling all 14 countries together, we estimate logistic regression models with the same set of independent variables in Model 1 for each country. For each model, we report the coefficient with its 95% confidence interval for Distributive Unfairness in Figure 11.4. The coefficient of Distributive Unfairness is statistically significant at the 0.05 level in 12 out of 14 countries (with the exception of Thailand and Mongolia). Therefore, the negative relationship between perceived distributive unfairness and regime support is quite robust for East Asian countries.

Conclusion

In this chapter, we investigate the relationship between citizens' perception of income distribution and their regime support in 14 East Asian countries and territories. We find that when citizens perceive their countries' income distribution to be more unfair, they are less supportive of the political regime and more supportive of regime change.

Our findings have an important implication for recent debates on democratic recession and authoritarian diffusion. In particular, we show that unfair income distribution harms regime stability in both democracies and autocracies via decreases in citizens' political support. As the income distribution becomes more unequal, the poor also perceive it to be more unfair and become more hostile toward their political systems. This discontent with the current regime fuels anti-regime momentum and even results in political instability and regime breakdown. The rise of anti-establishment populism and deepening political polarization are two typical consequences of this trend. Our finding further suggests that addressing the unfairness of income distribution is a key measure to reconcile the political conflicts between the rich and the poor in different regimes.

Finally, this article also connects to a growing literature on authoritarian politics that examines how leaders in authoritarian regimes use a variety of policy instruments to alleviate income inequality in order to preempt revolutionary threats from the masses. Chang and Wu (2016), for instance, extend the Heckscher-Ohlin model of international trade and show that leaders in authoritarian regimes have incentives to sign preferential trade agreements so as to enrich poor workers. In so doing, dictators can reduce the gap between the rich and the poor and consolidate their authoritarian rule. This article corroborates Chang and Wu's study and provides a micro-foundation on the relationship between inequality and citizens' regime support. Needless to say, how to fully unpack the complex relationship between inequality and regime stability awaits future research.

References

Acemoglu, Daron, and James A. Robinson. 2005. *Economic Origins of Dictatorship and Democracy*. New York: Cambridge University Press. doi:10.1017/cbo9780511510809.

Anderson, Christopher J., and Matthew M. Singer. 2008. "The Sensitive Left and the Impervious Right: Multilevel Models and the Politics of Inequality, Ideology, and Legitimacy in Europe." *Comparative Political Studies* 41 (4-5): 564-599. doi:10.1177/0010414007313113.

Blau, Judith R., and Peter M. Blau. 1982. "The Cost of Inequality: Metropolitan Structure and Violent Crime." *American Sociological Review* 47 (1): 114-129. doi:10.2307/2095046.

Boix, Carles. 2003. *Democracy and Redistribution*. New York: Cambridge University Press. doi:10.1017/cbo9780511804960.

Cederman, Lars-Erik, Kristian Skrede Gleditsch, and Halvard Buhaug. 2013. *Inequality, Grievances, and Civil War*. New York: Cambridge University Press. doi:10.1017/cbo9781139084161.

Chang, Eric C. C., and Wen-chin Wu. 2016. "Preferential Trade Agreements, Income Inequality, and Authoritarian Survival." *Political Research Quarterly* 69 (2): 281-294. doi:10.1177/1065912916636688.

Easton, David. 1965. *A Systems Analysis of Political Life*. New York: John Wiley and Sons.

Gimpelson, Vladimir, and Daniel Treisman. 2018. "Misperceiving Inequality." *Economics & Politics* 30 (1): 27-54. doi:10.1111/ecpo.12103.

Haggard, Stephan, and Robert R. Kaufman. 2012. "Inequality and Regime Change: Democratic Transitions and the Stability of Democratic Rule." *American Political Science Review* 106 (3): 495-516. http://www.jstor.org/stable/23275430.

Han, Sung Min, and Eric C. C. Chang. 2016. "Economic Inequality, Winner-Loser Gap, and Satisfaction with Democracy." *Electoral Studies* 44: 85-97. doi:10.1016/j.electstud.2016.08.006.

Houle, Christian. 2009. "Inequality and Democracy: Why Inequality Harms Consolidation But Does Not Affect Democratization." *World Politics* 61 (4): 589-622. doi:10.1017/s0043887109990074.

Kaufman, Robert R. 2009. "The Political Effects of Inequality in Latin America: Some Inconvenient Facts." *Comparative Politics* 41 (3): 359-379. doi:10.5129/001041509x12911362972359.

Krieckhaus, Jonathan, Byunghwan Son, Nisha Mukherjee Bellinger, and Jason M. Wells. 2014. "Economic Inequality and Democratic Support." *Journal of Politics* 76 (1): 139-151. doi:10.1017/S0022381613001229.

Kuhn, Theresa, Erika van Elsas, Armen Hakhverdian, and Wouter van der Brug. 2016. "An Ever Wider Gap in an Ever Closer Union: Rising Inequalities and Euroscepticism in 12 West European Democracies, 1975-2009." *Socio-Economic Review* 14 (1): 27-45. doi:10.1093/ser/mwu034.

Levitsky, Steven, and Daniel Ziblatt. 2018. *How Democracies Die*. New York: Crown.

Meltzer, Allan H., and Scott F. Richard. 1981. "A Rational Theory of the Size of Government." *Journal of Political Economy* 89 (5): 914-927. doi:10.1086/261013.

Nepal, Mani, Alok K. Bohara, and Kishore Gawande. 2011. "More Inequality, More Killings: The Maoist Insurgency in Nepal." *American Journal of Political Science* 55 (4): 886-906. doi:10.1111/j.1540-5907.2011.00529.x.

Przeworski, Adam, Michael E. Alvarez, Jose Antonio Cheibub, and Fernando Limongi. 2000. *Democracy and Development: Political Institutions and Well-Being in the World, 1950-1990*. New York: Cambridge University Press. doi:10.1017/cbo9780511804946.

Solt, Frederick. 2008. "Economic Inequality and Democratic Political Engagement." *American Journal of Political Science* 52 (1): 48-60. doi:10.1111/j.1540-5907.2007.00298.x.

Wu, Wen-chin, and Yu-tzung Chang. 2019. "Income Inequality, Distributive Unfairness, and Support for Democracy: Evidence from East Asia and Latin America." *Democratization* 26 (8): 1475-1492. doi:10.1080/13510347.2019.1656198.

12 Economic Performance, Regime Types, and Political Support
Chin-en Wu

In addition to their divergent levels of economic development, a defining feature of Asian countries is the heterogeneity of political development. Liberal democracies, electoral democracies, and authoritarian regimes all coexist in the region. As these countries in the region share geographical proximity and cultural similarity to some extent, this provides a good context for us to study the effect of regime type on political support.

Easton (1965) nicely distinguishes between diffuse and specific support. Specific support refers to the evaluation of the performance of a specific government, while diffuse support refers to the evaluation of a regime as a whole. Norris (1999) further distinguishes political support from specific to diffuse into four levels: incumbent government, governments as institutions, satisfaction with the performance of democracy, and support for democracy. In this chapter, we explore the mediating effect of regime type on the association between perceived economic performance and political support. For economic outputs, we focus on perceived overall economic performance and perceived fairness of income distribution in a country. For political support, we examine peoples' satisfaction with the incumbent government, the performance of democracy, and democratic support, which can be operationalized by support for democracy as a general concept, people's commitment to liberal democratic values, and endorsing the basic framework of democratic institutions.

To develop our current understanding of how perceived economic conditions and fairness of income distribution affects political support under different political regimes, this chapter uses the fifth wave of the Asian Barometer Survey (ABS). Based on the Freedom House democracy scores, we divide countries into three categories by their democratic levels. Countries are considered as liberal democracies if their average scores of political freedom and civil liberty are less than or equal to two. The liberal democracies are Japan, South Korea, Taiwan, Australia, and Mongolia. Countries are labeled as electoral democracies if their average scores are greater than two and less than five. The electoral democracies are India, Malaysia, Indonesia, and the Philippines. Elections in these countries are largely free and fair, but there are some significant flaws. Congress and the judiciary do not have sufficient oversight of the executive branch, and civil rights are still partially restricted. Countries are labeled as authoritarian regimes if their average scores are greater than or equal to five. The authoritarian regimes are Thailand, Myanmar, and Vietnam. In authoritarian regimes, governments hold nominal elections and allow only a limited space for civil society. Governments in these countries meddle in elections, control the mass media, and limit basic civil rights to protect their ruling status. Since the data from China is not available at this stage, it is not included.

In different political regimes, the build-in mechanisms that address popular grievances are different. As liberal democracies entail greater vertical, horizontal, and diagonal accountabilities, they are often considered to be capable of responding to people's needs. When accountability mechanisms are weak or absent, social and economic problems such as weak economic performance or distribution of income are less likely to be properly addressed (Rueschemeyer, Huber, and Stephens 1992). Therefore, it can be inferred that the disaffected people in the electoral and authoritarian regime are thus less satisfied with the existing political system and more likely to demand an overhaul to the political system. Citizens who are unhappy about economic conditions or distribution of income are more likely to endorse strengthening accountability mechanisms to deal with these issues. In other words, they tend to favor a more democratic form of government, hoping to address the economic woes.

An immediate question is the preferred contents of political reform. It depends on what the political system already has. For liberal democracies, the accountability mechanisms, the most effective way to address economic and social problems, are already in place; the disenchanted people see no reason to discard them. In electoral democracies, a basic democratic framework is largely in place but they are still short of a liberal democratic form of political system. Thus, the disenchanted people are more likely to favor core elements of liberal democracy such as the notions of freedom of organization and expression, equal rights to participate in politics, protection of civil liberties, checks and balances, and the rule of law. In authoritarian regimes, democratic institutions are generally absent, dissatisfied citizens are keen on some basic institutional framework of democracy such as elections and multi-party competition. They, however, do not necessarily embrace those liberal democratic values more than the satisfied citizens because these notions are not considered to be part of the basic institutional framework of democracy or are often far from many people's understanding of democracy.

Therefore, this chapter seeks to explore whether the effects of economic evaluations, state of the economy, and fairness of income distribution on political support are different across the three regime types. Specifically, we ask, does economic evaluation influence trust in the incumbent government and the political system differently in these three types of regimes? Next, will disaffection with the economic conditions translate into stronger support for democracy in electoral democracies and authoritarian regimes? Which form of democracy do they favor? Conversely, will disaffected people in liberal democracies reduce their commitment to the liberal democratic form of government?

Government Approval

We first examine the relationship between the economic conditions and approval of the incumbent's performance. The question we use to capture the state of the economy is: "How would you describe the change in the economic condition of our country over the last few years?" We group "much worse," "worse," and "about the same" as "worse" and "much better" and "better" as "better." For approval of the government, we use the question "How satisfied or dissatisfied are you with the [name of president, etc. current ruling] government?" to capture people's approval of the incumbent government. Figure 12.1 shows that in all three types of regime, people who are dispirited about the economic conditions over the past few years are less satisfied with government performance than those who perceive good economic conditions.

As can be seen, overall approval rates are comparatively low in liberal democracies when compared to electoral democracies and authoritarian regimes. Other than the baseline difference, the attitude gaps between satisfied and dissatisfied respondents are similar across political regimes. Political trust in authoritarian regimes always suffers from the validity problems that are associated with the intimidation effect and self-censorship. Chen and Shi (2001), however, argue that citizens' confidence in authoritarian governments exist even when the intimidation effect is taken into account. Rivetti and Cavatorta (2017) also posit that, considering the fast economic development, people who give high levels of political trust in authoritarian regimes are indeed satisfied with the economic performance of the government. In addition, asking respondents to evaluate the performance of incumbent political leaders is always sensitive in non-liberal democratic countries. By contrast, asking the perceived performance of the political system or the attitudes toward democracy is generally less sensitive.

Figure 12.1 Views of Nation's Economy and Satisfaction with the Government

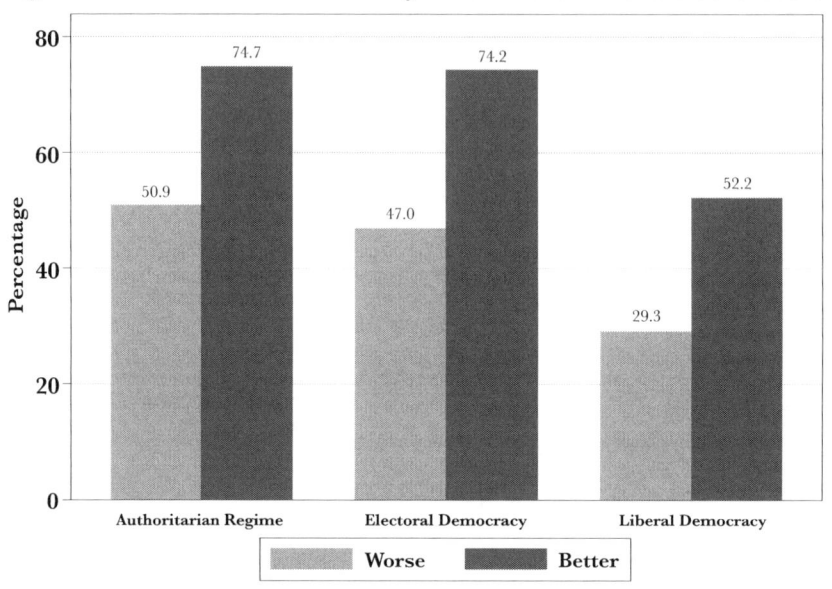

Source: Asian Barometer Survey. Author prepared.

Next, we examine the effect of perceived fairness of income distribution. We present respondents with the question, "How fair do you think income distribution is in the country?" The respondents answer on a four-point Likert scale (very unfair, somewhat unfair, somewhat fair, and very fair). We combine "very unfair" and "somewhat unfair" as "unfair" and "somewhat fair" and "very fair" as "fair." As seen in Figure 12.2, people who have positive views of income distribution are more likely to be satisfied with the government. The association between fairness of income distribution and satisfaction with government is greater in democracies than in authoritarian regimes. This is likely because the notion of fairness is the very foundation of liberal democracies which uphold freedom of speech, civil rights protection, and high level of fairness in electoral competition. Citizens under these regimes tend to attach great importance to the fairness of income distribution. Perceived unfair distribution of income is likely the result of lack of equal opportunity, social discrimination, rampant corruption, and unfair tax systems. These situations all contradict the notion of fairness, resulting in a larger satisfaction gap in liberal democracies.

Figure 12.2 Fairness of Income Distribution and Satisfaction with Governments

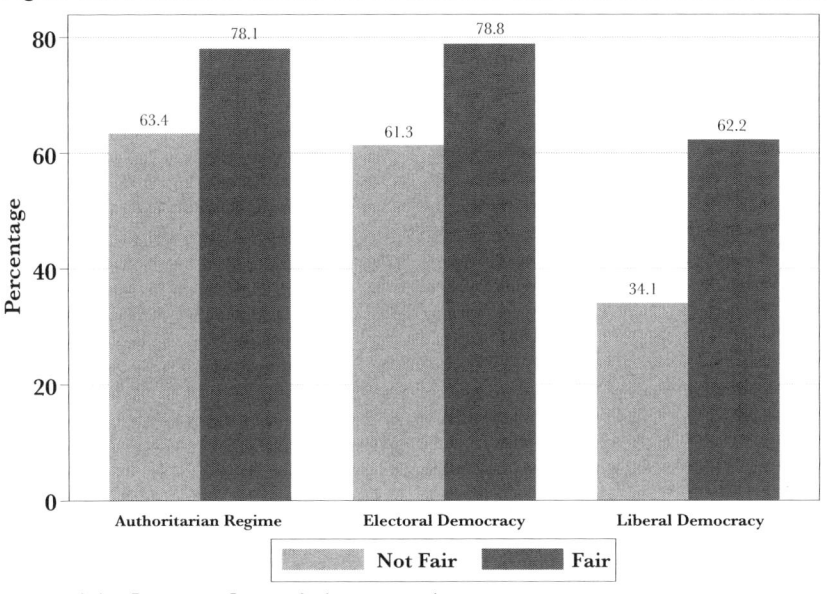

Source: Asian Barometer Survey. Author prepared.

In addition, in non-democracies, the above two figures suggest that the state of the economy is tied more closely with the approval of governments than fair distribution of income. As can be seen, the satisfaction gap is greater in Figure 12.1 than in Figure 12.2. In these regimes, economic performance assessment is more important to people's evaluation of government than fair distribution of income. The political structure of authoritarian regimes and even electoral democracies are inherently incongruent with the idea of fairness. Authoritarian governments do not construct legitimacy based on procedural fairness; instead, they tend to rely on performance. Governments promise to bring economic prosperity in exchange for support from citizenry. Citizens under this situation have to rely on economic performance to decide whether to trust the government. People are more likely to evaluate the government by assessing the overall economic performance.

Satisfaction with Democracy

Scholars argue that satisfaction with the way democracy works is dependent on context and influenced by short-term factors. Therefore, this concept is not an appropriate measure of support for democracy as a system but of how it works in practice (Linde and Ekman 2003). The meaning of satisfaction with the way democracy works in authoritarian regimes is less clear. It is best understood as people's general assessment of the functioning of the political system. Since electoral authoritarian and even authoritarian regimes like to call themselves democracies, people living under these regime types are most likely to answer the satisfaction with democracy question by referring to the function of their own political system.

The most frequently cited factors influencing satisfaction with the performance of democracy include democratic institutional performance such as equal treatment of people with different social backgrounds, the rule of law, vertical accountability, and horizontal accountability (Huang, Chang, and Chu 2008; Christmann and Torcal 2017) as well as institutional outputs such as human capital, health conditions, and macroeconomic performance, income inequality (Sarsfield and Echegaray 2005; Huang, Chang, and Chu 2008; Anderson and Singer 2008). It is normally assumed that people enjoying a higher level of material affluence tend to appreciate the performance of a democratic regime more, while people who perceive their material interests as faring significantly worse than others may become disappointed with the democratic system (Wagner, Dufour, and Schneider 2003). Higher income inequality is associated with a lower level of satisfaction with democracy (Anderson and Singer 2008). For satisfaction with democracy, we use the following question: "On the whole, how satisfied or dissatisfied are you with the way democracy works in the country?"

Figure 12.3 shows that people who are disgruntled about the economic conditions of their countries over the past few years tend to perceive a worse performance of democracy than those who perceive a good economy. This gap is larger in electoral democracies and authoritarian countries than in democracies. This finding shows that in democracies the contented and discontented respondents are quite close in their attitudes, suggesting that the short-term fluctuation of economic performance does not influence people's assessment of the performance of the political system as much. In contrast, in electoral democracies and authoritarian countries, overall economic performance appears to play a greater role in influencing satisfaction with how democracy works than in democracies.

Figure 12.4 shows that in all regimes, people who perceive that the distribution of income is fair tend to perceive a better performance of democracy than those who perceive an unfair distribution of income. It suggests that fairness of income distribution is an issue that affects satisfaction with the political system in all three regimes in an equal manner. Compared to Figure 12.3, the larger gap in democracies in this graph shows that people in democracies attach great importance to justice. Fairness of income distribution exerts greater influence on perceived democratic performance than the perceived overall economic performance.

Figure 12.3 Views of Nation's Economy and Satisfaction with Democracy

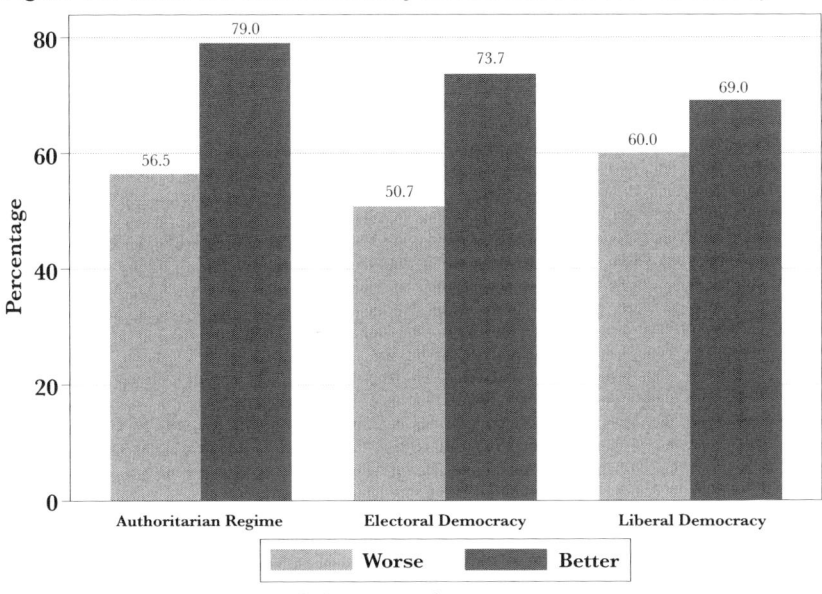

Source: Asian Barometer Survey. Author prepared.

Figure 12.4 Fairness of Income and Satisfaction with Democracy

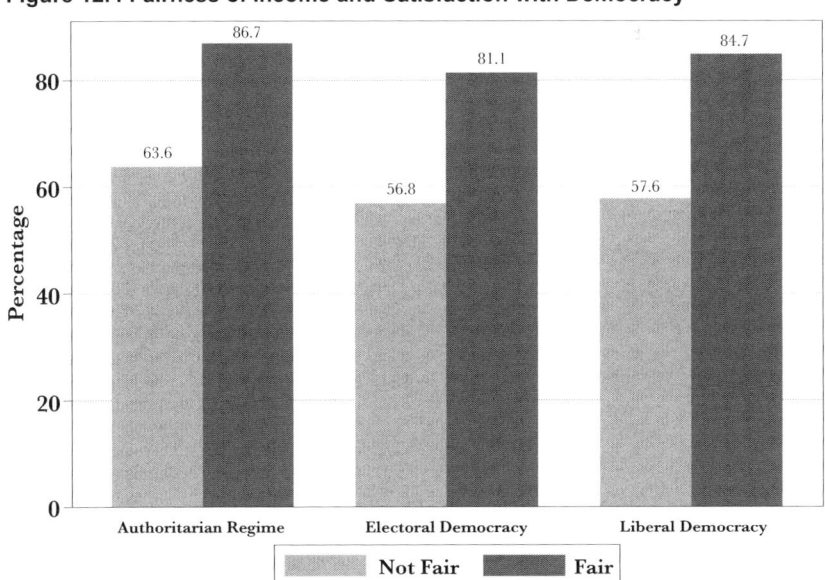

Source: Asian Barometer Survey. Author prepared.

The political structure of authoritarian regimes and even electoral democracies are inherently incongruent with the idea of fairness. These regimes are unwilling to adopt these accountability mechanisms such as clean and fair election, press freedom, freedom of association, resulting in unequal opportunity and rampant corruption. Although people tend to judge the performance of authoritarian governments by focusing on the overall economic outputs, the perceived unfairness of income distribution demonstrate the systematic flaws of such regimes. Therefore, it considerably reduces the disenchanted citizens' satisfaction with the overall performance of the political system.

Note that democratic satisfaction may also be influenced by the perceived function of democratic governance, which include vertical accountability, horizontal accountability, the rule of law, low levels of corruption, civil right protection, and equal treatment of people with different social backgrounds etc. These dimensions mainly concern the procedural performance of political systems. Conceptually, perceived governance may also be influenced by the economic performance such as macroeconomic performance, distribution of income, income levels etc. If we use economic evaluation to predict perceived governance, we find the two variables are not correlated, suggesting that people do not associate their economic evaluations with the perceived governance. In addition, we also find that the correlation between perceived governance and satisfaction with the way democracy works is not significant. It suggests that people do not evaluate the performance of political systems based on the perceived performance of governance. These findings suggest that the two concepts of satisfaction with democracy and perceived governance are not significantly overlapped.

Given people's attitudes toward economic performance and their satisfaction with the performance of the incumbent government and political system, will the disaffected citizens favor an alternative form of government to address the problems? Specifically, will disfavored economic conditions induce people to support democracy in electoral democracies and authoritarian regimes? Since people in authoritarian regimes cannot hold the rulers accountable for the poor economic performance, the only way to improve performance is to greatly strengthen the accountability mechanisms. Conversely, will disaffected citizens in liberal democracies reduce their commitment to the liberal democratic form of government? Since democratic institutions allow citizens to hold ill-suited politicians to account, the disenchanted voters have no reason to switch to the political institutions that do not allow people to do so. We will turn to those issues below.

Support for Democracy

To measure mass support for democracy, the conventional strategy asks respondents about their general support for democracy as an ideal political system. The abstract measure suffers from a validity problem as people's understanding of the concept of democracy varies across individuals and countries (Schedler and Sarsfield 2007). Many authoritarian regimes portray themselves as democracies (Márquez 2016). Because of the different meanings of democracy along with the social desirability problems, the abstract democracy question often over-estimates the aggregate support for democracy (Schedler and Sarsfield 2007; Kirsch and Welzel 2018). An alternative approach for measuring democratic support asks people their convictions of several core elements of liberal democracy such as freedom of organization and expression, equal rights to participate in politics, protection of civil liberties, checks and balances, and the rule of law. Thus, high liberal democratic values denote support for democratic institutions (Schedler and Sarsfield 2007). Welzel and Alvarez (2014) posit that using liberal democratic values to capture support for democracy can avoid the problem caused by divergent understandings of democracy. We also address these concerns by employing different measures of democracy, with some measures avoiding the "D-word." Those measures include liberal democratic values and attitudes toward the core institutions of democracy.

To measure people's support for democracy as a general concept, we first present respondents with the question, "Do you agree or disagree with the following statement: 'democracy may have its problems, but it is still the best form of government'?" Figure 12.5 shows there is no attitudinal difference in democratic support as a general concept across political regimes and between respondents of different evaluations of the economy. It demonstrates that people's support for democracy in this region is not tied to the perceived national economic conditions. Actually, a great majority of respondents, both contented and discontented, tend to endorse a democratic form of government in different types of political regimes. In liberal democracies, people who are not satisfied with the performance of the government or democratic system do not favor a non-democratic form of government more than the contended respondents. In electoral democracies and authoritarian countries, the disaffected citizens also do not favor democracy more than the satisfied ones.

Figure 12.5 Views of Nation's Economy and Support for Democracy

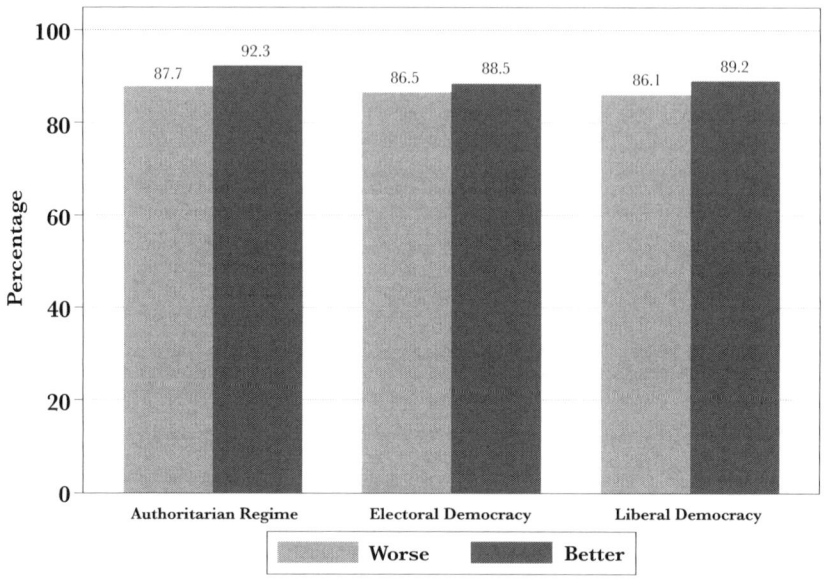

Source: Asian Barometer Survey. Author prepared.

Figure 12.6 suggests that people who hold a favorable view of the distribution of income in their countries are somewhat more likely to endorse a democratic form of government. The difference, however, is small. In addition, the pattern exists in liberal democracies, electoral democracies, and authoritarian countries. Figures 12.5 and 12.6 suggest that in democracies, although the discontented people are not satisfied with the ruling parties and the way democracy works in their countries, they do not intend to endorse alternative political systems. The two figures also show that in electoral democracies and authoritarian regimes, both contended and discontented respondents strongly endorse democracy as a general concept. Note that a great majority of people in these countries express support for democracy. However, the overwhelming support may be due to people's overly positive responses to the "D-word." Thus, we turn to liberal democratic values.

Next, we examine the relationship between perceived economic conditions and people's liberal democratic values. We employ a standard set of questions to measure liberal democratic values and use the mean as the cut-off point for high and low liberal democratic values.[1] Figure 12.7 shows that across regimes, people who perceived a worse national economic condition tend to embrace a higher level of democratic values, suggesting a greater support for democracy. Note that the gap in democratic values is greater in the electoral democracies than in authoritarian regimes and liberal democracies, suggesting that disenchanted people are more likely to endorse liberal forms of democracy in electoral democracies.

Figure 12.6 Fairness of Income Distribution and Support for Democracy

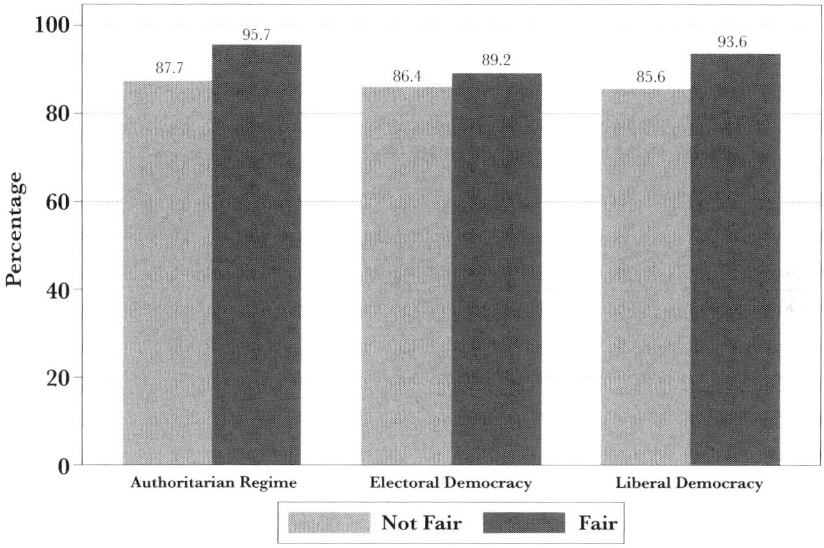

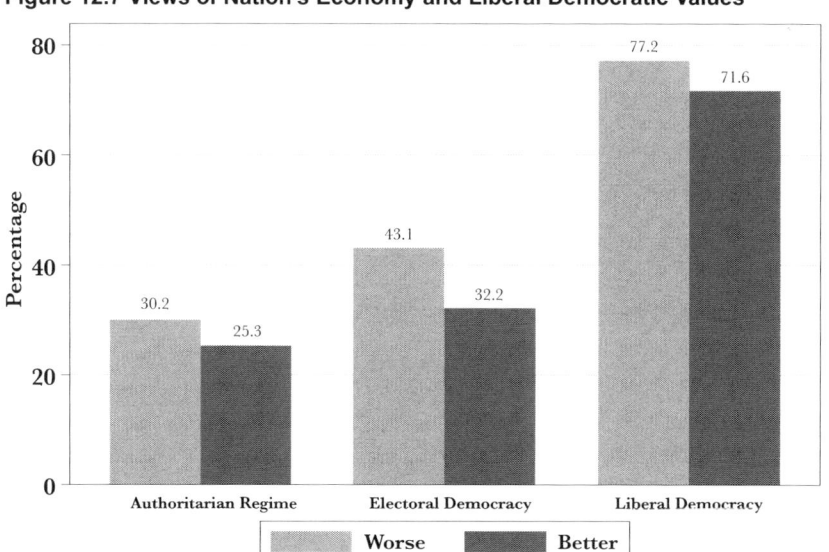

Source: Asian Barometer Survey. Author prepared.

Figure 12.7 Views of Nation's Economy and Liberal Democratic Values

Source: Asian Barometer Survey. Author prepared.

The pattern is even more clear when we look at the relationship between perceived fairness of income distribution and people's liberal democratic values. Figure 12.8 below shows that in electoral democracies and authoritarian regimes, people who perceive an unfair distribution of income tend to show a higher level of democratic values. The gap in democratic values is also particularly pronounced in the electoral democracies and less so in authoritarian regimes. In liberal democracies, people who are not satisfied with the performance of the economy are equally committed to the core values of liberal democracy. The pattern demonstrates that in non-liberal-democratic countries, especially in electoral democracies, people who are not satisfied with economic conditions, the national economic situation and income distribution, tend to embrace liberal democratic values. Liberal democratic values are people's convictions about the core principles of liberal democracies that uphold effective vertical and horizontal accountability and active civil society participation in the political decision-making process. Since multi-party competition and elections are already in place in electoral democracies, improvement in democratic development essentially means shifting to liberal democracy. Therefore, disaffected people in these countries are in favor of better democracy, which is revealed in higher liberal democratic values. They expect that making a transition to liberal democracy can enhance the accountability mechanisms, improving the overall economic condition and making income distribution fairer.

Figure 12.8 Fairness of Income Distribution and Liberal Democratic Values

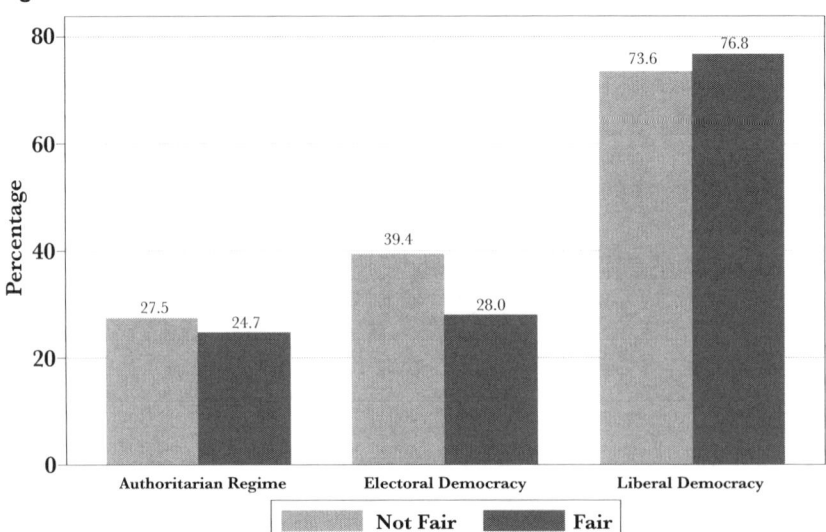

Source: Asian Barometer Survey. Author prepared.

In authoritarian regimes, as shown in the last two figures, the association between economic evaluation and democratic values is weaker than in electoral democracies.[2] Since the current political system is authoritarian, the most immediate and feasible improvement in democratic development is shifting to electoral democracy. Conversely, the liberal democratic model and its core principles is a distant goal that many people either do not consider them to be part of the basic democratic infrastructure or are not acquainted with. Therefore, perceived economic conditions are not significantly associated with liberal democratic values in these countries. Instead, people are most likely to envision electoral democracy.

Finally, we test the relationship between economic assessment and supporting the core institutions of democracy which include multi-party competition, direct election of government officials, and free press. To capture the concept of multi-party competition, we first ask respondents the question: "Only one political party should be allowed to stand for election and hold office." Figure 12.9 reports the percentage of respondents who reject this statement. As can be seen, the disaffected respondents in authoritarian regimes and electoral democracies are more likely to reject one-party rule. This relationship is strongest in authoritarian regimes.

Figure 12.9 Views of Nation's Economy and Multi-party Competition

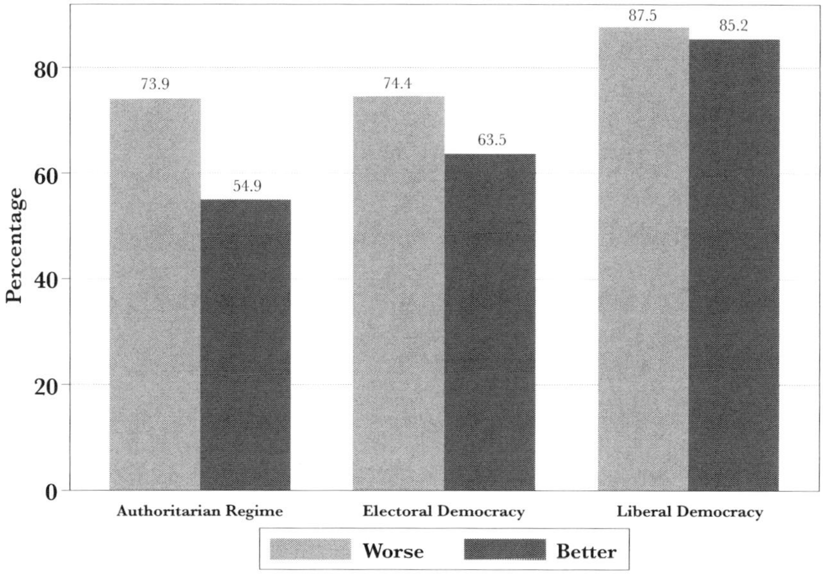

Source: Asian Barometer Survey. Author prepared.

In addition, we find evidence that economically dissatisfied respondents are more likely to believe that the media should have the right to publish news and ideas without government control. The relationship is also stronger in authoritarian regimes, but due to space limits, we do not report the results. Regarding the election of political leaders, we use a question that asks respondents to choose between two statements: 1) Political leaders are chosen by the people through open and competitive elections; and 2) Political leaders are chosen on the basis of their virtue and capability even without elections. Economically dissatisfied respondents are only slightly more likely to favor the first statement. However, note that 84 percent of respondents in authoritarian regimes concur with the first statement, against 72 percent in electoral democracies and 79 percent in liberal democracies. It appears that people in authoritarian regimes overwhelmingly welcome the idea of using elections to select political leaders. Taken together, this suggests that economically dissatisfied respondents in authoritarian regimes are more prone to supporting democracy, but mainly about the basic democratic infrastructure rather than the liberal democracy model.

In addition to the state of the economy, we examine the influence of fairness of income distribution. The pattern is less clear and mixed. It suggests that in authoritarian regimes the economic performance associates more closely with people's demand for democracy than the perceived fairness of income inequality. The most likely reason is that the authoritarian regimes in our sample are all developing economies. Rapid economic growth effectively improves the livelihood of citizens. Income inequality is still an emerging issue. People tend to place greater importance on economic development than fair distribution of income at this stage. Although deterioration of income distribution lowers people's satisfaction with the political system, it does not play a similar role as the state of the economy in inducing people to favor a more democratic form of government.

Conclusion

In different political regimes, people who are disgruntled about the state of the economy or the distribution of income tend not to approve of the incumbent government. The disaffected people are also more likely to perceive a worse performance of democracy. The effect of the economic factors on political support, however, depends on the political regimes. In non-liberal-democratic regimes, the perceived state of the economy exerts a greater influence on government performance than the perceived fairness of income distribution. The fairness of income distribution plays a more important role in liberal democracies. Conversely, the effect of national economic performance on the perceived performance of democracy is also larger in electoral democracies and in authoritarian regimes; while fairness issues exert similar effect in all three regimes.

We further examine the relationship between economic assessment and support for democracy. In liberal democracies, economic assessment is not correlated with support for democracy as a general concept and liberal democratic values. This suggests that people who are not satisfied with the performance of the economy do not favor a non-democratic form of government more than the contended respondents. In electoral democracies, economically disaffected citizens do not think that democracy is the best form of government more than the satisfied citizens. Actually, the data show that more than eighty percent of respondents in this region believe that democracy is the best form of government. Since this problem may suffer from social desirability problems, we then examine people's attitudes about liberal democratic values. In electoral democracies, dissatisfied citizens tend to embrace a higher level of liberal democratic values. As these countries already have a basic democratic framework, what they need is shifting toward liberal model of democracy. In authoritarian regimes, dissatisfied citizens do not embrace a higher level of liberal democratic values than satisfied citizens, but they favor building some basic framework of democracy if they find the state of economy not satisfied. However, in these countries most citizens view the state of the economy favorably. In electoral democracies and authoritarian regimes, except for Thailand, more than seventy percent of respondents think that the economy is getting better over the past few years. Sixty percent of Thais also perceive a good economic performance. It appears that the state of the economy is not likely to be the dominant factor that triggers democratic development in these countries in the near future.

Notes

1. These questions include: women should not be involved in politics as much as men; people with little or no education should have as much say in politics as highly-educated people; government leaders are like the head of a family; we should all follow their decisions; the government should decide whether certain ideas should be allowed to be discussed in society; harmony of the community will be disrupted if people organize lots of groups; when judges decide important cases, they should accept the view of the executive branch; if the government is constantly checked [i.e. monitored and supervised] by the legislature, it cannot possibly accomplish great things; if we have political leaders who are morally upright, we can let them decide everything; if people have too many different ways of thinking, society will be chaotic.
2. There are three countries in this category: Vietnam, Thailand, and Myanmar. The attitude gap in Vietnam is actually quite large. Disaffected Vietnamese are more likely to embrace liberal values than their satisfied counterparts.

References

Anderson, Christopher J., and Matthew M. Singer. 2008. "The Sensitive Left and the Impervious Right: Multilevel Models and the Politics of Inequality, Ideology, and Legitimacy in Europe." *Comparative Political Studies* 41 (4-5): 564-599. doi:10.1177/0010414007313113.

Chen, Xueyi, and Tianjian Shi. 2001. "Media Effects on Political Confidence and Trust in the People's Republic of China in the Post-Tiananmen Period." *East Asia* 19 (3): 84-118.

Christmann, Pablo, and Mariano Torcal. 2017. "The Political and Economic Causes of Satisfaction with Democracy in Spain—A Twofold Panel Study." *West European Politics* 40 (6): 1241-1266. doi:10.1080/01402382.2017.1302178.

Easton, David. 1965. *A Systems Analysis of Political Life*. New York: John Wiley and Sons.

Huang, Min-hua, Yu-tzung Chang, and Yun-han Chu. 2008. "Identifying Sources of Democratic Legitimacy: A Multilevel Analysis." *Electoral Studies* 27 (1): 45-62. doi:10.1016/j.electstud.2007.11.002.

Kirsch, Helen, and Christian Welzel. 2018. "Democracy Misunderstood: Authoritarian Notions of Democracy around the Globe." *Social Forces* 98 (1): 59-92. doi:10.1093/sf/soy114.

Linde, Jonas, and Joakim Ekman. 2003. "Satisfaction with Democracy: A Note on a Frequently Used Indicator in Comparative Politics." *European Journal of Political Research* 42 (3): 391-408. doi:10.1111/1475-6765.00089.

Márquez, Xavier. 2016. *Non-Democratic Politics: Authoritarianism, Dictatorship and Democratization*. London: Macmillan International Higher Education.

Norris, Pippa. 1999. "Introduction: The Growth of Critical Citizens?" In *Critical Citizens: Global Support for Democratic Government*, edited by Pippa Norris, 1-30.

Oxford: Oxford University Press.

Rivetti, Paola, and Francesco Cavatorta. 2017. "Functions of Political Trust in Authoritarian Settings." In *Handbook on Political Trust*, edited by Sonja Zmerli and Tom W.G. van der Meer. Cheltenham: Edward Elgar Publishing.

Rueschemeyer, Dietrich, Evelyne Huber, and John D. Stephens. 1992. *Capitalist Development and Democracy*. Chicago: The University of Chicago Press.

Sarsfield, Rodolfo, and Fabián Echegaray. 2005. "Opening the Black Box: How Satisfaction with Democracy and Its Perceived Efficacy Affect Regime Preference in Latin America." *International Journal of Public Opinion Research* 153-173. doi:10.1093/ijpor/edh088.

Schedler, Andreas, and Rodolfo Sarsfield. 2007. "Democrats with Adjectives: Linking Direct and Indirect Measures of Democratic Support." *European Journal of Political Research* 46 (5): 637-659. doi:10.1111/j.1475-6765.2007.00708.x.

Wagner, F. Alexander, Mathias Dufour, and Friedrich Schneider. 2003. "Satisfaction Not Guaranteed—Institutions and Satisfaction with Democracy in Western Europe." In *SSRN*. April. Accessed March 15, 2021. https://ssrn.com/abstract=396322.

Welzel, Christian, and Alejandro Moreno Alvarez. 2014. "Enlightening People: The Spark of Emancipative Values." In *The Civic Culture Transformed: From Allegiant to Assertive Citizens*, edited by Russell J. Dalton and Christian Welzel, 59-88. Cambridge: Cambridge University Press. doi:10.1017/cbo9781139600002.007.

13 Japanese Social Capital in Liberal Democracy 2003-2019: Focusing on Tolerance and Asian Style Political Culture

Ken'ichi Ikeda

During the first two decades of the 21st century, Japanese society experienced large political and economic upheavals: the rise and fall of political parties, two incumbent party changes (rare in postwar Japan), a difficult economic experience from the Lehman shock, and large-scale disasters in the Great East Japan Earthquake followed by the Fukushima nuclear plant accident. Despite those changes, as the Asian Barometer Survey (ABS) data show, the variables on which this chapter focuses are generally stable. Japanese people are deeply committed to liberal democracy and consider the current democracy to be stabilized. While distrust in politics is deep-rooted, the degree of detachment from authoritarianism is high, and the likelihood of supporting other systems is very small. Therefore, there is a great deal of repetition even if we update the chapter on Japan in the 2008 EAB book (Ikeda and Kohno, 2008) by adding the latest data.

Rather, we believe that a better description of where Japan is today would be to focus on how it faces the value dilemma between the West and Asia and how it is positioned between Asia and the West in the context of gradual changes in values. The focus here will be on investigating Japan's political culture in between East and West, by examining the structures of political and social tolerance that resonate the current global emphasis on tolerance for diversity.

The issue of conflict between Asian values and Western values has been an important theme for Japanese since the Meiji era (i.e., more than a century). Japanese insistence on "Out of Asia and into Europe 脱 亞 入 欧 " is still in an ongoing process and a debatable issue in its actual dynamics of political culture. Therefore, it would be worthwhile to discuss it in this chapter. We first review continuity and change in several variables concerning the basis of democracy and political culture: social capital variables (institutional trust and tolerance), political participation, political efficacy, evaluation of democracy, and the value orientations of Asians (what we call "Asian values"). Then we focus on analyses of political and social tolerance in the context of Asian political culture to clarify the Japanese position in this cultural sphere.

Institutional Trust

Institutional trust is at the core of the political community; it bonds a community together at low cost. Moreover, political systems, such as elections, social control, distribution of power and wealth, and sharing of information require confidence in a variety of institutions to function effectively and efficiently.

To clarify the structure of institutional trust, factor analyses[1] were conducted of the variables that represent its different aspects in each wave of the ABS Japan. Table 13.1 shows that the structure has been very stable for the past twenty years. There are three factors in Japanese perceptions of institutional trust: trust in politics and the national government, trust in social control institutions, and trust in the mass media. Although these bodies are stable, there has been some gradual decline in trust in the mass media and minor fluctuations in the low level of trust in public institutions throughout the period.

Table 13.1 Dimensions of Institutional Trust (2003-2019)

	Wave 1 (2003)			Wave 2 (2007)			Wave 3 (2011)			Wave 4 (2016)			Wave 5 (2019)		
	Fac1	Fac2	Fac3	Fac1	Fac2	Fac3	Fac1	Fac2	Fac3	Fac1	Fac2	Fac3	Fac1	Fac2	Fac3
President				0.17	0.57	-0.07	0.03	0.66	-0.02	0.71	0.15	-0.16	0.76	-0.03	-0.04
Court	0.1	0.47	0.03	0.61	0.14	-0.09	0.55	0.09	0.01	0.04	0.69	-0.07	0.2	0.43	0.03
National government	0.6	0.25	-0.05	0.26	0.59	-0.03	-0.06	0.84	0.01	0.78	0.16	-0.11	0.88	-0.05	-0.02
Political parties	0.95	-0.22	0.09	-0.16	0.86	0.08	-0.16	0.85	0.06	0.94	-0.21	0.13	0.78	-0.03	0.02
Parliament	0.84	-0.01	0.01	-0.07	0.86	0.06	0.08	0.71	-0.02	0.78	-0.03	0.12	0.77	-0.01	0.05
Civil service	0.64	0.11	-0.05	0.42	0.33	0.01	0.48	0.34	-0.13	0.19	0.55	-0.01	0.37	0.37	0.03
Military	-0.03	0.76	-0.07	0.65	0.03	-0.02	0.78	-0.17	-0.07	-0.01	0.73	-0.12	0.04	0.53	-0.09
Police	-0.04	0.78	-0.08	0.72	0	-0.08	0.78	-0.03	-0.06	-0.1	0.77	0.02	-0.02	0.73	-0.04
Local govenment	0.11	0.6	0.02	0.7	0.02	0.05	0.62	0.01	0.06	0.03	0.53	0.21	-0.06	0.78	-0.03
Newspaper	-0.02	-0.05	0.99	0.18	-0.08	0.78	0.05	-0.03	0.81	-0.05	-0.02	0.91	-0.05	-0.06	1
Television	0.03	0.01	0.68	-0.09	0.12	0.74	-0.08	0.02	0.82	0.02	-0.1	0.8	0.06	0.01	0.66
Election commission	-0.06	0.62	0.06	0.59	-0.05	0.09	0.54	-0.01	0.06	0.02	0.49	0.24	-0.03	0.69	-0.01
NGOs	-0.02	0.3	0.22	0.5	-0.08	0.11	0.27	0.04	0.18	0.02	0.22	0.31	-0.09	0.44	0.13
SS loadings	2.41	2.34	1.48	2.94	2.50	1.27	2.47	2.50	1.35	2.72	2.65	1.76	2.77	2.41	1.44
Proportion Var	0.20	0.20	0.12	0.23	0.19	0.10	0.19	0.19	0.10	0.21	0.20	0.14	0.21	0.19	0.11
Cumulative Var	0.20	0.40	0.52	0.23	0.42	0.52	0.19	0.38	0.49	0.21	0.41	0.55	0.21	0.40	0.51

SS loadings: Sum of squares of loadings
Source: Asian Barometer Survey. Author prepared.

Social Tolerance

Social tolerance is important in the practice of democracy in that heterogeneity, mutual tolerance, and discussion and consensus-building among diverse citizens are at the core of "making democracy work" (the title of Putnam's (1993) book on Italian democracy). It can be conceptualized as the perceived range of permissible heterogeneity of others in general interpersonal communication. More specifically, social tolerance concerns whether citizens perceive themselves to be free to dissent from others in their own interpersonal context.

Since the second wave, there has been a single measurement of the concept of social tolerance, "Would you have difficulty conversing with your friends or coworkers about politics if you had differing opinions?" Though the question uses "about politics," respondents are supposed to talk about it in a daily social environment. Then it is named "social" tolerance and is distinguished from "political" tolerance, which is a tolerable attitude under the given "political institutional context" defined in the next section. As shown in Figure 13.1, more than half of Japanese people are tolerant of opposing opinions, with some decline in tolerance between 2011 and 2016. In 2019, the direction of change reversed but did not return to its previous level, although in general the change is not large.

Figure 13.1 Social Tolerance (2007-2019)

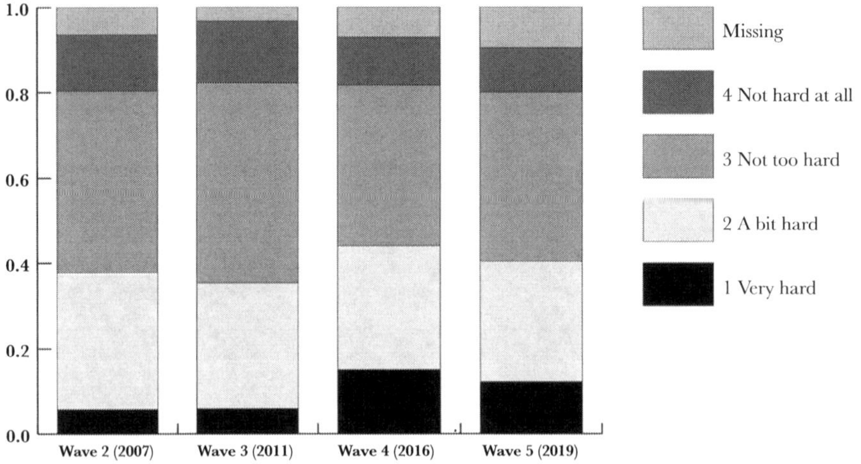

Source: Asian Barometer Survey. Author prepared.

Political Tolerance

In contrast with social tolerance, political tolerance is conceptualized as the perceived permissible heterogeneity of others in the institutional setting to which one belongs, in this chapter, Japan. Political tolerance is measured as the degree to which citizens perceive themselves free to express their opinions without fear or to participate in any group or organization without fear in a given political institutional setting, i.e., perceived formal degree of permissiveness of expressing oneself freely. In other words, this is the perceived tolerable range of actions concerning citizens' political creeds or voluntary affiliation. As shown in Figure 13.2,[2] on a 10-point scale (the summed mean of two variables), the Japanese have remained basically politically tolerant, although not sufficiently strongly in reference to the midpoint (5.5), over recent years.

Figure 13.2 Political Tolerance (2007-2019)

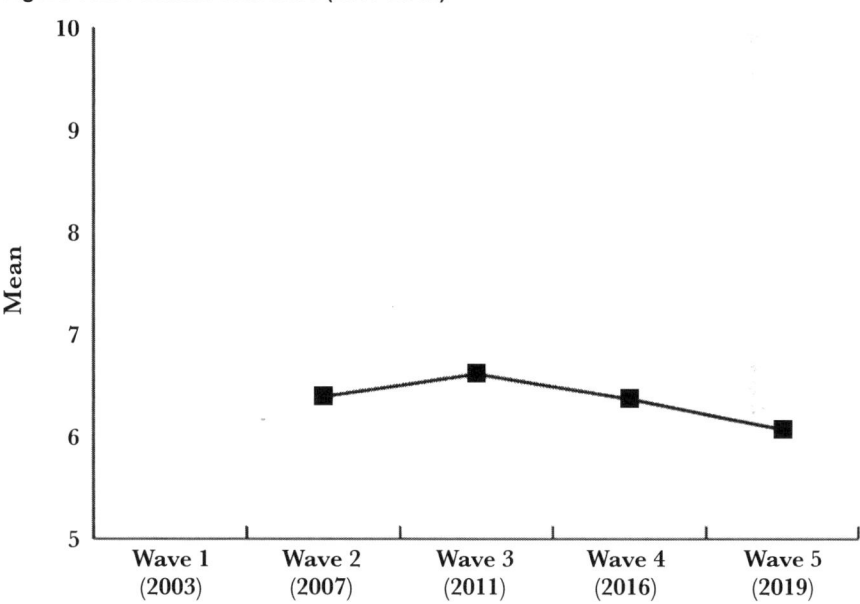

Source: Asian Barometer Survey. Author prepared.

Political Participation

The ABS measured a variety of activities related to political participation. We trace those that have been consistent over the five waves.

Figure 13.3 shows the proportions of the answers for five types of participation. As can be seen, trends in political participation have changed little, and they have remained low for 20 years in Japan. Involvement in local issues scored highest, followed by contact with politically powerful figures. The lowest frequency was observed in participation in demonstrations or protest marches.

Figure 13.3 Political Participation (2003-2019)

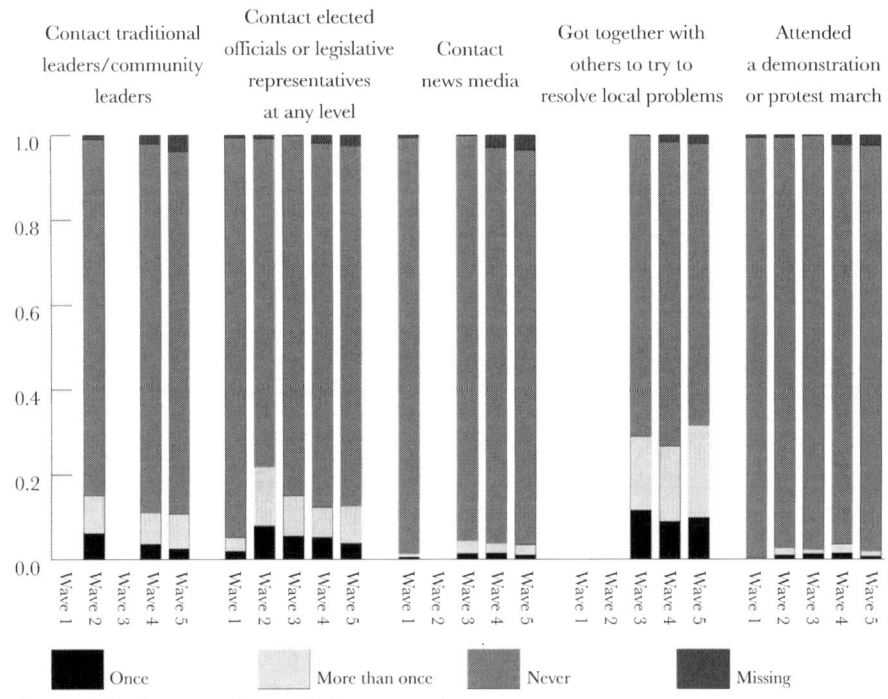

Source: Asian Barometer Survey. Author prepared.

Political Efficacy

In addition to actual involvement in politics by participation, citizens' perceived ability to influence politics—i.e., political efficacy—is essential for democracy to function. As previous studies have pointed out, political efficacy is divided into two dimensions: internal and external.

Political efficacy is measured using three items in the ABS: (E1) internal efficacy 1: "I think I have the ability to participate in politics," (E2) internal efficacy 2: "Sometimes politics and government seem so complicated that a person like me can't really understand what is going on," and (E3) external efficacy: "You can generally trust the people who run our government to do what is right." (If we focus on the word "trust," this question (E3) may be taken as a measure of "political trust," but it can also be read as a measure of the government's responsiveness to the will of the people in that "the people in charge of the government are doing the right thing by reflecting the will of the people," in other words, external efficacy.)

Figure 13.4 shows the mean scores of each variable on a four-point response scale; higher scores indicate greater political efficacy.[3] Although the ability perceived by Japanese people fluctuates somewhat, the general level of both aspects of efficacy is not high, i.e., below the midpoint (2.5). E2 (scale reversed) has been relatively stable for 20 years. On the other hand, E1 and E3 have changed in opposite directions in 2019. Scores on E1, which measures internal political efficacy, increased in the fifth wave. In contrast, those on E3, measuring external political efficacy, increased until the fourth wave but fell in the fifth wave.

Figure 13.4 Internal and External Political Efficacy (2003-2019)

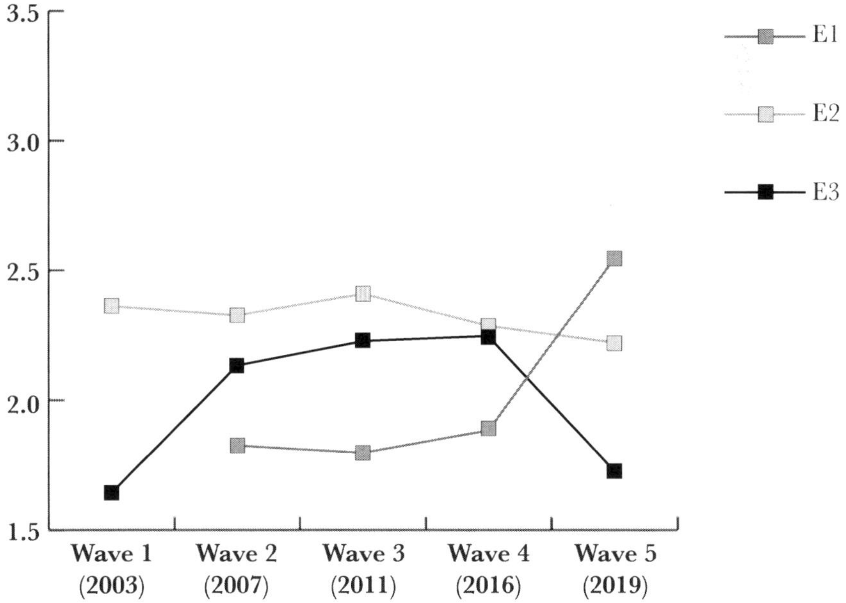

Source: Asian Barometer Survey. Author prepared.

Preference for Democracy

In the ABS, several different aspects of preference for democracy have been explored. Here we focus on three aspects: preference for democracy or authoritarianism, perception of democratic capability, and perception of the importance of democracy and economic growth.

Figure 13.5 shows that throughout the past two decades, Japan has been dominated by democracy supporters rather than authoritarians. Furthermore, Figure 13.6 shows that they also tend to rate democracy highly in terms of its capacity as a political system.

On the other hand, according to Figure 13.7, their opinions on the relationship between democracy and economic growth are roughly evenly divided. Although the pattern shows relative stability, economic growth was emphasized more strongly around the beginning of the 21st century. However, the emphasis changed slowly to democracy with an exception in 2011 (the third wave), when the survey was conducted after the Great East Japan Earthquake, an event that caused not only a disaster but also huge economic damage.

Figure 13.5 Preference for Democracy: Democracy/Authoritarianism (2003-2019)

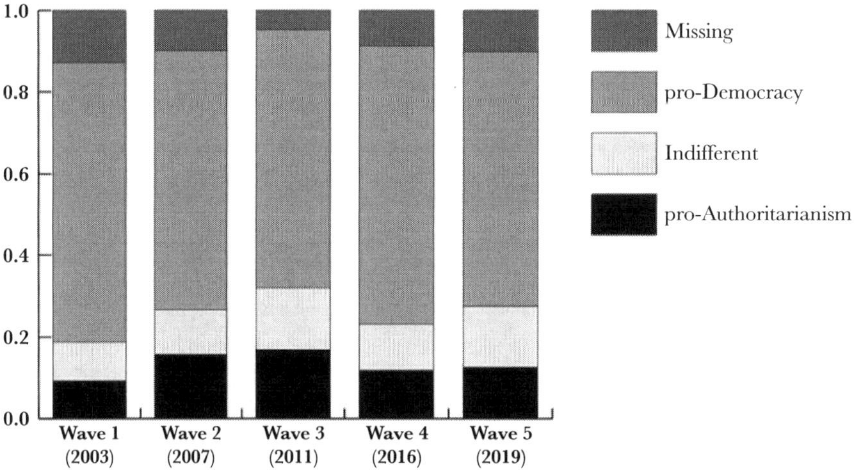

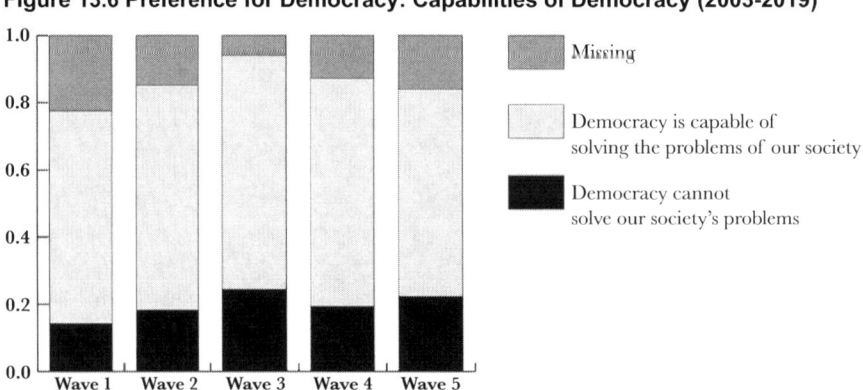

Source: Asian Barometer Survey. Author prepared.

Figure 13.6 Preference for Democracy: Capabilities of Democracy (2003-2019)

Source: Asian Barometer Survey. Author prepared.

Figure 13.7 Preference for Democracy: Economic Development vs. Democracy (2003-2019)

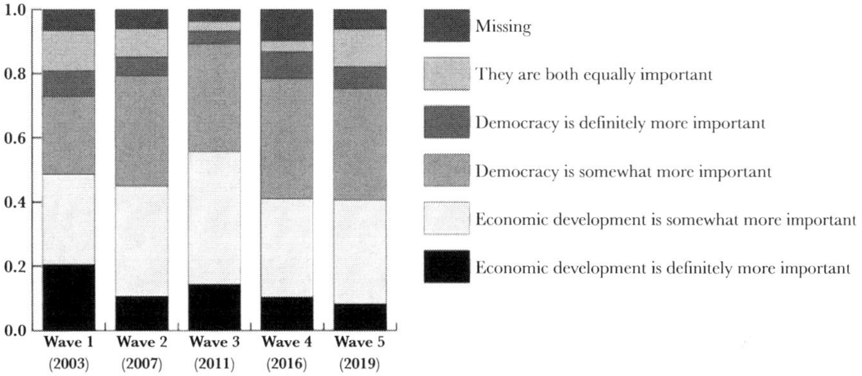

Source: Asian Barometer Survey. Author prepared.

Asian Values and Differences in Countries/Regions

Two dimensions of Asian values have been consistently observed in the five waves of the ABS throughout the country and regions covered, i.e., far beyond the geographical area of the Confucian tradition. These value orientations are found in both public and private aspects of Asian citizens' lives.

One dimension is a value orientation that emphasizes vertical social relationships (the vertical emphasis). Those who support this value are oriented toward accepting that those higher in the social hierarchy behave authoritatively and protectively toward those in lower positions. This is maintained because the relationship is thought to be reciprocal, in the sense that the superior (claims to) protects the inferior, and the inferior respects the superior and behaves accordingly.

The other dimension is a value orientation toward harmonious social relationships (the harmony orientation). Those who support this value are oriented toward emphasizing consensus or maintaining social harmony even in cases of potential conflict or disagreement.

All five waves of the ABS between 2001 and 2019 had several common questions on Asian values regarding private and social lives. Some variables were not measured in all five waves, and as the data from the second wave to the fifth wave will be the focus of this chapter (because of the main dependent variables), we show data from the second wave to the fifth wave here.

First, we examine the private aspect of Asian values. We have two questions on the vertical emphasis (on a four-point scale) throughout the four waves: "Even if parents' demands are unreasonable, children should still do what they ask"; and

"As a student, one should not question the authority of one's teacher." We had two questions on the harmony orientation: "For the sake of the family, the individual should put his personal interests second"; and "A person should not insist on his own opinion if his coworkers disagree with him."[4] Figure 13.8 shows the spread of responses from different countries on these two dimensions.

Figure 13.8 Scatterplots of Private Asian Values (2006-2019)[5]

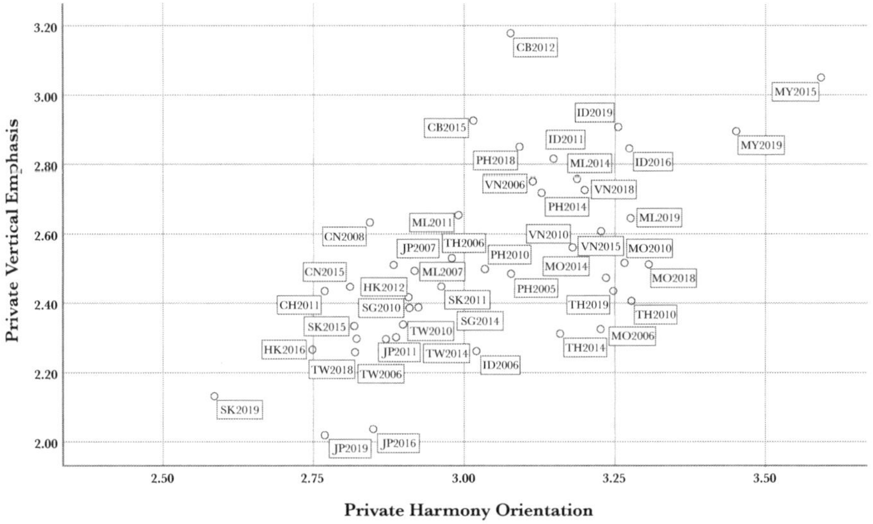

Source: Asian Barometer Survey. Author prepared.

Next, we examine the public aspect of Asian values. All four waves of the ABS have six questions on this aspect. A factor analysis revealed two dimensions corresponding to the vertical emphasis and the harmony orientation[6] Those that loaded highly on the vertical orientation consisted of the following items: "Government leaders are like the head of a family. We should all follow their decisions," "The government should decide whether certain ideas should be allowed to be discussed in society," "When judges decide important cases, they should accept the view of the executive branch," and "If we have political leaders who are morally upright, we can let them decide everything." Those questions with high factor loadings for harmony orientation were: "The harmony of the community will be disrupted if people are divided into many groups," "If the government is constantly checked by the legislature, it cannot possibly accomplish great things," and "If people have too many different ways of thinking, society will be chaotic."[7] Figure 13.9 shows the positions of countries and regions on these two dimensions.

Both figures clearly reveal that Japanese citizens, in a sense, remain outliers, especially those in the lower positions of vertical orientation in the public value sphere. On the other hand, in the private value sphere, their value orientation moved between the second wave and the fifth wave, from somewhat near the central position in Asia to an outlier, especially concerning the vertical emphasis value.

Figure 13.9 Scatterplots of Public Asian Values (2006-2019)

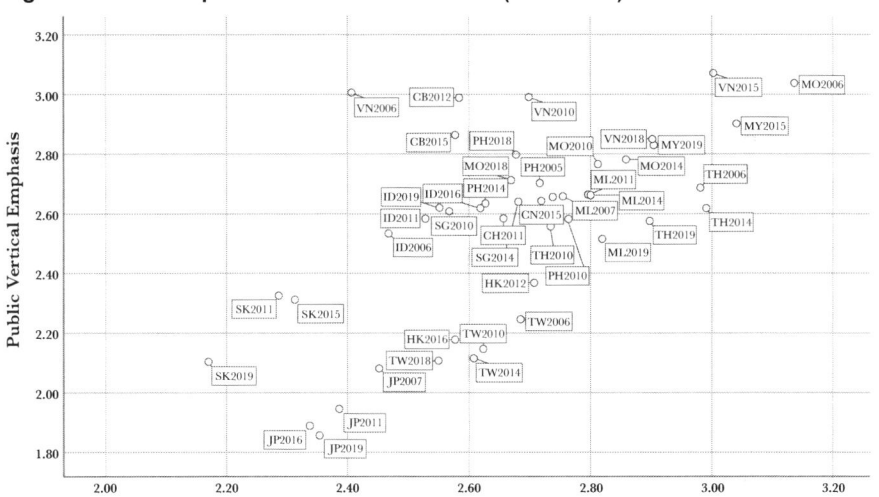

Source: Asian Barometer Survey. Author prepared.

The Values of Diversity and Tolerance

Paying full respect to the diversity of other citizens in one's society is closely interlinked with the basic values of liberal democracy. The values emphasize consensus-building through mutual exchange, discussion, and reconciliation of heterogeneous ideas and opinions expressed freely without fear of oppression. This is reflected in studies on liberal democracy from the viewpoint of social capital. These studies have remarked on the importance of tolerance for diversity or heterogeneity developed in horizontal social networks with mutual trust among citizens.

The political-cultural context of Asia, i.e., cultures that emphasize the values of hierarchical social relationships (vs. horizontal ones) and oriented toward homogeneity (vs. heterogeneity or diversity) may not be compatible with social capital theory, which could be bad news for liberal democracy.

Thus, to examine the possibility of incompatibility of the Asian political culture with liberal democracy and whether the Japanese are unusual Asian citizens as was discussed by authors such as Huntington (1996) and as has seen in the outlier positions of Japanese Asian value preferences in Figure 13.8 and 13.9, we explore the determinants of two dimensions of attitudes toward tolerance: acceptance of heterogeneity in interpersonal social networks (social tolerance) and acceptance of heterogeneity under given political institutions (political tolerance). This point is socially important in analyses with Japan as the focus. While moving away from Asian values, Japanese people have been considered to be socially and politically intolerant, which leads to their "unhappy life." One of the reasons why Japan's happiness ranked only 58th out of 156 countries in the World Happiness Report (2019; the year in which the ABS5 Japan survey was conducted) is reported to be due to their low tolerance (92nd: 32nd out of 36 OECD countries).

The Concept of Tolerance: Original Formulation

There is a well-known measure of tolerance created by Sullivan, Piereson, and Marcus (1982). Gibson (2013, 46) explains: "This technique allows respondents to pick the groups about which the tolerance questions are asked. Interviewees are instructed to identify their most disliked group(s) from a list provided to them. The tolerance questions are then tailored to the group the respondents identify as their foremost political opponents."

This technique is problematic, as shown in our 2009 article (Ikeda and Richey 2009). Sullivan's measure is based on a presumption of trust in the political institutions of the country. That is, it presupposes that the perceived robustness of the institution relates to whether it enables tolerance of the public actions of extremist groups.

Dual Faces of Tolerance

To define the tolerance concept systematically, we argue that human behavior has two types of social constraint: interpersonal and institutional (Ikeda 2007, Ikeda and Richey 2009). Based on these two types of constraint, there are two faces of tolerance: social tolerance and political tolerance.

As was mentioned above, social tolerance is derived from a perceived range of permissible heterogeneity in others in the context of interpersonal constraints. This does not presuppose institutional support but is based on personal trust for others so that a person can allow others to differ from themselves (in terms of viewpoints, opinions, etc.) as long as they can trust them.

On the other hand, Sullivan contends that political tolerance concerns a perceived permissible range of heterogeneity for others in one's institutional setting. This presupposes confidence in the given institution, such as a government or legal system. A person can be tolerant (or "put up with" something, in Sullivan's words) as long as the person has confidence in the given institution (e.g., in its ability to control extremists). We argue that political tolerance is influenced more by the public value orientation of citizens as it is more abstract in nature or is experienced less directly than social or personal constraints.

Hypotheses on Social/Political Tolerance
Hypotheses on Social Tolerance

Social tolerance will be constrained by one's real social network relationships. Then, in the Asian style of social relationships (which are compatible with Asian values), i.e., vertical/harmony-oriented social networks (rather than values), social tolerance will be reduced. Diversity of opinions and viewpoints is likely to be suppressed in these types of social networks.

Hypotheses on Political Tolerance

Political tolerance is rooted in the perception of confidence in a given institution so that it will be affected by value orientation. Thus, citizens who have a stronger Asian value orientation—i.e., a vertical/harmony orientation—will have less political tolerance for others' heterogeneous or diverse viewpoints.

Research Question (RQ) on Japanese Positions

Ikeda's analyses of the so-called "peculiarity" of Japanese political culture (2019, Chapter 4) revealed that while Japanese citizens are influenced by Asian values in a similar way to other Asian countries in regard to general trust and political participation (as dependent variables, i.e., they are constrained by harmony orientation and vertical emphasis), they deviate from other Asians in regard to institutional trust and evaluation of democracy, showing a tendency to follow the predictions of liberal democracy. The former values seem constrained by social context (with an Asian background), but the latter are influenced by the formal postwar institutional context, which gave Japan the longest liberal democratic history in Asia.

In line with these findings, we wonder whether (1) political tolerance is more easily predicted from westernized liberal democracy because of its institutional nature, whereas (2) social tolerance will be influenced by the Asian context because it occurs in people's social networks. This RQ is important in reference to the arguments concerning the conflict between Asian values and Western values in Japanese citizens presented in the beginning of this chapter.

Data and Measures

We use two survey datasets. The first is the merged dataset of the second to the fifth wave of the ABS, as the tolerance measures were only used in these waves. This includes eight surveys in the second wave, 13 in the third wave, 14 in the fourth wave, and 10 in the fifth wave.[8] The merged dataset consists of 45 surveys. The second dataset is from the fifth wave of the ABS, as the fifth wave dataset has variables on the Asian style of social relationships, which were not measured in the first four waves (10 countries and regions in the current analyses).

Measures of Tolerance
Tolerance Measures in the Second to the Fifth Wave of the ABS

In the ABS surveys, social tolerance and political tolerance are defined and measured as described above. Figure 13.10 shows a scatterplot of the two faces of tolerance using the second to fifth wave datasets. The Japanese are relatively high in political tolerance, but low in social tolerance.

Figure 13.10 Scatterplot of Social Tolerance and Political Tolerance (2007-2019)

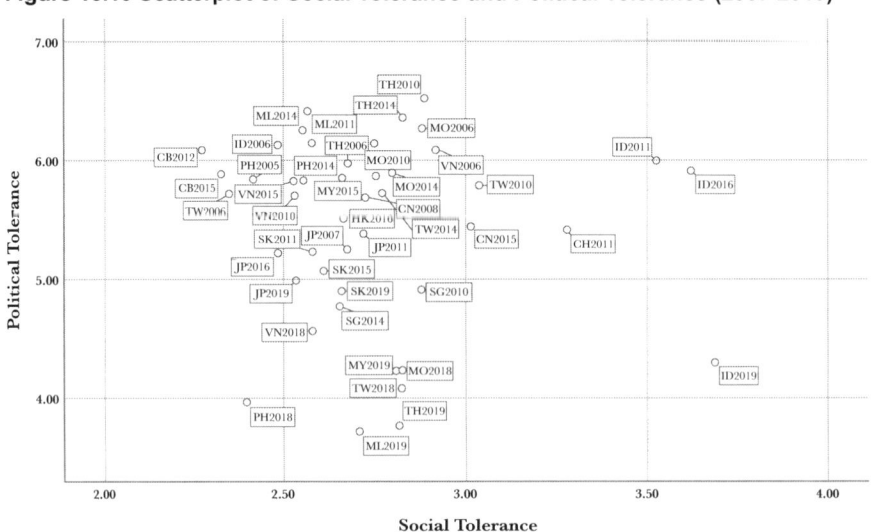

Source: Asian Barometer Survey. Author prepared.

Specific Social Network Characteristics and Measures in the Fifth Wave

The fifth wave includes two new measures of social network characteristics, network hierarchy perception and network heterogeneity perception. Using these variables, we were able to test the hypothesis on social tolerance.

The measurement proceeded as follows. After inquiring about the network size of the given respondent pool (number of people with whom the respondent has contact on weekdays), we asked: "Which of the following best describes your relations with most of your social contacts?" (the network hierarchy question). The result shows the dominance of the horizontal social network as shown below (%s are averages of W5 participant countries). However, about a seventh of respondents are in an interpersonal hierarchical context.

1. Most people's social status is higher than yours.   15.0%
2. Most people's social status is lower than yours.   7.6%
3. Most people's social status is equal to yours.   72.9% (DK/NA 4.5%)[9]

Then we asked, "Which of the following best describes the political views of the people with whom you have frequent contact?" (the network homogeneity/ heterogeneity question). The result shows that four out of 10 people have contact with politically heterogeneous others, and one out of four with like-minded others.

1. Virtually all of them have views similar to mine.   6.9%
2. A lot of them have views similar to mine.   19.7%
3. Only some of them have views similar to mine.   26.0%
4. Most of them have views different from mine.   13.3%
5. I don't know much about their political views.   27.3% (DK/NA 6.8%)[10]

Analyses
HLM Analysis of Political Tolerance (ABS2-5)

To gain insights into how political and social tolerance works in the Asian context as well as to examine whether Japanese are different from other Asians, we set the following independent variables at Level 1 (the individual level) in an HLM (Hierarchical Linear Modeling).

- Asian value orientations: vertical emphasis and harmony orientation[11]
- Social capital related variables: generalized trust,[12] personal trust,[13] social network size, social participation[14]
- Interest in politics, frequency of political discussions in daily life, internal and external political efficacy

- Demographic variables: living in an urban area, employment (dummy), gender, age, and education

Level 2 variables (45 country/region survey);

- For the intercept: Asian value orientations (mean of each survey), GDP per capita, Freedom House score, Japan dummy
- For the Asian value orientations: Japan dummy

As Table 13.2 shows, one of social capital variables, personal trust, was positively correlated with political tolerance, as were the political efficacy variables, both of which are as expected.

Table 13.2 HLM Analysis of Political Tolerance (2007-2019)[15]

	Coefficient	t-ratio
Level 1		
General trust	0.018	0.553
Personal trust	0.023	2.745**
Social network size	0.013	1.413
Interest in politics	-0.011	-0.843
Degree of political discussion	0.002	0.114
Internal political efficacy	0.021	1.889
External political efficacy	0.132	3.004**
Social participation	0.023	1.806
Public vertical emphasis value	0.256	4.046***
Japan dummy	-0.092	-0.570
Public harmony orientation value	0.092	3.515***
Japan dummy	-0.252	-2.584*
Living in urban area	0.012	0.378
Employed	-0.054	-2.336*
Gender (1 = male, 2 = female)	-0.006	-0.295
Age	0.003	1.851
Education	-0.013	-2.605**
Level 2		
Public vertical emphasis value	-0.309	-0.582
Public harmony orientation value	0.963	2.157*
GDP per capita	-8E-06	-1.266
Freedom House score	-0.064	-1.112
Japan dummy	-0.170	-0.560
Intercept	5.499	35.11***
No. of observations		45180
No. of (survey) countries		45

Note: Significance level p<0.05*, p<0.01**, p<0.001***

However, contrary to our prediction, both the Asian values, i.e. vertical emphasis and harmony orientation, positively affected political tolerance at Level 1 (and Level 2 for the harmony orientation). The effects of the Japanese dummy variables at Level 1 reduce tolerance in terms of harmony orientation, which shows Japanese citizens' opinions are more attuned to Putnamian ideas than to an Asian value disposition, though not strongly. The post hoc simulation depicted in Figure 13.11 (a), (b) clearly reveals that in terms of the role of harmony orientation (regression slope lines), Japanese people are different from those in most other Asian countries. On the other hand, the Japanese vertical emphasis value did not show any consistent pattern.

Figure 13.11 Post-hoc Simulation of Asian Values and Political Tolerance: Regression Slopes

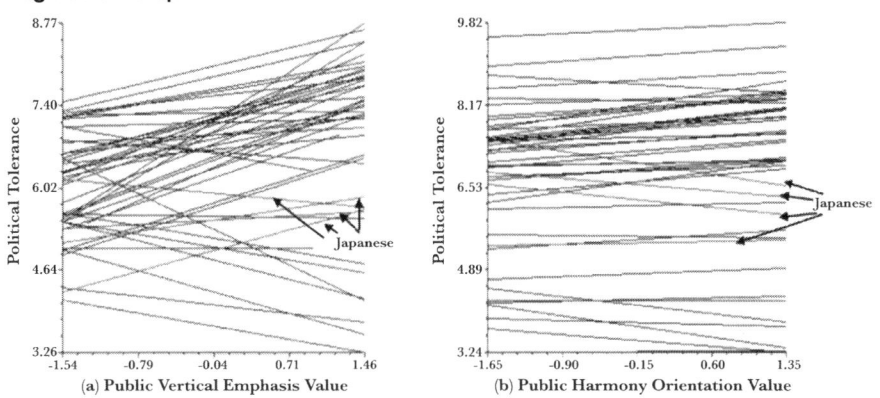

Source: Asian Barometer Survey. Author prepared.

Analysis of Social Tolerance (ABS5)

The analysis was conducted using the same variables as in Table 13.2, except that we added social network property variables.

As shown in Table 13.3, the social capital variables of general trust, personal trust, and social network size were strongly and positively correlated with social tolerance, as expected. On the other hand, talking about politics in daily life suppresses social tolerance, suggesting that politics is a source of possible conflict.

Table 13.3 HLM Analysis of Social Tolerance (2018-2019)

	Coefficient	t-ratio
Level 1		
General trust	0.08	3.68***
Personal trust	0.02	3.23***
Social network size	0.05	6.12***
Interest in politics	-0.02	-1.70
Degree of political discussion	-0.04	-2.23*
Internal political efficacy	0.00	-0.10
External political efficacy	0.01	1.01
Social participation	-0.01	-1.42
Private vertical emphasis value	-0.07	-2.47*
Japan dummy	0.02	0.22
Private harmony orientation value	0.01	0.32
Japan dummy	-0.04	-0.33
Vertical social network	0.01	0.43
Japan dummy	-0.18	-1.72
Social network homogeneity	0.04	2.86*
Japan dummy	-0.01	-0.20
Living in urban area	0.01	0.69
Employed	0.04	2.04*
Gender (1 = male, 2 = female)	-0.09	-4.83***
Age	0.00	2.38*
Education	0.01	2.60**
Level 2		
Private vertical emphasis value	0.22	0.41
Private harmony orientation value	1.11	1.55
GDP per capita	0.00	0.40
Freedom House score	-0.11	-2.02
Japan dummy	-0.22	-0.52
Intercept	2.88	26.54***
No. of observations		9583
No. of (survey) countries		10

Note: Significance level p<0.05*, p<0.01**, p<0.001***

As for the effects of social-value orientations, private vertical emphasis was negatively correlated with social tolerance. In contrast, social network homogeneity promoted social tolerance, but the effect of network verticality was insignificant. What we expected was that rather than value orientation, real network properties—specifically real-life social-relational properties—lead to intolerance, which was not supported: (1) the personal vertical emphasis value was significant (though the sign was negative and consistent with the Asian value hypothesis on the problematic nature of the value for tolerance), and (2) social network homogeneity was (unexpectedly) positive and significant.

Looking at the effects of Japanese dummy variables related to Asian values and social networks, we found only quasi-significance concerning vertical social networks. As shown in Figure 13.12 (a), (b), Japanese people are slightly more intolerant when the vertical (hierarchical) social relationship is stronger compared with other Asian people (a). However, we observe no clear effect of social network homogeneity (b).

Figure 13.12 Post-hoc Simulation of Asian Values and Social Tolerance: Regression Slopes

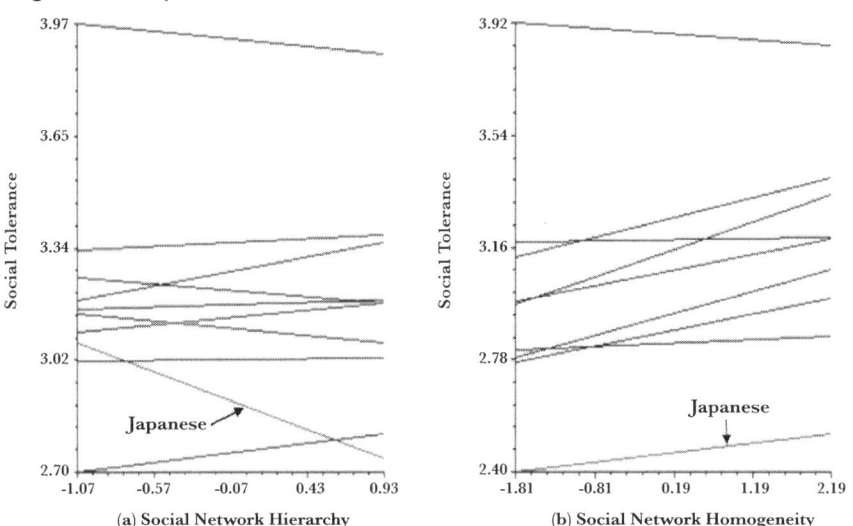

(a) Social Network Hierarchy   (b) Social Network Homogeneity

Source: Asian Barometer Survey. Author prepared.

Discussion: Implications for Diversity

Unexpectedly, concerning political tolerance derived from liberal democratic ideals, two types of public Asian values positively promoted tolerance. Recall that this type of tolerance is the perceived freedom of citizens in their own institutional setting. The results could be interpreted to mean that although further investigation is required, those who have value orientations consistent with the institutional cultural setting, i.e., those with a stronger vertical emphasis or who prefer harmony, perceive more freedom to exist, or judge the system to be more politically tolerant. In contrast, in terms of the harmony orientation for Japanese, the effect was reversed to some extent, i.e., consistent with liberal democratic prediction. No such pattern existed for vertical emphasis and the intercept for the Japan dummy was nonsignificant—they were no different from other Asians. In this sense, Japanese are torn between the East and the West.

As for social tolerance, the value of private vertical emphasis generally worked against it, consistent with the Western expectation. However, the effect of social network homogeneity was again in the reverse direction from the theoretical expectation. Why? Although the extent of political discussions suppresses social tolerance (shown in Table 13.3), in a homogeneous social network, discussions with people of politically different ideas are promoted. This seems to indicate tolerance of small differences, i.e., the minimum extent of political conversation with homogeneous others is perceived to be socially tolerant of different ideas. In other words, when citizens understand their social networks to be homogeneous, they can generously allow (slightly) heterogeneous others to talk politics, whereas if the networks are more heterogeneous, they cannot talk freely as it is risky to do so. This is very different from the ideal of social capital.

In conclusion, for the Japanese tolerance discussed in the RQ, we found patterns that were partially consistent with previous findings by Ikeda (2019); political tolerance was affected by a liberal democratic institutional context, whereas social tolerance seemed to be affected by social network properties with Asian cultural traditions.

Finally, in the larger Asian context, given the eclectic findings regarding the Japanese presented here, we wonder whether vertical emphasis and the harmony orientation could coexist with the idea of diversity. In other words, although we are apprehensive of the problems of vertical emphasis and harmony orientation, we ask is it possible to construct some standards or norms to allow more diversity within Asian cultural traditions? The Japanese case could provide a useful example of this for those who are citizens of Asian cultural tradition.

Notes

1. R version 4.0.2 (R core team, 2020) was used for the analysis in this section. The Psych and GPArotation packages were used for factor analyses. Factor analysis was performed with maximum-likelihood estimation and promax rotation.

2. In Wave 1, we had the same questions on political tolerance. However, the context of response was different, i.e. questions were asked to compare the political tolerance compared with the one before WWII. Then we are not able to show the mean score in Wave 1.

3. E1 was in the first wave survey as well. The reason why it was not shown relates to the context of the question. Respondents were asked to compare current perceived efficacy with that from before WWII.

4. Some waves had other related questions. We consistently observed these two dimensions in private life-value orientations.

5. Legend: JP: Japan, HK: Hong Kong, SK: South Korea, CH: Mainland China, MO: Mongolia, PH: Philippines, TW: Taiwan, TH: Thailand, ID: Indonesia, SG: Singapore, VN: Vietnam, CB: Cambodia, ML: Malaysia, MY: Myanmar.

6. Maximum likelihood method with varimax rotation was used. The Pearson correlation between the two dimensions was .166.

7. Because there is a 10 percent increase in the size of the target sample, if we use average values for those two dimensions (i.e., if there are missing answers, we calculate the average without them) instead of using factor loadings (i.e., no missing answers for relevant variables), we used the average values. The correlation of the average variable scores with factors is 0.7-0.8, which is sufficient.

8. Five survey datasets from the second wave could not be included in the analyses owing to the lack of the social tolerance variable in Hong Kong, Korea, Singapore, and Cambodia, and the lack of the external efficacy variable in China. In mid-2020, 12 fifth wave datasets were available, but we will not use the Indian or Australian data for analytical consistency. In addition, the Australian data do not have the social network property variables relevant to this chapter.

9. Percentages are from all 10 countries used in this paper.

10. To conduct multivariate analyses, we re-coded the network hierarchy question to set the responses in the first category at 3, those in the second at 1, and the others to 2. In a similar way, the responses to the network heterogeneity question were re-coded as follows: the responses in the first category were set to 5, those in the second to 4, those in the third to 2, those in the fourth to 1, and others (including those in the fifth) to 3.

11. Taking into account the consistency of the social context, two dimensions of public aspect of Asian values were set as independent variables when the dependent variable was political tolerance, and two dimensions of private aspect of Asian values were set as independent variables when the dependent variable was social tolerance. This is because the former is tolerance related to institutional constraints and the latter is tolerance in everyday interpersonal constraints.

12. We set the value of the answer "Most people can be trusted" to 2, and "You must be very careful in dealing with people" to 1.

13. Sum of trust in relatives, neighbors, and "other people you interact with."

14. Number of voluntary organizations to which the respondent belongs.

15. Table 13.2 and Table 13.3 show only fixed effects. Their random effects for the intercept as well as main Asian value variables and social network perceptions are statistically significant except vertical social network perception in Table 13.3.

References

Gibson, J. L. 2013. "Measuring Political Tolerance and General Support for Pro-Civil Liberties Policies: Notes, Evidence, and Cautions." *Public Opinion Quarterly* 77 (S1): 45-68. Oxford: Oxford University Press. doi:10.1093/poq/nfs073.

Huntington, Samuel. 1996. *The Clash of Civilizations and the Remaking of World Order*. New York: Simon & Schuster.

Ikeda, Ken'ichi. 2007. *Seiji No Riariti to Shakai Shinri: Heisei Koizumi Seiji No Dainamikkusu = Political Reality and Social Psychology: The Dynamics of the Koizumi Years*. Tōkyō: Bokutakusha (In Japanese).

—. 2019. *Touchi No Fuan to Nihon Seiji No Riariti: Seikenkoutai Zengo No Teiryu To Kokusai Hikaku Bunmyaku = The Reality of Contemporary Japanese Politics and Anxiety over Governance: Factors for Incumbent Changes and Their International Context*. Tōkyō: Bokutakusha (In Japanese).

Ikeda, Ken'ichi, and Masaru Kohno. 2008. "Japanese Attitudes and Values toward Democracy." In *How East Asians View Democracy*, edited by Yun-han Chu, Larry Diamond, Andrew J. Nathan, and Doh Chull Shin, 188-219. New York: Columbia University Press.

Ikeda, Ken'ichi, and Sean Richey. 2009. "The Impact of Diversity in Informal Social Networks on Tolerance in Japan." *British Journal of Political Science* 39 (3): 655-668. https://ideas.repec.org/a/cup/bjposi/v39y2009i03p655-668_00.html.

Putnam, Robert. 1993. *Making Democracy Work: Civic Traditions in Modern Italy*. Princeton, N. J.: Princeton University Press.

Sullivan, John, James Piereson, and George E. Marcus. 1982. *Political Tolerance and American Democracy*. Chicago: The University of Chicago Press.

14 Australia Compared in the "Asian Century"
Jill Sheppard

Australia joined the Asian Barometer Survey (ABS) project in 2017, in the early years of what Australian Prime Ministers, international organizations, and commentators have called the "Asian Century." Certainly, economic trade patterns are converging on Asia (Wang 2019), but domestic politics in Australia are also intractably focused on our northern neighbors. Whether the issue is trade relations with China or negotiating maritime borders with Timor Leste, Australian domestic and foreign policies are intractably aligned with the region.

However, fully immersing ourselves in Asia is outside the comfort zone of many Australian citizens. In 2019, 21 percent of Australians believed that the country's relations with Asia had "gone too far;" 56 percent believed that relations were about right, and 22 percent that relations were not yet close enough (Cameron and McAllister 2020). Feelings toward Asia are marked by generational gaps: 48 percent of Australians between 18 and 24 years of age want closer relations with Asia, but only 28 percent of Australians aged 65 or older (and only 16 percent of those aged between 35 and 44) do.

Variation in attitudes toward Asia and the Asian Century mirror the diversity of Australian society. British settlement has shaped many of our political and social traditions, but at the 2016 Census of the Australian population, 28 percent of the country had been born overseas, and a further 21 percent had parents who were born overseas. Although British heritage dominates much of the country's political and social institutions, migration from Asia—particularly China and India —makes up an increasing proportion of Australia's population growth.

However, little research has explored how closely the attitudes of Australian citizens mirror those of citizens of Asian countries. Australia's entry to the ABS presents a new opportunity to both examine Australians' views toward culture, society, and democracy, and to compare those views across a range of east and south-east Asian countries. The Asian Barometer Survey (fifth wave) was conducted in Australia between October 2018 and January 2019, via a self-complete questionnaire taken either online or via hardcopy mail. The sampling frame was all registered addresses in Australia, with letters sent to all sampled households.

The response rate was 32 percent of all valid households, with a total of 1630 respondents. The final data are weighted by gender, education, age, internet and telephone access, and location.

This chapter provides an overview of cultural and political values in Australia, with an emphasis on intergenerational differences, as well as comparison with other ABS countries. Ultimately, it argues that Australian values are quite distinct from those of many Asian countries, but they closely resemble certain values emerging among young Taiwanese citizens. These common bonds represent an opportunity for both countries to learn from each other and collaborate on democratic design and reform. Second, the chapter finds that there are warning signs in Australians' democratic orientations, but that fundamentally they remain supportive of democratic institutions and processes. The largest challenge for Australian political leaders and policymakers is the large minority of Australians who equate democracy with social and economic equality, and the associated consequences for democratic support in times of crisis.

Australian Values

Liberal democracy is entrenched in Australian society, and values of individual liberty, rule of law, and egalitarianism inform the national identity. The Australian government requires new migrants to acknowledge understanding that:

> Australian society values respect for the freedom and dignity of the individual, freedom of religion, commitment to the rule of law, Parliamentary democracy, equality of men and women and a spirit of egalitarianism that embraces mutual respect, tolerance, fair play and compassion for those in need and pursuit of the public good; Australian society values equality of opportunity for individuals, regardless of their race, religion or ethnic background; the English language, as the national language, is an important unifying element of Australian society (Department of Home Affairs 2020).

Certainly, these values reflect how many Australians view their society. Former Prime Minister John Howard famously described his ideal Australia as "relaxed and comfortable" (see for example Brett 2005). An associated view of Australia—"associated with masculinity and sport, what might be seen as working-class activities (saying 'g'day', barbecues, beer-drinking, sports)" (Austin and Fozdar 2018)—has dominated the culture until recently, as younger generations have come to embrace more progressive, multicultural values.

"Traditional values" in the Australian context have reflected the British settler influence: horizontal egalitarianism is a central element, while vertical or intergenerational respect is secondary at best. Reverence for military achievements, and the associated traits of "physical prowess, bravery, stoicism in the face of adversity, mateship, anti-authoritarianism, innovation, and practicality" is common throughout Australian society, across all generations. The capacity for sport to provide a "level playing field" for Australians of all social classes, races, and backgrounds to compete speaks to the same set of values: in Australia, anyone can succeed (see for example Ward 2010).

Australian identity has rarely been associated with what might be considered Confucian values (Inglehart and Welzel 2005), or "paternalistic meritocracy" (Shin 2011). ABS data from 2018 allow us to examine, for the first time, whether values of paternalistic meritocracy are common among Australian residents and how they are distributed within the population. To begin, Figure 14.1 shows the level of agreement with key ABS measures capturing these values. Australians are most likely to agree with the statement that "when dealing with others, a person should not only focus on their own immediate interests but also plan for the future." Similarly, we see high rates of agreement that "developing a long-term relationship is more important than securing your immediate interests" and that "a person should not be preoccupied with temporary gains and losses." We might view these as reflective of an anti-hedonistic or short-term orientation.

Group harmony features prominently among Australians' values in the ABS: a majority of Australians express group-based values over individual ones. In total, 54 percent agree or strongly agree that individual interests could be sacrificed for the national interest, and 59 percent that they could be sacrificed for the group's collective interest. Two-thirds of all respondents agree that an individual should put individual interests aside for family interests.

Paternalistic values such as siding with one's mother in a dispute with a wife and preferring a male child over a female child are much less prevalent among Australians. Just under half (47 percent) agree that children should respect parents' unreasonable demands, 48 percent that students should not question their teachers' authority, and 63 percent agree that people should avoid conflict even in the face of disagreement. In contrast, they exhibit signs of more liberal meritocracy: only 21 percent agree with the statement that wealth and success (or poverty and failure) are determined by fate. This finding resonates with common Australian notions of egalitarianism and equality of opportunities (if not necessarily equality of outcomes).

Figure 14.1 Values of Paternalistic Meritocracy among Australians, Asian Barometer Survey (2018)

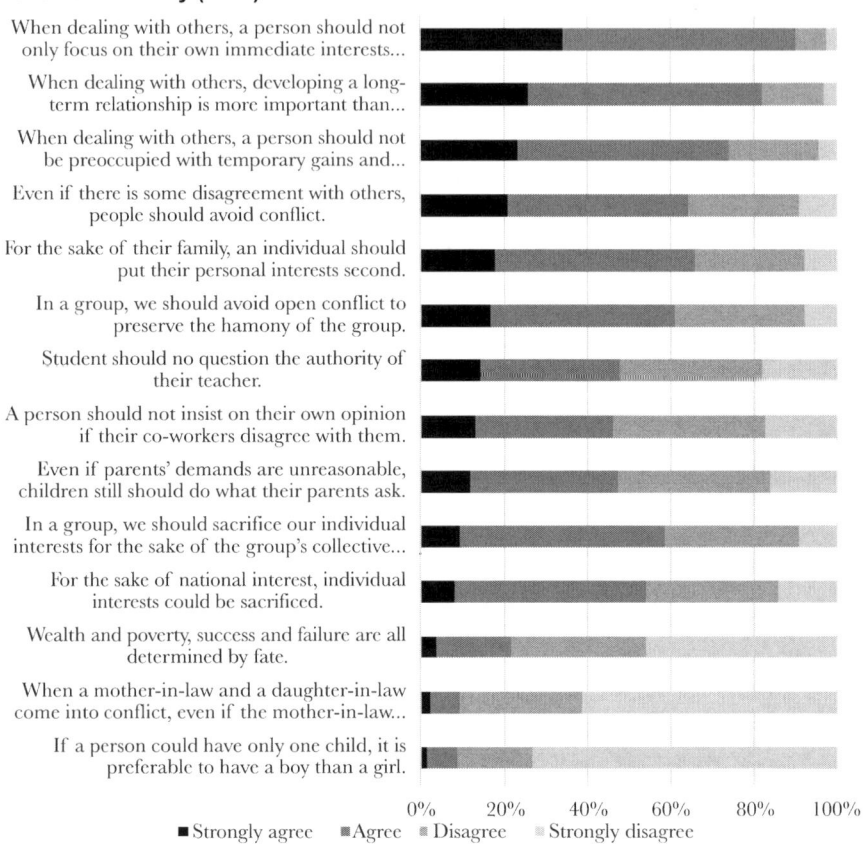

Table 14.1 Agreement with Statements among Australians (Percentage Respondents by Age Group), Asian Barometer Survey (2018)

	18-24	25-34	35-44	45-54	55-64	65-74	75+
When dealing with others, a person should not only focus on their own immediate interests but also plan for the future.	91	89	88	93	91	87	92
When dealing with others, developing a long-term relationship is more important than securing your immediate interests.	90	77	81	82	82	84	79
When dealing with others, a person should not be preoccupied with temporary gains and losses.	70	64	83	74	75	77	76
Even if there is some disagreement with others, people should avoid conflict.	71	56	60	61	60	75	80
For the sake of their family, an individual should put their personal interests second.	58	59	65	70	66	74	73
In a group, we should avoid open conflict to preserve the harmony of the group.	63	54	54	60	58	72	81
Students should not question the authority of their teacher.	29	33	53	52	52	62	62
A person should not insist on their own opinion if their co-workers disagree with them.	39	40	40	50	48	56	61
Even if parents' demands are unreasonable, children still should do what their parents ask.	28	38	53	47	51	58	67
In a group, we should sacrifice our individual interests for the sake of the group's collective interest.	60	49	64	59	59	63	61
For the sake of national interest, individual interests could be sacrificed.	48	51	58	47	57	57	64
Wealth and poverty, success and failure are all determined by fate.	28	20	19	16	17	27	36
When a mother-in-law and a daughter-in-law come into conflict, even if the mother-in-law is in the wrong, the husband should still persuade his wife to obey his mother.	11	6	7	9	8	13	16
If a person could have only one child, it is preferable to have a boy than a girl.	10	10	5	7	9	11	13

Source: Asian Barometer Survey. Author prepared.

Explicitly paternalistic attitudes show the largest variation by age group, among Australians (Table 14.1). Where only 29 percent of respondents aged between 18 and 24 agree that students should not question their teachers' authority, 62 percent of respondents aged 65 and over agree. Similarly, only 28 percent of the youngest respondents agree that children should accept their parents' unreasonable demands, compared with 67 percent of the oldest respondents. Young Australians are also much less likely to agree that they should avoid disagreements with co-workers. "Young people lack respect for authority" is not a particularly interesting finding. Indeed, these generational differences in attitudes to authority provide some support for the external validity of the ABS data. What is perhaps more striking is the lack of age-group differences in responses to the other measures of paternalistic meritocracy. While the oldest respondents are most likely to agree with paternalistic statements (e.g., that mothers take precedence over wives, or that a son if preferable to a daughter), the differences are minor and largely statistically insignificant. For the most part, there appears little difference in values among Australian adults of all ages.

Comparing the Australian results internationally, it is easiest if we treat these variables as one scale of paternalistic-meritocratic values. Although at face value, these measures seem to cluster around long-term interests, group harmony, paternalism, and meritocracy, the full battery of variables is a more reliable scale than any smaller sub-scales. Accordingly, we can combine the battery into a scale of paternalistic-meritocratic values with confidence that we are measuring a cohesive expression of values (Cronbach's alpha = 0.73).[1] The resulting additive scale is divided by 42 (the maximum value of the additive scale), to create a variable ranging from 0 to 1. The mean value of this variable (among Australian respondents) is 0.38, with a standard deviation of 0.12.

Among the first tranche of country studies in the fifth wave of the ABS, Australian respondents generally report the lowest rates of paternalistic meritocracy values (Figure 14.2), followed closely by Taiwan. This is as expected, given the earlier discussion about Australian national identity and strong cultural norms of egalitarianism and opportunity. However, there is a noticeable difference in the values of the youngest and oldest Taiwanese respondents, compared with very similar values among Australians of all ages. This may suggest that paternalistic values are rare and stable in Australia, but only emerging in Taiwan. Alternatively, it may represent a within-lifecycle phenomenon (rather than generational replacement), and that Taiwanese become more paternalistic as they age. These ABS data suggest that Australia is not so far removed from its democratic neighbors in east Asia.

Figure 14.2 Mean Paternalistic Meritocracy Values by Age Group (scaled from 0 to 1) in First Tranche of Country Studies, Asian Barometer Survey Fifth Wave (2018)

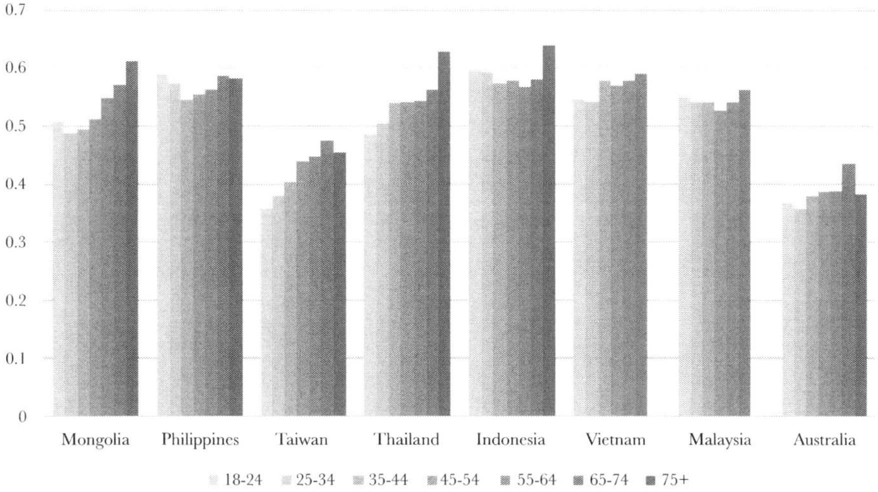

18-24   25-34   35-44   45-54   55-64   65-74   75+

Source: Asian Barometer Survey. Author prepared.

Democracy and Political Institutions

Australian democracy is very well entrenched, but the country has recently experienced some signs of the backsliding evident in other consolidated democratic systems. Since 2007, the Australian Election Study (AES) has found satisfaction with democracy has fallen from 86 percent to only 59 percent in 2019 (Cameron and McAllister 2020). The view that people in government can be trusted has fallen from 43 percent in 2007 to 25 percent in 2019. As of 2019, only 15 percent of Australians agree that politicians know what ordinary people think. The percentage of Australians who believe that government is run for a few big interests (rather than for all people) has increased from 38 percent in 2007 to 56 percent in 2019— the highest level since the AES began in 2019.

In this context, the ABS provides a deeper look at attitudes to democracy and political institutions in Australia. Although on the surface we might expect all Australians to be consistently democratic in their views, we know from existing evidence that democratic support is much more nuanced. Accordingly, I replicate Chu and Huang's (2010) typology of democratic orientations: consistent democrats, critical democrats, non-democrats, and superficial democrats. Following Chu and Huang, I create two scales of democratic orientation: democratic legitimacy and liberal-democratic values.

The legitimacy scale comprises four measures,[2] with a Cohen's alpha reliability score of 0.553. Those measures are whether democracy is always preferable to other kinds of government (three ordinal responses), whether democracy is always suitable for Australia (a ten-item scale), whether democracy is capable of solving Australia's problems (four ordinal responses), and whether democracy is more important than economic development (four ordinal responses). The scale was created by adding (positively scored) responses to all four questions, resulting in a variable ranging from four to 21. The median value is 17, and so to replicate Chu and Huang's dichotomous high/low measure of support for democratic legitimacy, scores 17 and over are coded as "high," and 16 and lower coded "low." The intention in this analysis is to create a benchmark of Australian data for future reference, not to compare Australian results to existing pan-Asian analyses.

The second measure in Chu and Huang's typology comprises questions of liberal democratic values. Seven questions make up this scale: whether government is like the head of a family and we should all follow it; whether the government should decide that certain ideas are allowed to be discussed in a society; whether the harmony of a society will be disrupted if people organize lots of groups; whether judges should accept the government's view in deciding important cases; whether government can achieve great things if constantly monitored by a parliament; whether morally sound leaders should be allowed to decide everything; and whether too many people deciding things will cause social chaos. Each variable has four possible ordinal responses, from "strongly agree" to "strongly disagree." The additive scale of these variables results in a measure of liberal democratic values ranging from 7 to 28. The scale is highly reliable with a Cohen's alpha of 0.82, and the median is 21. Accordingly, all respondents scoring 22 and higher are categorized as "high" on the liberal democratic scale, and all those scoring 21 and lower are categorized as "low," per the Chu and Huang model.

Following Chu and Huang (2010), I assign Australian respondents to categories in a two by two matrix of high and low legitimacy democrats, and high and low liberal democrats. The resulting distribution of democratic orientations is shown in Table 14.2. Among the four categories, most Australians are either consistent democrats (high on the liberal democratic scale and high on the democratic legitimacy scale) or non-democrats (low with regard to liberal democratic values, and with regard to democratic legitimacy). In fact, non-democrats are the biggest section of the population, comprising 33 percent of respondents.

Table 14.2 Democratic Orientations among Australians, Asian Barometer Survey (2018)

	Low liberal-democratic	High liberal-democratic
Low legitimacy	32.90%	16.90%
High legitimacy	19.80%	30.40%

Source: Asian Barometer Survey. Author prepared.

It is important to remember that these categories represent dichotomies within the Australian population. This does not suggest that 33 percent of Australians hate democracy and long for revolution; rather, it represents the distribution of democratic attitudes using median positions as a cut-off. It shows us that few Australians who espouse liberal democratic values without embracing legitimate democratic institutions (i.e., high liberal-democratic, but low legitimacy, or "critical democrats"): only 17 percent populate this category. Likewise, only 20 percent fall into the "superficial democrat" category: 20 percent report high orientations toward democratic legitimacy, but low liberal democratic values. We might describe these Australians as essentially authoritarian in their views toward democracy.

This analysis represents a benchmark from which to study future trends in democratic attitudes in Australia. Where Chu and Huang compare Asian states cross-sectionally, the most salient analysis of Australian democracy is probably longitudinal: assessing not how citizens of an established democracy compare with those of new and emerging democracies, but how they change over time. Indeed, Chu and Huang conduct some multi-wave analyses of their subject countries; this approach informs how we will monitor Australian opinion in future years.

In a similar vein, we can also examine how Australians view the concept of democracy in 2018. ABS data show that Australians believe the most essential elements of democracy are freedom from corruption, provision of basic necessities to citizens, and the ability to choose government via free and fair elections (see Figure 14.3). Close behind these are multi-party competition, freedom of speech, and the provision of certain public services (namely law and order and job opportunities).

While democratic processes are therefore considered the most essential to democracy, social and economic outcomes are also prominent in how Australians view democracy. The potential tension between democratic inputs and outputs, such as they are measured here, has not been closely examined in Australia. However, it is a common phenomenon throughout East Asian nations, and is widely viewed as a "weak" indication of democratic support: if support for democracy is dependent on social or economic outcomes, that support should decline in the face of economic recession, social unrest, or any number of other crises over which governments have limited control (see for example, Norris 2011).

Figure 14.3 Response to Four Questions Asking "If You Have to Choose from the Following, Which Would You Choose as the Most Essential Characteristic of a Democracy?"

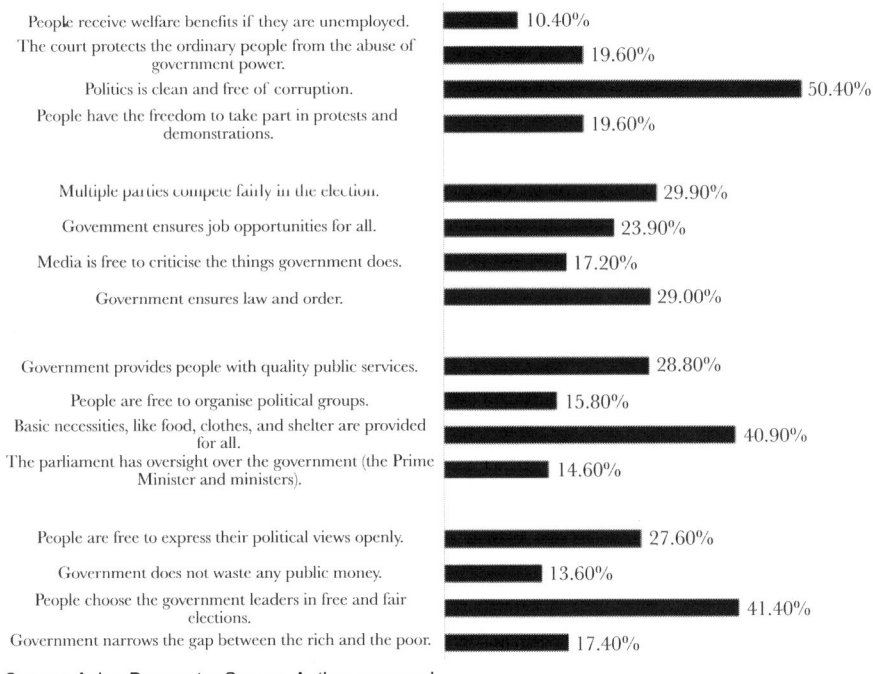

People receive welfare benefits if they are unemployed.	10.40%
The court protects the ordinary people from the abuse of government power.	19.60%
Politics is clean and free of corruption.	50.40%
People have the freedom to take part in protests and demonstrations.	19.60%
Multiple parties compete fairly in the election.	29.90%
Government ensures job opportunities for all.	23.90%
Media is free to criticise the things government does.	17.20%
Government ensures law and order.	29.00%
Government provides people with quality public services.	28.80%
People are free to organise political groups.	15.80%
Basic necessities, like food, clothes, and shelter are provided for all.	40.90%
The parliament has oversight over the government (the Prime Minister and ministers).	14.60%
People are free to express their political views openly.	27.60%
Government does not waste any public money.	13.60%
People choose the government leaders in free and fair elections.	41.40%
Government narrows the gap between the rich and the poor.	17.40%

Source: Asian Barometer Survey. Author prepared.

Australians who believe that socioeconomic outcomes are the most essential features of democracy are the least likely to believe that Australia is currently a democratic state (Table 14.3). Those respondents who selected freedom to protest, multi-party elections, parliamentary oversight, and freedom of association are the most likely to believe that Australia is a full democracy. At the other end of the scale, respondents who view job opportunities, economic equality, and the provision of shelter, food, clothes, and welfare benefits are the least likely to agree that Australia is a full democracy. Of those who think narrowing the gap between rich and poor is one of the most essential elements of democracy, a full third believe that Australian democracy has "major problems." Across the full sample of Australians, 13 percent believe the country is a full democracy, 64 percent that it is a democracy with minor problems, 21 percent that it is a democracy with major problems, and only 2 percent believe it is not a democracy at all.

The vast majority of Australians believe that democracy—however they understand it—is currently suitable for Australia, and that Australia will still be a democracy in ten years' time. On the ABS's 10-point scales, 85 percent of respondents selected six or higher on the question of whether democracy is currently suitable for Australia, and 62 percent selected six or higher on whether Australia will be a democracy in ten years' time. Three in four respondents—73 percent—selected six or higher on the question of whether Australia is currently a democracy. Likewise, 61 percent are satisfied with the way democracy works in Australia, and 12 percent are very satisfied.

Table 14.3 Assessment of Australian Democracy, According to Most Essential Characteristic of a Democracy (%)

	A full democracy	A democracy, but with minor problems	A democracy, with major problems	Not a democracy
Government ensures job opportunities for all.	5.5	67.50%	25.40%	1.60%
Government narrows the gap between the rich and the poor.	7.3	53.60%	34.50%	4.60%
Basic necessities, like food, clothes, and shelter are provided for all.	8.9	64.70%	24.80%	1.60%
People receive welfare benefits if they are unemployed.	10.10%	62.70%	22.80%	4.40%
Politics is clean and free of corruption.	10.40%	62.00%	25.30%	2.30%
Media is free to criticize the things government does.	10.50%	64.80%	21.30%	3.40%
Government does not waste any public money.	11.00%	65.70%	20.00%	3.30%
The court protects the ordinary people from the abuse of government power.	12.10%	67.00%	20.60%	0.30%

(Continuing on the next page)

Table 14.3 Cont.

	A full democracy	A democracy, but with minor problems	A democracy, with major problems	Not a democracy
Government ensures law and order.	13.20%	68.20%	17.00%	1.60%
People are free to express their political views openly.	13.50%	66.40%	19.00%	1.20%
Government provides people with quality public services.	13.90%	64.10%	18.60%	3.40%
People choose the government leaders in free and fair elections.	15.10%	66.30%	17.00%	1.50%
People are free to organize political groups.	15.90%	63.30%	20.00%	0.80%
The parliament has oversight over the government (the Prime Minister and ministers).	18.00%	62.70%	17.10%	2.20%
Multiple parties compete fairly in the election.	19.40%	57.00%	21.60%	1.90%
People have the freedom to take part in protests and demonstrations.	20.70%	67.00%	10.40%	1.90%
Rows sum to 100%				

Source: Asian Barometer Survey. Author prepared.

In sum, then, although there are some clear fissures in democratic support among Australians, they do not appear to be fundamental, nor do they suggest that Australian democracy is fragile. There is some evidence of superficial democratic support, as well as a core group of Australians who display little support for either democratic legitimacy nor for liberal-democratic values. Future waves of the ABS in Australia will shed light on whether this group is growing in size or becoming smaller. They will also allow closer comparison of multi-dimensional democratic orientations in Australia and our northern neighbors in Asia. We also observe a large minority of outcome-focused democrats in Australia, whose support for democracy in principle might crumble in the face of social or economic crises. This poses challenges for Australian political leaders and policymakers, just like it does in countries across Asia.

Conclusion

Entering the Asian Barometer Survey project has opened new frontiers in understanding Australian values and democratic support in the context of the Asian Century. It is also particularly timely: migration from Asia—particularly from India and China—into Australia is the fastest growing part of the Australian population. It is increasingly naïve to study Australia and its citizens without reference to Asia.

Indeed, this chapter has found that Australian values share important similarities to what we have previously considered "Confucian" or paternalistic-meritocracy values. Despite what we know—or think we know—about Australian identity, the ABS have shown that Australia has much in common with Taiwan, and particularly young, democratized Taiwanese generations. Australians—across all age groups—and young Taiwanese express values of long-term planning and meritocracy and reject paternalism and the primacy of group harmony. Future waves of the ABS will show whether these similarities continue, or whether Australian and Taiwanese values are more different than they have appeared here.

ABS data have also shown that support for democracy in Australia is broad but has some weak spots. As in democracies throughout the world, a large minority of Australians believe that social and economic equality are fundamental democratic principles, and these individuals show the least confidence that Australia is currently a democracy, or that our democratic systems are working well. Similarly, around a third of Australians demonstrate both low support for democratic legitimacy and low rates of liberal-democratic values. While these findings cannot suggest much about how Australia compares with our Asian neighbors or whether these "non-democrats" are increasing or decreasing in number, Australia's involvement in future ABS waves will provide vital insights into the country's identity and democracy.

Notes

1. The comparative battery only comprises 12 variables; two questions ("When dealing with others, a person should not be preoccupied with temporary gains and losses" and "When dealing with others, a person should not only focus on their own immediate interests but also plan for the future") were not asked in the entire first tranche of Wave 5 countries. The Cohen's alpha for the 12-item is 0.78 in the comparative, 8-country dataset.
2. Chu and Huang (2010) use a five-item scale, but one of those five measures ("To what extent do you want your country to be democratic now?") was not asked in the fifth wave.

References

Austin, Catherine, and Farida Fozdar. 2018. "Australian National Identity: Empirical Research since 1998." *National Identities* 20 (3): 277-298.

Brett, Judith. 2005. *Quarterly Essay 19 Relaxed & Comfortable: The Liberal Party's Australia*. Melbourne: Black Inc.

Cameron, Sarah, and Ian McAllister. 2020. "Australian Election Study, 1987-2019 Trends." *Australian Election Study, 1987-2019 Trends*. ADA Dataverse.

Chu, Yun-han, and Min-hua Huang. 2010. "The Meanings of Democracy: Solving an Asian Puzzle." *Journal of Democracy* 21 (4): 114-122.

Department of Home Affairs. 2020. "Australian Values Statement." In *Australian Values Statement*. https://immi.homeaffairs.gov.au/form-listing/forms/1281.pdf.

Inglehart, Ronald, and Christian Welzel. 2005. *Modernization, Cultural Change, and Democracy: The Human Development Sequence*. Cambridge: Cambridge University Press.

Norris, Pippa. 2011. *Democratic Deficit: Critical Citizens Revisited*. Cambridge: Cambridge University Press.

Shin, Doh Chull. 2011. *Confucianism and Democratization in East Asia*. Cambridge: Cambridge University Press.

Wang, Huiyao. 2019. "In 2020, Asian Economies Will Become Larger than the Rest of the World Combined—Here's How." *World Economic Forum*. https://www.weforum.org/agenda/2019/07/thedawn-of-the-asian-centur.

Ward, Tony. 2010. *Sport in Australian National Identity: Kicking Goals*. London: Routledge.

15 Intensity of Trust in Institutions in India: The Emerging Paradox

Shreyas Sardesai and Sandeep Shastri

A dominant narrative in academic literature on trust and confidence of citizens in a country's core institutions is its linkages with measuring the success of democracy (Easton 1965; Miller 1974; Crozier, Huntington, and Watanuki 1975; Dalton 2004). A healthy representative democracy is said to contain, as an essential prerequisite, institutions that are trusted. Cultural theories of democracy have emphasized that a civic culture with high levels of institutional and interpersonal trust is vital for the stability of democratic systems and for "making democracy work" (Verba and Almond 1963; Putnam 1993; Inglehart 1997). Such trust is also seen as contributing to citizens' commitment to democratic values and the rejection of authoritarian appeals. They view institutional trust to be an extension of interpersonal trust that is embedded in society, learned early in life, and projected onto political institutions much later. These cultural theories have been challenged by the institutional theories of democracy that suggest that citizens' trust toward institutions be a rational response to institutional performance (Jackman and Miller 1996; Hetherington 1998; Mishler and Rose 2005), linked largely to economic issues, but also rooted in their perception on the reduction of corruption, the adherence to the rule of law, and civil liberties. Of late, some scholars have also argued that the decline in trust levels in Western democracies may not necessarily be a challenge. It could well be due to the greater political sophistication and cognitive mobilization of citizens (Norris 1999). Some have even viewed distrust and skepticism of institutions as a welcome development for democracy (Warren 1999; Hardin 1999; Bruno 2017; van der Meer 2017; Mishler and Rose 1997; Cleary and Stokes 2006). Warren (1999, 310), for instance, makes the argument that distrust is an important feature of the democratic process and that it offers a basis for "healthy suspicion of power upon which the vitality of democracy depends." The reports of the Global Barometer Survey in South Asia also endorse this perspective. In its reporting of the 2013 Survey, the Report stated that "the lukewarm trust in institutions... announce the arrival of a critical citizen... Citizens are not awed by institutions... (the) relationship is firmly within the domain of democratic questioning" (Shastri,

Palshikar, and Kumar 2017, 53).

Nonetheless, while most researchers continue to bolster the assumption that trust is necessary for the vibrancy of democracy, there is an increasing concern that rising distrust in political institutions in many democracies, as captured by public opinion surveys and as reflected in the rise of anti-establishment populist movements and leaders in many parts of the world, can have major consequences for the stability and quality of democracy. Dalton (2004, 157), for instance, in his influential study *Democratic Challenges, Democratic Choices: The Erosion of Political Support in Advanced Industrial Societies* was of the opinion that "there are legitimate reasons to worry that such trends (of rising political distrust) may erode the vitality of democracy or eventually may undermine the democratic process itself."

In the context of this dominant theoretical consensus among political scientists that views a high degree of citizens' trust in political institutions as being conducive for democracy, the case of present-day India, when analyzed through the prism of the India component of the Global Barometer Survey in 2019 as compared with the trends in earlier rounds of the survey, makes for interesting reading. When the trends in citizen trust in institutions as evidenced from the survey are analyzed, two trends are patently visible. Firstly, the levels of trust in individual institutions have increased over time. Secondly, non-elected institutions tend to evoke greater trust as compared to elected institutions. While elected institutions do not enjoy as high levels of trust as non-elected institutions, the level of trust even in elected institutions has witnessed an increase. Indian citizens, as this chapter will show, indicate higher levels of confidence in their institutions over time. What however makes this high trust in institutions among Indians paradoxical is the parallel narrative by independent analysts highlighting how institutions such as the judiciary, the military, the police, the election commission, and the media have lost much of their independence in the present political context (Palshikar 2019; Ganguly 2020, Varma 2018; Misra 2018; Hasan 2018; Ahmad 2020; Mehta 2019a, 2019b). Recently, the annual Democracy Index by the Economist's Intelligence Unit has now downgraded India to the position of a "flawed democracy" (The Economist 2020), Freedom House's Freedom in the World report has downgraded India's status from a "Free" country to "Partly Free" (Freedom House 2021) and Varieties of Democracy or V-Dem has labelled India as an "Electoral Autocracy" (V-Dem 2021). Put simply, is Indian citizens' perception of the functioning of democratic institutions in the country at odds with critical journalistic, academic, and expert commentary on the state of Indian democracy?

This chapter will discuss in detail the important trust-related survey findings evidenced in the India Component of the Global Barometer Survey and seek to explain this apparent paradox. It will also try to offer reasons as to why this may be so.

The Order of Trust in 2019

It may be useful to highlight the political context of 2019, the time around which the survey was conducted. This year saw an important national election. The survey was undertaken a few months after the elections, in which the ruling BJP under the leadership of Narendra Modi was voted back to power. The questionnaire had a list of fourteen questions that sought to tap the levels of trust expressed by the respondents toward fourteen selected institutions. These institutions were carefully selected to cover a wide spectrum of important players in the political process.

The findings broadly indicate a reasonably high degree of trust in most of the institutions. While one does concede significant differences in the intensity of trust expressed toward the selected institutions, the trend more or less conforms to earlier studies. The military or the armed forces emerged as the most trusted institution. Close to nine of every ten respondents expressed strong or moderate trust in the armed forces (Table 15.1). Interestingly, the military was the only institution for which the distrust percentage was found to be in single digits. Next in the hierarchy of trust came the office of the Prime Minister[1] and the judiciary or the courts. Both institutions were found to be trusted by nearly four-fifths of the respondents. A little less than half strongly trusted them, and one-thirds moderately trusted them.

While television, an important and dominant source of news in the country, was also found to be trusted by four-fifths of the respondents, the intensity of trust in it was lower compared to the trust reposed by citizens in the prime minister and the courts. This is because the proportion of those trusting it moderately was greater than the proportion of those trusting it strongly. In the case of all the remaining institutions too—the election commission, the national government, the newspapers, the parliament, the police, the local government, civil service, NGOs, political parties and the internet—moderate trust was found to be greater than strong trust. In the hierarchy of trust, particularly when seen exclusively through the lens of "strong trust," internet and political parties emerged as the least trusted of all, with only one of every six respondents having strong faith or confidence in them. Political parties in fact were the only institution for whom there was greater strong distrust than strong trust. In the case of all other institutions, deep distrust was lower than deep trust.

Table 15.1 Extent of Trust-distrust in Institutions in October 2019 (High-to-low Order Based on the "Strong Trust" Figures)

	Strong Trust	Some Trust	TOTAL TRUST	Some Distrust	Strong Distrust	TOTAL DISTRUST	No Response
Military	68	19	87	6	3	9	4
Prime Minister	47	31	78	9	9	18	4
Courts	46	33	79	11	5	16	5
Television	38	41	79	7	3	10	11
Election Commission	34	35	69	13	8	21	10
National Government	33	35	68	15	9	24	8
Newspapers	30	42	72	10	3	13	15
Parliament	30	35	65	15	9	24	11
Police	29	37	66	17	14	31	3
Local Govt	28	40	68	17	11	28	4
Civil Service/Govt Officials	26	39	65	18	10	28	7
NGOs	19	33	52	19	11	30	18
Political Parties	16	32	48	26	20	46	6
News on Internet	16	30	46	16	11	27	27

Note: Figures are percentages.
Source: Global Barometer Survey. Authors prepared.

Overall, if the data were to be analyzed in terms of net trust,[2] political parties emerged as the least trusted institution with a net trust of just two percentage points (Table 15.2). This conforms to the pattern of trust noticed in earlier studies also. News gleaned from the internet was the second most distrusted with a net trust of just nineteen percentage points. Non-governmental organizations were the third most distrusted institutions with a net trust of 22 percentage points. The police and the civil service found themselves at the bottom of the net trust hierarchy, although they fared much better in comparison with the bottom three. The three most trusted institutions in terms of net trust were the military (respondents were 78 percentage points more likely to trust it than distrust it), television (66 percentage points), and the courts (63 percentage points). Net trust in the prime minister and newspapers was close behind that of the judiciary. Falling somewhere in the middle of the net trust hierarchy were the election commission, the national government, the parliament, and the local government in urban and rural India. Net trust in all four was found to be somewhere in the middle, between 40 and 50 percentage points. It was thus neither too high nor too low.

Table 15.2 Net Trust in Institutions

	Net Trust (trust minus distrust) in percentage points
Military	+78
Television	+66
Courts	+63
Prime Minister	+60
Newspapers	+59
Election Commission	+48
National Government	+44
Parliament	+41
Local Government	+40
Civil Service	+37
Police	+35
NGOs	+22
News on Internet	+19
Political Parties	+2

Source: Global Barometer Survey. Authors prepared.

Longitudinal Analysis (2004, 2013, and 2019)

Since the India component of the Global Barometer Survey series had asked the same "trust in institutions" questions in the previous rounds of the study (in 2004 and 2013), a longitudinal analysis of responses is undertaken. The analysis found not much change at the top and the bottom of the trust ladder. The military continued to be the most trusted institution during all three rounds (Tables 15.3 & 15.4). Similarly, just as they were least trusted in 2019, political parties were also at the bottom of the trust hierarchy in 2004 and 2013. What is also particularly significant is that there was hardly any institution that did not witness a rise in trust levels over this period of time spanning a decade and a half. A comparison of responses in 2004, 2013, and 2019 suggests that nearly all institutions in 2019 saw people's confidence and trust in them going up compared to the past and this was true in the case of both methods of calculating trust, net trust, and net of high trust. Moreover, in the case of most institutions about which questions of trust had been asked in all three rounds, the rise in people's trust in them has been steadily increasing. This is however not true for the national government and the local government, both of which saw a fall in trust levels in 2013.

The increase in net trust in the police during the period under study was to the tune of 31 percentage points, a rise that is greater than the rise recorded for any other institution (Table 15.3). In other words, despite being among the least trusted institutions, the police at the same time also made the most impressive gains. The other institutions that recorded a significant rise in trust were the courts, the prime minister, the national government, and the military.

Table 15.3 Net Trust in Institutions over the Years

	2004	2013	2019	*What's the trend?*	*Rise in net trust between 2013 and 2019*
Military	+60	+68	+78	*Rise*	*+10*
Courts	+37	+47	+63	*Rise*	*+16*
Prime Minister	NA	+46	+60	*Rise*	*+14*
Election Commission	+39	NA	+48	*Rise*	
National Government	+48	+27	+44	*Fall-Rise*	*+17*
Parliament	+23	+33	+41	*Rise*	*+8*
Local Government	+40	+27	+40	*Fall-Rise*	*+13*
Civil Service/Govt Officials	+12	+28	+37	*Rise*	*+9*
Police	-2	+4	+35	*Rise*	*+31*
Political Parties	-7	-12	+2	*Fall-Rise*	*+14*

Note: Net trust here is trust minus distrust.
Source: Global Barometer Survey. Authors prepared.

Table 15.4 Order of Institutions (2004, 2013 & 2019) Based on Net of Trust-distrust Shown in Table 15.3

2004	2013	2019
MILITARY	MILITARY	MILITARY
NATIONAL GOVT	COURTS	COURTS
LOCAL GOVT	PRIME MINISTER	PRIME MINISTER
ELECTION COMMISSION	PARLIAMENT	ELECTION COMMISSION
COURTS	CIVIL SERVICE	NATIONAL GOVT
PARLIAMENT	NATIONAL GOVT	PARLIAMENT
CIVIL SERVICE	LOCAL GOVT	LOCAL GOVT
POLICE	POLICE	CIVIL SERVICE
POLITICAL PARTIES	POLITICAL PARTIES	POLICE
		POLITICAL PARTIES

Source: Authors prepared.

Making Sense of the Paradox
A Macro Picture of Trust

In order to make sense of the paradox of rising trust, a comprehensive index of trust in eleven institutions[3] was created drawings from the findings of the survey done in 2013 and 2019. Only those institutions were chosen for constructing the index which were included in both rounds of the study to permit comparability. The trust index that was constructed was based on a summated score of responses given by the interviewees to the questions regarding each of the eleven institutions.[4]

When doing this exercise, it was found that not only was trust in institutions at an aggregate or overall level high in both rounds of the survey, it also registered a significant increase of nine percentage points between the two rounds (Table 15.5). Whereas a little over half the respondents were found to have "high trust" in institutions in 2013, the proportion of those having "high trust" went up to three-fifths in 2019. This rise in "high trust" was found to have come at the expense of a drop in "moderate trust" and "low trust" as well as the proportion of those who had been non-committal. There was also a fairly sharp four percentage point fall in the share of respondents who did not express an opinion on any of the eleven questions. It could be argued therefore that the already high trust in institutions recorded in 2013 increased even further in 2019, and only a tiny fraction of the population distrusted institutions with great intensity.

Table 15.5 Trust Index (From Questions on Eleven Institutions Asked in Both 2013 and 2019)

	2013	2019
Non-committal	5	1
Low Trust	8	5
Moderate Trust	35	33
High Trust	52	61

Items used: military, television, courts, prime minister, newspapers, national government, parliament, local government, civil service, police, political parties
Source: Global Barometer Survey. Authors prepared.

High Institutional Trust Does Not Necessarily Foster a Democratic Sentiment

The India component of the Global Barometer Surveys found that higher trust in institutions does not necessarily make people more favorable to the idea of democracy. A comparative analysis of the 2013 and 2019 data shows that predisposition toward an authoritarian government has gone up not only among those with low trust in institutions but even among those with moderate and high trust in institutions. In 2013, respondents with high trust in institutions were 3.6 times more likely to prefer democracy over authoritarianism when given a choice between the two. This likelihood reduced to 2.3 times in 2019 (Table 15.6). Among those with moderate trust in institutions, the drop in the probability to choose democracy over authoritarianism has fallen from five times to 1.6 times. Responses to another question asked in the survey that sought views on dictatorship yielded similar results. When respondents were asked whether they agreed or disagreed with the proposition that "we should get rid of parliament and elections and have a strong leader decide things," more than half of those with high trust in institutions and a little less than half of those with moderate trust in institutions agreed with the proposition. Both these figures of agreement were lower in 2013 (Table 15.7). Thus, an already high predisposition toward a dictatorship or autocracy among those with moderate and high trust in institutions seems to have increased even further, and this suggests that trust in institutions may not necessarily be an endorsement of democracy as it exists.

Table 15.6 Proclivity for Authoritarian Government by Trust in Institutions (2013 vs. 2019)

	2013				2019			
	Democracy always preferable	In some situations authoritarian govt preferable	Does not matter	NR	Democracy always preferable	In some situations authoritarian govt preferable	Does not matter	NR
Low Trust	19	3	14	64	23	9	11	57
Moderate Trust	45	9	18	28	35	21	13	31
High Trust	54	15	16	15	52	22	11	15
Non Committal	15	2	9	74	4	2	10	84
Overall	**46**	**11**	**16**	**27**	**44**	**21**	**11**	**24**

Source: Global Barometer Survey. Authors prepared.

Table 15.7 Proclivity toward Dictatorship by Trust in Institutions (2013 vs. 2019)

Would you disapprove or approve of the statement "We should get rid of parliament and elections and have a strong leader decide things"?

	2013				2019			
	Strongly agree	Some what agree	Some what disagree	Strongly disagree	Strongly agree	Some what agree	Some what disagree	Strongly disagree
Low Trust	7	10	7	11	11	18	15	14
Moderate Trust	14	22	17	22	15	30	16	18
High Trust	20	26	17	23	25	28	14	22
Non Committal	4	7	6	2	4	6	4	2
Overall	**16**	**22**	**16**	**21**	**21**	**28**	**14**	**20**

Note: Figures of no response to the question have not been shown in the table.
Source: Global Barometer Survey. Authors prepared.

Regime and Personality Effect

What could be possibly causing trust in institutions and democratic sentiment to vary at the same time? We believe that the leadership of Prime Minister Narendra Modi could be an external explanatory factor. Modi has repeatedly and consciously attempted to portray himself as a strong and decisive leader. He has also been displaying traits of authoritarianism. It is therefore quite possible that most respondents, a large number of whom were Modi and BJP supporters, showed both proclivities—support for dictatorship and high trust in institutions—at the same time. Since Modi has an authoritarian streak, it is quite likely that his many supporters, favor less democracy/favor an authoritarian government, even as they show a high trust in "democratic" institutions that are functioning under his regime.

In fact, a greater attachment of the people to the regime of Narendra Modi compared to the previous Manmohan Singh government does help explain the unexpectedly high level of trust in institutions in 2019. The SDI 2019 survey found 25 percent or one in every four respondents to be "very satisfied" with the work done by the Central government as opposed to 8 percent or less than one in every ten who were "very dissatisfied" (Table 15.8). In other words, complete satisfaction with the Narendra Modi-led BJP-NDA government's performance was three times greater than complete dissatisfaction. When compared with the 2013 SDI survey that had asked the same question to respondents with respect to the then Manmohan Singh-led Congress-UPA government, the 2019 data represents a complete reversal of the pattern. Back in 2013, voters had been nearly thrice as likely to be utterly dissatisfied with the Singh government's performance as they were fully satisfied, 20 percent to 8 percent. Considering that both rounds of the survey also found satisfaction with the Central government to have a clear linear relationship with trust levels in institutions—the greater the satisfaction, the more the trust (Table 15.9), these vastly differing satisfaction levels assume significance in understanding as to why there was higher trust in institutions in 2019.

Table 15.8 Satisfaction Levels with the Central Government (2013 vs. 2019)

	Manmohan Govt (last year of second term) 2013	Modi Government (first year of second term) 2019
Very Satisfied with Central Govt	8	25
Somewhat Satisfied with Central Govt	38	42
Somewhat Dissatisfied with Central Govt	16	16
Very Dissatisfied with Central Govt	20	8

Note: The rest of the respondents did not respond to/answer the question.
Source: Global Barometer Survey. Authors prepared.

Table 15.9 Trust in Institutions by Satisfaction with Central Government (2013 vs. 2019)

	2013			2019		
	Low Trust	Moderate Trust	High Trust	Low Trust	Moderate Trust	High Trust
Very Satisfied with Central Government	4	26	69	2	21	77
Somewhat Satisfied with Central Government	6	29	63	4	31	65
Somewhat Dissatisfied with Central Government	7	34	56	4	41	54
Very Dissatisfied with Central Government	7	52	38	14	54	32

Source: Global Barometer Survey. Authors prepared.

To put it in simpler terms, the fact that there were far more people satisfied with the ruling government's performance in 2019 than in 2013 was bound to have resulted in an increase in the proportion of those trusting institutions since the survey data clearly suggests that a greater satisfaction with the government's performance leads to greater institutional trust. In addition to this, what is also significant is that the effect of satisfaction on trust seems to have been far greater in 2019 than in 2013. Those fully satisfied with the Modi government in 2019 showed greater "high trust" in institutions than those fully satisfied with the Singh government in 2013 (77-69 percent); similarly, those fully dissatisfied with the Modi government showed greater "low trust" than those fully dissatisfied with the Singh government (14-7 percent; Table 15.9). This basically indicates that the regime effect in 2019 was stronger than it was in 2013 and that the perception about government in 2019 determined people's responses to the trust questions more than it did in 2013. The higher than before trust in institutions could be because people viewed their functioning through the prism of the Modi/his government and thus did not want to rate them poorly.

Conclusion

From the above analysis, two very clear trends are evident. In the first place, citizens tend to bestow the greatest trust on non-elected Indians as compared to elected institutions. Secondly, over time, the level of trust in institutions has registered a steady rise.

The latest round of the India component of the Global Barometer survey was conducted in the autumn of 2019. In this round, it was found that people's overall trust in institutions exceeded their overall distrust. This pattern was noticed with respect to all institutions about which trust levels were sought. A comparison with the data from the 2013 round suggests that there is not a single institution that has not seen people's confidence in it increase in the last six years. This needs to be explained keeping in mind an important political context. The latest round of the survey was held a few months after the BJP, under the leadership of Prime Minister Modi, was returned to power.

The National Election Study 2019 Survey shows that there was a visible pro-incumbency sentiment and support for the leadership of the prime minister. This factor could have had a clear impact in terms of the display of trust in institutions. It is important to highlight that the levels of satisfaction with the incumbent BJP government (2014-2019) led by Narendra Modi were much higher than the satisfaction with the previous Manmohan Singh-led government (2004-2014). When the 2013 survey was undertaken, the Manmohan Singh government was toward the end of its second term and anti-incumbency sentiment had clearly set in. Since the survey also finds trust in institutions to be correlated with government satisfaction, greater institutional trust in 2019 is thus only to be expected. People's higher trust in institutions thus seems to be to a large extent a function of their endorsement of the ruling party and the government.

Elections also produce an expectation overload and its impact remains for a few months after the government comes to power. In the Report on the 2013 round of the study, the South Asia study reported that democratic institutions "are prone to generate a high level of expectations" toward the political establishment (Shastri, Palshikar, and Kumar 2017, 55). This factor could have contributed to the rise in levels of trust across institutions.

The higher trust in non-elected institutions as compared to elected ones also merit attention. In the Report on the 2013 study in South Asia, it was underscored that this trend could well be on account of the insulated manner in which non-elected institutions function. This "often evokes trust that often borders on respect, admiration and even a bewilderment that flows from limited information about their functioning and working style." When it comes to elected institutions, "their working and scrutiny is much more in the public domain and thus evoked both greater criticism and cynicism" (Shastri, Palshikar, and Kumar 2017).

The conduct of the 2019 survey just as the excitement of an election was settling down could have impacted the rise in the levels of trust in institutions. The demonstration of higher levels of trust in non-elected institutions could well be a perception which flows from watching the working of institutions from a distance. As citizens are much more "connected" with elected institutions, a critical approach to the same is clearly apparent.

Notes

1. The role of Prime Minister Modi in ensuring the victory of his party (BJP) in the 2019 elections may have been a key factor to explain the high levels of trust in the Prime Minister in 2019. It was evident that in the National Election Study 2019, it was reported that one thirds of those who voted for the BJP would have changed their party preference if Modi were not the Prime Ministerial candidate of the BJP. (Shastri 2019)
2. Net trusted calculated as the difference between the total proportion of trust (strong and moderate combined) and the proportion of distrust (strong and moderate combined).
3. Military, courts, parliament, prime minister, national government, local government, political parties, police, civil service, television, and newspapers.
4. The answer categories of "strongly trust" in 2019 and "great deal of trust" in 2013 were assigned a score of 4. The answers "somewhat trust" in 2019 and "quite a lot of trust" in 2013 were assigned a score of 3. The responses "somewhat distrust" in 2019 and "not much trust" in 2013 were given a score of 2 and the answer category of "strongly distrust" in 2019 and "no trust at all" in 2013 was assigned a score of 1. A non-response to a question in both rounds was assigned a score of 0. The scores of all 11 questions were summed up. The resulting summated scores for each respondent ranged from 0 to 44. The summated scores were distributed across four newly created categories that indicated different degrees of trust. Respondents with summated scores ranging from 30 to 44 were categorized as having "high trust." Those with summated

scores that ranged from 15 to 29 were categorized as having "moderate trust." Finally, respondents with summated scores ranging from 1 to 14 were labeled as having "low trust." Those with summated scores that totaled 0 were deemed as being "non-committal," that is these are respondents who did not answer any of the eleven questions related to trust in institutions.

References

Ahmad, Aijaz. 2020. "Strictly Technical." *London Review of Books*. Vol. 42. No. 6. March 19. https://www.lrb.co.uk/the-paper/v42/n06/aijaz-ahmad/strictly-technical.

Bruno, Jonathan R. 2017. "Vigilance and Confidence: Jeremy Bentham, Publicity, and the Dialectic of Political Trust and Distrust." *American Political Science Review* 111 (2): 295-307. New York: Cambridge University Press. doi: 10.1017/S0003055416000708.

Cleary, Matthew R., and Susan Stokes. 2006. *Democracy and the Culture of Skepticism: The Politics of Trust in Argentina and Mexico*. New York: Russell Sage Foundation.

Crozier, Michel, Samuel P. Huntington, and Joji Watanuki. 1975. *The Crisis of Democracy*. Vol. 70. New York: New York University Press.

Dalton, Russell J. 2004. *Democratic Challenges, Democratic Choices: The Erosion of Political Support in Advanced Industrial Democracies*. Oxford: Oxford University Press. doi: 10.1093/acprof:oso/9780199268436.001.0001.

Easton, David. 1965. *A Systems Analysis of Political Life*. New York: John Wiley.

Freedom House. 2021. "Freedom in the World 2021, Democracy under Siege." by Sarah Repucci and Amy Slipowitz. https://freedomhouse.org/sites/default/files/2021-02/FIW2021_World_02252021_FINAL-web-upload.pdf.

Ganguly, Sumit. 2020. "An Illiberal India?" *Journal of Democracy* 31 (1): 193-202. doi: 10.1353/jod.2020.0016.

Hardin, Russell. 1999. "Do We Want Trust in Government?" In *Democracy and Trust*, edited by Mark E. Warren, 22-41. Cambridge: Cambridge University Press. doi: 10.1017/CBO9780511659959.002.

Hasan, Zoya. 2018. "Our Institutions Are at Risk under Modi." *Rediff.com*. December 19. https://www.rediff.com/news/column/our-institutions-are-at-risk-under-modi/20181219.htm.

Hetherington, Marc J. 1998. "The Political Relevance of Political Trust." *American Political Science Review* 92 (4): 791-808. New York: Cambridge University Press. doi: 10.2307/2586304.

Inglehart, Ronald. 1997. *Modernization and Postmodernization: Cultural, Economic, and Political Change in 43 Societies*. Princeton: Princeton University Press.

Jackman, Robert W., and Ross A. Miller. 1996. "The Poverty of Political Culture." *American Journal of Political Science* 40 (3): 697-716. doi: 10.2307/2111790.

Mehta, Pratap Bhanu. 2019a. "Pratap Bhanu Mehta at Express Adda: 'I Think Real Challenge Will Begin After Lok Sabha Election.'" *The Indian Express*. May

07. https://indianexpress.com/article/india/pratap-bhanu-mehta-lok-sabha-elections-narendra-modi-bjp-congress-5713762/.

—. 2019b. "Serial Authoritarianism Picks Out Targets One by One, and Tires Out Challenges." *The Indian Express*. October 10. https://indianexpress.com/article/opinion/columns/sedition-charge-against-celebrities-mob-lynching-narendra-modi-6061361/.

Miller, Arthur H. 1974. "Political Issues and Trust in Government: 1964-1970." *American Political Science Review* 68 (3): 951-972. doi: 10.2307/1959140.

Mishler, William, and Richard Rose. 1997. "Trust, Distrust and Skepticism: Popular Evaluations of Civil and Political Institutions in Post-Communist Societies." *The Journal of Politics* 59 (2): 418-451. Austin: University of Texas Press. doi: 10.1017/S0022381600053512.

—. 2005. "What Are the Political Consequences of Trust? A Test of Cultural and Institutional Theories in Russia." *Comparative Political Studies* 38 (9): 1050-1078. doi: 10.1177/0010414005278419.

Misra, Satish. 2018. "ModiGovt@4: Institutions Take a Big Hit." *Observer Research Foundation*. May 25. https://www.orfonline.org/expert-speak/modi-t4-institutions-take-big-hit/.

Norris, Pippa. 1999. *Critical Citizens: Global Support for Democratic Government*. Oxford: Oxford University Press.

Palshikar, Suhas. 2019. "History Will Judge Modi Govt on How It Handles Critical Issues." *Outlook*. May 25. https://www.outlookindia.com/magazine/story/india-news-in-lieu-of-an-agenda/301658.

Putnam, Robert D. 1993. *Making Democracy Work: Civic Traditions in Modern Italy*. Princeton: Princeton University Press.

Shastri, Sandeep. 2019. "The Modi Factor in the 2019 Lok Sabha Election: How Critical Was It to the BJP Victory?" *Studies in Indian Politics* 7 (2): 206-218. doi: 10.1177/2321023019874910.

Shastri, Sandeep, Suhas Palshikar, and Sanjay Kumar. 2017. *State of Democracy in South Asia (SDSA): Report II*. Bangalore: Jain University Press.

The Economist. 2020. "Global Democracy Has Another Bad Year." *The Economist Intelligence Unit's Democracy Index*. January 22. https://www.economist.com/graphic-detail/2020/01/22/global-democracy-has-another-bad-year.

V-Dem. 2021. "Autocratization Turns Viral, Democracy Report 2021." V-Dem Institute at the University of Gothenburg. https://www.v-dem.net/static/website/files/dr/dr_2021.pdf.

Van der Meer, Tom W. G. 2017. "Political Trust and the 'Crisis of Democracy.'" In *Oxford Research Encyclopedia of Politics*. https://oxfordre.com/politics/view/10.1093/acrefore/9780190228637.001.0001/acrefore-9780190228637-e-77.

Varma, Subodh. 2018. "How Modi Government Is Destroying Key Indian Institutions." October 27. https://www.newsclick.in/how-modi-government-destroying-key-indian-institutions.

Verba, Sidney, and Gabriel Almond. 1963. *The Civic Culture: Political Attitudes and Democracy in Five Nations*. Princeton: Princeton University Press.

Warren, Mark E. 1999. "Democratic Theory and Trust." In *Democracy and Trust*, edited by Mark E. Warren, 310-345. Cambridge: Cambridge University Press.

16 Election Losers and Support for Democracy: Challenges to Democratic Consolidation in Taiwan

Yu-tzung Chang and Yun-han Chu

As we enter the twenty-first century, the third wave of democratization has come to a halt, with only a handful of annual changes between democracies and non-democracies (Freedom House 2021; V-dem 2021). Behind this phenomenon, there are many issues that are worth exploring in depth.

Ten years ago, Bruce Gilley (2009) argued that most of the third wave democracies were established on unstable foundations, and even a minor shock may lead to a democratic reversal and a return to authoritarianism. Gilley also pointed out that the research focus of democratization scholars has started to switch to authoritarian resilience. These scholars criticized the transitions paradigm for its teleological bias. Democracy is not the only path for global political development. Scholars must also be aware of the nature of authoritarianism, as well as its resilience and its particular institutional arrangements (Chu et al. 2020).

Ten years later, scholars' concerns about democratic regression have extended to include Western democracies. People all over the world are dissatisfied with the performance of democracy in their own countries (Chu et al. 2020; Foa et al. 2020, 2022). They question both the basic values of democracy and how democracy works in practice and no longer consider it to be the best choice. More seriously, growing numbers of people regard non-democratic systems as viable alternatives (Foa and Mounk 2016, 2017). The analysis of the Asian Barometer Survey recently conducted in these countries reveals that pluralities of their citizenries are psychologically disposed to realign themselves with a hybrid or autocratic system. It also reveals that democratic learning and socioeconomic modernization, two significant influences on democratic consolidation, do little to keep East Asians from joining in the deconsolidation movement (Shin 2021).

More recently, academics have begun to challenge claims of crisis of democracy, with different views on democratic resilience. "Resilience" means the ability of a social (political) system to cope with, survive, and recover from complex challenges and crises. According to Vanessa A. Boese et al. (2021), "democratic resilience" has two processes. One is to prevent the decline of democracy and to avoid the process of authoritarianism. Robert C. Lieberman et al. (2021) convened a number of political scholars to publish a book last year, divided into five parts, to discuss whether democracy can stand the test and demonstrate its democratic resilience in the face of an increasingly polarized American society.

How has Taiwan's democracy developed, and how is its path similar to other countries? The main purpose of this study is to analyze whether there is any difference in supporters' attitudes toward Taiwan's democracy between the winning and losing camps over the past twenty years. This is an important issue because democracy must reflect public opinion through regular elections. Through the election process, democracies aggregate the individual choices of voters and reward or punish political parties and politicians. Elections are also competitions with both election winners and election losers. Past research has shown that the different political experiences and outcomes of political elites and their supporters, whether they are electoral winners or losers, or the ruling majority or the opposition minority, determine how people evaluate the existing democratic system (Anderson et al. 2005).

Why Are Losers Important?

The attitudes of election losers toward the democratic system are more important than those of election winners. Supporters of election winners will mostly be satisfied with the outcome of the election, and they can expect the future incumbent to promote policies that benefit them or that they agree with. This being the case, they have no reason to oppose or question the rules of the democratic game (Miller and Listhaug 1999). Election winners are still worthy of research because they have the authority to enact all kinds of policies and laws. However, focusing only on election winners greatly limits our understanding of the sustainability and stability of democracy. It does not tell us why after one election is held, elections become an established mode of political participation in the future. In fact, the collective decision made by the voters may create tensions within society. This is because the results of the election divide the electorate into winners and losers, and there is a conflict of interest between the two sides. The most fundamental reason is the disproportionate distribution of the benefits between the winners and losers of the election (the election itself is like a zero-sum game). A number of important studies have shown that the rules of the democratic game are often viewed as the rules of the majority. But democracies rarely have rule by an absolute majority. Instead, the majority are more likely to be voters who did not vote for the winning party (or candidate) than those who voted for the winning party (or candidate). Many modern democracies apply the plurality rule, leading to a government that is only supported by a minority (Anderson et al. 2005).

Another problem is that the attitudes of the election losers toward the democratic system are often less clear-cut or firm (Nadeau and Blais 1993). For example, if the same party loses again and again in democratic elections, they may begin to question the legitimacy of the democratic system. As well as disappointment and dissatisfaction with the outcome of the election, in order to protect their own interests, election losers may do everything in their power to prevent election winners from implementing their policy proposals. In some cases, voters who find themselves on the losing side may decide no longer to vote in elections or even boycott elections. In more extreme cases, they may initiate political and social movements that seek to violently overthrow governments that they consider "unfair" and "unjust."

Therefore, a key principle of liberal democracy is that the power of the executive (winners) must be limited while minorities (losers) must be protected. This fits with the general distinction regarding the degree to which being on the side of the winners or losers and subsequently being part of the majority or minority shapes peoples' views about politics in general. While winners generally feel satisfied with democracy, losers tend to be more skeptical. More generally, winners seek consistency between their choice for the winning party and the actions of their party (van der Brug et al. 2021).

For a long time, scholars, including those in Taiwan, have been concerned with the electoral winners and their supporters, analyzing their strategies in winning elections, or the deciding factors of their votes, as well as the impact and consequences of their victory on future policy. However, there has been less analysis about election losers and their supporters (Shepsle 2003). Riker (1983) is one of the few scholars that has observed election losers over a long time period. Riker argues that the direction of a county's political interactions is actually set by the losers of elections. Therefore, the most important factor for the functioning and survival of democracy is not the victory of the winners, but the self-restraint of the losers; the losers must accept both the results of the election which they dislike and the process which produced them in order for democracy to survive.

Research Design

The concept of democratic support was given renewed attention in the late twentieth century through the study of democratic consolidation. However, democratic consolidation itself is a multifaceted and controversial concept (Schneider 1995). Fortunately, since Linz and Stepan's (1996, 6) proposed definition of the concept of democratic consolidation, this academic debate has gradually subsided. Linz and Stepan argued that democratic consolidation can be defined from three levels: behavioral, attitudinal, and constitutional. In terms of behavior, no political group has seriously tried to overthrow the democratic system, or achieve the goal of dividing the country through increased domestic or international violence. In terms of attitudes, even if they are facing a serious political and economic crisis, the vast majority of the people still believe that democracy is the only game in town, and any political changes must be based on democratic procedures. In terms of constitutional arrangements, all political actors are accustomed to resolving domestic political conflicts through existing norms, and consider violation of these norms to be ineffective and costly. By defining democratic consolidation in terms of popular attitudes toward democracy, Linz and Stepan change the orientation of research on third-wave democratization. Therefore, the concept of support for democracy or democratic legitimacy has become one of the most important and indispensable themes in the study of democratic consolidation (Bratton, Mattes, and Gyimah-Boadi 2005; Chu et al. 2008; Shi and Lu 2010).

Mishler and Rose (2005) identify three ways of defining the concept of support for democracy: popular support for democracy, popular evaluation of democratic performance, and popular democratic ideals and beliefs. Evaluation of democratic performance as a measure of citizens' attitudes toward democracy is currently used by many cross-national longitudinal research projects, including the Eurobarometer, the Comparative Study of Electoral Systems (CESS), and the International Social Survey Programme (ISSP). However, as Linde and Ekman (2003) clearly show, it is not ideal to measure popular democratic values solely in terms of "satisfaction with democracy," which only measures how democracy works in practice and is highly dependent on the specific political context when the question is asked.

Overall, democratization scholars have mainly defined the concept of support for democracy in terms of directly measuring citizens' attitudes toward democracy, or indirectly through democratic ideas and beliefs. Schedler and Sarsfield (2007) refer to the former as the direct measures and the latter as the indirect measures of support for democracy. Schedler and Sarsfield criticize the direct measure from a methodological perspective, pointing out that democracy is a highly complex and abstract concept, and every citizen has a different understanding of democracy. It is not appropriate or correct to measure people's support for democracy directly without dealing with the fundamental question of what democracy is. Therefore, the indirect measures of support for democracy are more suitable. However, if the concept of support for democracy excludes attitudes and only uses political values as indirect measures, it may not be possible to fully grasp the different orientations of citizens toward democracy. In other words, there may be an internal inconsistency between the two measurement methods. For example, although some citizens may be deeply committed to democratic values, they may not necessarily prefer a democratic system or believe that democracy is superior to other systems. Conversely, some citizens, while not deeply committed to democratic values, may prefer a democratic system and believe that democracy is better than other alternatives.

How can we create a scale for direct support for democracy? Based on a review of the literature, Chu et al. (2008) measure support for democracy on six dimensions: detachment from authoritarianism, preference for democracy, desirability of democracy, suitability of democracy, efficacy of democracy, and priority of democracy. However, this chapter excludes detachment from authoritarianism because detachment from authoritarianism does not necessarily indicate support for democracy. Citizens may have a depoliticized orientation that is detached from both authoritarianism and democracy. In addition, efficacy of democracy and priority of democracy are not necessarily related to support for democracy. Many surveys in Western countries have found a distinction between belief in the legitimacy of democracy and the evaluation of its actual performance. Growing numbers of citizens in Western countries identify with democracy but are dissatisfied with the democratic performance of their countries. Scholars refer to these people as "critical citizens" (Klingemann 1999; Norris 1999). Therefore, direct support for democracy in this chapter is measured using three items: desirability, suitability, and preferability.

Measures of Direct Support for Democracy

ddem1: What level of democracy would you like Taiwan to have now? (1-10)

ddem2: How suitable do you think democracy is for Taiwan? (1-10)

ddem3: Democracy is always better than other system of government. (1-10)

1. No matter what, democracy is always better than other systems of government.

2. In some cases, an autocratic government (i.e. authoritarian government) may be better than a democracy.

3. To me, it doesn't matter if it is a democracy or not.

Indirect support for democracy does not actively prompt the word "democracy," but instead measures whether citizens have democratic ideals and beliefs. In this regard, this chapter argues that democracy must have two basic systems of accountability: vertical accountability and horizontal accountability. The former is the concept of citizenship, and the latter is the concept of checks and balances between institutions.

Measures of Indirect Support for Democracy

idem1: Government leaders are like the head of a family; we should all follow their decisions.

idem2: The government should decide whether certain ideas should be allowed to be discussed in society.

idem3: When judges decide important cases, they should accept the view of the executive branch.

idem4: If the government is constantly checked by the legislature, it cannot possibly accomplish great things.

Data Analysis

Table 16.1 shows the descriptive statistics for the seven indicators over the five waves of the Asian Barometer Survey. From the data, direct measures of direct support for democracy, desirability of democracy, and suitability of democracy scored highly, but preferability of democracy did not. The four indicators measuring indirect support for democracy tend to be positive. Of these, three indicators scored relatively highly, while the item on the legislature checking the government had a lower score due to the frequent stalemate and paralysis in the Legislative Yuan.

Table 16.1 Descriptive Statistics

	Median(p50)	mean	sd	min	max
ddem1	8.0000	8.0845	1.71	1.0	10.0
ddem2	7.0000	7.0242	2.04	0.0	10.0
ddem3	2.0000	2.2310	0.84	1.0	3.0
idem1	3.0000	2.8569	0.60	1.0	4.0
idem2	3.0000	2.8888	0.59	1.0	4.0
idem3	3.0000	2.7517	0.69	1.0	4.0
idem4	2.0000	2.3734	0.65	0.0	4.0
N	7441				

Note: Don't know and refused are coded as missing values.
Source: Asian Barometer Survey, 2000-2018. Authors prepared.

Figure 16.1 Changes in the Three Indicators of Direct Support for Democracy

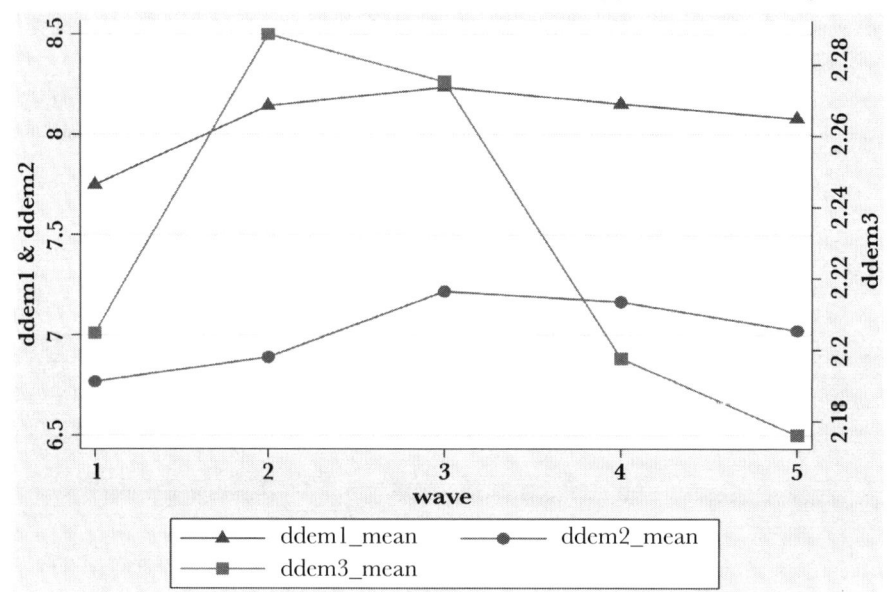

Source: Asian Barometer Survey. Authors prepared.

Figure 16.1 shows direct support for democracy over the five survey waves. In Figure 16.1, the indicator for preference for democracy has been falling since the second wave, and is now lower than in the first wave. The other two indicators are much more stable.

Figure 16.2 shows indirect support for democracy over the five survey waves. In Figure 16.2, all four indicators show a trend of stable growth. There has been a dramatic change in preference for democracy, which has been falling since the second wave, and is now lower than in the first wave. There has been less change in the remaining two indicators which have been relatively stable. However, the concept of the legislature acting as a check on the executive is gradually increasing.

This chapter carries out confirmatory factor analysis (CFA) on the seven items to test whether the data meets the criteria of unidimensionality and local independence in the IRT model. Kline (1998) proposes four indicators of model fit: chi square/degree of freedom ratio (χ^2/df), standardized root mean square residual (SRMR), Tucker-Lewis Index (TLI), and comparative fit index (CFI). The chi square/degree of freedom ratio is <3, RMSEA value is <.06, and CFI and TLI values >.95. Therefore, the data has a good model fit. Figure 16.3 shows that the indicators are all consistent with the theoretical deductions.

Figure 16.2 Changes in the Four Indicators of Indirect Support for Democracy

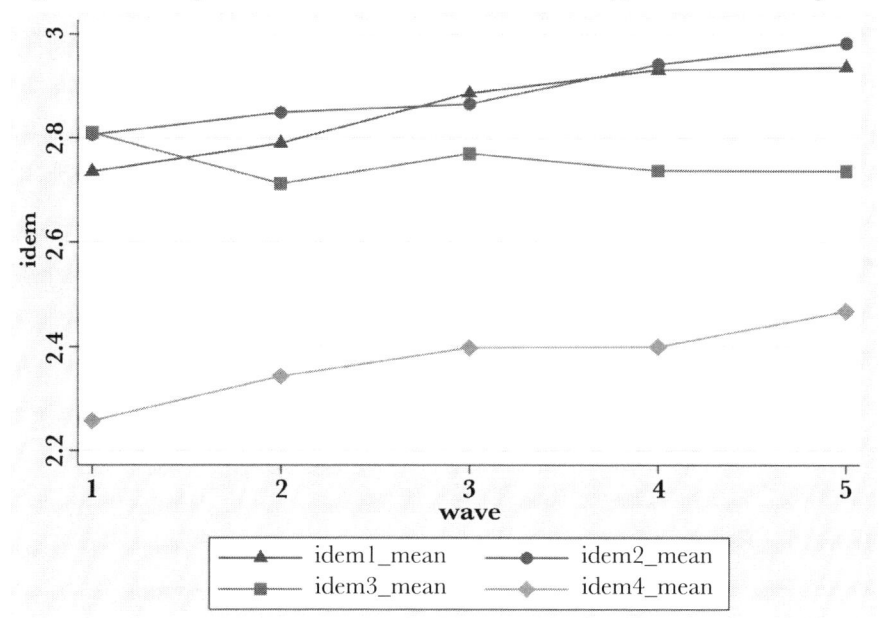

Source: Asian Barometer Survey. Authors prepared.

Figure 16.3 Confirmatory Factor Analysis

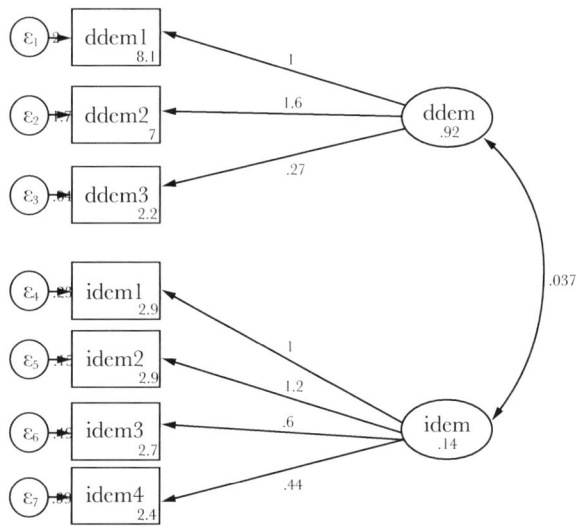

Estimation: Maximum likelihood with missing value
CFI: 0.988, TLI: 0.980, RMSEA: 0.023 (all pass)
Source: Authors prepared.

Changes in Losers and Winners between Each Wave
The Gap between Losers and Winners in Each Wave

Figure 16.4 shows the estimated distribution of winners and losers at 25 percent, 50 percent, 75 percent, and 90 percent direct support for democracy and indirect support for democracy. In the four figures, we find that regardless of the percentage, there is no major difference in their basic distribution of winners and losers. Losers scored less than winners on measures of direct democracy, but winners also scored less than losers on measures of indirect democracy. Van der Brug et al. (2021) find consistent support for our research, which predicts that supporters of governing parties are less likely to favor liberal democracy (indirective support for democracy) than are supporters of opposition parties. People who support the government in power are always less willing to constrain the executive than are those who support the opposition. In some cases, the differences are substantial. In response to this finding, it is necessary for us to construct conceptual types for deep analysis.

Figure 16.4.1 Median Direct Support for Democracy (Left), Indirect Support for Democracy (Right)

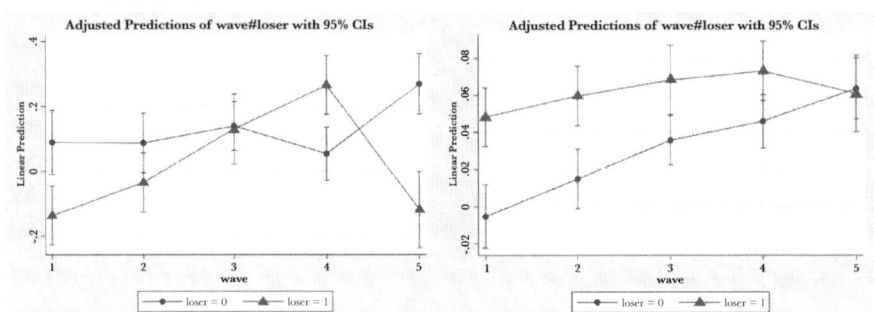

Source: Authors prepared

Figure 16.4.2 25% Direct Support for Democracy (Left), Indirect Support for Democracy (Right)

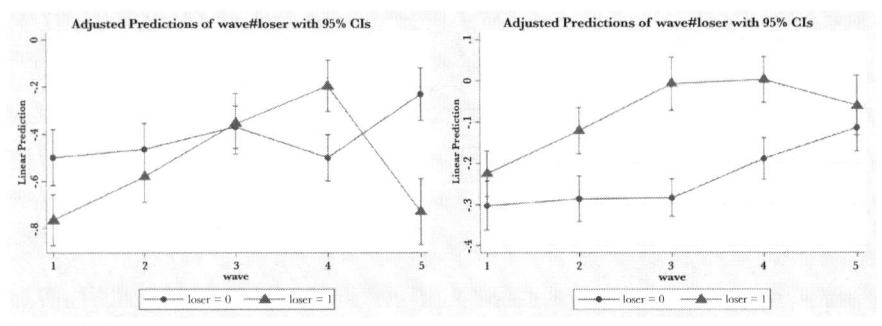

Source: Authors prepared.

Figure 16.4.3 75% Direct Support for Democracy (Left), Indirect Support for Democracy (Right)

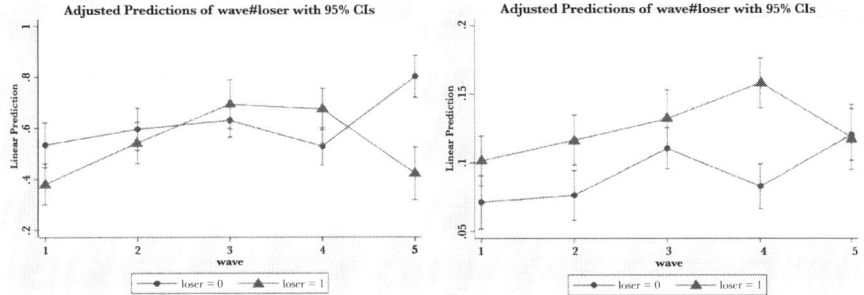

Source: Authors prepared.

Figure 16.4.4 90% Direct Support for Democracy (Left), Indirect Support for Democracy (Right)

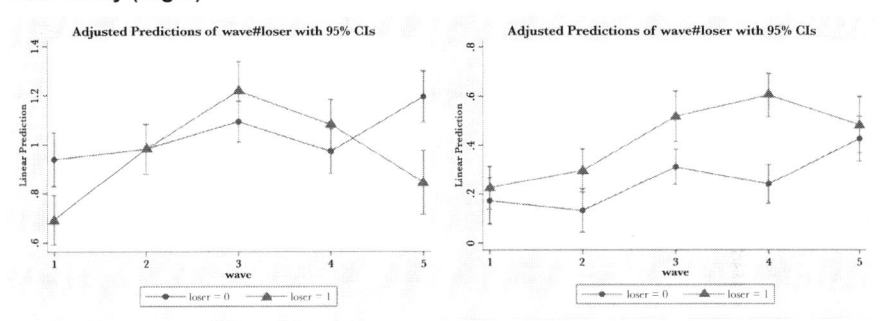

Source: Authors prepared.

Comparison of the Types of Support for Democracy

Using the results of factor analysis, this chapter goes on to construct four different types of support for democratic institutions. The method uses these two factors extracted through factor analysis as two different axes, and finally four different types of support for democracy can be distinguished. Attitude (2 x 2 = 4). The construction process is as follows: because the two aspects are composed of two measurement questions, in theory, in each aspect, at least the positive orientation must be answered before this aspect is classified as a positive orientation (that is, equal to 2 points), the rest are classified as negative orientation (i.e. between -2 and 0). Secondly, find out the corresponding factor analysis value greater than 0, which is used as the cutpoint of the classification. Finally, we can divide the attitudes of Taiwanese masses' political support into the following four different types.

Consistent Democrats: ddem_cfa>=0.0859533 & idem_cfa>=0.0539951

Superficial Democrats: ddem_cfa>=0.0859533 & idem_cfa<0.0539951 or no response to indirect support for democracy

Non-Democrats: ddem_cfa<0.0859533 & idem_cfa<0.0539951 or no response to direct support for democracy and indirect support for democracy

Critical Democrats: ddem_cfa<0.0859533 & idem_cfa>=0.0539951 or no response to direct support for democracy

Table 16.2 to Table 16.4 present the basic statistical findings for the four types of support for democracy.

Table 16.2 Descriptive Statistics for the Four Types

	mean	sd	min	max
con_dem	0.29	0.45	0.0	1.0
sup_dem	0.22	0.41	0.0	1.0
non_dem	0.30	0.46	0.0	1.0
cri_dem	0.22	0.41	0.0	1.0
N	7510			

Source: Asian Barometer Survey. Authors prepared.

Table 16.3 Descriptive Statistics for the Four Types (Losers)

	mean	sd	min	max
con_dem	0.33	0.47	0.0	1.0
sup_dem	0.17	0.38	0.0	1.0
non_dem	0.28	0.45	0.0	1.0
cri_dem	0.23	0.42	0.0	1.0
N	2247			

Source: Asian Barometer Survey. Authors prepared.

Table 16.4 Descriptive Statistics for the Four Types (Winners)

	mean	sd	min	max
con_dem	0.29	0.45	0.0	1.0
sup_dem	0.25	0.43	0.0	1.0
non_dem	0.30	0.46	0.0	1.0
cri_dem	0.18	0.38	0.0	1.0
N	2865			

Source: Asian Barometer Survey. Authors prepared.

Figure 16.5 The Ratios of the Four Types of Support for Democracy in Each Wave

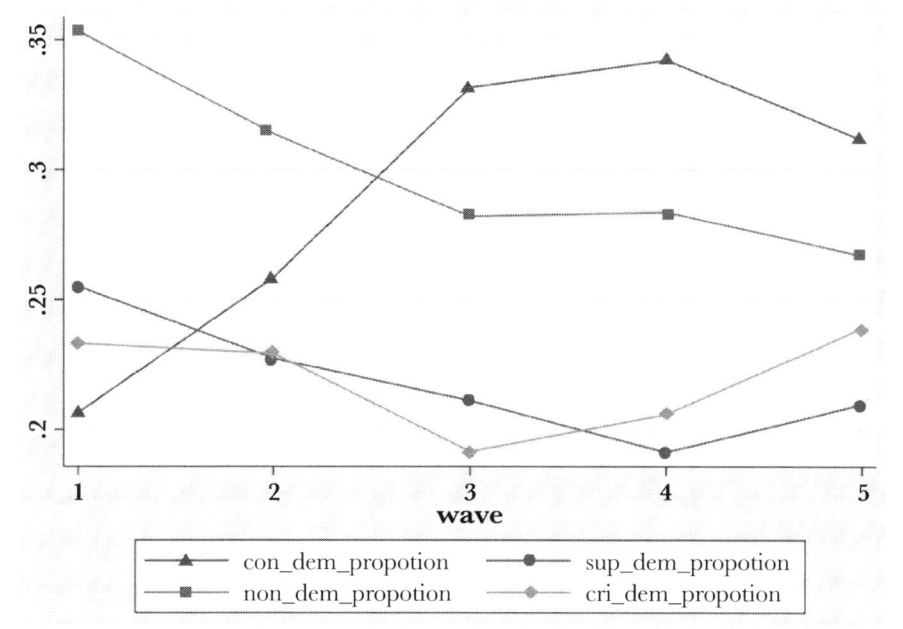

Source: Asian Barometer Survey. Authors prepared.

Figure 16.5 shows the overall analysis for the four types of support for democracy. The figure shows a steady decline in the ratio of Non-Democrats. There has also been a slight increase in the number of Critical Democrats, although the ratio is not large. There is a trade-off between Superficial Democrats and Consistent Democrats: when one group has a high ratio, the other group tends to have a low ratio.

Figures 16.6 and 16.7 illustrate the variation in the four types of support for democracy between the winners and losers. Among winners, there is a large increase in Consistent Democrats and a large decrease in Non-Democrats. Among losers, the pattern is the opposite. There is increase in Critical Democrats and a large increase in Non-Democrats.

Figure 16.6 The Ratios of the Four Types of Support for Democracy in Each Wave (Losers)

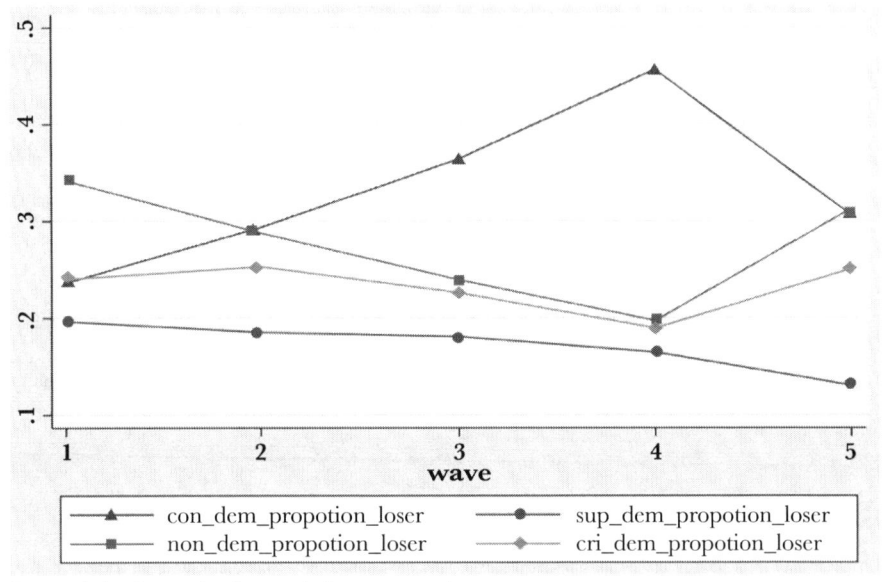

Source: Asian Barometer Survey. Authors prepared.

Figure 16.7 The Ratios of the Four Types of Support for Democracy in Each Wave (Winners)

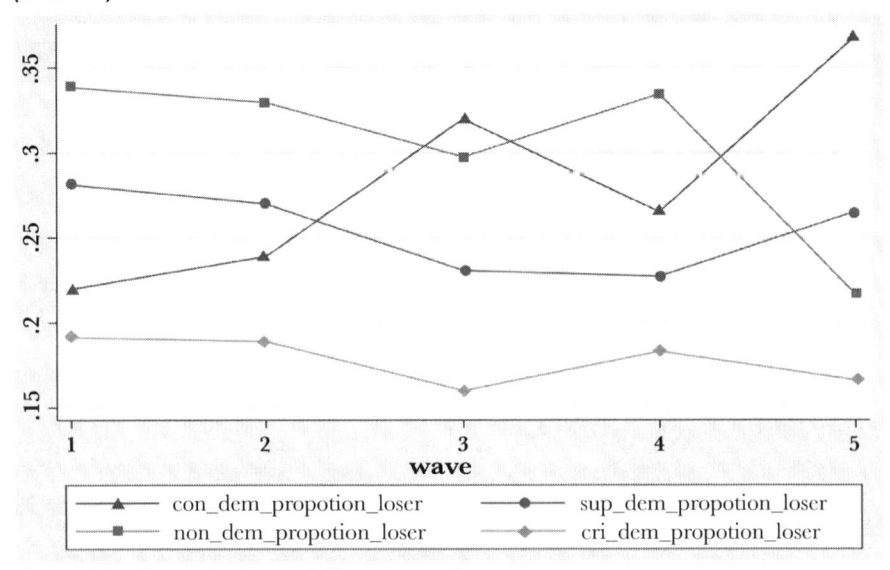

Source: Asian Barometer Survey. Authors prepared.

Our findings show that belonging to the winning or losing camps in elections does have an effect on support for democracy. Among elections losers, there are more Critical Democrats followed by Non-Democrats, and relatively few Consistent Democrats. Among election winners, there are more Consistent Democrats. Future research can control for other possible explanatory factors to determine whether belonging to the losing or winning camp in elections is still an important factor determining support for democracy in Taiwan.

Conclusion

Critical Democrats are equivalent to what Western societies call critical citizens. Since the 1960s, there have been a number of critical citizens in Western society. At the time, scholars believed that this was a problem arising from contradictions in the inherent structure of capitalist democracy (Geissel, 2008). However, after the 1990s, scholars believed that critical citizenship had positive effects on democracy. Dalton (2004) pointed out that critics of democracy have a driving force for the deepening process of democracy. Welzel and Inglehart (2008) pointed out that democracy requires political elites to make commitment to democratic rules, but the demand and criticism of democracy by the general public is an indispensable factor for the deepening and consolidation of democracy.

With the results of Taiwan's 2016 presidential election, there was a third party rotation, which weakened the support of the pan-blue camp supporters for the democratic system. However, as Przeworski said, the most value of democracy lies in its "uncertainty." Even if the losing camp loses this election, they believe that in the next election, as long as they work harder, there will be chances of winning (Przeworski, 1991:19-26). For a democracy to survive, everyone must feel that the party they support has a chance of winning in the future. After three party rotations in Taiwan, supporters of different camps have tasted the taste of winning and losing the election, which may help cultivate citizens' positive attitude toward democracy. Of course, this inference needs to be corroborated by future data.

References

Anderson, Christopher J., André Blais, Shaun Bowler, Todd Donovan, and Ola Listhaug. 2005. *Losers' Consent: Elections and Democratic Legitimacy*. New York: Oxford University Press.

Boese, Vanessa A., Amanda B. Edgell, Sebastian Hellmeier, Seraphine F. Maerz, and Staffan I. Lindberg. 2021. "How Democracies Prevail: Democratic Resilience as a Two-stage Process." *Democratization* 28 (5): 885-907.

Bratton, Michael, Robert Britt Mattes, and Emmanuel Gyimah-Boadi. 2005. *Public Opinion, Democracy, and Market Reform in Africa*. New York: Cambridge University Press.

Chu, Yun-han, Larry Diamond, Andrew Nathan, and Doh Chull Shin, eds. 2008. *How East Asians View Democracy*. New York: Columbia University Press.

Chu, Yun-han, Kai-Ping Huang, Marta Lagos, and Robert Mattes. 2020. "A Lost Decade for Third-wave Democracies?" *Journal of Democracy* 31 (2): 166-181.

Dalton, Russel. J. 2004. *Democratic Challenges, Democratic Choices: The Erosion of Political Support in Advanced Industrial Democracies*. New York: Oxford University Press.

Foa, Roberto Stefan, and Yascha Mounk. 2016. "The Danger of Deconsolidation: The Democratic Disconnect." *Journal of Democracy* 27 (3): 5-17.

—. 2017. "The Signs of Deconsolidation." *Journal of Democracy* 28 (1): 5-16.

Foa, Roberto Stefan, A. Klassen, M. Slade, A. Rand, and R. Collins. 2020. *The Global Satisfaction with Democracy Report 2020*. Cambridge: Centre for the Future of Democracy.

Foa, Roberto Stefan, Yascha Mounk, and Andrew Klassen. 2022. "Why the Future Cannot be Predicted." *Journal of Democracy* 33 (1): 147-155.

Freedom House. 2021. Freedom in the world 2020, "Leaderless Struggle for Democracy." https://freedomhouse.org/report/freedom-world/2020/leaderless-struggle-democracy.

Geissel, Brigitte. 2008. "Do Critical Citizens Foster Better Governance? A Comparative Study." *West European Politics* 31 (5): 855-873.

Gilley, Bruce. 2009. "Democratic Triumph, Scholarly Pessimism." *Journal of Democracy* 21 (1): 160-167.

Kline, Rex B. 1998. *Principles and Practices of Structural Equation Modeling*. New York: Guilford Press.

Klingemann, Hans-Dieter. 1999. "Mapping Political Support in the 1990s: A Global Analysis." In *Critical Citizens: Global Support for Democratic Governance*, edited by Pippa Norris, 31-56. New York: Oxford University Press.

Lieberman, Robert C., Suzanne Mettler, and Kenneth M. Roberts, eds. 2021. *Democratic Resilience: Can the United States Withstand Rising Polarization?*. New York: Cambridge University Press.

Linde, Jonas, and Joakim Ekman. 2003. "Satisfaction with Democracy: A Note on a Frequently Used Indicator in Comparative Politics." *European Journal of Political Research* 42 (3): 391-408.

Linz, Juan, and Alfred Stepan. 1996. *Problems of democratic transition and consolidation: Southern Europe, South America, and post-communist Europe*. Baltimore: John Hopkins University Press.

Miller, and Ola Listhaug. 1999. "Political Performance and Institutional Trust." In *Critical Citizens: Global Support for Democratic Government*, edited by Pippa Norris, 204-16. New York: Oxford University Press.

Mishler, William, and Richard Rose. 2005. "What Are the Political Consequences of Trust?" *Comparative Political Studies* 38 (11): 1050-1078.

Nadeau, Richard, and André Blais. 1993. "Accepting the Election Outcome: The Effect of Participation on Losers' Consent." *British Journal of Political Science* 23 (4): 553-563.

Norris, Pippa. 1999. "Global Communications and Cultural Identities." *Harvard International Journal of Press/Politics* 4 (4): 1-7.

Przeworski, Adam. 1991. *Democracy and the Market: Political and Economic Reform in Eastern Europe and Latin American*. Cambridge: Cambridge University Press.

Riker, William H. 1983. "Political Theory and the Art of Heresthetics." In *Political Science: The State of the Discipline*, edited by Ada W. Finifter, 47-68. Washington D.C.: American Political Science Association.

Schedler, Rodolfo, and Andreas Sarsfield. 2007. "Democrats with Adjectives: Linking Direct and Indirect Measures of Democratic Support." *European Journal of Political Research* 46 (5): 637-659.

Schneider, Ben Ross. 1995. "Democratic Consolidations: Some Broad Comparisons and Sweeping Arguments." *Latin American Research Review* 30 (2): 215-234.

Shepsle, Kennet A. 2003. "Losers in Politics (and How They Sometimes Become Winners): William Riker's Heresthetic." *Perspective on Politics* 1 (2): 307-315.

Shi, Tianjian, and Jie Lu. 2010. "The Shadow of Confucianism." *Journal of Democracy* 21 (4): 123-130.

Shin, Doh C. 2021. "Democratic Deconsolidation in East Asia: Exploring System Realignment in Japan, Korea, and Taiwan." *Democratization* 28 (1): 142-160.

V-Dem. 2021. "Autocratization Turns Viral: Democracy Report 2021." https://www.v-dem.net/static/website/files/dr/dr_2021.pdf.

Van der Brug, Wouter, Sebastian Popa, Sarah Hobolt, and Hermann Schmitt. 2021. "Democratic Support, Populism, and the Incumbency Effect." *Journal of Democracy* 32 (4): 131-145.

Welzel, Christian, and Ronald Inglehart. 2008. "The Role of Ordinary People in Democratization." *Journal of Democracy* 19 (1): 126-140.

17 South Korea's Embattled Democracy
Jung-ah Gil and Chong-Min Park

Over the past three decades since the democratic transition in 1987, South Korea (hereafter Korea) has maintained an electoral democracy. If democracy is characterized by universal suffrage, free and fair elections, and multiparty competition (Dahl 1971), the prevailing system of government in Korea meets the minimal standards of "thin" democracy. With four peaceful transfers of political power since the democratic transition, Korea has already passed the "two-turnover test" of democratic consolidation (Huntington 1991). More remarkable is that such democratic progress has been made despite the worst economic crisis in its modern history in the late 1990s. Even amid the global "democratic recession" in the 2000s, Korean democracy hardly lost its resilience and vibrancy.

Korea's steady institutional democratization is confirmed by expert-based assessments of democracy. The Polity5 Project evaluates regime authority characteristics on a 21-point scale ranging from -10 (hereditary monarchy) to +10 (consolidated democracy), with -10 to -6 corresponding to autocracies, -5 to +5 to anocracies, and +6 to +10 to democracies. In each of the first ten years after the transition, Korea received a Polity score of +6. In each of twenty-one years from 1998 to 2018, it received a score of +8, two notches below the maximum score. After the three decades of democratic rule, the political regime in Korea is rated as a nearly, if not fully, consolidated democracy.

Freedom House's *Freedom in the World* assigns the designation "electoral democracy" to countries that meet certain minimum standards for political rights and civil liberties. Since the publication of *Freedom in the World 1996-1997*, Korea has been designated as an electoral democracy. Freedom House assesses the condition of political rights and civil liberties on a 7-point scale with 1 (most free) to 7 (least free). The average score for political rights and civil liberties determines an overall status of "free" (1.0-2.5), "partly free" (3.0-5.0), and "not free" (5.5-7.0). Korea received an average combined score of 2.5 in each of the first five years of democratic rule (1988-1992); a score of 2.0 in each of the next eleven years (1993-2003); a score of 1.5 in each of the next nine years (2004-2012); and a score of 2.0 in each of eight years (2013-2020). Although the rating of political rights has been downgraded over the past years, Korea remains a "free" country.

How do, then, ordinary Koreans view their prevailing system of government? How do they evaluate the democratic quality of the regime? How do they view democracy and its authoritarian alternatives? How supportive are they of liberal democratic norms? By addressing these questions, we examine the mass-level attitudinal foundation of democracy in Korea, one of the successful third-wave democracies in East Asia. For the purpose of this chapter, we utilize two public opinion survey series—the Asian Barometer Survey (hereafter ABS) and the Korea Democracy Barometer (hereafter KDB).[1]

Regime Performance
Level of Democracy

In accord with expert-based assessments, most Koreans consider their prevailing system of government largely a democracy. When asked, "How much of a democracy the country is," those who replied, "a full democracy" constituted only a tiny minority over a decade (5 percent in 2006, 4 percent in 2011, 5 percent in 2015, and 4 percent in 2019). Yet, those who answered "a democracy, but with minor problems" accounted for 56 percent in 2006, 63 percent in 2011, 61 percent in 2015, and 67 percent in 2019, whereas those who answered "a democracy, with major problems," 34 percent in 2006, 29 percent in 2011, 30 percent in 2015, and 26 percent in 2019. In contrast, those who chose "not a democracy" represented the smallest group (2 percent in 2006, 2011, and 2015, and 1 percent in 2019). Notable is that among those who found their democracy flawed, those indicating minor problems far outnumbered those indicating major ones, and the gap between them widened from 22 percent in 2006 to 34 percent in 2011, 32 percent in 2015, and 41 percent in 2019. After three decades of democratic rule, two in three Koreans believe that the prevailing system of government is either a full or slightly flawed democracy.

Democratic Quality

Since democratic institutional performance is multidimensional, we examine how Koreans evaluate the prevailing system of government in terms of core liberal democratic principles—popular control, electoral competition, freedom, and checks and balances (see Table 17.1).[2]

Table 17.1 Evaluation of Democratic Quality

Survey Item	2006	2011	2015	2019
Agree: People have the power to change a government they don't like; Citizens are able to remove a government they don't like through elections (2019)	44	51	43	63
Disagree: Between elections, the people have no way of holding the government responsible for its actions	36	35	37	50
Both	*16*	*17*	*12*	*27*
Agree: Political parties/candidates in our country have equal access to the mass media during the election period; Parties/candidates not in power have opportunities to be elected into government (2019)	66	65	60	59
Say: Our elections always or most of the time offer the voters a real choice between different parties/candidates	47	51	45	35
Both	*35*	*35*	*28*	*21*
Agree: People are free to speak what they think without fear	57	52	50	53
Agree: People can join any organization they like without fear	64	66	56	56
Both	*41*	*36*	*32*	*41*
Disagree: When government leaders break the laws, there is nothing the court can do	43	40	50	58
Say: The legislature is capable of keeping government leaders in check	53	50	56	53
Both	*25*	*22*	*30*	*32*

Source: 2006 ABS Korea (N = 1,212); 2011 ABS Korea (N = 1,207); 2015 ABS Korea (N = 1,200); and 2019 ABS Korea (N = 1,268). Authors prepared.

Popular Control

We begin with popular control or accountability. When asked about electoral accountability, 44 percent in 2006, 51 percent in 2011, and 43 percent in 2015 agreed with the statement, "People have the power to change a government they don't like." In 2019, 63 percent agreed with the statement "Citizens are able to remove a government they don't like through elections." When asked about non-electoral accountability, 36 percent in 2006, 35 percent in 2011, 37 percent in 2015, and 50 percent in 2019 disagreed with the statement, "Between elections the people have no way of holding the government responsible for its action." Those giving affirmative responses to both statements accounted for 16 percent in 2006, 17 percent in 2011, 12 percent in 2015, and 27 percent in 2019, indicating an upward trend. Yet, even after three decades of democratic rule, only one in four Koreans approve of regime performance in popular control.

Electoral Competition

We turn to electoral or political competition. When asked about public contestation for power, 66 percent in 2006, 65 percent in 2011, and 60 percent in 2015 agreed with the statement "Political parties or candidates have equal access to the mass media during the elections." In 2019, 59 percent agreed with the statement, "Parties or candidates not in power have opportunities to be elected into government." When asked "How often the elections offer the voters a real choice between different parties or candidates," 47 percent in 2006, 51 percent in 2011, 45 percent in 2015, and 35 percent in 2019 replied either "always" or "most of the time." Those giving affirmative responses to both questions accounted for 33 percent in 2006, 35 percent in 2011, 28 percent in 2015, and 21 percent in 2019, suggesting a downward trend. Even after three decades of democratic rule, only one in five Koreans approve of regime performance in political competition.

Freedom

We turn to liberal rights of speech and association. When asked about freedom of speech, 57 percent in 2006, 52 percent in 2011, 50 percent in 2015, and 53 percent in 2019 agreed with the statement, "People are free to speak what they think without fear." When asked about freedom of association, 64 percent in 2006, 66 percent in 2011, and 56 percent in both 2015 and 2019 agreed with the statement, "People can join any organization they like without fear." By combining favorable responses to both questions, we assess overall evaluation of liberal rights of speech and association. Those who agreed with both statements accounted for 41 percent in 2006, 36 percent in 2011, 32 percent in 2015, and 41 percent in 2019, indicating little improvement over a decade. After three decades of democratic rule, only two in five Koreans feel that liberal rights of speech and association are protected.

Checks and Balances

We turn to legislative and judicial checks on the executive branch. When asked about legislative checks, 53 percent in 2006, 50 percent in 2011, 56 percent in 2015, and 53 percent in 2019 said that the National Assembly was either "very capable" or "capable" of keeping the government in check. When asked about judicial checks, 43 percent in 2006, 40 percent in 2011, 50 percent in 2015, and 58 percent in 2019 agreed with the statement, "When government leaders break the laws, there is nothing the court can do." Those giving affirmative responses to both questions accounted for 25 percent in 2006, 22 percent in 2011, 30 percent in 2015, and 32 percent in 2019, suggesting only slight improvement. Nonetheless, after three decades of democratic rule, only one in three Koreans consider checks and balances effective.

Overall, after three decades of democratic rule, none of the four liberal democratic dimensions examined enjoys majority approval. In the eyes of ordinary citizens, Korea's prevailing system of government remains weak, especially in institutions of democratic accountability.

Institutional Trust

Trust in political institutions is used as one of the key indicators of regime affect. Of political institutions, the parliament and political parties constitute core institutions of representation. For each institution, citizen confidence had declined dramatically for the second decade of democratic rule, before it turned around in the early 2010s. Those who had either "a great deal of trust" or "quite a lot of trust" in the National Assembly plummeted from 49 percent in 1996 to 21 percent in 1997 amid Korea's worst economic crisis. The proportion further declined to 15 percent in 2003 and 7 percent in 2006 and then slightly rose to 11 percent in 2011 and 12 percent in both 2015 and 2019, below the pre-economic crisis levels. In the 2010s, on average, about one in ten had confidence in the legislative branch of government. A similar trajectory was found for political parties. Those who had either "a great deal of trust" or "quite a lot of trust" in political parties plunged from 29 percent in 1996 to 19 percent in 1997. The proportion further declined to 15 percent in 2003 and 9 percent in 2006 and then rose slightly to 12 percent in 2011, 16 percent in 2015, and 15 percent in 2019, below the pre-economic crisis levels. In the 2010s, on average, about one in ten had confidence in political parties.

All things considered, after three decades of democratic rule, a large majority of Koreans consider their prevailing system of government a full or somewhat flawed democracy. Yet, only a small minority approve of the regime's democratic quality and express some degree of trust in institutions of representation.

Support for Democracy
Preference for Democracy

After three decades of democratic rule, public preference for democracy appears to be entrenched. As presented in Figure 17.1, those who chose "Democracy is always preferable to any other kind of government" steadily fell from 65 percent in 1996 to 54 percent in 1998, 45 percent in 2001, and 43 percent in 2006 and then bounced back to 66 percent in 2011, 63 percent in 2015, and 71 percent in 2019. A decade-long decline in the wake of the 1997 economic crisis was followed by a dramatic reversal in the early 2010s. The average level of democratic preference across three surveys conducted during the 2000s was 46 percent, whereas it was 67 percent across three surveys conducted during the 2010s, indicating a huge increase. More remarkable is that this growth took place amid a global democratic recession.

As noted in Figure 17.1, the largest drop in democratic preference occurred in the wake of the 1997 economic crisis, suggesting that economic performance has a huge influence. However, a sudden rise in the wake of the Great Recession in the late-2000s challenges any simplistic economic accounts. If economic performance matters most, preference for democracy should have further declined or at least stayed low in the wake of a global economic downturn. Other events that occurred between 2006 and 2011 should be responsible for the upturn in democratic preference. An obvious candidate is the 2007 presidential election through which an unpopular incumbent was removed through the ballot box. This collective experience of popular accountability seems to convince ordinary Koreans that democracy is better than its alternatives (Park 2014).

Figure 17.1 Preference for Democracy and Rejection of Authoritarian Rule

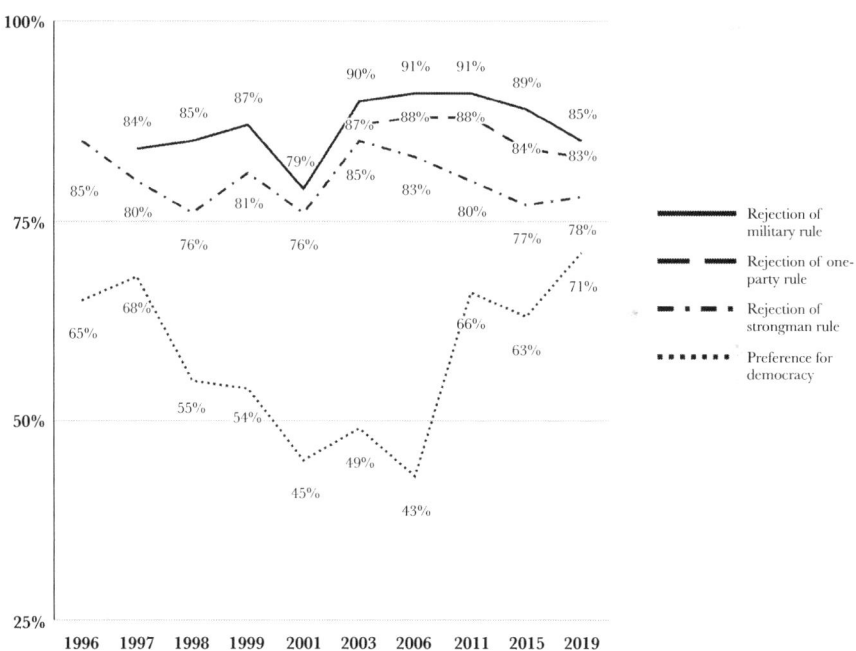

Source:1996 KDB (N = 1,000); 1997 KDB (N = 1,117); 1998 KDB (N = 1,010); 1999 KDB (N = 1,007); 2001 KDB (N = 1,005); 2003 ABS Korea (N = 1,500); 2006 ABS Korea (N = 1,212); 2011 ABS Korea (N = 1,207); 2015 ABS Korea (N = 1,200); and 2019 ABS Korea (N = 1,268). Authors prepared.

Rejection of Authoritarian Rule

As shown in Figure 17.1, public rejection of strongman rule is widespread. Those who disagreed with the statement "We should get rid of parliament and elections and have a strong leader decide things" accounted for 85 percent in 1996, 80 percent in 1997, 75 percent in 1998, 81 percent in 1999, 76 percent in 2001, 85 percent in 2003, 83 percent in 2006, 80 percent in 2011, 77 percent in 2015, and 78 percent in 2019. Popular opposition to strongman rule declined in the wake of the economic crisis of 1997 but bounced back as the country emerged from its worst economic crisis. In the 2010s, on average, more than three in four remain opposed to replacing democratic institutions of accountability with strongman rule.

Popular opposition to military rule is more widespread. Those who disagreed with the statement "The military should come in to govern the country" accounted for 84 percent in 1997, 85 percent in 1998, 87 percent in 1999, 79 percent in 2001, 90 percent in 2003, 91 percent in both 2006 and 2011, 89 percent in 2015, and 85 percent in 2019. Even right after the economic crisis in 1997, public rejection of military rule turned out to be robust. In the 2010s, on average, less than nine in ten remain opposed to military intervention in politics.

Popular rejection of one-party rule also proved to be prevalent. In 2003, 87 percent disagreed with the statement, "No opposition party should be allowed to compete for power." Those who disagreed with the statement "Only one political party should be allowed to stand for election and hold office" accounted for 88 percent in both 2006 and 2011, 84 percent in 2015, and 83 percent in 2019. In the 2010s, on average, more than four in five remain opposed to party dictatorship in favor of a competitive, multiparty political system.

In sum, popular detachment from authoritarian rule is firmly entrenched as the third decade of democratic rule ends, indicating, at the very least, popular support for institutions of minimalist democracy. An overwhelming rejection of dictatorship among the population suggests that the democratic method of selecting government leaders is widely accepted as "the only game in town."

Support for Democratic Norms

Support for democracy and rejection of authoritarian rule may be shallow unless they are accompanied by attachment to liberal democratic norms. In this section, we examine support for core liberal democratic norms—political equality, popular control, checks and balances, and social pluralism (see Table 17.2).

Table 17.2 Support for Liberal Democratic Norms

Survey Item	2003	2006	2011	2015	2019
Disagree: Government leaders are like the head of a family; we should all follow their decisions	53	60	60	63	72
Disagree: If we have political leaders who are morally upright, we can let them decide everything	37	34	41	43	66
Both	*25*	*23*	*28*	*32*	*52*
Disagree: When judges decide important cases, they should accept the view of the executive branch	69	72	67	68	68
Disagree: If the government is constantly checked by the legislature, it cannot possibly accomplish great things	54	57	62	57	67
Both	*39*	*46*	*48*	*44*	*55*
Disagree: Harmony of the community will be disrupted if people organize lots of groups	65	55	59	62	68
Disagree: If people have too many different ways of thinking, society will be chaotic	53	52	56	58	65
Both	*39*	*36*	*42*	*43*	*52*

Source: 2003 ABS Korea (N = 1,500); 2006 ABS Korea (N = 1,212); 2011 ABS Korea (N = 1,207); 2015 ABS Korea (N = 1,200); and 2019 ABS Korea (N = 1,268). Authors prepared.

Popular Control

Popular control, a core principle of democracy as rule of the people, rejects the idea that some political leaders possess superior competence to make collective decisions for the people. When asked about rule by paternalistic leaders, 53 percent in 2003, 60 percent in 2006, 60 percent in 2011, 63 percent in 2015, and 72 percent in 2019 disagreed with the statement, "Government leaders are like the head of a family; we should all follow their decision." When asked about rule by moral leaders, 37 percent in 2003, 34 percent in 2006, 41 percent in 2011, 43 percent in 2015, and 66 percent in 2019 disagreed with the statement, "If we have political leaders who are morally upright, we can let them decide everything."[3] Those who disagreed with both statements accounted for 23 percent in 2006, 32 percent in 2015, and 52 percent in 2019, suggesting an upward trend. Yet, even after three decades of democratic rule, only one in two believe that people are the best judges of their own interests, suggesting ambivalence toward popular sovereignty.

Checks and Balances

Separation of powers and checks and balances embody the liberal idea of limited government. When asked about legislative checks, 54 percent in 2003, 57 percent in 2006, 62 percent in 2011, 57 percent in 2015, and 67 percent in 2019 disagreed with the statement, "If the government is constantly checked by the legislature, it cannot possibly accomplish great things."[4] When asked about judicial checks, 69 percent in 2003, 72 percent in 2006, 67 percent in 2011, 68 percent in 2015, and 68 percent in 2019 disagreed with the statement, "When judges decide important cases, they should accept the view of the executive branch." Those who disagreed with both statements accounted for 39 percent in 2003, 46 percent in 2006, 48 percent in 2011, 44 percent in 2015, and 55 percent in 2019. Although the trend appears to be upward, public support for institutions of horizontal accountability is not that high.

Social Pluralism

A vibrant pluralist civil society or public sphere is essential for liberal political order. When asked about associational activism, 65 percent in 2003, 55 percent in 2006, 59 percent in 2011, 62 percent in 2015, and 68 percent in 2019 disagreed with the statement, "Harmony in the community will be disrupted if people organize lots of groups."[5] When asked about the marketplace of ideas, 53 percent in 2003, 52 percent in 2006, 56 percent in 2011, 58 percent in 2015, and 65 percent in 2019 disagreed with the statement, "If people have too many different ways of thinking, society will be chaotic."[6] Those who disagreed with both statements accounted for 39 percent in 2003, 36 percent in 2006, 42 percent in 2011, 43 percent in 2015, and 52 percent in 2019. Public support for social pluralism surged in the late 2010s after a decade of stagnation. Nonetheless, after three decades of democratic rule, only one in two remains supportive of a pluralistic civil society.

Overall, after the three decades of democratic rule, at least one in two Koreans appear to be attached to core liberal democratic norms. Notable is that support for specific liberal democratic norms remains lower than support for democracy as an undifferentiated whole.

By Way of Conclusion: Dangers of Democratic Erosion

Considering the evidence presented above, Korea's democracy appears to be consolidated in the mass-level attitudinal dimension (Linz and Stepan 1996; Diamond 1999). After three decades of democratic rule, an overwhelming majority of the population reject any common form of authoritarian rule as an alternative to democracy. A large majority of the population believe that democracy is always preferable to any other kind of government. Although only a small minority approve of the regime's democratic quality and have confidence in institutions of representation, political discontent hardly deters ordinary Koreans from supporting democracy or rejecting authoritarian rule. Yet, public attachment to liberal democratic norms has yet to be entrenched. In view of the fact that support for democracy is broad and rejection of authoritarian rule is overwhelming, there is no doubt that an electoral, if not liberal, democracy, has become "the only game in town" in Korea. Yet, low public attachment to liberal democratic norms suggests that Korea's democracy remains vulnerable to the tyranny of the democratic but illiberal majority.

Recent political developments cause concern about democratic erosion in Korea. A massive wave of political protest denouncing misgovernment, which has been dubbed the "Candlelight Revolution," resulted in the impeachment of a sitting President in late 2016 and brought a leftist opposition party to power in mid-2017. Considering the actions that the government has taken since then, Korea's democracy appears to be in the incremental process of erosion (Ginsburg and Huq 2018). What is happening in Korea seems reminiscent of what has happened in Poland and Hungary.[7]

With public opinion on its side in the wake of the "Candlelight Revolution," the president and the parliamentary majority have taken actions to weaken institutions of horizontal accountability and to politicize state institutions, especially rule-of-law institutions. The government has pursued its political agenda more aggressively in the wake of the ruling party's landslide victory in the National Assembly election in 2020 amid the coronavirus pandemic.

First, the government has sought to weaken or dismantle liberal institutions of checks and balances. The courts are stocked with loyalists, which allows them to make pro-government controversial rulings. The legislature controlled by the ruling party hardly serves as an independent check on executive power. As both the judiciary and the parliament cease to be separated from the executive branch, the system of checks and balances appears to be breaking down.

Second, by overemphasizing democratic control, the president and the parliamentary majority politicize state institutions. They have undermined the independence of unelected bodies as "the internal executive safeguards of democratic rule." Notably, under the pretext of prosecution reform, the president and the ruling party have weakened the autonomy and impartiality of law-enforcing institutions. The police, which are more vulnerable to political intervention, have been given investigation power. A new agency, which would be vulnerable to presidential influence, has been established to investigate high-ranking officials, including public prosecutors and judges. Law-enforcing state agencies and independent regulatory bodies have become politicized as their key posts are filled with loyalists. These politicized institutions are deployed against political opponents and critics, leading to selective rule of law.

Third, the government has regulated independent media and mobilized public media, which makes public discourse biased in favor of its political agenda. The government has used libel prosecution to limit the flow of information critical of the president and the government and assaulted liberal rights of speech and association, targeting anti-government segments of civil society including anti-North Korea groups. The government has employed the selective enforcement of laws and regulations to shape the environment of public discourse, which renders the playing field uneven.

In the wake of the "Candlelight Revolution," the government has taken actions to turn institutions of horizontal accountability and rule-of-law institutions into an instrument of executive control, indicating that Korea's democracy is in the dangerous process of democratic erosion. The system of separation of powers and checks and balances is in crisis. The impartiality of rule-of-law institutions is in danger. Liberal rights of speech and association are in retreat. With a weak rule of law and a façade of checks and balances, democracy in Korea seems to be on the verge of degenerating into the tyranny of majority rule or "stealth authoritarianism" (Varol 2018).

Overall, Korea's thin democracy is consolidated in the mass-level attitudinal dimension after three decades of democratic rule. Yet, the supply of democracy remains far short of public demand for democracy. Despite increasing mass support for democracy and persistent rejection of authoritarian rule over decades, Korea's democracy appears to be in retreat because of illiberal actions taken by the president and the parliamentary majority. Korea's democracy is under attack from the very people who seize power in the wake of the so-called "Candlelight Revolution."

Acknowledgements

This work was supported by the Ministry of Education of the Republic of Korea and the National Research Foundation of Korea (NRF-2018S1A3A2075609).

Notes

1. This study uses the ABS's five surveys (2003, 2006, 2011, 2015, and 2019) and the KDB's three surveys (1996, 1997, and 2001). For the ABS, see http://asianbarometer.org. For the KDB, see Shin and Lee (2006).
2. For the multidimensionality of democratic quality, see Diamond and Morlino (2004).

3. The 1997 KDB reports that only 39 percent of respondents disagreed with the statement "We can leave things to morally upright leaders."
4. The 1997 KDB reports that only 39 percent of respondents disagreed with the statement "If a government is often restrained by an assembly, it will be unable to achieve great things."
5. In view of the 1997 KDB report that only 34 percent of respondents agreed with the statement "Too many competing groups would undermine social harmony," there is a huge increase in public support for associational activism over the last three decades.
6. In view of the 1997 KDB report that only 35 percent agreed with the statement "Too many diverse opinions would undermine social order," there is a huge rise in public support for the marketplace of ideas over the last three decades.
7. For the trajectory of democratic erosion in Hungary and Poland, see Halmai (2018) and Sadurski (2018), respectively.

References

Dahl, Robert A. 1971. *Polyarchy: Participation and Opposition*. New Haven: Yale University Press.

Diamond, Larry. 1999. *Developing Democracy: Toward Consolidation*. Baltimore: Johns Hopkins University Press. https://www.ebook.de/de/product/3752190/larry_diamond_developing_democracy_toward_consolidation.html.

Diamond, Larry, and Leonardo Morlino. 2004. "The Quality of Democracy: An Overview." *Journal of Democracy* 15 (4): 20-31. doi:10.1353/jod.2004.0060.

Ginsburg, Tom, and Aziz Huq. 2018. *How to Save a Constitutional Democracy*. Chicago: The University of Chicago Press.

Halmai, Gábor. 2018. "A Coup Against Constitutional Democracy: The Case of Hungary." In *Constitutional Democracy in Crisis?*, edited by Mark A. Graber, Sanford Levinson, and Mark Tushnet, 243-256. Oxford: Oxford University Press.

Huntington, Samuel. 1991. *The Third Wave: Democratization in the Late Twentieth Century*. Norman: University of Oklahoma Press.

Linz, Juan J., and Alfred Stepan. 1996. *Problems of Democratic Transition and Consolidation: Southern Europe, South America, and Post-Communist Europe*. Baltimore: Johns Hopkins University Press.

Park, Chong-Min. 2014. "South Korea's Disaffected Democracy." In *Democracy in Eastern Asia: Issues, Problems and Challenges in a Region of Diversity*, edited by Edmund Fung and Steven Drakeley. Oxfordshire: Routledge.

Sadurski, Wojciech. 2018. "Constitutional Crisis in Poland." In *Constitutional Democracy in Crisis?*, edited by Mark A. Graber, Sanford Levinson, and Mark Tushnet, 257-276. Oxford: Oxford University Press.

Shin, Doh Chull, and Jaechul Lee. 2006. "The Korea Democracy Barometer Surveys: Unraveling the Cultural and Institutional Dynamics of Democratization, 1997-2004." *Korea Observer* 37 (2): 237-275.

Varol, Ozan O. 2018. "Stealth Authoritarianism in Turkey." In *Constitutional Democracy in Crisis?*, edited by Mark A. Graber, Sanford Levinson, and Mark Tushnet, 339-354. Oxford: Oxford University Press.

18 The Development of Democracy in Mongolia: The Perspective of Ordinary Citizens

Damba Ganbat

Thirty years ago, on July 29, 1990, the first democratic and multiparty elections were held in Mongolia after seventy years of a communist political regime. On December 10, 1989, the first democratic gathering in which Mongolian people have exercised their right to express those views freely and criticize the ideology under one-party society, took place on International Human Rights Day. The Mongolian Democratic Union (MDU) organized the country's first-ever peaceful protest. This four-hour-long protest started the transition to democracy, and it has officially marked the beginning of the democratic development of Mongolia. Owing to the fact that this protest was the turning point for Mongolians that no one would dare to imagine, a free and democratic multiparty election was held after eight months.

However, the events during these eight months have fundamentally changed our society. Having questioned the ideology of the communist regime, the initial gathering led to further rallies of tens of thousands of people beyond the capital city Ulaanbaatar. Moreover, these demonstrations evolved into a political hunger strike due to the harassment and arrests by the authorities.

Thanks to the struggle in the streets, the slogans touched the hearts of thousands of people. Consequently, the ruling party had no choice but to acknowledge that they had lost the support of the public. In March 1990, the leadership of the ruling party resigned and sat at a round table with the activists of the democratic movement to discuss the future of Mongolia. Samuel Huntington (1991, 13) characterized Mongolia's transition to democracy as a process of "transplacement," mainly because democratization resulted from joint action by groups both in and out of power.

Indeed, there was no representation of the democratic movement in government until the first election in 1990. The authorities amended the 1960 Constitution, declaring the end of a one-party rule and enacted a multiparty system to allow for democratic elections. Democratic movements have not only monitored the authorities' actions and put pressure on them, they also held roundtables with them to present their own demands. Thus, the first ever competitive multiparty democratic election was held in Mongolia in July 1990.

During the first democratic election in 1990, the communist party, with a history stretching back seven decades, competed with five democratic parties that had been in existence for only five months. At that time, there were very few candidates from the new parties who genuinely represented the Mongolian people, especially those in the countryside. It was inevitable that the Mongolian People's Revolutionary Party (MPRP) would gain as many as 343 seats (80 percent) in the 430-seat People's Great Khural. Independent candidates won fifty-one seats, or around 20 percent, whereas the newly established democratic parties won only 8 percent of all the seats.

Members of the lower house, or State Baga Khural, were elected according to a proportional representation system from party lists. The MPRP won 66 percent of the seats, while the Democratic Party, the Social Democratic Party of Mongolia, and the Mongolian National Progressive Party took 26 percent, 8 percent, and 6 percent respectively. The democratic movement that had started one year earlier now had its first representatives in both houses of the parliament.

Since Mongolia had its first democratic constitution in 1992, a total of twenty-three general elections have been held in Mongolia, including the recent election in 2020. Specifically, eight parliamentary elections, seven presidential elections, and eight local parliamentary elections have been held.

There were eight political parties and two coalitions in the first parliamentary elections in 1992, while thirteen political parties and four coalitions participated in 2020, which marks the record for the highest numbers of both political parties and coalitions. In eight parliamentary elections from 1992 to 2020, it can be seen that the numbers of political parties have dramatically increased to thirteen in the last election (2020).

While about 293 candidates from political parties, coalitions, and independents ran for 76 parliamentary seats in the 1992 election, there were 302 candidates in 1996, 602 in 2000, 244 in 2004, 356 in 2008, 544 in 2012, 498 in 2016, and 606 in the 2020 election (Table 18.1).

Table 18.1 Number of Parties and Candidates in the Parliamentary Elections (1992-2020)

Parliamentary Elections	Political Parties	Coalitions	Candidates
1992	8	2	293
1996	5	2	302
2000	13	3	602
2004	7	1	244
2008	12	1	356
2012	11	2	544
2016	12	3	498
2020	13	4	606

Source: General Election Commission of Mongolia. www.gec.gov.mn. Author prepared.

Ikh Khural (parliament) elections were regularly held during the communist era, but each constituency was required to elect a candidate for the ruling party. Voting was mandatory, and people were legally obligated to fulfill their civic duty. It was no surprise that the election turnout was maintained around 99.99 percent, which can be considered as a tool for party control. In contrast, voting is voluntary today in Mongolia, but voter turnout still remains high (Figure 18.1).

Figure 18.1 Parliamentary Election Turnout (1992-2020)

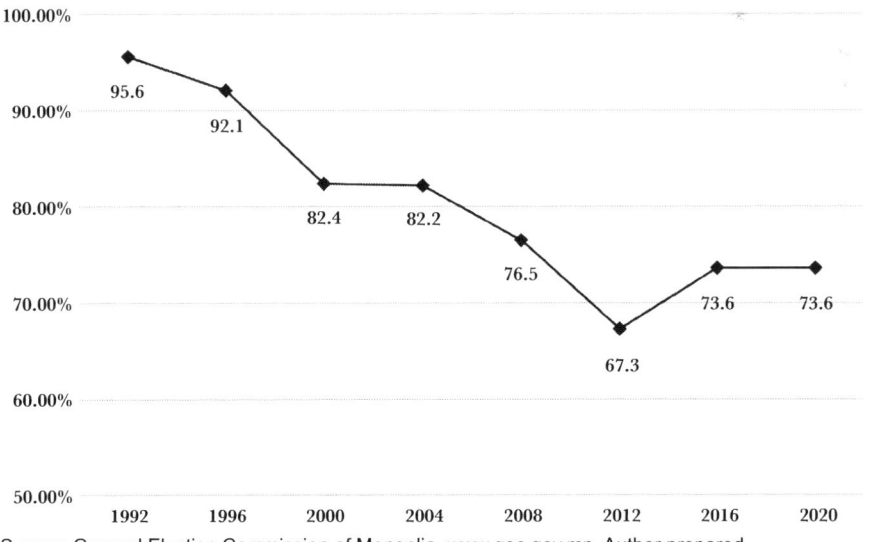

Source: General Election Commission of Mongolia. www.gec.gov.mn. Author prepared.

Figure 18.2 "How Often Do You Think Our Elections Offer the Voters a Real Choice between Different Parties/Candidates?" (2006-2018)

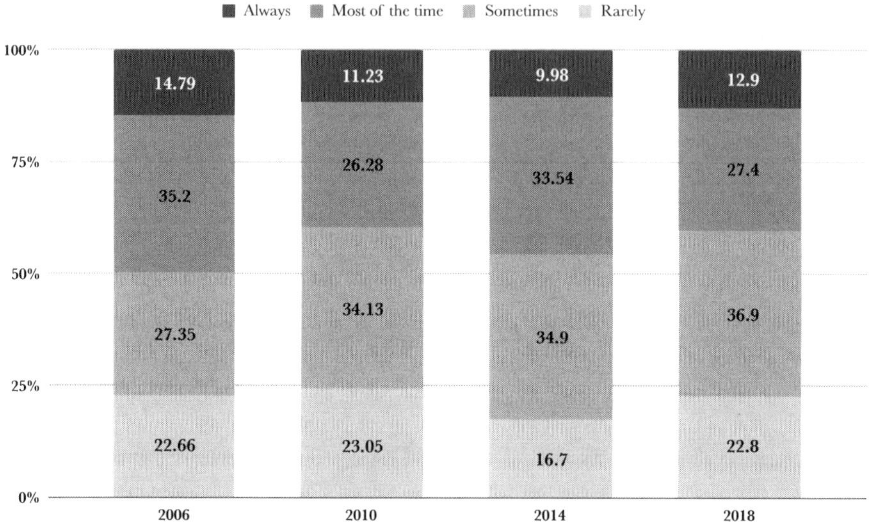

Source: Asian Barometer Survey. Author prepared.

Despite the high turnout, public opinion about elections remains negative. Many Mongolians still believe that the elections in Mongolia do not always represent them. Namely, 50 percent of respondents believed that the 2003 election (when the first wave was conducted) provided them the opportunity to choose, and this percentage has dropped to 40 percent in 2018 (the fifth wave, Figure 18.2).

What has happened in Mongolia is the first successful transition from totalitarian communism to democracy in Asia. Mongolia is the only post-communist country outside Eastern Europe that scores high in terms of political rights, civil liberties, and press freedom. Furthermore, no one can say that Mongolia's democratic political process is dominated by a few powerful politicians, a common occurrence among third-world nations. Mongolia may be considered to be "one of the more remarkable outliers of the post-communist universe in regards to democratization," because it is "the only third wave of democracy east of the Balkans that avoided political erosion and successfully consolidated democracy" (Fritz 2002). Among the family of third-wave democracies, Mongolia is often regarded as "one of the least likely cases" to have undergone a successful transition (UNDP in Mongolia 2020: 27, cited by Pomfret (2000, 149) and Fish (1998, 128)). Despite this assessment, the country is consistently ranked as democratic and free by international observers.

Figure 18.3 Freedom Rating, Mongolia (1999-2018)

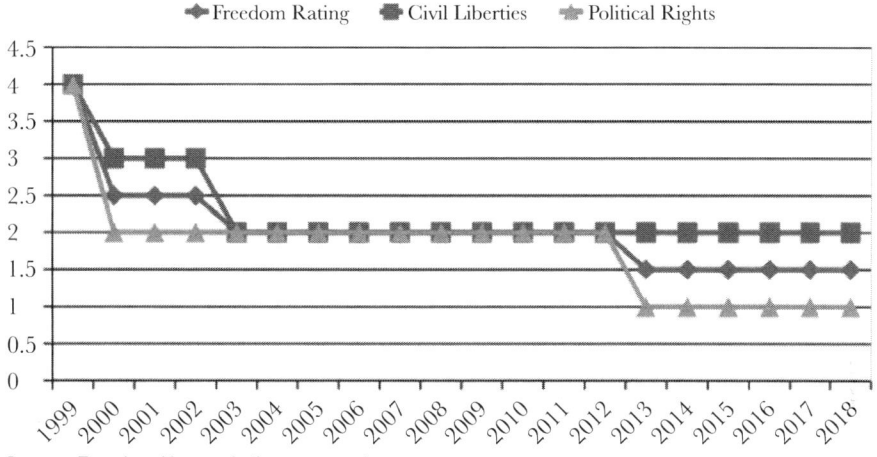

Source: Freedom House. Author prepared.

Freedom House publishes an annual report on levels of freedom which ranks countries' political rights and civil liberties on a scale of 1 (most free) to 7 (least free). As shown in Figure 18.3, in 2003 (the first wave), Mongolia received a freedom rating score of 2.0 and was rated "free," with a score of 2.0 for both political rights and civil liberties (Figure 18.3).

At that time, Mongolia, in common with other electoral democracies, did not receive the perfect score for freedom that many advanced Western democracies were awarded. Furthermore, Freedom House considered Mongolia to be an "electoral democracy," indicating that it possessed the basic properties of a democracy, such as a competitive multiparty system, universal adult suffrage, regularly contested elections, and equal access to the electorate for major political parties. Fifteen years later in 2018, when the fifth wave was conducted, Mongolia's freedom rating had risen to 1.5, and it was also rated as "free," with a political rights score of 1.0 and a civil liberties score of 2.0.

Evaluation of Democracy

There is always a positive correlation between the human development index and freedom and human rights. For instance, in the late 1990s, Mongolia scored 2.5 for political freedom and 3.0 for civil liberties. This correlates with a score of 0.66 on the human development index (UNDP 2020; Freedom House 2020). However, eighteen years later, in 2018, the country's political freedom score was 1.5, civil liberties was 2.0, and its human development index had increased to 0.74 (Freedom House 2020; UNDP 2020). Although these numbers are not sufficient to prove that political and human developments are progressing hand in hand in Mongolia, it is still a very positive trend.

Democracy allows people to live their lives freely and to make their own choices. That is why political development and economic development are seen as being closely linked and are studied in conjunction with each other on a theoretical level and in real life. As a new democracy, Mongolia has fundamentally changed its previous one-party system and dismantled its centrally planned economy, a process that is commonly referred to as a "dual transition."

However, there are some issues that demand our attention, judging from the unequal distribution of income in Mongolia. For example, in the 1990s, Mongolia's Gini coefficient was 30.3, but by 2006 it had increased to 36.5. After that, it improved slightly, decreasing to 33.1 in 2010. However, the index crept up again to 39 in 2014 (National Statistics Office of Mongolia 2020). Although some indexes show a negative trend, this dual transition, which started in the 1990s, still receives a positive evaluation from the public, according to successive waves of the ABS.

In 2003, when the first wave of the ABS was conducted, 77.5 percent of the population agreed that democracy was capable of solving the problems in Mongolian society (Figure 18.4). Although the level of approval declined over the following waves of the ABS, two-thirds of respondents still said that democracy was capable of solving society's problems in all five waves.

Figure 18.4 Democracy Is Capable of Solving Problems (2003-2018)

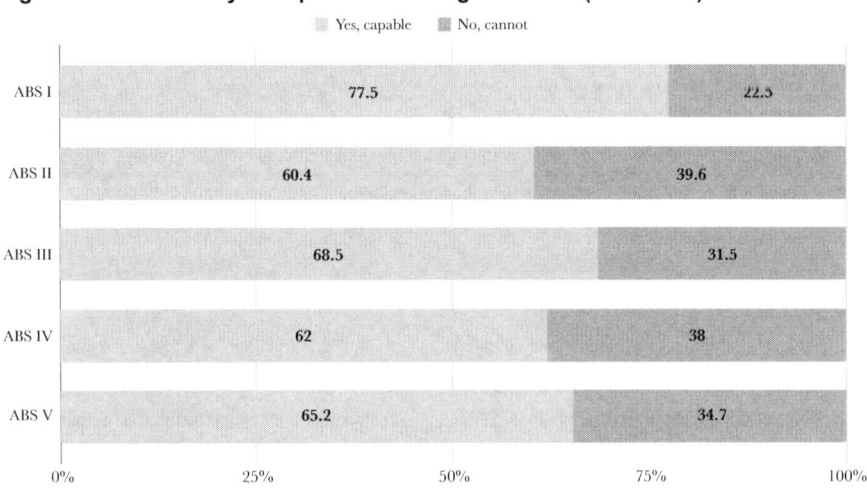

Source: Asian Barometer Survey. Author prepared.

Figure 18.5 Economic Development vs. Political Freedom (2003-2018)

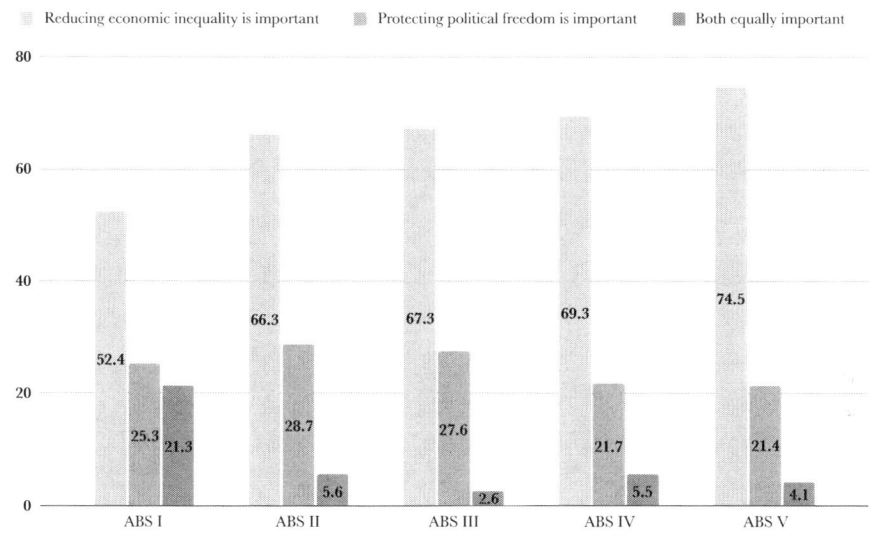

Source: Asian Barometer Survey. Author prepared.

In the years when an ABS was conducted, the majority of respondents indicated that they put economic development before democracy, with the percentage of respondents who put economic development first being two to three times higher than the percentage of respondents who preferred democracy. In recent years, this trend has become more prominent judging from how respondents answered the question, "If you had to choose between reducing economic inequality and protecting political freedom, which would you say is more important?" There was a much more marked difference in the percentages of respondents preferring economic development and political freedom in Mongolia (Figure 18.5). Since 2003, most ABS respondents in Mongolia have been concerned about socioeconomic problems in their country, while issues related to political rights and civil liberties are considered to be less important.

This political and economic dual transition still receives a positive evaluation from the public according to the ABS. For example, in 2003, two-thirds of respondents agreed with the statement, "Democracy may have its problems, but it is still the best form of government," and in the most recent poll in 2018, that percentage increased to 75.3 percent (including those who answered "strongly agree" and "agree," see Figure 18.6).

Figure 18.6 The Best Form of Government (2003-2018)

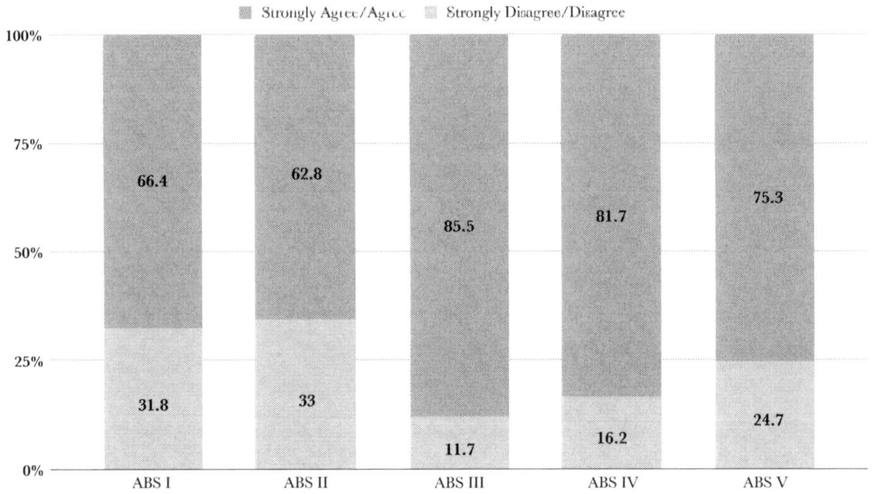

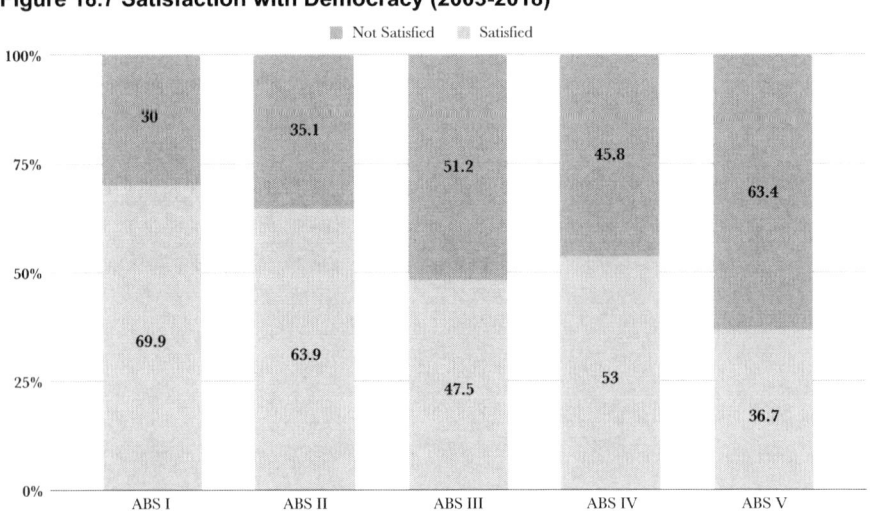

Source: Asian Barometer Survey. Author prepared.

However, Mongolians are highly critical of the way that democracy has been realized in their country. Over the years in which polls have been conducted, the percentage of respondents who have said they were not satisfied with the way democracy works in Mongolia has increased from 30 percent to 63.4 percent (Figure 18.7).

Figure 18.7 Satisfaction with Democracy (2003-2018)

Source: Asian Barometer Survey. Author prepared.

Commitment to Democracy

Support for democratic politics goes beyond a cognitive or behavioral capacity to engage in a democratic system. Citizens with limited experience of democracy may remain nostalgic about the hierarchical order of the communist system and consequently may have a combination of democratic and totalitarian proclivities (Rose and Mishler 2000). Therefore, it is incumbent upon new democracies to foster a citizenry that will endorse the legitimacy of democracy and actively choose it over totalitarianism and other antidemocratic alternatives. Only then can "incomplete" democracies endure and grow into complete ones. In this section, I focus on Mongolians' orientation in favor of democracy and against its alternatives.

How strongly are ordinary Mongolians attached, in principle, to democracy as a system of government? How strongly are they committed to its practices? These questions address the desirability of democracy, the suitability of democracy, preference for democracy, the efficacy of democracy, and the priority that should be given to democracy. Positive or pro-democratic responses to the questions are considered, individually and collectively, to measure the specific and general level of commitment to democratic governance.

The vast majority (92-94 percent) of Mongolians articulated a clear desire for democracy, producing a score of 6 or above (10 = complete democracy). More notably, a plurality of one-third (30 percent) expressed a desire for complete democracy (10 on the scale). It is evident that at least in principle, most Mongolians want to live in a democracy rather than in any of its alternatives.

Desirability is not enough, however, to build a democratic nation. Democracy has to be accepted as suitable for the nation's socioeconomic and other conditions. A large majority said that democracy is suitable for their nation, and more than one-quarter said that it was completely suitable (10 on the ladder scale). Thus, in addition to believing that democracy is a desirable form of government, many Mongolians also perceive democracy to be suitable for their society. In order to gauge whether there is general support for democracy as a viable political system, the ABS survey asked respondents whether or not they believe "democracy is capable of solving the problems facing the country." A substantial majority replied in the affirmative, asserting democracy's efficacy. This percentage is, however, lower than the percentages expressing desire for democracy and belief in the suitability of democracy, and what is notable is that the percentage declined over the years 2003-2018 (from 78 percent to 65.6 percent) (Table 18.2).

Table 18.2 Support for Democracy as a Viable Political System in Mongolia (2003-2018)

(Percentage of respondents)	First Wave	Second Wave	Third Wave	Fourth Wave	Fifth Wave
Desirable for our country now	91.6	94.4	-	-	75.3
Suitable for our country now	86.3	84.4	84.1	73.5	74.4
Effective in solving problems	78.4	77.0	74.6	63.0	65.6
Preferable to all other kinds of government	57.1	39.7	48.4	43.7	36.9
Should have priority over economic development	48.6	28.0	28.2	25.6	22.4
Mean number of items	*3.6*	*3.2*	*2.4*	*2.2*	*2.1*

Source: Asian Barometer Survey. Author prepared.

To determine whether Mongolians remain attached to communist rule, the ABS asked respondents if they would always prefer democracy to authoritarian rule or authoritarianism over democratic rule, or if they had no preference at all. There has been a downward trend in desire for democracy (Figure 18.8). Furthermore, the number of people who answered, "Under some circumstances, an authoritarian government can be preferable to a democratic one" has been growing at a steady rate during the last decade. From this, we can draw the preliminary conclusion that 40 percent of the population, or more than one-third, would not oppose a non-democratic regime, compared to 27.9 percent fifteen years ago. The percentage of people who answered, "Democracy is always preferable to any other kind of government" decreased from 56 percent to 37 percent. In other words, in the first wave (2003), a majority (56 percent) expressed a preference for democratic rule over authoritarian rule, while a minority (28 percent) expressed feelings of nostalgia for communism (choosing authoritarian rule over democratic rule).

A small minority (16 percent) of Mongolians said they did not believe that regime type matters. What is noteworthy about these findings is that more than one-third of Mongolians expressed a preference for non-democratic rule over democracy. The situation had changed by the time of the next wave of the ABS. Preference for authoritarianism had grown, and in the fifth wave (2018), it reached as high as 41 percent, while supporters of democracy were in a minority. Over the years, those who expressed a preference for democracy were under 50 percent. Based on all the ABS data to date, we can calculate that an average of around 40 percent of Mongolians prefer democracy over authoritarianism, and 30 percent prefer authoritarianism to democracy, while one out of four Mongolians do not believe that the regime type matters.

Figure 18.8 Democracy vs. Authoritarianism (2003-2018)

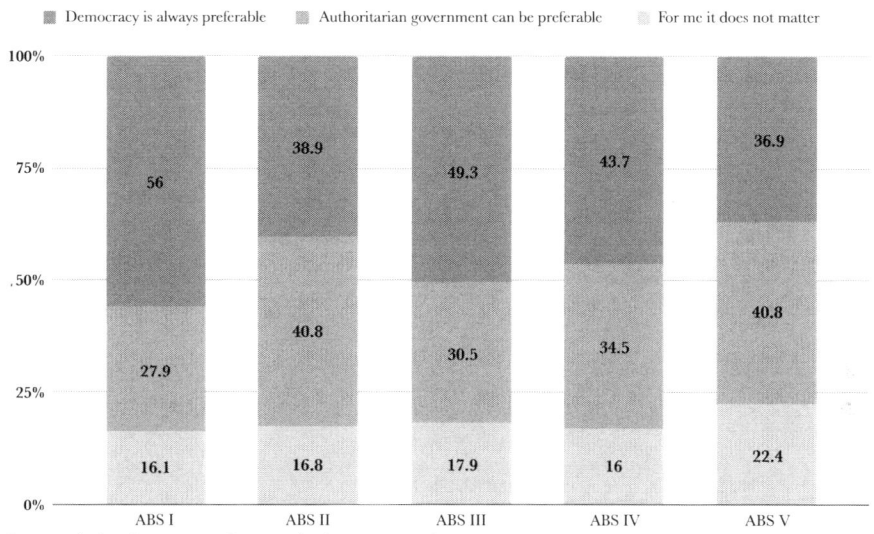

Source: Asian Barometer Survey. Author prepared.

Table 18.2 displays the percentages of Mongolians who have expressed positive views about the desirability, suitability, and efficacy of democracy, prefer democracy to authoritarianism and give priority to democracy. These percentages clearly show that Mongolians, like citizens of other new democracies, are more supportive of democracy as a political ideal than as a political enterprise. Even among those who embrace democracy as the best method of governance, it is not widely regarded as a highly salient development goal.

However, Mongolians are highly critical regarding the democracy in their country. Over the years in which the ABS have been conducted, the percentage of respondents who have said that democracy in Mongolia, for instance, has major problems has increased from 39.5 to 52.1 (Figure 18.9).

Figure 18.9 How Much Democracy (2003-2018)

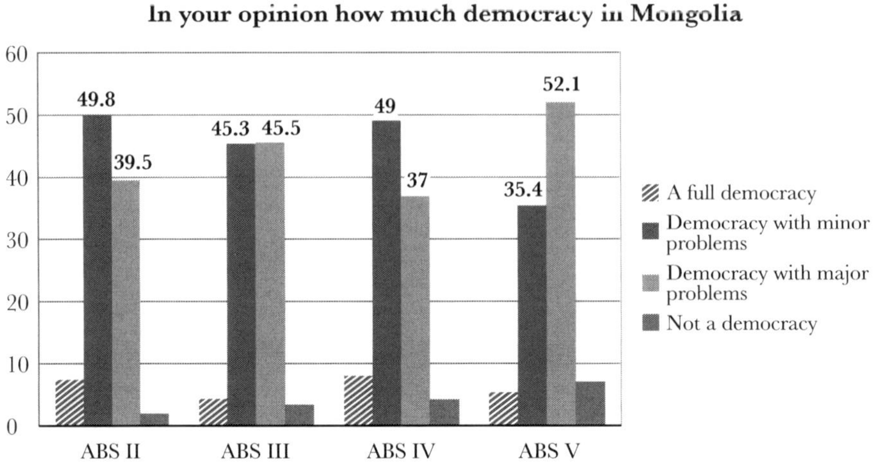

In your opinion how much democracy in Mongolia

Source: Asian Barometer Survey. Author prepared.

Conclusion

Mongolia was in the past considered to be a "least likely" case for democratization compared to other countries in the "fourth wave" (Doorenspleet 1999, 2001) and in the Central Asian region (Fish 1998, 2001; Sabloff 2002; Fritz 2002). Now, its political system meets most of the minimal and procedural criteria for democracy outlined by analysts such as Diamond (1999) and Przeworski et al. (2000), in that it has a competitive and developed political party system and has achieved peaceful and regular transfers of power over nine successive parliamentary elections and seven presidential elections. It was classified as "least likely" because it lacked the standard prerequisites for democracy from a modernization perspective and also lacked certain cultural factors that were seen as essential for the development of democracy. Despite these handicaps, however, Mongolia has managed to establish a democratic regime, although most of its post-communist neighbors have become largely undemocratic.

In addition to these developments, Mongolia still needs to confront important challenges associated with deficiencies in civil and political rights and a lack of basic resources for the provision of economic and social rights.

The majority of Mongolians still believe in the principle of democracy and that democracy and a free-market economy are the keys to Mongolia's development. In order to move beyond what theorists call electoral democracy, Mongolia has to overcome many challenges. From the ABS data, we can see that not all the values of liberal democracy have taken root in Mongolian society. In particular, there is a pressing need for legal procedures and practices to control corruption and the institution of a horizontal system of responsibility.

The Mongolian people have expressed a desire for a government that is more responsive to their needs rather than one that tends to employ non-democratic methods. The electoral system needs to be adjusted in such a way as to push out "dirty" politics, and steps need to be taken to crack down on bribe taking by politicians and to regulate election campaigning. Another area highlighted by the ABS data is the importance of separating the judiciary from politics and guaranteeing judges' immunity from prosecution. All of these factors have a direct impact on the legitimacy of democracy, and in the long run they serve as the foundation of a sustainable, democratic system.

References

Diamond, Larry. 1999. *Developing Democracy: Toward Consolidation*. Baltimore: Johns Hopkins University Press.

Doorenspleet, Renske. 1999. "Reassessing the Three Waves of Democratization." *World Politics* 52 (3): 384-406.

—. 2001. "The Fourth Wave of Democratization: Identification and Explanation." Ph.D. dissertation, University of Leiden.

Fish, M. Steven. 1998. "Mongolia: Democracy without Prerequisites." *Journal of Democracy* 9 (3): 127-141.

—. 2001. "The Inner Asian Anomaly: Mongolia's Democratization in Comparative Perspective." *Communist and Post-Communist Studies* 34 (3): 323-338.

Freedom House. 2020. *Freedom in the World 2020 Mongolia*. Accessed July 8, 2020. https://freedomhouse.org/country/mongolia/freedom-world/2020.

Fritz, Verena. 2002. "Mongolia: Dependent Democratization." *The Journal of Communist Studies and Transition Politics* 18 (4): 75-100.

Huntington, Samuel. 1991. *The Third Wave: Democratization in the Late Twentieth Century*. Norman: University of Oklahoma Press.

National Statistics Office of Mongolia. 2020. *Mongolian Statistical Information Service*. Accessed July 8, 2020. http://www.1212.mn/en.

Pomfret, Richard. 2000. "Transition and Democracy in Mongolia." *Europe-Asia Studies* 52 (1): 149-160. doi:10.1080/09668130098316.

Przeworski, Adam, Michael E. Alvarez, Jose Antonio Cheibub, and Fernando Limongi. 2000. *Democracy and Development: Political Institutions and Well-being in the World, 1950-1990*. New York: Cambridge University Press.

Rose, Richard, and William Mishler. 2000. *Regime Support in Non-Democratic and Democratic Contexts*. Glasgow: University of Strathclyde.

Sabloff, Paula L. W. 2002. "Why Mongolia? The Political Culture of an Emerging Democracy." *Central Asian Survey* 21 (1): 19-36.

UNDP. 2020. *National Human Development Report 2019*. Accessed July 8, 2020. https://www.undp.org/mongolia/publications/human-development-report-2019#.

19 Mass Support for the Political System: Indonesia's Democracy 2006-2019

The extent to which Indonesia's democracy can survive, or even better, to consolidate, is a crucial issue as the country is relatively new,[1] contains diverse primordial identities, especially based on ethnicity, region, and religion,[2] is socio-economically a developing country,[3] and a Muslim nation whose counterparts in the world are mostly non-democracies. It is moreover in a global situation of stagnation or perhaps a declining trend of democratization,[4] during an era of democratic deficit worldwide which is believed to threaten democratic sustainability (Norris 2011).

One way to diagnose the problem is to check the extent to which the citizens support the political system. This system support, in the framework created by David Easton, includes several dimensions of the political system, from more specific to more diffuse: government performance, trust in political institutions, assessment of democratic performance, support of regime principles, and positive attitude toward the political community or nation-state (Norris 2011).

This chapter's first task is to explore the extent to which the people support the political community, regime principles, positively assess regime performance, have trust in political institutions, such as the presidency, parliament, courts, the military, police, etc., and positively evaluate government performance.

The political culture approach is an appealing starting point to explain system support in Indonesia, in particular the democratic preferences and performance in Indonesia, as the country is a Muslim-majority nation. Democracy is a rare phenomenon in such countries. Why does democracy work in this particular Muslim country? What went right (or wrong) with Indonesian Muslims?

The political culture perspective emphasizes the importance of traditions or civilizations. The main source of civilization is religion. For example, Huntington's human civilizations are closely associated with religions: Western civilizations (Protestantism and Catholicism), Latin American, Orthodox Christian, the Eastern world (Buddhism, Confucianism, Hinduism), Islam, sub-Saharan Africa, and others (Huntington 1997).

Relying on history, many studies in the political science literature posit that separation between church and state is a critical foundation for a modern polity, which is the basis for the existence of nation-states and democracy in the modern world (cf. Bendix 1978). This foundation does not exist in Muslim history and societies. The ideas of nation-state and democracy are alien to the community, or at least are weak or unstable (Huntington 1997; Kedourie 1994). In addition, in the civic culture perspective, civic engagement is believed to be crucial to strengthen the modern political system. Social trust, a component of civic engagement or social capital, spills over into political trust, which is believed to strengthen democracy. Social trust, rooted in civilizations, stabilizes democracy and generally the political system (Inglehart 1988).

Some students of Muslim community and history believe that civil society is alien to the Muslim community (Gellner 1994; Lewis 2002). If this proposition is correct, we cannot expect a contribution from the Muslim community toward an increase in civic engagement, which would strengthen political trust, and finally, the political system.

Political Community

Political community, in the form of the nation-state, is a basic element of a modern political system. It is a precondition for any regime, democratic or non-democratic. Regime stability or consolidation is not likely without the stability of the nation-state on which the regime is built (Linz and Stepan 1996).

In the context of contemporary Indonesia, the regime is a democracy. That democracy cannot be stable or consolidated if the nation-state is not stable. One way to assess the stability of the nation-state is to observe the extent to which the masses are positively oriented toward the nation-state. In the public opinion survey literature, this positive orientation is the extent to which the people in general are proud to be citizens of the country, or are loyal to the nation-state regardless of its imperfections.

Our surveys found that most people were very proud of being citizens of the country. Only a very small proportion state the opposite (not very proud or not proud at all).[5] This very proud attitude is very consistent and has significantly increased in the last 13 years. In 2006, 70.6 percent of the population stated that they were very proud to be citizens of the country. This percentage increased very significantly to be 84.7 percent in 2019. In addition, most Indonesians are not willing or not willing at all to live in another country.[6] This sentiment increased very significantly from 50.7 percent in 2006 to 66.5 percent in 2019. They are loyal to their own country regardless of its imperfections (Figure 19.1). These findings indicate that almost all Indonesians are positively and strongly oriented toward the political community, which is a basic requirement for the existence and stability of a political system and its democratic regime. At this most diffuse level of the political system, Indonesia probably does not face a serious problem.[7]

This finding is important for comparative studies but even more so for students of Indonesian politics. Many believed that the country would fall apart as political freedom or democracy was introduced. The term "balkanization" was heard frequently in discussions of the country's probable future. Freedom, it was thought, would open divisions and conflicts along primordial lines. As is well-known, Indonesia is very diverse primordially, particularly in the huge number of ethnic and regional groups. Primordially-driven separatist elements were expected to emerge and become a major threat to the integrity of the nation-state.

Indonesian nationality was believed to be weak due to the lack of a national-level primordial component, especially an ethnic one. There is no single majority ethnic group in the country. The largest, the Javanese, is less than fifty percent (around 41 percent). Even the name, Indonesia, was invented quite recently, and introduced by an Orientalist in the nineteenth century (Earl 1850; Logan 1850). There was no entity called Indonesia in the archipelago, then named Netherlands India, before it was proclaimed as a nation-to-be in 1928 by an anti-colonial movement. Indonesia was thus produced by an anti-colonial movement and ultimately by a revolution from 1945-49. It was never and is not now a fixed ethnic group, but rather a historically produced or imagined community (Anderson 2006).

Figure 19.1 Attitudes toward the Political Community (%)

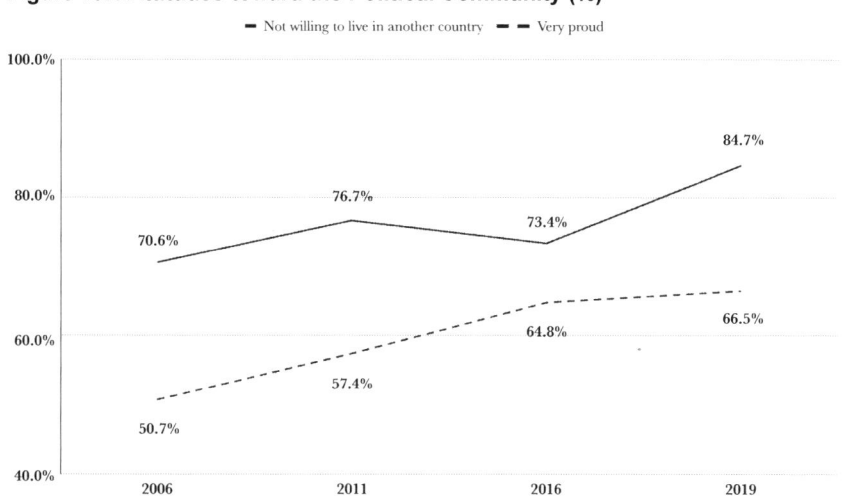

Source: Asian Barometer Survey. Author prepared.

To be sure, there is a primordial element that may serve to blend or unite the diverse ethnic and regional groups to become a nation. That is Islam, the religion of the vast majority (87%). Islam is argued by some, both Indonesians and outside observers, to bind the ethnically and regionally diverse groups to be a nation, even though Islam is also a relatively recent arrival in the islands (Kroef 1958). It only arrived in the thirteenth century and became a dominant religion in the country in the sixteenth century (Ricklefs 1991). Among some Muslim and nationalist leaders, "Loving the nation is a part of the faith" has become a popular slogan.[8]

Islam, anti-colonialism, and the revolution for independence against Dutch colonial rule have denoted the national identity with the label Indonesia. In addition, Indonesians share a national language, Bahasa Indonesia or Indonesian, which is also a uniting factor. The adoption of Indonesian, originally the native language of only a small group, is also a quite recent development. It was officially proclaimed to be the national language as the country was proclaimed independence from colonialism in 1945 (Kridalaksana 1991).

Despite its recent formation, Indonesians' national identity is probably not as weak as some students of Indonesian politics have assumed. Indonesia, at least, still exists as a sovereign state. Attitudinally, almost all of the people are positively oriented toward Indonesia as a nation-state or a modern political community, and this sentiment increased in the last 13 years (see Figure 19.1).

Regime Principles: Democratic Support

In addition to support for the political community, a political system requires a political regime, or form of government, to make it work successfully. Mass support for a political regime is believed to make the regime stable and effective, regardless of regime type, democratic or non-democratic.

Since the collapse of authoritarianism in 1998, Indonesia has turned out to be a democracy even though it is still not consolidated. In Freedom House's judgment, Indonesia is not yet fully, but only a partly free country (Freedom House 2020). It was, however, fully free from 2006-2014, but was reduced to partly free when the civil liberty component regressed (Freedom House 2020). An indicator of democratic consolidation or stability can be observed in the extent to which a majority of the people attitudinally prefer democracy to any other regime (Linz and Stepan 1996). In the last four public opinion surveys, a majority of Indonesians have, in fact, preferred democracy to any other regime.[9] The trend declined slightly (by about 4 percent) from 2006 to 2011, but has recovered in the last survey (75.8 percent). (Figure 19.2).

Figure 19.2 Democratic Support (%)

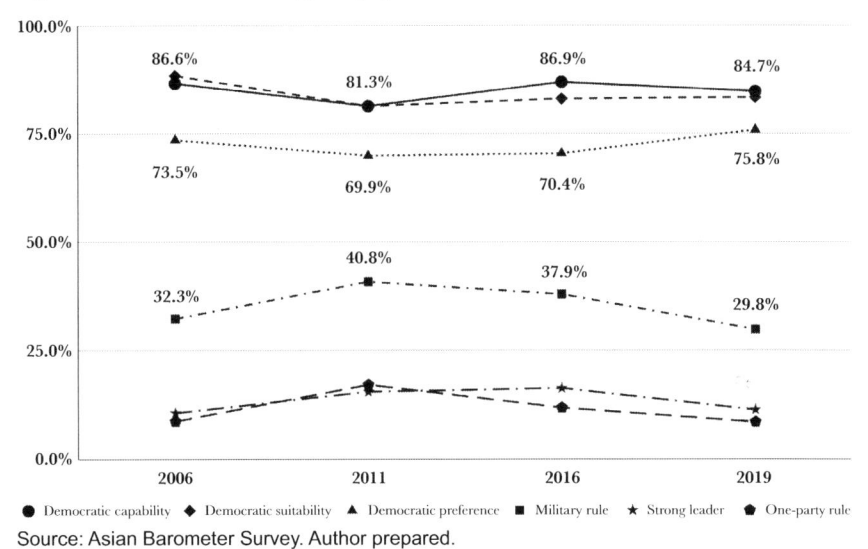

Source: Asian Barometer Survey. Author prepared.

Preference for democracy may be also gauged by some other measures. First, democratic preference is about a belief in the extent to which democracy is considered capable of solving the problems in a country. Over the period of thirteen years (2006-2019), a majority of the people, in fact, consistently believe that democracy is capable of resolving problems.[10] Consistent with these attitudes, a majority of the people disagree with the idea that a strong leader without elections and parliament,[11] a one-party system,[12] unelected expert leadership,[13] or a military government are preferable.[14] In addition, a majority of the people think that democracy is suitable for the country, and they believe that democracy is capable of resolving problems in the country (Figure 19.2). These attitudes were consistent over the period.

At more diffuse levels, i.e., support for political community and regime principles, Indonesians are mostly oriented positively toward the system. This positive orientation indicates that at those levels Indonesia attitudinally does not face the problem of system stability and consolidation.

Democratic Performance

How about attitudes toward a less diffused component of the system, i.e., the regime or democratic performance? The concern is with how democracy works and has been implemented in the country. Many studies have found that attitudes at this level are commonly less positive relative to the more diffuse elements of the system (Norris 2011).

However, in the last thirteen years, a majority of Indonesians have evaluated democratic performance positively. They are very or fairly satisfied with the way democracy had worked in the archipelago. They increasingly think that Indonesia is a full democracy, or a democracy with only some minor problems (Figure 19.3).

Figure 19.3 Democratic Performance (%)

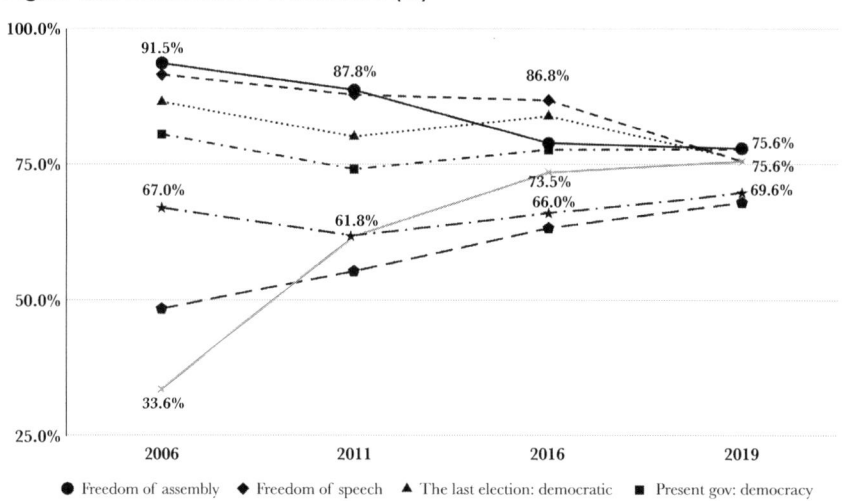

Source: Asian Barometer Survey. Author prepared.

Their ratings on a ten-point scale of democraticness of the nation indicate that democratic performance is positive. Since Indonesian democracy was revived in 1998, there have been five national elections to elect parliamentary members involving dozens of political parties and four direct presidential elections. How free and fair were those elections? Freedom House judged Indonesia a fully free country in terms of political freedom, a measure in which the performance of national elections is a crucial component (Freedom House 2020). From the people's assessment, a majority thought that the elections were fully free and fair or free and fair with minor problems (Figure 19.3).

Democratic performance refers not only to political freedom but also to civil liberty. This component is crucial to Indonesia as it makes Indonesia only a partly free country (Freedom House 2020). Civil liberty refers to freedom of expression and belief, associational rights, the rule of law, and personal autonomy or individual rights.

One measure of freedom of belief is freedom to believe or to disbelieve in a religion or God, or to practice one's own religion. This measure is problematic in Indonesia as the Constitution formally forbids citizens to be disbelievers or atheists. A citizen is, therefore, not allowed to publicly express that he or she is an atheist.[15]

Not only at the constitutional level but also in more practical terms, many Indonesian adherents to minority religions still experience attacks on their religious freedom. Incidents regarding religious intolerance often emerge in society, and the state is unable to protect the victims. Minority religious groups such as Shi'a or Ahmadiyya, for example, still experience terror from members of the majority Sunni community, and the state fails to protect their religious freedom (Mujani 2019).

However, if asked whether the people in the country can practice their own faith or religion without fear, a vast majority state that they do think people are free to practice their own faith.[16] This proportion is similar to responses on comparable issues of being able to participate in any organization and speak honestly and without fear about what they think is right (Figure 19.3). However, there had been a significant decline in the people's assessment of freedom of speech and assembly in the period, even though most of them were positive about the issues.

From the people's evaluation of democratic or regime performance, we can conclude that Indonesian democracy is in general performing well, at least at the political rights dimension of the polity.

Trust in Political Institutions

Political trust is less diffuse than regime performance in the hierarchy of the political system. It refers to political institutions such as the presidency, the parliament, parties, courts, the military, etc. Positive orientations toward or trust in these institutions are believed to be crucial for the stability of a political system (Inglehart, 1997, 1988).

In the case of Indonesia, trust in institutions varies significantly, depending on the object of trust. In 2006-2019, the greatest trust had been in the armed forces (above 85%), followed by civil servants, the presidency, national and local governments, the police, the courts, and parliament. Only in terms of political parties does the level of trust not reach a majority (Figure 19.4).

Compared to democratic performance, political trust on average is lower because trust in political parties has been very low relative to other political institutions. In addition, trust in parliament had on average been lower. It is interesting to explore why trust in political parties and parliament among the masses had been much lower relative to the armed forces or civil servants for example.

Figure 19.4 Trust in Political Institutions (%)

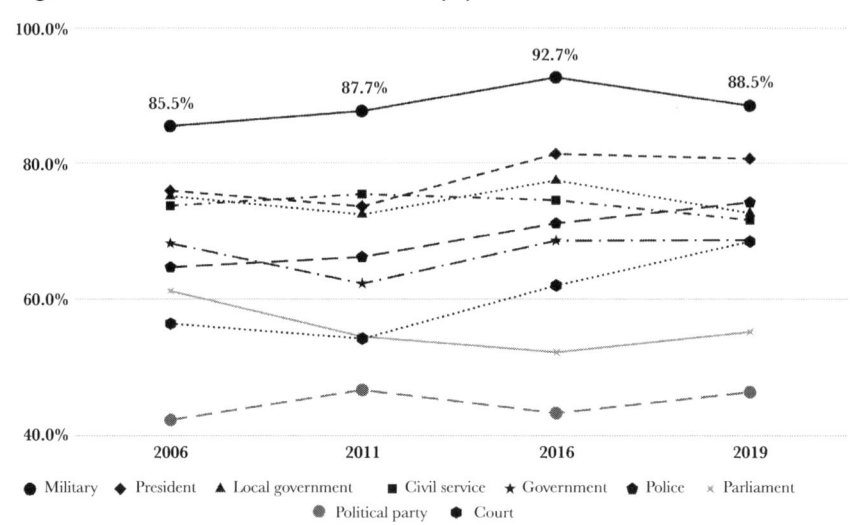

Source: Asian Barometer Survey. Author prepared.

Government Performance

In the hierarchy of the political system, government performance is naturally more dynamic relative to institutional trust. This dynamic is reflected in public assessment about government performance. The assessments include the extent to which the central and local governments have worked, about corruption in government and about government fight against corruption (Figure 19.5).[17]

The masses' assessment of central government performance had been, on average, positive. In fact, there was a tendency to be more positive in the period between 2006 and 2019. In addition, the people had positive perceptions about corruption in the local government. However, the people were less positive about corruption in the central government even though this negative sentiment declined somewhat (Figure 19.5). In addition, the masses, in general, were positive about the government's fight against corruption in the country, and this positive perception increased over the period (Figure 19.5).

However, after the election in 2019, and after the last survey in 2019, the government and the parliament have revised the role of Komisi Pemberantasan Korupsi (Corruption Eradication Commission) or KPK, a special institution responsible specifically for preventing and cracking down on corruption in the country. This institution was powerful and popular. Anti-corruption activists protested against the revision as it is believed to weaken the KPK. Prior to the revision, mass media reported corruption cases on an almost daily basis. Nowadays, after the revision, reported cases of corruption have dramatically declined. This decline is not associated with the decline of corruption cases but rather because of the worse performance of the KPK to crack down corruption in the country as it has been weakened institutionally by the government and parliament.[18]

Figure 19.5 Government Performance (%)

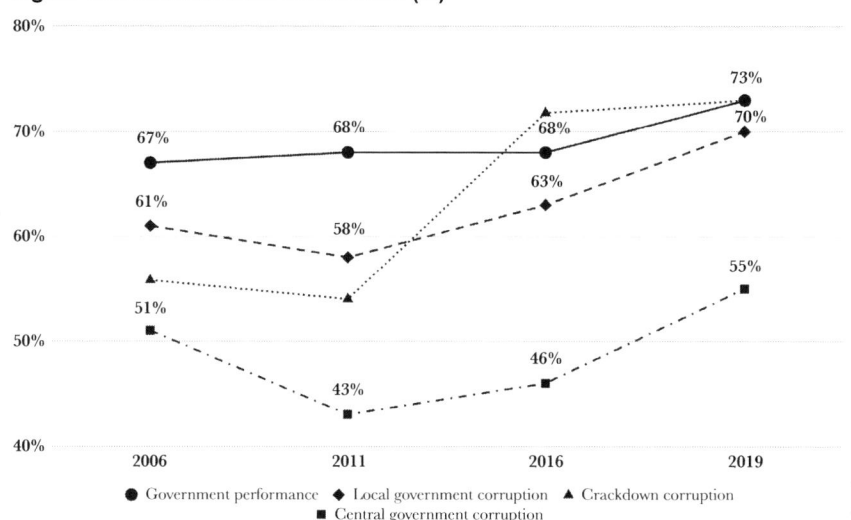

Source: Asian Barometer Survey. Author prepared.

Conclusion

From a political system perspective, a congruent relationship between the political system and the mass attitudes toward the system is required to make the system stable and work. Do Indonesians support the system, including political community, regime principles, regime performance, institutional trust, and government performance?

The four nationwide public opinion surveys in the last thirteen years of Indonesian democracy suggest some important findings. First, the people are mostly oriented positively toward the political system. They support the nation-state or political community, prefer democracy to any other type of regime, positively assess regime performance, trust most political institutions, and evaluate government performance positively. The positive orientations, in general, have increased over thirteen years.

These findings suggest that the propositions that the components of the political system, i.e., nation-state, democracy, political trust, and government performance, are alien to Muslims, are not persuasive in the case of Indonesia, whose citizens are almost all Muslims. Muslims in the country are positively oriented toward the nation-state and democracy as a political regime. In addition, they in general positively evaluate the regime performance, trust the political institutions, and positively assess the government performance. The political system and the Muslim masses are congruent. From a political culture perspective, this congruence indicates that Indonesian democracy is likely to be stable and has the potential to consolidate. A further study is suggested to explain the congruence between the masses and political system to predict if the system is likely to consolidate.

Notes

1. Democracy was first attempted in 1955 when the first free election for parliament was held. It failed to survive. The parliament was dissolved and a non-elected President Sukarno took over the government. Democracy reemerged in 1998, after 43 years of authoritarianism, as a response to an economic crisis that the authoritarian government was unable to handle. The next free election was in 1999, followed by regular elections at five-year intervals ever since.

2. Indonesia's population according to the World Bank estimate was 257.6 million in 2015. (http://data.worldbank.org/country/indonesia). It is the fourth most populous country, after the People's Republic of China, India, and the United States. It is the most populous Muslim country, and the third largest democracy, after India and the United States. Indonesia is an archipelago consisting of thousands of islands and hundreds of ethnic groups. None of the ethnic groups constitutes a majority of the population. The Javanese are the largest (about 41%), followed by the Sundanese (about 15%). According to the last census in 2010, a majority of the population (87.18%) are Muslim; the rest are Protestants (6.96%), Catholics (2.91%), Hindus (1.69%), Buddhists (0.72%), Confucians (0.5%), and others (0.51%). See Badan Pusat Statistik. 2010. *Sensus Penduduk 2010.*

3. The Human Development ranking which measures socioeconomic development considers Indonesia a medium human development country, ranked 110, in 2015. The GDP per capita is US$9,254. See UNDP, 2015 (Human Development Report 2015: Work for Human Development).

4. Freedom House 2016.

5. In the figure only response "very proud" was reported. Wordings in the surveys

are: "How proud are you to be a citizen of the country? Are you very proud, somewhat proud, not very proud, or not proud at all?"

6. In the figure, only responses "not willing" or "not willing at all" were reported. Wordings in the surveys: "Given the chance, how willing would you be to go and live in another country? Very willing, willing, not willing, not willing at all."

7. It is true that Indonesia continues to face separatist movements, the largest ones being in Papua and Aceh. So far, at least, these movements have not been able to win independence. The separatist movement in Aceh has dramatically declined since peace agreement between the Free Aceh movement or Gerakan Acheh Merdeka (GAM) and Indonesian government was signed, and the rebels began to turn their weapons over to international monitors in 2005 (see https://www.cfr.org/backgrounder/indonesia-aceh-peace-agreement). On the contrary, the separatist movement in Papua is still persistent, see https://www.abc.net.au/news/2020-05-12/west-papua-secret-war-with-indonesia-for-independence/12227966.

8. http://www.republika.co.id/berita/dunia-islam/khazanah/15/03/15/nl8f3g-pbnu-cinta-tanah-air-sebagian-dari-ima

9. Wordings in the surveys: "Which of the following statements comes closest to your own opinion? 1) Democracy is always preferable to any other kind of government; 2) Under some circumstances, an authoritarian government can be; 3) For people like me, it does not matter whether we have a democratic or non-democratic regime."

10. "Which of the following statements comes closer to your own view? 1) Democracy is capable of solving the problems of our society; 2) Democracy cannot solve our society's problems."

11. "We should get rid of parliament and elections and have a strong leader decide things." (Strongly agree, somewhat agree, somewhat disagree, or strongly disagree)

12. "Only one political party should be allowed to stand for election and hold office." (Strongly agree, somewhat agree, somewhat disagree, or strongly disagree)

13. "We should get rid of elections and parliaments and have experts make decisions on behalf of the people." (Strongly agree, somewhat agree, somewhat disagree, or strongly disagree)

14. "The army (military) should come in to govern the country." (Strongly agree, somewhat agree, somewhat disagree, or strongly disagree)

15. The first pillar in the Indonesian Constitution (*Undang-Undang Dasar*), whose preamble contains Five Pillars (*Pancasila*) is "Belief in the one and only God."

16. In a series of nation-wide public opinion surveys, we frequently ask how the people assess the practice of religious freedom in the country. Almost everybody stated that the people practice their religions or beliefs without fear: about 96.3% in 2006, 90,6% in 2010, and 91.8% in 2014.

17. Government performance: "very satisfied" and "somewhat satisfied." National corruption: Not much corruption in the national government. Local corruption: not much corruption in the local governments. Crack down corruption: Doing its best.
18. See https://www.cnnindonesia.com/nasional/20190926052107-12-434098/ kpk-26-poin-dalam-uu-kpk-baru-memperlemah-kerja.

References

Anderson, Benedick. 2006. *Imagined Communities: Reflections on the Origin and Spread of Nationalism*. New York: Verso Books.

Bendix, Reinhard. 1978. *Kings or People: Power and the Mandate to Rule*. Berkeley: University of California Press.

Earl, George S. W. 1850. "On The Leading Characteristics of the Papuan, Australian and Malay-Polynesian Nations." *Journal of the Indian Archipelago and Eastern Asia* 4: 172-181.

Freedom House. 2016. "Freedom in the World 2016 Anxious Dictators, Wavering Democracies: Global Freedom under Pressure." https://freedomhouse.org/report/freedom-world/2016/anxious-dictators-wavering-democracies-global-freedom-under-pressure.

—. 2020. "Freedom in the World 2020 A Leaderless Struggle for Democracy." https://freedomhouse.org/report/freedom-world/2020/leaderless-struggle-democracy.

Gellner, Ernest. 1994. *Conditions of Liberty: Civil Society and Its Rivals*. London: Hamish Hamilton.

Huntington, Samuel. 1997. *The Clash of Civilizations and the Remaking of World Order*. New York: Simon and Schuster.

Inglehart, Ronald. 1997. *Modernization and Postmodernization: Cultural, Economic, and Political Change*. Princeton: Princeton University Press.

. 1988. "The Renaissance of Political Culture." *American Political Science Review* 82 (4): 1203-1230. doi: 10.2307/1961756.

Kedourie, E. 1994. *Democracy and Arab Political Culture*. Portland: Frank Cass.

Kridalaksana, Harimurti. 1991. *Masa Lampau Bahasa Indonesia: Sebuah Bunga Rampai*. Yogyakarta: Penerbit Kanisius.

Kroef, Justus M. Van Der. 1958. "The Role of Islam in Indonesian Nationalism and Politics." *Political Research Quarterly* 11 (1): 33-54. doi:10.1177/10659129580 1100103.

—. 2002. *What Went Wrong?: Western Impact and Middle Eastern Response*. Oxford New York: Oxford University Press.

Linz, Juan J., and Alfred Stepan. 1996. *Problems of Democratic Transition and Consolidation: Southern Europe, South America, and Post-Communist Europe*. Baltimore: Johns Hopkins University Press.

Logan, James Richardson. 1850. "The Ethnology of the Indian Archipelago: Embracing Enquiries into the Continental Relations of the Indo-Pacific Islanders." *Journal of the Indian Archipelago and Eastern Asia* 4: 252-347.

Mujani, Saiful. 2019. "Explaining Religio-Political Tolerance among Muslims: Evidence from Indonesia." *Studia Islamika* 26 (2): 319-351. doi:10.15408/sdi. v26i2.11237.

Norris, Pippa. 2011. *Democratic Deficit: Critical Citizens Revisited*. Cambridge: Cambridge University Press.

Ricklefs, Merle Calvin. 1991. *Islam in the Indonesian Social Context*. Clayton, Victoria: Centre of Southeast Asian Studies, Monash University.

20 Philippine Citizen Attitudes toward Democracy

Linda Luz Guerrero, Iremae D. Labucay, and Steven Rood

The five waves of the Asian Barometer Survey (ABS) have spanned a tumultuous time in the Philippines. The first wave came after the extra-constitutional ouster of populist Joseph Estrada and his replacement by the presumably more technocratic Gloria Macapagal-Arroyo. The second wave came in the wake of a widely publicized scandal as Macapagal-Arroyo was accused of cheating in order to be elected in her own right in 2004. The third wave came at the end of her long and by then deeply unpopular administration, with enthusiasm building for her replacement in the May 2010 elections. The fourth wave came in the middle of the Benigno Aquino III administration, just as the Supreme Court issued a ruling disallowing his budgetary practice that was widely seen as corrupt (rather than technocratic). The fifth wave was more than two years into the administration of Rodrigo Roa Duterte, widely seen as a populist and an unabashed purveyor of strong-man tactics. Many see the election in 2016 of Duterte as part of a global trend and a drastic repudiation of a liberal democratic arc that spanned 1992 to 2016 (beginning with the administration of Fidel V. Ramos).

The Philippines is a hyper-presidential system, with the rhythm of politics being timed to election cycles and the presidential term (normally six years). The resulting shifts in citizen attitudes are seen in Figure 20.1 using all five waves of the Asian Barometer Survey.[1] At the beginning of the long Arroyo administration[2] there were high levels of satisfaction—Filipinos on occasion congratulated themselves that it had taken only a couple of years to oust Estrada as opposed to the fourteen years of Marcos authoritarianism before the 1986 People Power Revolution ousted him. Subsequently, satisfaction with (and trust in) Arroyo dropped in the context of multiple political controversies but rebounded under the presidency of Aquino. This rebound continues to very high levels under the Duterte administration, much to the dismay of those who criticize his actions relevant to human rights, including a War on Drugs that has caused thousands of deaths.

In the fifth wave, there seems to be a shift that goes beyond the presidency—institutional trust is up across the board for many different institutions. The time series in Figure 20.2 is much less volatile since it focuses more on institutions than personalities. Again, the increase during the Duterte administration is impressive, and across the board (though the change in response categories must be noted).[3]

Figure 20.1 Presidential Satisfaction and Trust, Philippines (2002-2018)

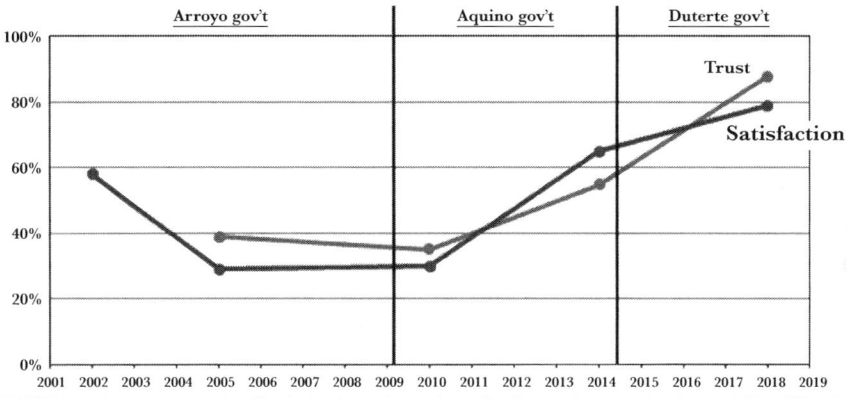

TRUST: I'm going to name a number of Institutions. For each one, please tell me how much trust you have in them (THE PRESIDENT). (TRUST FULLY, TRUST A LOT, TRUST SOMEWHAT, DISTRUST SOMEWHAT, DISTRUST A LOT, DISTRUST FULLY) SATISFACTION: How satisfied or dissatisfied are you with the (NAME OF THE PRESIDENT) government? Are you VERY SATISFIED, SOMEWHAT SATISFIED, SOMEWHAT DISSATISFIED, VERY DISSATISFIED?
* Trust (2004-2014) = % A great deal of trust + % Quite a lot of trust; * Trust (2018) = % Trust fully + % Trust a lot + % Trust somewhat
** Satisfied (2002-2018) = % Very satisfied + Somewhat satisfied
Source: Asian Barometer Survey. Authors prepared.

Figure 20.2 Trust in Institutions, Philippines (2002-2018)

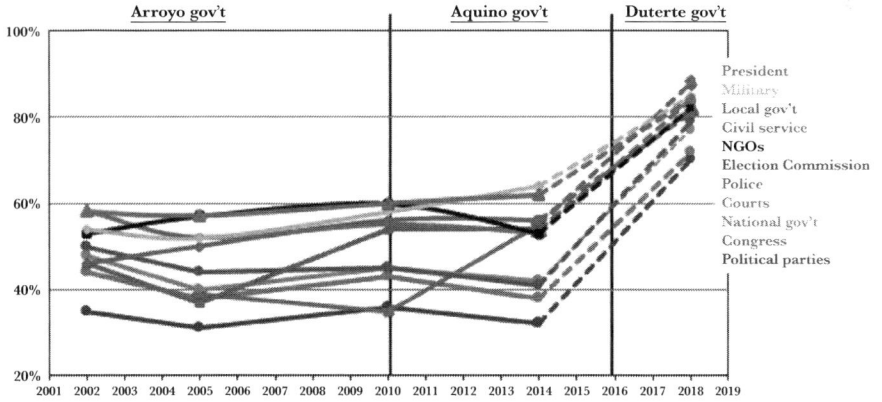

2002-2014: I'm going to name a number of Institutions. For each one, please tell me how much trust you have in them. Is it A GREAT DEAL OF TRUST, QUITE A LOT OF TRUST, NOT VERY MUCH TRUST, or NONE AT ALL?
2018: I'm going to name a number of Institutions. For each one, please tell me how much trust you have in them. (Trust fully, Trust a lot, Trust somewhat, Distrust somewhat, Distrust a lot, Distrust fully)
* Trust (2004-2014) = % A great deal of trust + % Quite a lot of trust
* Trust (2018) = % Trust fully + % Trust a lot + % Trust somewhat
Source: Asian Barometer Survey. Authors prepared.

Attitudes toward Democracy

Along the same lines, satisfaction with the way democracy has worked has increased as seen in Figure 20.3. After a decline in the middle of the Arroyo administration, beginning in 2010 (perhaps in anticipation of the impending election), the rating increased, reaching record levels by the middle of Duterte's administration which is due to end in 2022.

Figure 20.3 Satisfaction with the Way Democracy Works, Philippines (2002-2018)

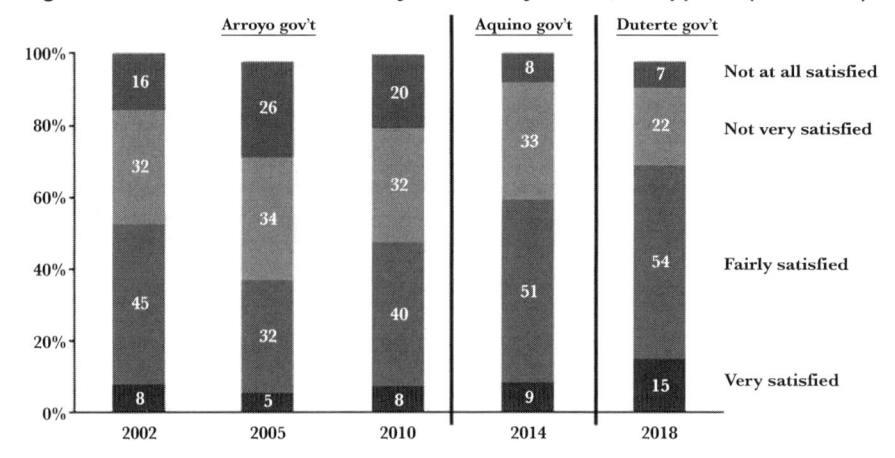

Q. On the whole, how satisfied or dissatisfied are you with the way democracy works in the country?
Source: Asian Barometer Survey. Authors prepared.

Beginning with the second wave, the extent of democracy in the Philippines as evaluated by Filipinos (Figure 20.4) shows the low point in satisfaction with democracy. Since that point, citizens have continually been more approving in judging how democratic the Philippines is. The improvement continued under the administration of Duterte, with more citizens judging the Philippines as either a "full democracy" or one with "minor problems." Interestingly, the rise from 4 percent to 7 percent saying the Philippines is "not a democracy" is statistically significant even in the face of the rise in positive responses. Perhaps this is a small segment of the citizenry that is concerned with the more publicized violations of democratic norms that are discussed next.

For those attuned to the international discourse about the Philippines, this is a striking set of findings. Much journalistic attention has been given to the spectacle of the War on Drugs, with thousands killed in police operations and thousands more killed in murky circumstances. Similarly, recent attention has been drawn internationally to threats of the freedom of the press, including pressure on the

Rappler online website's corporate registration and a criminal conviction of its editor for cyberlibel. Most recently, the largest broadcast network in the Philippines was closed in mid-2020 and denied a franchise at the initiative of Duterte who complained of its unfair treatment during his 2016 electoral campaign and its critical coverage of his War on Drugs.

Figure 20.4 Evaluating Democracy in the Philippines (2005-2018)

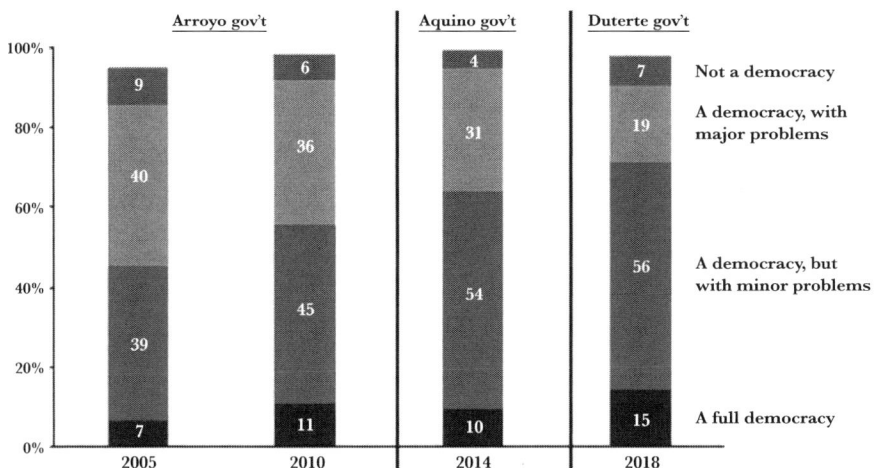

Q. In your opinion how much of a democracy is the Philippines (A FULL DEMOCRACY, A DEMOCRACY, BUT WITH MINOR PROBLEMS, A DEMOCRACY, WITH MAJOR PROBLEMS, NOT A DEMOCRACY...)?
Source: Asian Barometer Survey. Authors prepared.

International observers worry that the Duterte administration is a reversal of democratic norms and acceptance of populism. While the examination of the rise of such attitudes is beyond the scope of this short chapter, this can be illustrated by the recent rise in preference for leaders making the decisions rather than implementing what voters want in Figure 20.5.

Figure 20.5 Institutional Preferences: Government Leaders, Philippines (2010-2018)

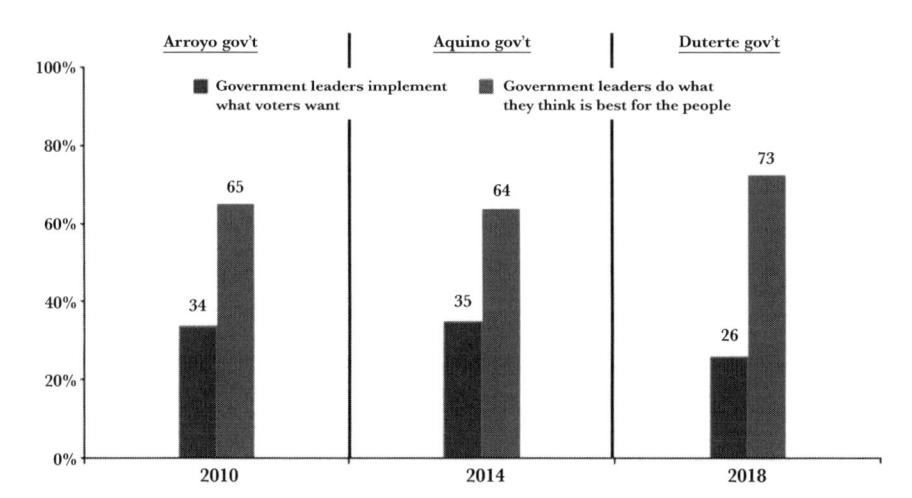

Q82. Let's talk for a moment about the kind of government you would like to have in this country, which of the following statements do you agree with most?
Government leaders implement what voters wants; Government leaders do what they think is best for the people.
Source: Asian Barometer Survey. Authors prepared.

Beyond journalistic coverage of the current dispensation under Duterte, there are numerous institutions that have been reporting macro-declines in democracy in the Philippines. Freedom House, Economist Intelligence Unit, World Justice Project, Reporters without Borders, and Human Rights Watch have all issued warnings. A summary of many indicators to measure the state of democracy across the world is provided by the International Institute for Democracy and Electoral Assistance (International IDEA) in its report issued late in 2019. The Philippines was one of the two countries (along with India) that was classified under "Moderate Democratic Backsliding" (although still within the category of Democracies). In particular, the declines in civil liberties being discussed with regard to the media and extrajudicial killings were registered as part of the backsliding.[4]

The disjuncture between the increasingly positive attitudes of Filipinos and the discourse among international observers of the Philippines may arise from how Filipinos define "democracy." In the first wave, an open-ended question, "What for you is the meaning of 'democracy'?" was asked (and never again in any of the subsequent waves). In that survey, almost two-thirds of respondents gave answers related to freedom and civil liberties (Abueva and Guerrero 2003, slide 3).

Figure 20.6 Essential Characteristics of Democracy in the Fifth Wave, Philippines (2018)

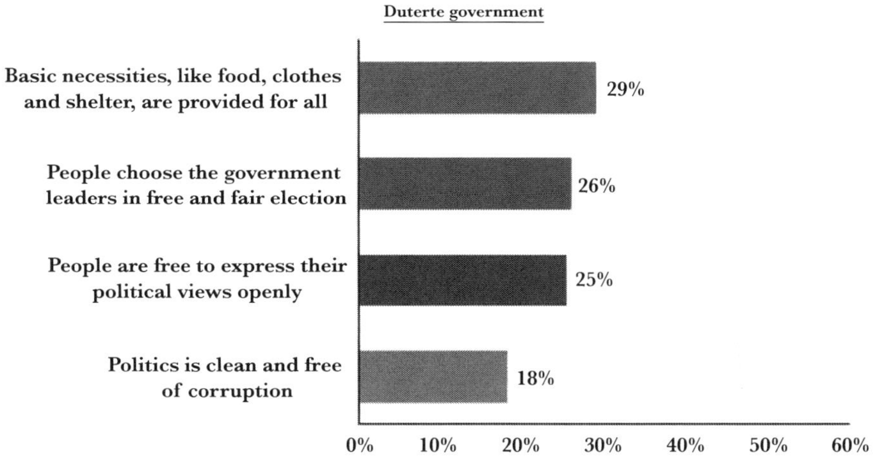

Duterte government

Q98. If you have to choose only one, which of the following do you think is the most essential element of a democracy?
Source: Asian Barometer Survey. Authors prepared.

In 2018, respondents in the fifth wave were asked a forced-choice question about the most important characteristic of a democracy (Figure 20.6), and the provision of basic necessities was the modal answer, followed closely by the free expression of political views and free and fair elections (which together accounted for just over half of the respondents). The statistical time series analysis of definitions of democracy is somewhat hampered by the changes in format and wording changes (Shin and Kim 2018).

Along with freedom of expression, Filipinos have consistently supported freedom of the media by a two-thirds margin, as we see in Figure 20.7. The slight reduction under President Rodrigo Duterte might be a one-time fluctuation or may reflect his rhetorical attacks on the press.

Figure 20.7 Institutional Preferences: Media Freedom, Philippines (2010-2018)

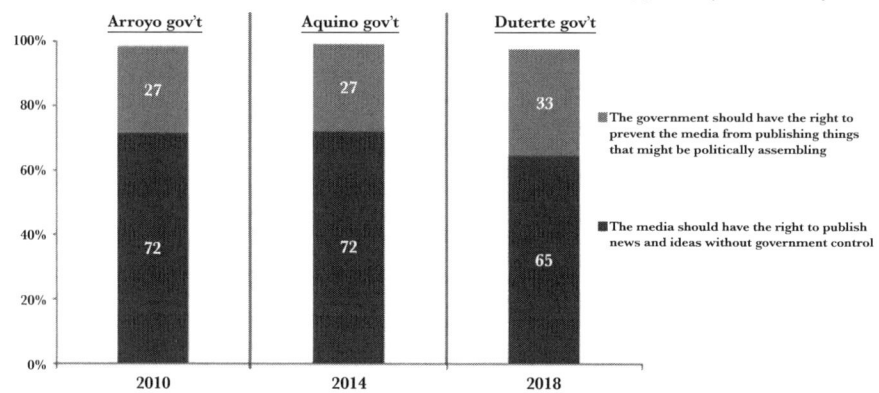

Q84. Let's talk for a moment about the kind of government you would like to have in this country, which of the following statements do you agree with most? Choose the first or the second statement. (SHOW CARD) Do you STRONGLY AGREE or JUST AGREE with your chosen statement? (1. The media should have the right to publish news and ideas without government control. 2. The government should have the right to prevent the media from publishing things that might be politically assembling.)

Source: Asian Barometer Survey. Authors prepared.

Narrowing the forced choice to "democracy" versus "economic development," it is observed in Figure 20.8 that the Filipino citizenry continually stressed economic development more than democracy, with between 72 and 78 percent over the years of all five Waves of the Asian Barometer. A similar emphasis on economic factors, reducing economic inequality, over protecting political freedom has been consistent over Waves 3, 4, and 5 (Figure 20.9).

In point of fact, the underlying economic condition of the Philippines had been continually improving for the past few years—until the coronavirus pandemic brought the economy to its knees with record unemployment. After decades of disappointing economic growth and high and stagnant poverty—especially in the context of the rapid development of its Asian neighbors—in the past decade, the Philippines has dramatically improved its performance. This improvement was examined in a 2018 edited book entitled, *The Philippine Economy: No Longer the East Asia Exception?* (Clarete, Esguerra, and Hill 2018)

Figure 20.8 Importance of Democracy versus Economic Development, Philippines (2002-2018)

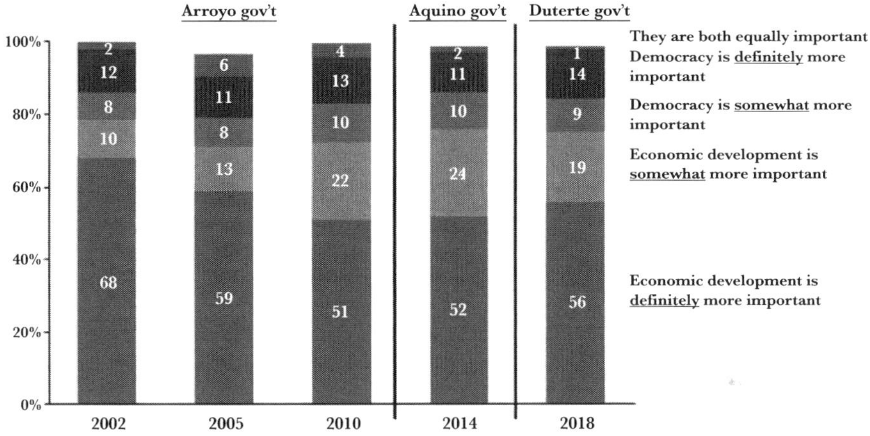

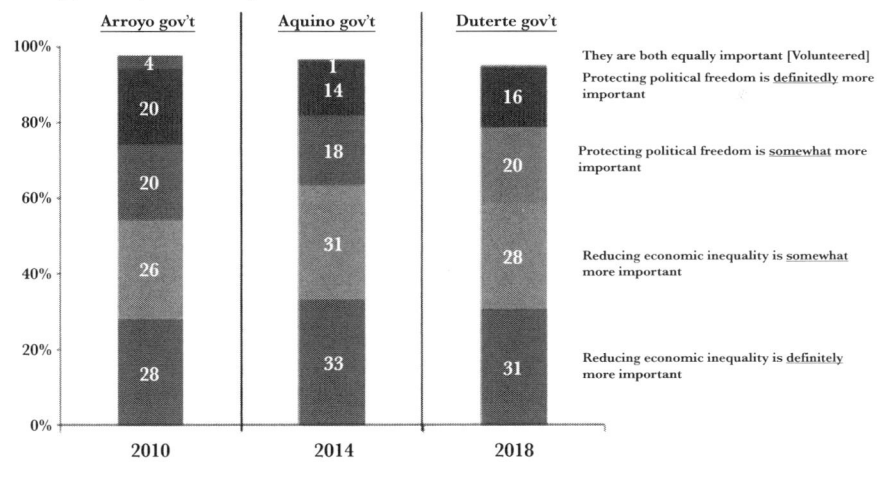

Q134. If you had to choose between democracy and economic development, which would you say is more important?

Source: Asian Barometer Survey. Authors prepared.

Figure 20.9 Reducing Economic Inequality versus Protecting Political Freedom, Philippines (2010-2018)

Q135. If you had to choose between reducing economic inequality and protecting political freedom, which would you say is more important?

Source: Asian Barometer Survey. Authors prepared.

And this improvement was reflected in citizen attitudes over the five Waves of the Asian Barometer as seen in Figure 20.10. By 2018 record numbers were evaluating economic conditions favorably. Roughly two-thirds were feeling their family's economic situation was good and expect it to be better in the future; almost as many felt that way about the country.

In sum, by the fifth wave, Filipinos were satisfied with democracy and trusted their institutions, particularly the President. What they mean by democracy is a mixture of liberal pluralist procedural requirements (elections and freedom of speech and the media) and substantive outcomes (basic necessities provided; lack of corruption, reduced economic inequality). When forced to choose, they prioritize economic development over democracy; since the economy had been performing well in the run-up to the fifth wave of the Asian Barometer, their positive views of democracy in the Philippines (Figure 20.4) were reinforced.

Figure 20.10 Evaluating Economic Conditions, Philippines (2002-2018)

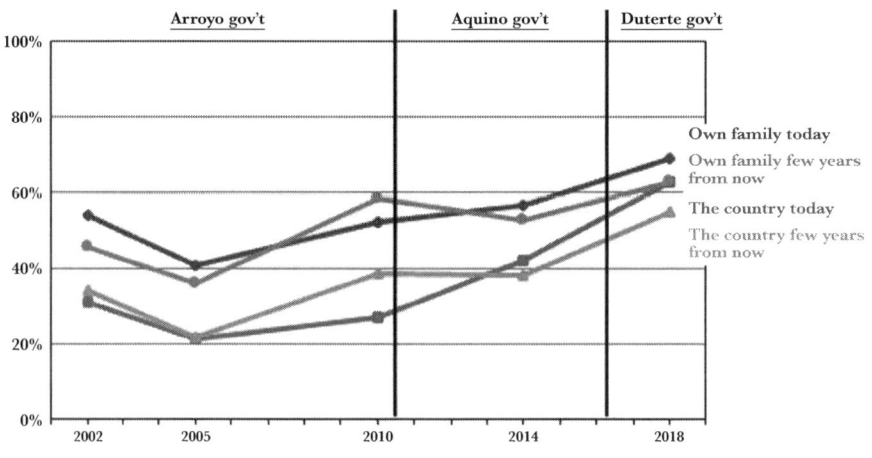

Q1. How would you rate the overall economic condition of our country today? VERY GOOD, GOOD, SO-SO (NOT GOOD NOR BAD), BAD, VERY BAD

Q3. What do you think will be the state of our country's economic condition a few years from now? MUCH BETTER, A LITTLE BETTER, ABOUT THE SAME, A LITTLE WORSE, MUCH WORSE

Q4. As for your own family, how do you rate the economic situation of your family today? VERY GOOD, GOOD, SO-SO (NOT GOOD NOR BAD), BAD, VERY BAD

Q6. What do you think will be the economic situation of your family a few years from now? MUCH BETTER, A LITTLE BETTER, ABOUT THE SAME, A LITTLE WORSE, MUCH WORSE

Source: Asian Barometer Survey. Authors prepared.

Democratic Deconsolidation

This characterization of the views of the citizenry tends to be in contradiction to the general views of analysts on the character of the current government. The recent survey of the political, administrative and security moves of Duterte, by Iglesias and Ordones, asserts the democratic erosion as "Duterte led a process of democratic deconsolidation by explicitly renouncing democracy, skirting constitutional restraints on the presidency, orchestrating violence and committing gross human rights violations." (Iglesias and Ordones 2019)

To answer more directly the "decline of democracy" thesis, the fifth wave instituted a six-question "deconsolidation" battery. The question battery was: "Do you agree or disagree with the following statements?" (In what follows, strongly agree and somewhat agree are labeled "agree" while somewhat disagree and strongly disagree are labeled as "disagree.")

1. Under a democratic system, the country endures poor economic performance.
2. Democratic regimes are indecisive and full of problems.
3. Democratic systems are not effective at maintaining order and stability.
4. The citizens in our country are not prepared for a democratic system.
5. Democracy negatively affects social and ethical values in our country.
6. As long as a government can solve our country's economic problem, it does not matter if it is democratic or not democratic.

Filipino citizens tended to agree with these statements, with percentages ranging from 78 percent agreeing with the last statement down to only 63 percent agreeing with the fourth statement, that citizens are not prepared.[5] However, the relation between these sentiments and attitudes toward democracy are not at all clear. Cross tabulations between these items and items more directly tapping into democracy generally do not show significant relationships (assuming an ordinal level of measurement, Table 20.1). For instance, in Figure 20.8, we saw that Filipinos consistently find economic development more important than democracy, but in no case are the deconsolidation items significantly related to these attitudes. Similarly, in Figure 20.5, we show that respondents in the fifth wave were increasingly likely to allow government leaders to do what they think best rather than implementing what voters want. None of the items in the deconsolidation battery are related to such attitudes.

When data that depicts citizens' increasing satisfaction with democracy are considered, we do find a significant relationship with deconsolidation items four (citizens unprepared), five (negatively affects values), and six (if economic problems are solved, democracy doesn't matter) is seen. The gamma values ranging from .120 to .167; these values, though low, are all statistically significant at the .01 level. The difficulty in interpreting these findings is that the direction of relation is counter-intuitive—those who give the "deconsolidated" answer of agreeing with items four, five, and six tend to be more satisfied with democracy. This is hardly evidence of deconsolidation of democracy among the citizenry.

However, there is an important item that is indeed correlated with all the items in the deconsolidation battery, the classic political efficacy probe: "Sometimes politics and government seem so complicated that a person like me can't really understand what is going on." Figure 20.11 shows that the inefficacious response (combining the "somewhat agree" and "strongly agree") is a majority in all five waves of the Asian Barometer. By the fifth wave, this response was at a record high and cross tabulation analysis produces unanimous positive correlations. The gammas in this set of tables range from .146 to .217, all six being significant beyond the .01 level, and the direction of relationship is substantively very intuitive. In each case, the "deconsolidation" response is associated with the inefficacious response. Table 20.1 displays the gamma values for cross-tabulations between democracy indicators and deconsolidation.

Figure 20.11 Political Efficacy, Philippines (2002-2018)

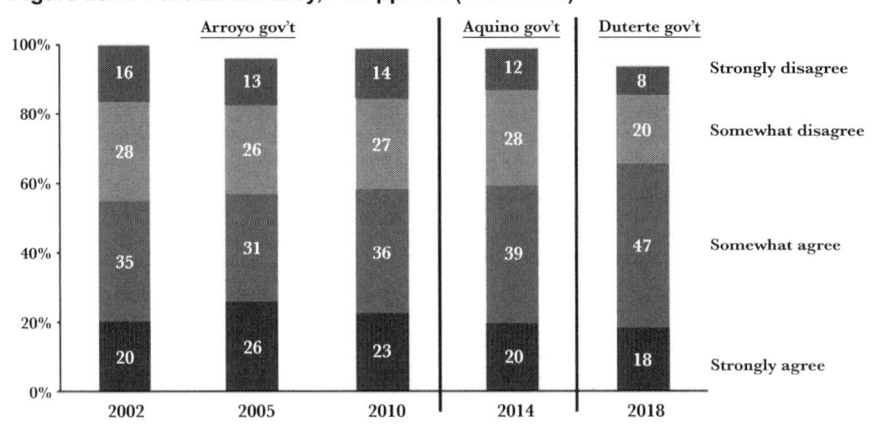

Q142. I have here some statement. For each statement, would you say you STRONGLY AGREE, SOMEWHAT AGREE, SOMEWHAT DISAGREE, or STRONGLY DISAGREE? (SHOWCARD) "Sometimes politics and government seem so complicated that a person like me can't really understand what is going on."

Source: Asian Barometer Survey. Authors prepared.

Table 20.1 Gamma Values for Cross Tabulations between Democracy Indicators and Deconsolidation Options

Wave 5 (2018)

Deconsolidation Item Battery	Democracy Indicators			
	"If you had to choose between democracy and economic development, which would you say is more important?"	"Government leaders do what they think is best for the people" versus "government leaders implement what the voters want."	"On the whole, how satisfied are you with the way democracy works in your country?"[a]	"Sometimes politics and government seem so complicated that a person like me can't really understand what is going on."[b]
Under a democratic system, the country endures poor economic performance.	n.s.	n.s.	n.s.	.208***
Democratic regimes are indecisive and full of problems.	n.s.	n.s.	n.s.	.157***
Democratic systems are not effective at maintaining order and stability.	n.s.	n.s.	n.s.	.167***
The citizens in our country are not prepared for a democratic system.	n.s.	n.s.	.120**	.217***
Democracy negatively affects social and ethical values in our country.	n.s.	n.s.	.141**	.160***
As long as a government can solve our country's economic problem, it does not matter if it is democratic or not democratic.	n.s.	n.s.	.167**	.146***

* $p < .05$; ** $p < .01$; *** $p < .001$; n.s. = not significant.
a. Positive values mean those most satisfied with democracy are more likely to agree with deconsolidation item.
b. Positive values mean those giving "inefficacious" response agree with deconsolidation item.

The association between inefficacy and the deconsolidation items sheds an interesting light on what might seem a worrisome trend exhibited in Figure 20.12—a decrease in the proportion saying democracy is always preferable, from a majority opinion to one held by just over one-third of citizens. An inspection of Figure 20.12 will reveal that this decline is not due to an increase in the willingness to countenance authoritarianism but rather due to an increase in the feeling that the distinction does not matter for people such as the respondent.[6]

Figure 20.12 Preference for Democracy versus Authoritarianism, Philippines (2002-2018)

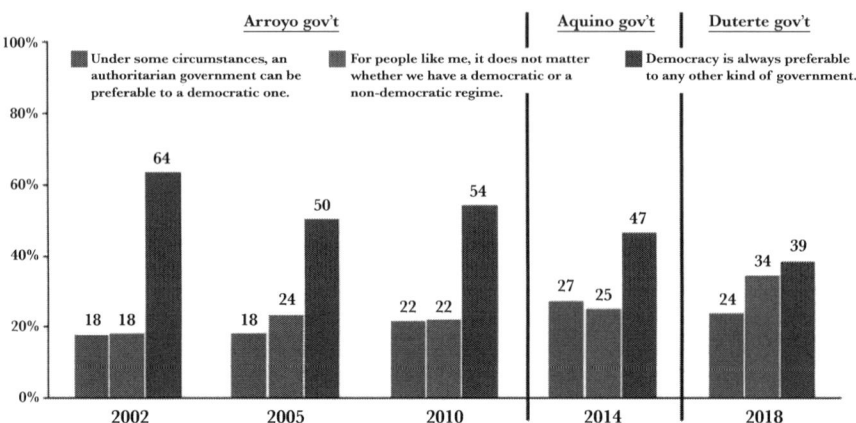

Q132. Which of the following statements comes closest to your own opinion?
Source: Asian Barometer Survey. Authors prepared.

In short, the "deconsolidation" that is being picked up in the Philippines by the fifth wave battery of items is not so much a rejection of democracy or an embrace of authoritarianism, but could be instead a reflection of a decrease in political efficacy.

Conclusion

By examining a number of items over the years, we have characterized Filipino attitudes toward democracy. First, Filipinos are satisfied with democracy. Second, they trust their institutions, particularly the President. Third, liberal pluralist elements in their conception (elections and freedom of speech and the media) are balanced by a concern with substantive outcomes (basic necessities provided; lack of corruption, reducing economic inequality). Fourth, when forced to choose, Filipinos prioritize economic development over democracy. Note that the economy had performed well for years before the fifth wave, so general feelings of citizen satisfaction were quite high, including more than two-thirds feeling that the Philippines is a full democracy, or one with minor problems.

The interpretive puzzle is driven by concerns over the discursive, transgressive style of Duterte, the decline in official respect for human rights under his administration (as monitored by international organizations), and his dislike of any constraints on his behavior. This leads many to fear an authoritarian turn in Philippine politics, and they project that concern onto citizen attitudes. However, what is seen is not so much endorsement of authoritarianism but a decline in political efficacy. This does translate into a decline in the proportion of citizens finding democracy always preferable (though it remains the modal opinion to be sure). If such a decline makes the defense of democracy less robust, the coming years (the next general election is scheduled for 2022) could be fraught.

Notes

1. The president was only added to the battery of trust questions beginning in the second wave.
2. As Arroyo had ascended to the presidency in 2001 from her position as vice president, she was not constrained from running in 2004 by the constitutional prohibition on running for a second term.
3. Observers of Philippine politics will not be surprised that "political parties" rank last in this series. Political parties in the Philippines are generally temporary agglomerations of convenience for the purpose of contesting elections, which are immediately re-formed once the outcome (particularly for president) is known.
4. International Institute for Democracy and Electoral Assistance, *The Global State of Democracy 2019: Addressing the Ills, Reviving the Promise* (International Institute for Democracy and Electoral Assistance 2019), 10. A specific discussion of the War on Drugs is found on page 187, Box 4.3.
5. Some countries in the fifth wave had a wider range of responses: In Indonesia 81 percent of respondents agreed with the first statement and only 28 percent agreeing with the fifth statement about negative effects on social and ethical values. Mongolia had roughly the same pattern though with a narrower range, agreeing most with "poor economic performance" (72 percent and 59 percent, respectively) and agreeing least with negative effects on values (41 percent and 33 percent, respectively).
6. This substantive finding does tend to bolster the notion that the relationship between inefficacy and deconsolidation is not due to response set (the tendency to agree with any item). The statistical case against response set is seen in all the non-significant results discussed above, where response set would have produced a positive result. However, "response set" as a possibility could help account for the counter-intuitive finding with respect to satisfaction with democracy, though that investigation is beyond the scope of this chapter.

References

Abueva, Jose, and Linda Luz Guerrero. 2003. "What Democracy Means for Filipinos." *A Comparative Study of Democracy, Governance and Development: Working Paper Series No. 5*. http://www.asianbarometer.org/publications/5fdff49cf0df14 1fd15414c7d3fe325c.pdf.

Clarete, Ramon L., Emmanuel F. Esguerra, and Hal Hill. 2018. *The Philippine Economy: No Longer the East Asia Exception?* Singapore: ISEAS-Yusof Ishak Institute. https://www.ebook.de/de/product/34624302/the_philippine_ economy.html.

Iglesias, Sol, and Lala Ordones. 2019. "The Philippines 2018-2019: Authoritarian Consolidation under Duterte." *Asia Maior* Vol. 30. Torino (TO): Asia Maior.

International Institute for Democracy and Electoral Assistance. 2019. *The Global State of Democracy 2019: Addressing the Ills, Reviving the Promise*. Stockholm: International IDEA. doi:10.31752/idea.2019.31.

Shin, Doh Chull, and Hannah June Kim. 2018. "How Global Citizenries Think about Democracy: An Evaluation and Synthesis of Recent Public Opinion Research." *Japanese Journal of Political Science* 19 (2): 222-249. doi:10.1017/ S1468109918000063.

21 Political Identity, System Support, and Perceptions of Government Performance in Hong Kong

Wai-man Lam, Ngok Ma, and Stan Hok-wui Wong

Hong Kong has undergone significant political changes in recent years. Among other things, the rise of a new Hong Kong political identity led to rising currents of self-determination and localism that brought about more stringent control from Beijing. Disillusionment with the lack of progress in democratization, and the declining legitimacy of the existing political system, brought increasingly radical challenges to the Hong Kong government. All of these are effectively revealed in the anti-extradition protests in 2019, which led to a strong response from the Beijing regime as in the enactment of the National Security Law for Hong Kong in 2020.

This chapter analyzes the changing intertwined relationships of Hong Kong people's political identity, system support, and perceptions of the Hong Kong government, using various waves of Asian Barometer Hong Kong survey data. The results showed a declining pride in the identity as a Chinese citizen, particularly among the young people, by 2019. The diffuse system support for the regime has also declined, partly due to worsening evaluation of government performance in civil liberties and responsiveness as well as disappointment at the democratic development of the city.

Background

The first four waves of Asian Barometer surveys (ABS) in Hong Kong were conducted in 2001, late 2007, late 2012, and early 2016 respectively. Fieldwork for the fifth wave in 2019 was first delayed due to the Anti-Extradition protests and later halted by the outbreak of COVID-19. These five surveys corresponded to different periods of political development in Hong Kong. During the first wave (2001) Hong Kong was under the impact of the Asian Financial Crisis, as pre-handover worries about undue intervention from Beijing temporarily subsided. This was a period when economic concerns dominated in Hong Kong society.

Major dissatisfaction against the Tung Chee-hwa administration and the proposal of the National Security Ordinance led to a major outburst in the 500,000-people anti-government demonstration on July 1, 2003.

The second wave took place amidst renewed optimism in 2007, as the economy had recovered and the unpopular Tung had been replaced by the pragmatic and moderate Donald Tsang in 2005. The years 2007-2008 were a period of high popularity for both the Chinese and the Hong Kong government. On the other hand, the 2003 rally was an empowering experience for the younger generation, rekindling the democracy movement (Lee and Chan 2008). It also kick-started a new wave of post-materialist movements led by a new generation of activists (Chan 2005; So 2008).

By the time of the third wave (2012), the optimism in 2007-2008 has largely vanished. With the autocratic turn of China after the 2008 Beijing Olympics, the political gap between China and Hong Kong was further widened. With the lack of progress in democratization feeding a trend of radicalization, the 2012 Legislative elections witnessed a rise of radical and anti-China groups (Ma 2015). Beijing's conservative formula for the 2017 Chief Executive election, which was deemed undemocratic by the opposition, sparked the Umbrella Movement in September 2014. The Umbrella Movement, where protesters occupied three urban sites for seventy-nine days, polarized and mobilized Hong Kong society. The fourth wave survey, conducted between February and April 2016, captured the impacts of the Umbrella Movement on political values in Hong Kong. The Umbrella Movement had stimulated political awareness and enhanced efficacy, but the futility of the movement also brought a sense of helplessness among some people. It also drove more people onto the road of radicalism and localism, as more young people believed that the prospects for democratic reform under "One Country, Two Systems" did not look hopeful (Lam 2017).

The fifth wave survey had been postponed to September 2019 because of the anti-extradition protests. The fieldwork went on amidst the protests but was later halted in early 2020 due to the outbreak of COVID-19. By June 2020, 473 interviews were completed, which significantly reflect the changes in people's political identity and government evaluation since the fourth wave. In terms of scale, scope, and impact, the anti-extradition protests were undeniably unprecedented. The youth activism, persistence and radicalization of protest tactics, as well as the internationalization of lobbying and contention, shook the world and led to strong response from the regime. The struggle brought intense distrust in the government, the police force, and even the judiciary, and heightened anti-China sentiments, which prompted Beijing to enact the National Security Law for Hong Kong in June 2020.

Table 21.1 showed the survey results by the Public Opinion Program of Hong Kong University (HKUPOP). The percentage that identifies as Chinese or Hongkonger fluctuated over the years, but there was a consistent trend of stronger identification with Hong Kong and weaker identity with China in recent years.

Table 21.1 Political Identity in Hong Kong (1997-2020)

Date of Survey	Hongkonger	Chinese	Mixed Identity	Other	Don't Know
June 4-1, 2020	50.5%	12.6%	35.9%	0.0%	1.0%
June 17-20, 2019	52.9%	10.8%	35.8%	0.0%	0.5%
June 4-7, 2018	40.7%	17.8%	38.8%	0.5%	2.2%
June 13-15, 2017	37.3%	20.9%	40.0%	1.4%	1.0%
June 10-16, 2016	41.9%	17.8%	38.0%	1.3%	0.9%
June 15-18, 2015	36.3%	22.1%	40.5%	0.3%	0.8%
June 6-12, 2014	40.2%	19.5%	38.7%	0.2%	1.3%
June 10-13, 2013	38.2%	23.0%	36.3%	1.1%	1.6%
June 13-20, 2012	45.6%	18.3%	34.3%	1.1%	0.7%
June 21-22, 2011	43.8%	23.5%	31.7%	0.4%	0.6%
June 9-13, 2010	25.3%	27.8%	46.0%	0.4%	0.5%
June 8-13, 2009	24.7%	29.3%	45.3%	0.2%	0.4%
June 11-13, 2008	18.1%	38.6%	42.5%	0.1%	0.7%
June 8-12, 2007	23.4%	26.4%	48.5%	0.3%	1.4%
June 13-15, 2006	24.8%	34.6%	40.0%	0.3%	0.3%
June 6-8, 2005	24.0%	36.4%	35.9%	0.5%	3.3%
June 7-11, 2004	28.0%	33.0%	35.5%	0.4%	3.1%
June 13-18, 2003	36.7%	29.0%	31.1%	0.7%	2.5%
June 4-5, 2002	32.2%	32.5%	31.1%	0.4%	3.9%
June 1-5, 2001	36.1%	28.4%	31.6%	0.0%	3.8%
June 7-8, 2000	35.5%	22.8%	36.9%	0.7%	4.1%
June 8, 1999	39.9%	17.0%	36.2%	0.6%	6.3%
June 3-4, 1998	34.2%	24.8%	37.3%	0.2%	3.4%
August 26-27, 1997	34.9%	18.6%	44.9%	0.4%	1.3%

Source: data from HKUPOP site and PORI, "Identification of oneself as a Hongkonger / Chinese / mixed identity" (Chinese in Hong Kong or Hongkonger in China).
https://www.hkupop.hku.hk/english/popexpress/ethnic/eidentity/poll/datatables.html,
https://www.pori.hk/pop-poll/ethnic-identity/q001. Authors prepared.

Methodology

In this chapter, we examine the changing political identity in Hong Kong and the factors that drive the change. We postulate that the changing identity and the legitimacy of the current political system is driven by the changing evaluation of government performance, freedom, and equal treatment of classes. The following analysis utilizes the data of the five waves of ABS in Hong Kong conducted in 2001, 2007, 2012, 2016, and 2019 (473 cases).

Dependent Variables

We have four dependent variables of interest:

(1) *Pride in Chinese Identity* from the question of "How proud are you to be a citizen of China?" (4-points: very proud = 4, somewhat proud = 3, not very proud = 2, not proud at all = 1)

(2) *Pride in Hong Kong Identity* from the question of "How proud are you to be a citizen of Hong Kong?" (4-points: very proud = 4, somewhat proud = 3, not very proud = 2, not proud at all = 1)

(3) *Diffuse System Support 1* from the question: "Thinking in general, I am proud of our system of government." (4-points: strongly agree = 4, somewhat agree = 3, somewhat disagree = 2, strongly disagree = 1)

(4) *Diffuse System Support 2* from the question: "A system like ours, even if it runs into problems, deserves the people's support." (4-points: strongly agree = 4, somewhat agree = 3, somewhat disagree = 2, strongly disagree = 1)

Independent Variables

We have identified six variables of interest related to evaluation of government performance and civil liberties in Hong Kong. We also include the major demographic variables for analysis.

Government Attributes

(1) *Responsiveness* from the question: "How well do you think the government responds to what people want?" (4-points: very responsive = 4, largely responsive = 3, not very responsive = 2, not responsive at all = 1)

(2) *Non-Transparency* from the question: "How often do government officials withhold important information from the public view?" (4-points: rarely = 1, sometimes = 2, most of the times = 3, always = 4)

(3) *Power Abuse* from the question: "How often do you think government leaders break the law or abuse their power?" (4-points: never/rarely = 1, sometimes = 2, most of the times = 3, always = 4)

(4) *Equal Treatment of Classes* from the question: "Rich and poor people are treated equally by the government." (4-points: strongly agree = 4, somewhat agree = 3, somewhat disagree = 2, strongly disagree = 1)

Civil Liberties

(1) *Freedom of Speech* from the question: "People are free to speak what they think without fear." (4-points: strongly agree = 4, somewhat agree = 3, somewhat disagree = 2, strongly disagree = 1)

(2) *Freedom of Assembly* from the question: "People can join any organization they like without fear." (4-points: strongly agree = 4, somewhat agree = 3, somewhat disagree = 2, strongly disagree = 1)

(3) *Demographics*: Age, Age Squared, Education, Income, Birthplace, Marital Status and Gender

For gender effect, we include a dummy variable for female. Marital status as a dummy variable is assigned a value of "1" to a married respondent and "0" otherwise. We operationalize birthplace with a dummy variable with code "1" for Hong Kong and "0" otherwise. Because people may change their political attitudes during the course of life, we include age squared to capture non-linear effect of age on a certain attitude.

Analysis and Discussion
Age and Identity

Table 21.2 demonstrates the changes of pride in Chinese identity and pride in Hong Kong identity across the five waves. Consistent with the HKUPOP results, the pride in a Chinese citizen has decreased over the years, from 3.05 in 2007 to 2.57 in 2019 on a 4-point scale. In contrast, pride in Hong Kong Identity has remained quite constant: from 3.12 in 2007 to 3.04 in 2019.

Table 21.2 Pride in Chinese and Hong Kong Identity across Five Waves

Wave	Pride in Chinese Identity	Pride in Hong Kong Identity
First wave (2001)	-	-
Second wave (2007)	3.051216	3.128464
Third wave (2012)	2.909683	3.154057
Fourth wave (2016)	2.727099	3.097952
Fifth wave (2019)	2.579208	3.042697

Source: Asian Barometer Survey. Authors prepared.

Is the rise of the younger generation in Hong Kong politics a valid explanation of identity changes? Table 21.3 and Figures 21.1 and 21.2 show the changes in pride in Chinese Identity and Hong Kong Identity across five waves and age groups of (1) below 35, (2) 35 to 60, and (3) above 60. While the pride in Hong Kong

Identity has remained relatively constant across waves and age groups, the pride in being a citizen of China has been consistently low among those below 35, and has declined across all age groups since the fourth wave. This more or less supports the common view that the younger generation has been more supportive of Hong Kong autonomy and more rejective of Chinese identity.

Table 21.3 Age and Identity across Waves of Surveys

Wave	Age Group	Pride in Chinese Identity	Pride in Hong Kong Identity
First wave	1	-	-
	2	-	-
	3	-	-
Second wave	1	2.977528	3.081967
	2	3.047962	3.134118
	3	3.129032	3.16129
Third wave	1	3.138889	3.266055
	2	3.052257	3.205543
	3	2.754128	3.091892
Fourth wave	1	2.347015	3.084211
	2	2.737946	3.063953
	3	3.046205	3.164596
Fifth wave	1	2.084337	3.052632
	2	2.656051	3.062147
	3	2.756098	3.017341

Source: Asian Barometer Survey. Authors prepared.

Figure 21.1 Pride in Chinese Identity, Age, and Waves of Surveys

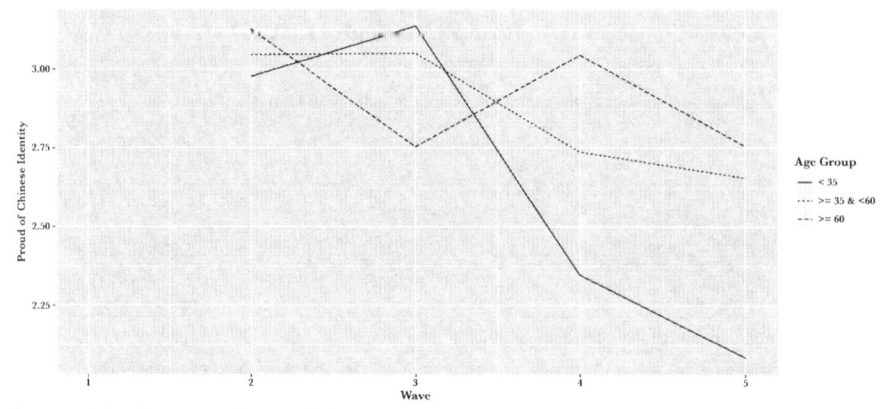

Source: Asian Barometer Survey. Authors prepared.

Figure 21.2 Pride in Hong Kong Identity, Age, and Waves of Surveys

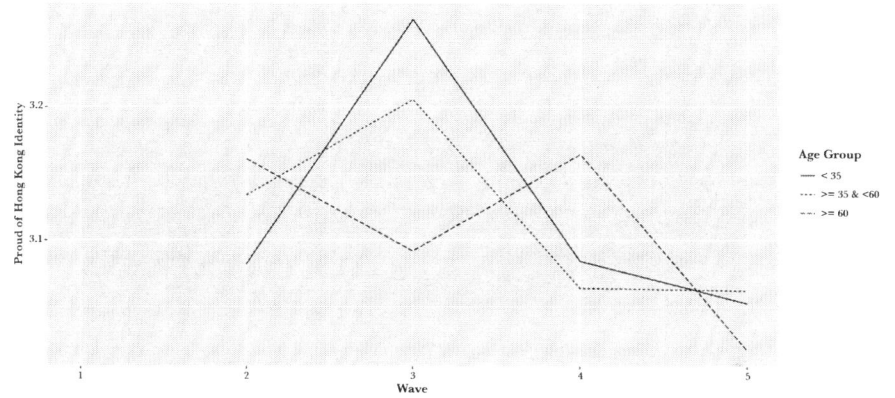

Source: Asian Barometer Survey. Authors prepared.

Tables 21.4 and 21.5 show the results of the ordered logistic regression analysis. For each of the dependent variables of interest, we regressed it, firstly, with demographic variables; secondly, we added the first three variables of government attributes (responsiveness, non-transparency, and power abuse) and the two variables of civil liberties (freedom of speech and freedom of assembly); and lastly, we added the last variable of government attributes, equal treatment of classes.

Pride in Chinese Identity

Table 21.4 shows that the three demographic variables birthplace, age and age squared, and gender are consistently significant. The negative coefficients for birthplace indicate that those not born in Hong Kong felt more proud of being a Chinese citizen. Age and age squared are also strong predictors in all three specifications. The older the person, the prouder he or she feels being a Chinese citizen. The positive effect of age and the negative effect of age squared (Table 21.3) means that the effect of age is weakened as people get older. The effect of gender is also significant across the three specifications, with males more likely to be proud of their Chinese identity. Both education and income affect the pride in Chinese identity in two specifications. The negative coefficients indicate that those with less education and lower income tend to be more proud of being a Chinese citizen.

Specification 2 includes five factors, including three government attributes variables and two civil liberties variables. All except power abuse and freedom of assembly are important predictors. Those who consider the government very responsive and rarely hide information from public view, and also those who consider people to be enjoying freedom of speech tend to be more proud of being a Chinese citizen. The addition of the last variable in specification 3 does not weaken the importance of the previous variables. Those who considered rich and poor people to be treated equally by the government tended to be more proud of their Chinese identity.

Table 21.4 Ordered Logistic Regression Analysis of Proud of Chinese Identity

	How proud are you to be a citizen of China?		
	(1)	**(2)**	**(3)**
Demographics			
Age	0.083**	0.070**	0.084**
	(0.013)	(0.015)	(0.018)
Age Squared	-0.001**	-0.001**	-0.001**
	(0.000)	(0.000)	(0.000)
Education	-0.048*	-0.056*	-0.048
	(0.021)	(0.023)	(0.026)
Income	-0.132**	-0.076	-0.116*
	(0.037)	(0.041)	(0.048)
Born in Hong Kong	-0.719**	-0.524**	-0.553**
	(0.088)	(0.098)	(0.111)
Married	-0.026	-0.208	-0.285*
	(0.094)	(0.110)	(0.127)
Female	-0.187*	-0.246**	-0.262*
	(0.081)	(0.091)	(0.105)
Wave	-0.395**	-0.239**	-0.101
	(0.042)	(0.050)	(0.090)
Government Attributes			
Responsiveness	-	0.661**	0.611**
		(0.082)	(0.092)
Non-Transparency	-	0.480**	-0.501**
		(0.064)	(0.078)
Power Abuse	-	-0.084	-0.057
		(0.063)	(0.081)
Equal Treatment of Classes	-		0.277**
			(0.081)
Civil Liberties			
Freedom of Speech	-	0.499**	0.504**
		(0.110)	(0.123)
Freedom of Assembly	-	0.193	0.155
		(0.103)	(0.111)

(Continuing on the next page)

Table 21.4 Cont.

	How proud are you to be a citizen of China?		
	(1)	**(2)**	**(3)**
Cutoff Point 1	-3.010**	-0.843	0.550
	(0.378)	(0.584)	(0.758)
Cutoff Point 2	-1.703**	0.654	2.028**
	(0.378)	(0.588)	(0.761)
Cutoff Point 3	1.576**	4.282**	5.428**
	(0.377)	(0.602)	(0.777)
Cutoff Point 4	-	-	-
Number of Observations	2602	2085	1527

Notes: (1) The estimation strategy is ordered logistic regression. (2) Standard errors are in parentheses. (3) * $p < 0.05$, ** $p < 0.01$.

Pride in Hong Kong Identity

Findings shown in Table 21.5 about pride in Hong Kong identity are rather different from those discussed above. None of the demographic variables predicts the pride in Hong Kong identity, except income which is significant only in specification 4. Responsiveness and freedom of assembly are the only two significant predictors. Those who considered the government more responsive and that people are enjoying freedom of assembly tended to exhibit greater pride of being a Hong Kong citizen. Our list of variables apparently cannot explain pride in Hong Kong Identity, which is worthy of further examination.

Table 21.5 Ordered Logistic Regression Analysis of Proud of Hong Kong Identity

	How proud are you to be a citizen of Hong Kong?		
	(4)	**(5)**	**(6)**
Demographics			
Age	0.011	-0.007	-0.016
	(0.015)	(0.016)	(0.019)
Age Squared	-0.000	0.000	0.000
	(0.000)	(0.000)	(0.000)
Education	0.003	0.014	0.005
	(0.021)	(0.024)	(0.027)
Income	-0.101*	-0.075	-0.073
	(0.040)	(0.045)	(0.053)
Born in Hong Kong	-0.108	-0.062	-0.037
	(0.091)	(0.100)	(0.113)
Married	0.129	0.152	0.122
	(0.101)	(0.113)	(0.132)
Female	-0.154	-0.177	-0.170
	(0.086)	(0.096)	(0.110)
Wave	-0.068	0.108*	0.007
	(0.044)	(0.054)	(0.092)

(Continuing on the next page)

Table 21.5 Cont.

	How proud are you to be a citizen of Hong Kong?		
	(4)	**(5)**	**(6)**
Government Attributes			
Responsiveness	-	0.333**	0.278**
		(0.086)	(0.095)
Non-Transparency	-	-0.064	-0.061
		(0.066)	(0.078)
Power Abuse	-	0.054	0.057
		(0.064)	(0.079)
Equal Treatment of Classes	-		0.069
			(0.080)
Civil Liberties			
Freedom of Speech	-	0.137	0.076
		(0.126)	(0.136)
Freedom of Assembly	-	0.401**	0.394**
		(0.119)	(0.129)
Cutoff Point 1	-4.438**	-1.961**	-2.577**
	(0.423)	(0.611)	(0.779)
Cutoff Point 2	-2.916**	-0.424	-1.143
	(0.410)	(0.618)	(0.777)
Cutoff Point 3	0.966*	3.526**	2.596**
	(0.407)	(0.634)	(0.785)
Cutoff Point 4	7.579**	9.958**	8.802**
	(1.055)	(1.166)	(1.223)
Number of Observations	2698	2151	1582

Notes: (1) The estimation strategy is ordered logistic regression. (2) Standard errors are in parentheses. (3) $* p < 0.05$, $** p < 0.01$.

Table 21.6 System Support across Five Waves

Wave	Diffuse System Support 1	Diffuse System Support 2
I (2001)	-	-
II (2007)	-	-
III (2012)	2.44486	2.423474
IV (2016)	2.501942	2.441006
V (2019)	2.162162	2.124717

Source: Asian Barometer Survey. Authors prepared.

System Support

Table 21.6 shows that the scores of diffuse system support 1 and 2 were both low and declining. Diffuse system support 1 dropped from 2.44 in 2012 to 2.16 in 2019. Diffuse system support 2 dropped from a score of 2.42 in 2012 to 2.12 in 2019.

Diffuse System Support 1

Tables 21.7 and 21.8 show the results of the ordered logistic regression analysis of system support. Same as above, for each of the dependent variables, we regressed it, firstly, with demographic variables. We then added the first three variables of government attributes (responsiveness, non-transparency, and power abuse) and the two variables of civil liberties (freedom of speech and freedom of assembly); lastly, we added the equal treatment of classes variable.

Table 21.7 shows that Education and Income are consistent significant predictors, with the less educated and lower income groups tended to be more proud of the system of government. Birthplace and marital status are significant only in specification 7. Comparatively, perceptions of government as responsive, government as transparent and people having freedom of speech are consistent and important predictors. The perception of equal treatment of classes also predicts system support. Its introduction into specification 9 does not affect much the effects of other predictors.

Table 21.7 Ordered Logistic Regression Analysis of Diffuse System Support 1

	Thinking in general, I am proud of our system of government.		
	(7)	**(8)**	**(9)**
Demographics			
Age	0.017	0.006	0.006
	(0.014)	(0.016)	(0.016)
Age Squared	-0.000	-0.000	-0.000
	(0.000)	(0.000)	(0.000)
Education	-0.083**	-0.067**	-0.061*
	(0.022)	(0.025)	(0.025)
Income	-0.146**	-0.115*	-0.109*
	(0.040)	(0.046)	(0.046)
Born in Hong Kong	-0.248**	-0.145	-0.151
	(0.091)	(0.103)	(0.104)
Married	0.235*	0.099	0.056
	(0.104)	(0.121)	(0.121)
Female	0.121	0.011	0.029
	(0.087)	(0.097)	(0.098)
Wave	-0.120	0.069	0.015
	(0.064)	(0.079)	(0.079)
Government Attributes			
Responsiveness	-	0.570**	0.553**
		(0.081)	(0.081)
Non-Transparency	-	-0.376**	-0.338**
		(0.074)	(0.074)

(Continuing on the next page)

Table 21.7 Cont.

	Thinking in general, I am proud of our system of government.		
	(7)	**(8)**	**(9)**
Power Abuse	-	-0.028	-0.020
		(0.073)	(0.075)
Equal Treatment of Classes	-	-	0.392**
			(0.081)
Civil Liberties			
Freedom of Speech	-	0.511**	0.510**
		(0.132)	(0.134)
Freedom of Assembly	-	0.010	-0.090
		(0.131)	(0.136)
Cutoff Point 1	-2.589**	-0.480	0.034
	(0.461)	(0.693)	(0.690)
Cutoff Point 2	-0.678	1.667*	2.218**
	(0.456)	(0.698)	(0.695)
Cutoff Point 3	2.166**	4.647**	5.228**
	(0.471)	(0.715)	(0.714)
Cutoff Point 4	-	-	-
Number of Observations	1915	1579	1561

Notes: (1) The estimation strategy is ordered logistic regression. (2) Standard errors are in parentheses. (3) * $p < 0.05$, ** $p < 0.01$.

Diffuse System Support 2

Same as above, education and income are the most significant variables predicting diffuse regime support 2. Similarly, the less educated and lower income groups tended to have greater system support. Birthplace and age exhibit effects only in specification 10. Like the above analysis, perceptions of government responsiveness, transparency, freedom of speech, and equal treatment of classes are important predictors (Table 21.8).

Table 21.8 Ordered Logistic Regression Analysis of Diffuse System Support 2

	A system like ours, even if it runs into problems, deserves the people's support.		
	(10)	**(11)**	**(12)**
Demographics			
Age	0.041**	0.023	0.020
	(0.014)	(0.015)	(0.016)
Age Squared	-0.000**	-0.000	-0.000
	(0.000)	(0.000)	(0.000)
Education	-0.135**	-0.128**	-0.119**
	(0.023)	(0.026)	(0.026)
Income	-0.131**	-0.109*	-0.102*
	(0.040)	(0.044)	(0.044)

(Continuing on the next page)

Table 21.8 Cont.

	A system like ours, even if it runs into problems, deserves the people's support.		
	(10)	**(11)**	**(12)**
Born in Hong Kong	-0.356**	-0.178	-0.209*
	(0.092)	(0.105)	(0.106)
Married	-0.025	-0.085	-0.104
	(0.104)	(0.117)	(0.119)
Female	-0.049	-0.118	-0.133
	(0.088)	(0.098)	(0.098)
Wave	-0.193**	0.102	0.047
	(0.068)	(0.084)	(0.085)
Government Attributes			
Responsiveness	-	0.751**	0.722**
		(0.093)	(0.094)
Non-Transparency	-	-0.223**	-0.184*
		(0.076)	(0.077)
Power Abuse	-	-0.014	-0.001
		(0.075)	(0.077)
Equal Treatment of Classes	-	-	0.430**
			(0.079)
Civil Liberties			
Freedom of Speech	-	0.510**	0.506**
		(0.119)	(0.120)
Freedom of Assembly	-	0.157	0.056
		(0.109)	(0.110)
Cutoff Point 1	-3.153**	0.256	0.733
	(0.469)	(0.697)	(0.701)
Cutoff Point 2	-1.031*	2.661**	3.178**
	(0.460)	(0.705)	(0.710)
Cutoff Point 3	2.346**	6.219**	6.762**
	(0.469)	(0.719)	(0.724)
Cutoff Point 4	-	-	-
Number of Observations	1924	1597	1581

Notes: (1) The estimation strategy is ordered logistic regression. (2) Standard errors are in parentheses. (3) * p < 0.05, ** p < 0.01.

Overall Discussion

Simply put, the older, those not born in Hong Kong, and male are more likely to express pride in identity as a Chinese citizen, with education and income having a partial effect. The predictors for pride in Hong Kong identity is inconclusive from our findings. In our data, the pride in Chinese identity and in Hong Kong identity do not contradict each other, unlike some other previous findings (Steinhardt, Li, and Jiang 2018).

The less educated, lower income groups and those not born in Hong Kong tend to register greater system support. The prediction powers of the demographic variables, in descending order, are income (9 out of 12 specifications), education (8 out of 12 specifications), birthplace (6 out of 12 specifications), age (4 out of 12 specifications), gender (3 out of 12 specifications), and marital status (2 out of 12 specifications).

Perception of government responsiveness can predict all four dependent variables. This echoes with our earlier analysis of the growing youth activism: changing identity and declining trust was induced by the government's neglect of the demand for democratic reform. Perception of non-transparency and freedom of speech (both 6 out of 8 specifications) are the next most effective predictors. Power Abuse is not a significant predictor at all.

Conclusion

Our results more or less illustrate the plight of the Hong Kong government. The younger generation has a weaker identity with China. They are dissatisfied with the current political system because of its performance in civil liberties (freedom) and responsiveness (democracy). The declining system support fuels the drastic direct actions in recent years to defend their freedom and fight for democracy. The support base of the government is reduced to those who are older, have lower income, and lower education, which is unlikely to grow in influence in time, except a change of immigration policies (Wong, Ma, and Lam 2018; Wong et al. 2019). The gap between institutional performance and societal aspirations can grow larger, which may bring more governance problems and challenges to the system in the future.

Acknowledgements
The authors thank the General Research Fund (Ref: 746812 and 14614815) and the Faculty Development Scheme (Ref: UGC/FDS16/H05/18) of the Research Grants Council of Hong Kong for the funding support of the projects.

References
Chan, Kin-man. 2005. "Civil Society and the Democracy Movement in Hong Kong: Mass Mobilization with Limited Organizational Capacity." *Korea Observer* 36 (1): 167-182.

Lam, Wai-man. 2017. "Hong Kong's Fragmented Soul: Exploring Brands of Localism." In *Citizenship, Identity and Social Movements in the New Hong Kong*, edited by Wai-man Lam and Luke Cooper, 72-93. London: Routledge.

Lee, Francis L. F., and Joseph M. Chan. 2008. "Making Sense of Participation: The Political Culture of Pro-democracy Demonstrators in Hong Kong." *The China Quarterly* 193: 84-101. doi: 10.1017/S0305741008000052.

Ma, Ngok. 2015. "The Rise of 'Anti-china' Sentiments in Hong Kong and the 2012 Legislative Council Elections." *The China Review* 15 (1): 39-66. https://www.jstor.org/stable/24291928.

So, Alvin Y. C. 2008. "Social Conflict in Hong Kong After 1997: The Emergence of a Post-modernist Mode of Social Movements?" In *China's Hong Kong Transformed: Retrospect and Prospects Beyond the First Decade*, 233-251. Hong Kong: City University of Hong Kong Press.

Steinhardt, H. Christoph, Linda Chelan Li, and Yihong Jiang. 2018. "The Identity Shift in Hong Kong Since 1997: Measurement and Explanation." *Journal of Contemporary China* 27 (110): 261-276. doi: 10.1080/10670564.2018.1389030.

Wong, S. H. W., K. C. Lee, K. Ho, and H. D. Clarke. 2019. "Immigrant Influx and Generational Politics: A Comparative Case Study of Hong Kong and Taiwan." *Electoral Studies* 58: 84-93. doi: 10.1016/j.electstud.2018.12.008.

Wong, S. H. W., N. Ma, and W. M. Lam. 2018. "Immigrants as Voters in Electoral Autocracies: The Case of Mainland Chinese Immigrants in Hong Kong." *Journal of East Asian Studies* 18 (1): 67-95. doi: 10.1017/jea.2017.29.

22 Dynamics of Thais' Political Values and Orientation toward Democracy

Thawilwadee Bureekul and Ratchawadee Sangmahamad

Thailand has experienced more coup d'états than any other country, and since 1932 Thailand has had thirteen successful military coups, twenty constitutions, and twenty-eight national elections. In the period 1932 to 2020, there has on average been a coup d'état every 6.7 years, a new constitution every 4.4 years, and 3.1 years between elections. Meanwhile, between late 2013 and early 2014, anti-government protests were held in Bangkok and disrupted the subsequent general election in February 2014. The anti-government protests sought a government without influence from the Shinawatra family and viewed the then Prime Minister Yingluck Shinawatra as a puppet to her brother, Thaksin Shinawatra. While Thaksin was the most popular Prime Minister in Thai history, he was convicted of corruption charges in 2008 and has lived in self-imposed exile from the country since 2006. Later in 2010, a series of political protests were held in favor of the Shinawatra family, making it clear that both Thai elites and rural workers were protestors. The incumbent Prime Minister, former General and head of a military junta, General Prayuth Chan-o-cha, has been in power since the May 2014 coup d'état. An election was held in 2019 through which Prime Minister Prayuth Chan-o-cha was able to form a coalition government while Prayuth Chan-o-cha was appointed as Prime Minister by the Thai parliament.

This chapter examines support for democracy in Thailand over five different waves of the Asian Barometer Survey, a cross-national research program that gauges public opinion. More specifically, the chapter explores the factors affecting satisfaction with the way democracy functions in Thailand.

Literature Review
Political Culture

Almond and Verba (1963) define political culture as referring to individuals' attitudes that affect their behavior in the political system. In other words, political culture subjectively defines political activities and processes at the individual level.

Moreover, political culture shapes political activities and behaviors at the individual and group level (Almond and Verba 1963). Political culture provides the core for political participation behavior at the individual level while it also describes value patterns and understanding at the group level to ensure the cohesiveness of institutions. Pye (1965), Almond and Powell (1978) redefined the scope of the definition of political culture as the set of attitudes, beliefs, and feelings toward contemporary political issues (Almond and Powell 1978; Fuchs 1998).

Political culture can be identified at two levels, the elite level and the citizen level (Almond and Verba 1963). However, political culture can be seen in different groups or ethnicities within a country. Furthermore, it is not necessary for all members of a nation to hold the same political culture characteristics, and different groups can have their own particular political culture (David, Paletz, and Lipinkski 1994). Accordingly, there can be multiple political cultures within a single country.

The concept of political culture is based on the belief that culture has an impact directly and indirectly on the citizen's behavior on political activities and political structure. Almond and Verba (1963) proposed three types of psychological orientations that affect political culture on the basis of citizens' attitudes and values: 1) Cognitive orientations refer to citizens' knowledge and attitudes toward political activities and processes; 2) Affective orientations imply feelings based on individuals' emotions about political activities including their context, as well as political processes such as the government's performance, role, and authority; and 3) Evaluation orientations refer to how individuals evaluate the political process, including their opinions about political issues (Ishiyama 2012).

Moreover, Almond and Verba (1963) proposed three types of political culture: 1) Parochial culture refers to the situation where citizens only know and realize the existence of government; 2) Subject political culture refers to circumstances where citizens pay no attention to political activities, with the citizen not realizing that they are part of political activities. They only realize that they are subject of government; and 3) Participation culture refers to situations where citizens are involved in the political process as well as the inputs and outputs of government processes, for instance, where citizens can share their opinions with the government and political parties. These types of political culture are known as civic culture (Dalton and Welzel 2015).

Role of Political Culture in Democratic Institutions

Political culture can be explained as a precondition for and consequence of the democratic process. A pro-democratic political culture is typically based on high levels of participation in the political process, as well as citizens holding certain self-expression values. In this sense, political culture is an important factor determining the characteristics of government institutions (Draško and Džihić 2019; Inglehart and Welzel 2005).

Inglehart and Welzel (2003) argued that political culture emphasizes individual expression, tolerance, trust, and participation processes in political activities as the main elements of democratic political institutions. Inglehart and Welzel (2003) also argued that self-expression and GDP per capita positively affect the democratic process (Adkisson and McFerrin 2014). This is in contrast with Anderson's (1998) finding that indicators for political and economic performance have a greater effect on satisfaction with democracy than aspects of political culture since culture changes slowly and political values are deeply embedded.

In addition, transparency is understood to be an important characteristic of democratic institutions. Dahler-Larsen and Boodhoo (2019) propose that culture positively affects the transparency of institutions and that higher levels of evaluation culture are associated with greater government transparency.

Modernization, Globalization, and Political Value Changes

Globalization has created a sort of global village, in which all locations around the world have been compressed. As a consequence, globalization has resulted in an intensification of the consciousness of the world being considered as a whole. Moreover, globalization has affected the evolution of modern communications, resulting in changes in the political values and cultural orientations of both individuals and groups. Accordingly, it can be seen that political values change largely on the basis of fundamental characteristics of society. In other words, it can be concluded that the process of globalization has significantly affected personal convictions, including individuals' values, beliefs, and attitudes, which are aspects of political culture (Dalton and Klingemann 2007).

Supporting Research

Rystina (2013) analyzes youth attitudes toward politics in Kazakhstan by investigating the effect of attitudes and education level on political participation and satisfaction with democracy. Educationally disadvantaged youth were found to participate less than older individuals with a higher level of education. Moreover, youth with a higher level of education tend to have positive attitudes toward and trust in the political process (Rystina 2013).

In addition, differences were also found in the way gender affects political values. Gender is found to influence political values and is associated with differences in political behavior. This situation is referred to as the traditional gender gap. This finding is supported by research into the African context, in which African women and men have slightly different preferences in relation to political and economic issues and when evaluating the government (Logan and Bratton 2006). Besides, women are more concerned about political issues, have a stronger tolerance for one-party systems, and show less support for multiparty competition in democratic systems (Logan and Bratton 2006).

Moreover, personality traits at the individual level and the procedures of state institutions are found to significantly relate to satisfaction and participation in the political process. Individuals with a degree of satisfaction tend to participate more in the political process because they believe that they can influence the political process. Moreover, citizen satisfaction levels in relation to personality traits are reflected by their participation in the democratic process and activities (Matei 2009). In addition, the governing system can also affect citizens' democratic attitudes and their satisfaction with the democratic process. Markovik (2010) shows that socialism, the governing system of the Republic of Macedonia, is the dominant political ideology, and almost 80 percent of students had socialist attitudes, affecting their political behavior. Moreover, they also show that democratic attitudes are influenced by the degree of openness to new ideas (Markovik 2010).

In summary, political culture is an important part of determining values and behaviors related to the political process. These also include trust in political institutions and satisfaction with the democratic regime. Thus, not only the individuals, but the entire population is affected. Yet, there may be different political values among different groups. Those with different financial resources may develop different worldviews, with well-off citizens valuing post-materialist values and the poor emphasizing economic security. This study aims to understand how the difference in demographic characteristics affects political values, which in turn affect their attitudes toward democracy and the government. This section answers the research question: Over the past two decades, how do demographic characteristics as well as the dynamics of different political values affect the direction of democratic preferences?

Data Collection

This study presents data from face-to-face interviews undertaken in 2001, 2006, 2010, 2014, and 2018 (see Table 22.1 and Figure 22.1) by the Asian Barometer

Survey of Democracy, Governance, and Development in Thailand, as conducted by King Prajadhipok's Institute. All the interviewees were at least 18 years old on the date of the interview and represented a true sample of eligible Thai voters. Moreover, probability sampling was utilized to randomly select survey respondents.

Table 22.1 Summary of Asian Barometer Surveys and Political Events in Thailand (2001-2019)

Year	Survey (Wave)	Period of Data Collection	Prime Minister	Sample Size	Political Event	Period of Event
2001	1	October-November, 2001	Thaksin Shinawatra	1,546	Election	January 6, 2001
2005			Thaksin Shinawatra		Election	February 6, 2005
2006	2	April-September, 2006	Thaksin Shinawatra	1,546	Election (void)	April 2, 2006
					Coup d'état	September 19, 2006
			Surayud Chulanont		Interim government	October 1, 2006
					Constitution of the Kingdom of Thailand (Interim) 2006	October 1, 2006
2007			Surayud Chulanont		Constitution of the Kingdom of Thailand 2007	August 24, 2007
					Election	December 23, 2007
2008			Samak Sundaravej			January 29, 2008
			Somchai Wongsawat		Election (void)	September 8, 2008
			Abhisit Vejjajiva			
2010	3	August- December, 2010	Abhisit Vejjajiva	1,512		
2011					Election	July 3, 2011
2014	4	August- October, 2014	General Prayuth Chan-o-cha	1,200	Coup d'état	May 22, 2014
					Election (void)	February 2, 2014
					Constitution of the Kingdom of Thailand (Interim) 2014	July 22, 2014

(Continuing on the next page)

Table 22.1 Cont.

Year	Survey (Wave)	Period of Data Collection	Prime Minister	Sample Size	Political Event	Period of Event
2017					Constitution of the Kingdom of Thailand 2017	April 6, 2017
2018	5	December 2018-February 2019	General Prayuth Chan-o-cha	1,200		
2019			General Prayuth Chan-o-cha		Election	March 24, 2019

Source: Authors prepared.

It should be noted that an election was held at the beginning of 2001 before the first wave survey. Meanwhile, the 2006 data collection for the second wave was completed during the same month as the coup d'état of September 19, 2006. Similarly, there were political events leading up to the May 22, 2014 coup d'état, including demonstrations, road protests, voting disruption, and an invalidated election during the third wave of the survey. The period in which the fourth wave was conducted included the May 22, 2014 coup d'état to remove an interim government that was formerly headed by Yingluck Shinawatra. General Prayuth Chan-o-cha then became leader of the National Council for Peace and Order (NCPO), the military junta which governed Thailand between May 22, 2014 and July 10, 2019 after the election in 2019. Therefore, during the fourth and fifth waves, Thailand was governed by a military junta under the 2014 interim constitution and the later 2017 constitution.

This chapter sought to investigate the dynamics of Thais' political values and their orientations toward democracy over the past two decades.

Findings

The findings of this chapter are divided into three sections. The first section describes the attitudes of Thai people toward democracy and government, the second section explores support for democracy in Thailand, and the final section discusses the factors that affect how democracy works in Thailand.

1. The attitudes of Thai people toward democracy and the government

1-1 Satisfaction with democracy and the government
The results in Table 22.2 show that between 2001 and 2018, satisfaction with the way democracy works decreased from 90.4 percent in 2001 to 74.2 percent in 2018.

Table 22.2 Satisfaction with Democracy and Government in Thailand (2001-2018)

Very satisfied and satisfied	Survey Year				
	2001	2006	2010	2014	2018
The way democracy works	90.4	83.6	82.5	79.5	74.2
The current government	89.7	81.4	68.4	90.2	62.8

Source: Asian Barometer Survey. Authors prepared.

When Thaksin Shinawatra was elected in 2001, satisfaction with the current government was very high at 89.7 percent. However, satisfaction decreased continuously in 2006 and 2010 due to the 2005-2006 military coup d'état and the 2010 protests, which resulted in at least 90 deaths and 2,000 wounded (Human Rights Watch 2011, 376). Government satisfaction was at its highest in 2014 at 90.2 percent after the government promulgated the interim Thai constitution on July 22, 2014, yet it decreased to the lowest recorded level in 2018 when it reached 62.8 percent, conforming to the level of trust in the performance of the Prime Minister, as shown in Table 22.3.

Table 22.3 Trust in the Thai Prime Minister (2001-2018)

The questions	Survey Year				
	2001	2006	2010	2014	2018
A great deal of trust and quite a lot of trust in the prime minister	-*	69.9	64.7	75.5	70.2

Source: Asian Barometer Survey. Authors prepared.

1-2 Level of democracy under the present Thai government
Respondents were asked, "Where would you place our country under the present government," using a 10-point Likert scale, ranging from 1 for completely undemocratic through to 10 for completely democratic. The findings in Table 22.4 show that the interviewees considered Thailand to be trending toward undemocratic, falling from a score of 8.21 in 2001 to 5.74 points in 2018.

From Table 22.4, there is a statistical difference between regions in terms of how people perceive the level of democracy in Thailand. The trend for the perception of democracy in Thailand's Central, Northeastern, and Southern regions follow the same pattern, albeit with fluctuations from 2001 to 2018 (Figure 22.1). Meanwhile, in Bangkok, Thailand was perceived to become more democratic throughout this period, while Thailand's Northern region perceived the level of democracy to decrease continuously.

Table 22.4 Results for "Where Would You Place Our Country under the Present Government?" (2001-2018) by Region on a 10-point Likert Scale

Survey Year	Regions					Total	Sig.
	Bangkok	North	Center	Northeast	South		
2001	7.59	8.32	7.91	8.62	8.06	8.21	***
2006	7.31	7.76	7.48	7.75	6.56	7.46	***
2010	8.68	7.45	7.91	8.49	7.14	8.00	***
2014	6.06	6.90	7.13	6.36	7.06	6.68	***
2018	7.40	5.85	4.60	6.02	5.84	5.74	***

* sig at < .05; ** sig. at < .01; *** sig. at <.001
a significant at the .05 level

Figure 22.1 Regional Perspectives on the Democratic State of Thailand, Compared by Survey Period

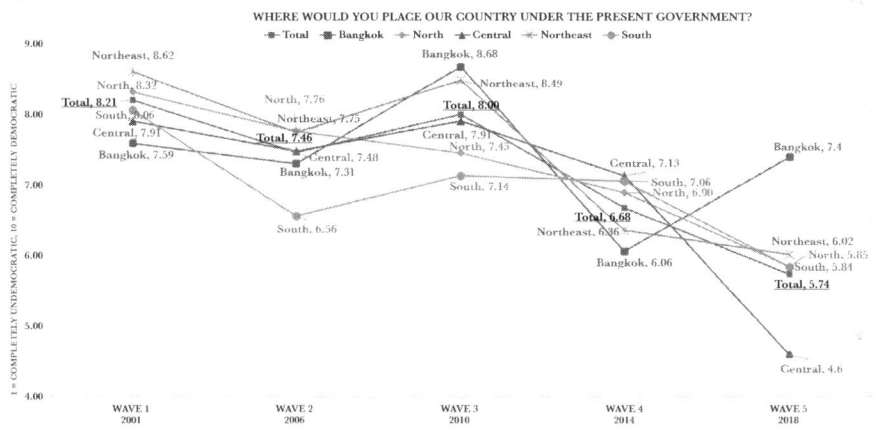

Source: Asian Barometer Survey. Authors prepared.

2. Measurement of support for democracy

Commitment to democracy: Testing undemocratic forms of government

In order to determine support for or commitment to democracy, respondents were asked to rate the following statements from 1 to 4, in which 1 indicates strong acceptance and 4 indicates strong disapproval:

"We should get rid of parliament and elections and have a strong leader to decide things (strong leader)."

"Only one political party should be allowed to stand for election and hold office (single party)."

"The army (military) should come in to govern the country (military government)."

"We should get rid of elections and parliaments and have experts make decisions on behalf of the people (technocracy)."

Higher scores indicate a greater level of support for democracy out of a maximum of 16, equating to a total commitment to democracy.

Table 22.5 presents the mean of commitment toward several approaches of democratic government, compared to region of residence. It can be seen that in 2001, region had a significant influence on attitudes toward having a strong leader, single-party system, or military government. The mean score for military government was the highest among these three approaches for those living in Bangkok and outside of Bangkok. Region of residence also affected these three approaches in 2006, in which the mean score for a single-party system was the highest among these three approaches for those living in Bangkok, while the mean for a single-party system and military government were highest outside Bangkok. Conversely, the effect of region of residence during the 2010 survey influenced support for having a strong leader and single-party system. Similarly, region of residence affected attitudes toward a military government and technocracy in 2014 and single-party system and technocracy in 2018.

Table 22.5 Mean of Commitment to Democratic Government, Compared by Region of Residence (2001-2018)

Year	Residence	Strong Leader	Single Party System	Military Government	Technocracy	Support for Democracy (16 of total)
2001	BKK	3.44	3.25	3.51	3.25	13.43
	Non-BKK	3.12	2.70	3.25	3.19	12.19
	Sig	*0.000****	*0.000****	*0.000****	*0.445*	*0.000****
	Total	3.15	2.76	3.27	3.20	12.38
2006	BKK	2.85	2.98	2.92		11.24 (8.32)#
	Non-BKK	3.03	3.13	3.13		12.15 (9.05)#
	Sig	*0.013**	*0.031**	*0.003***		*0.000****
	Total	3.00	3.11	3.11	*-**	12.28[9.22]**
2010	BKK	3.37	3.55	3.18	3.44	13.09
	Non-BKK	3.12	3.26	3.31	3.30	12.51
	Sig	*0.007***	*0.001***	*0.115*	*0.091*	*0.048**
	Total	3.15	3.28	3.30	3.32	13.05
2014	BKK	2.67	2.82	2.74	2.69	9.98
	Non-BKK	2.85	2.9	2.4	2.89	10.62
	Sig	*0.092*	*0.432*	*0.001***	*0.001***	*0.071*
	Total	*2.83*	*2.89*	*2.42*	*2.87*	*11.01*
2018	BKK	3.27	2.93	3.35	3.07	12.61
	Non-BKK	3.29	3.25	3.32	3.30	13.21
	Sig	*0.730*	*0.001***	*0.626*	*0.022**	*0.086*
	Total	*3.29*	*2.93*	*3.02*	*3.47*	*13.17*

(1 = **support** the other approaches to government, 4 = **support for democracy**)
* sig at < .05; ** sig. at < .01; *** sig. at <.001
Note: Because the final question was not asked in 2006, this figure has been adjusted in line with the other responses for that year.

3. Factors affecting satisfaction with how democracy works in Thailand

We analyzed the variables that influence the level of satisfaction with the way democracy works in Thailand. Regression analysis was then undertaken with other independent variables, including support for democracy, level of corruption and bribe-taking in local and national governments, level of satisfaction with the current government, following political news, political interest, level of trust in the Prime Minister and the national government, and the overall economic condition. The control variables include gender, age, income, educational level, and resident in Bangkok or outside Bangkok.

From Table 22.6, it can be seen that factors including support for democracy, perception of corruption in local government, citizen satisfaction toward the current government, the level of interest in politics, trust, the overall economic condition, and demographic factors affect citizen satisfaction with the way democracy works throughout the survey period.

The results indicate that the overall economic condition positively affected citizen satisfaction with democracy in 2006 and 2018. That means that if people rated the overall economic situation as good, they were satisfied with the way democracy works. A higher level of trust in the Prime Minister and national government also affected citizen satisfaction with democracy in 2001, 2006, and 2018. Furthermore, the level of interest in politics had a positive influence in 2001, 2010, and 2014. However, following the news had a negative effect in 2014, with respondents who regularly followed political news less satisfied with the democracy works. Citizen satisfaction positively impacted citizen satisfaction with democracy in 2001 and 2018, whereas it had a negative impact in 2006. Citizens' perception of corruption in the national government had a positive effect on citizen satisfaction with democracy in 2014 only. Moreover, the perception of corruption in local government had a positive effect in 2001 and 2018. Furthermore, support for democracy also positively influenced citizen satisfaction with democracy in 2018, but negatively in 2014.

Table 22.6 Significant Factors Affecting Satisfaction with the Way Democracy Works in Thailand, Compared by Survey Period

Model	Correlation Coefficients (sig.)				
	2001	2006	2010	2014	2018
Support for Democracy				-.039***	.036***
Level of corruption and bribe-taking in the local government	.071**				.136***

(Continuing on the next page)

Table 22.6 Cont.

Model	Correlation Coefficients (sig.)				
	2001	**2006**	**2010**	**2014**	**2018**
Level of corruption and bribe-taking in the national government				.078*	
Level of satisfaction with the current Government	.226***	-.212***			.197***
Follow the political news				-.085**	
Political interest	.105***		.100*	.153***	
Trust in the Prime Minister	-		.076*		.099**
Trust in the national government	.079***		.117**		.132***
Gender (female = 0, male = 1)	.095**				
Age			.005*		
Household Income	-.049**				.058***
Overall economic condition of country		.109***	.084**	.078**	.115***
Residence area (Non-BKK = 0, BKK = 1)			.198*		
Level of education				-.108**	
Constant	*1.906*	*2.153*	*1.523*	*2.485*	*-0.057*
R²	*.154*	*.214*	*.095*	*.154*	*.428*

* sig at < .05; ** sig. at < .01; *** sig. at <.001, - = No question in this survey

For residence area, it is found that citizens living in Bangkok were more satisfied with democracy than citizens living outside Bangkok in 2010. Demographic factors (gender, age, education, and average household income) also affected citizen satisfaction with democracy in several years. In 2001, males were more satisfied with democracy than females. Meanwhile, older age groups were more satisfied than younger groups with the way democracy works in Thailand in 2010.

In addition, low-income households were satisfied with the way democracy worked in Thailand in 2001, while high-income households were satisfied in 2018. Meanwhile, level of education had a negative effect on citizen satisfaction with democracy in 2014, meaning that those with a lower level of education were more satisfied with the way democracy worked than those with a higher level of education.

Conclusion

The chapter shows that citizens' socioeconomic status is a very important factor. The data suggest that the interviewees placed higher priority on human security, especially in terms of their prosperity. Further, economic development is considered to be the government's responsibility. Therefore, if people have a good degree of well-being and the country's economy is well-developed, people are likely to pay more attention to politics and, in turn, be more satisfied with the government and the way democracy works.

References

Adkisson, Richard V., and Randy McFerrin. 2014. "Culture and Good Governance: A Brief Empirical Exercise." *Journal of Economic Issues* 48: 441-450. doi:10.2753/jei0021-3624480218.

Almond, Gabriel, and Bingham Powell. 1978. *Comparative Politics: A Developmental Approach*. Boston: Little Brown and Co.

Almond, Gabriel, and Sidney Verba. 1963. *The Civic Culture*. Princeton: Princeton University Press.

Anderson, Christopher. 1998. *Political Satisfaction in Old and New Democracies*. Institute for European Studies Working Paper, Binghamton. New York: Citeseer.

Dahler-Larsen, Peter, and Adiilah Boodhoo. 2019. "Evaluation Culture and Good Governance: Is There a Link?" *Evaluation* 25 (3): 277-293. doi:10.1177/1356389018819110.

Dalton, Russell J., and Christian Welzel. 2015. "Political Culture and Value Change." In *The Civic Culture Transformed*, edited by Russell J. Dalton and Christian Welzel, 1-16. New York: Cambridge University Press. doi:10.1017/cbo9781139600002.003.

Dalton, Russell J., and Hans-Dieter Klingemann. 2007. *The Oxford Handbook of Political Behavior*. New York: Oxford University Press.

David, Paletz, and Daniel Lipinkski. 1994. *Political Culture and Political Communication*. Barcelona: Duke University.

Draško, Gazela Pudar, and Vedran Džihić. 2019. "Introduction: The Quest for a New Political Culture." In *Political Culture in Southeast Europe: Navigating between Democratic and Authoritarian Beliefs and Practices*, 3-5. Sarajavo: Friedrich Ebert Stiftung. https://library.fes.de/pdf-files/bueros/sarajevo/15414.pdf

Fuchs, Dieter. 1998. *The Political Culture of Unified Germany*. WZB Discussion Paper, Berlin: Wissenschaftszentrum Berlin für Sozialforschung (WZB). http://hdl.handle.net/10419/56478.

Human Rights Watch. 2011. *World Report 2011*. New York: Human Rights Watch.

Inglehart, Ronald, and Christian Welzel. 2003. "Political Culture and Democracy: Analyzing Cross-Level Linkages." *Comparative Politic* 36 (1): 61-79. doi:10.2307/4150160.

—. 2005. *Modernization, Cultural Change, and Democracy: The Human Development Sequence*. New York: Cambridge University Press.

Ishiyama, John T. 2012. *Principles of Political Science Series*. West Sussex: Blackwell Publishing.

Logan, Carolyn, and Michael Bratton. 2006. *The Political Gender Gap in Africa: Similar Attitudes, Different Behaviors*. Working Papers, Afrobarometer.

Markovik, Marijana. 2010. "Political Attitude and Personality in a Democratic Society." *The Western Balkans Policy Review* 1 (1): 168-184. http://hdl.handle.net/20.500.12188/13625.

Matei, Oana. 2009. *Political Culture and Public Administration in Arad-Romania*. Arad: Western University.

Pye, Lucian W. 1965. *Political Culture and Political Development*. Princeton: Princeton University Press.

Rystina, Indira Sadybekovna. 2013. "Evolution of the Political Culture of the Youth of Kazakhstan." *Procedia-Social and Behavioral Sciences* 89: 413-417. doi:10.1016/j.sbspro.2013.08.869.

23 Thriving Opposition and Political Empowerment in Cambodia Before the 2017 Party Ban

Min-hua Huang

Since the restoration of the monarchy in 1993, modern Cambodia had gone through a bumpy journey with limited but substantive progress toward democratization until late 2017, when the main opposition party was outlawed and banned from politics (Hookway and Narin 2017). This was followed by a total sweep of the seats and more than three-fourths of the votes for the ruling party in the 2018 general election (Sochua 2019). However, authoritarian strongman Hun Sen's crackdown on the opposition, who were accused of treason, destroyed the country's democratic mechanisms and left it with a one-party system akin to China and Vietnam (Morgenbesser 2019), departing from the trajectory of a slow but vibrant democratic development characterized by a growing civil society and strong opposition forces (Norén-Nilsson 2019). For the five general elections prior to 2018, the opposition was competitive with Hun Sen's Cambodian People's Party (CPP) with the ratio of the seats as follows: 48 percent vs. 43 percent (1993), 48 percent vs. 52 percent (1998), 41 percent vs. 59 percent (2003), 21 percent vs. 73 percent (2008), and 45 percent vs. 55 percent (2013), despite the many doubts that international observer groups cast about the integrity of the elections. Therefore, Hun Sen's purge of opposition leaders and parties can be viewed as a preemptive strike to obliterate any political challenge and ensure his grasp of power that has already lasted four decades can continue into the future.

This chapter will briefly review Cambodia's democratization by presenting public opinion data collected by the Asian Barometer Survey (ABS) in 2007, 2012, and 2015. Unfortunately, due to the mounting political persecution after 2018, it was not possible to carry out the fifth wave of the survey in the country. However, our analysis of the data from three waves of the survey can illuminate the political attitudes and democratic orientations of Cambodian citizens in the context of the country's troubled democracy.

Socioeconomic Background

Cambodia remains one of the least developed countries in the world. However, despite its low-income status, the country has enjoyed substantial economic growth since the early 2000s. According to World Bank WDI indicators, from 2003 to 2020, the average annual growth in GDP per capita was 5.9 percent, with only two years of negative growth in 2009 (-1.4 percent) and 2020 (-4.5 percent) due to the global financial crisis in 2008-2009 and the COVID-19 pandemic respectively. Between 2010 and 2019, the country had steady economic growth of between 5 percent and 6 percent. GDP per capita increased 2.5 times from US$507 to US$1269 (constant 2010 US$) between 2003 and 2019. At the same time, the poverty rate (poverty headcount ratio at national poverty lines, WDI indicator) also fell rapidly from 50.2 percent (2003) to 13.5 percent (2014), and the unemployment rate, based on WDI, fell from around 1.3 percent before 2008 to 0.1 percent after 2016 until the outbreak of the pandemic. Overall, the country's socioeconomic conditions have improved significantly, and Cambodia enjoys a late-comer advantage in the global economy like other ASEAN countries such as Vietnam, the Philippines, and Indonesia.

Does the country's strained political situation bias Cambodia citizens' assessment of their economic condition downward? As Table 23.1 shows, Cambodians are generally rational when evaluating the country's overall economic condition, with a similar proportion consistently viewing the economic condition as getting worse over the three survey waves, a small increase in the proportion believing the country's economic condition is about the same, and a small decline in the proportion believing the country's economic condition is getting better. The decline in the proportion of respondents who believe the country's economic condition is getting better can be explained by the ratchet effect, with citizens who are accustomed to steady economic growth increasing their expectations for economic performance. When respondents were asked about their own household's economic condition, there was a similar pattern, with a growing ratio of negative assessments (from 17 percent to 30 percent) and a decline in positive assessments (from 48 percent to 32 percent). Nonetheless, the percentage of positive and neutral assessments combined were around 70 percent or above, which signifies that Cambodians did perceive improvement in their socioeconomic conditions despite growing political tension.

Table 23.1 Assessment of the Change in the Economic Condition

	Overall Economic Condition			Household Economic Condition		
	Second Wave (2007)	Third Wave (2012)	Fourth Wave (2015)	Second Wave (2007)	Third Wave (2012)	Fourth Wave (2015)
Become Worse	27%	27%	26%	17%	28%	30%
About the Same	19%	27%	31%	34%	31%	37%
Got Better	53%	46%	42%	48%	40%	32%

Source: ABS Cambodia Survey 2007, 2012, 2015. Author prepared.

A key political measure is how Cambodians evaluated the capacity and responsiveness of Hun Sen's government. As shown in Figure 23.1, more than 50 percent of the respondents across three waves gave positive assessments toward Hun Sen's government when answering how likely the government was to be able to solve the country's most important problem. A similar result was found for the responsiveness measure, despite a conspicuous drop in 2015 from nearly 50 percent or above beforehand to only 35 percent. This drop signaled increasing political discontent after the close election in 2013 and subsequent controversy.

Figure 23.1 Assessment of Government Capacity and Responsiveness

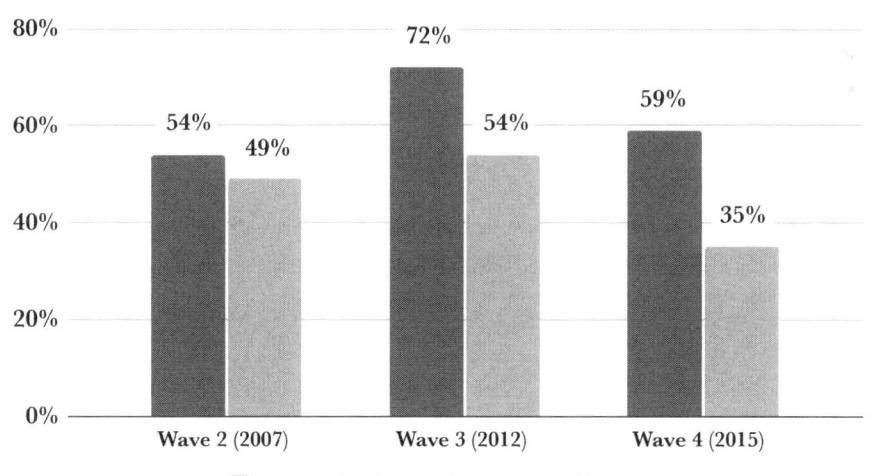

Source: ABS Cambodia Survey 2007, 2012, 2015. Author prepared.

The Growth of Civil Society and Political Participation

The strong performance of the opposition parties in the general elections prior to 2018 reflected the country's thriving civil society, and Cambodian citizens did place high hopes in the electoral mechanisms to practice democracy. This was manifested in the near 70 percent of positive responses when respondents were asked how often elections offer a real choice between different parties or candidates, as shown in Figure 23.2. Only less than 15 percent of the respondents gave negative answers, which suggested that people still believe in electoral competition to make a substantial difference in politics despite frequent accusations of election fraud and obstruction.

The growth of civil society is also shown in the attitude that people believe they have the right to join social organizations, even though political repression is commonplace and widely known. As Figure 23.3 makes evident, an overwhelming percentage of respondents believed they have the right to join any organization they like without fear. The number was consistently above 80 percent across the three survey waves. Such universal consensus was shared between supporters of both the opposition and the ruling party. To a large extent, this explains why Hun Sen launched a legal coup to pre-empt the electoral threat of the opposition before the 2018 election (Chheang 2017). The concept of citizen politics through the right to participate in civil society organizations had become rooted in people's minds. This genuine democratic idea threatened the CPP's election prospects. Therefore, overriding it with a treason charge was the only way to ensure the ruling party's unchallenged re-election without staging a military coup.

Figure 23.2 Elections Offer the Voters a Real Choice between Different Parties or Candidates

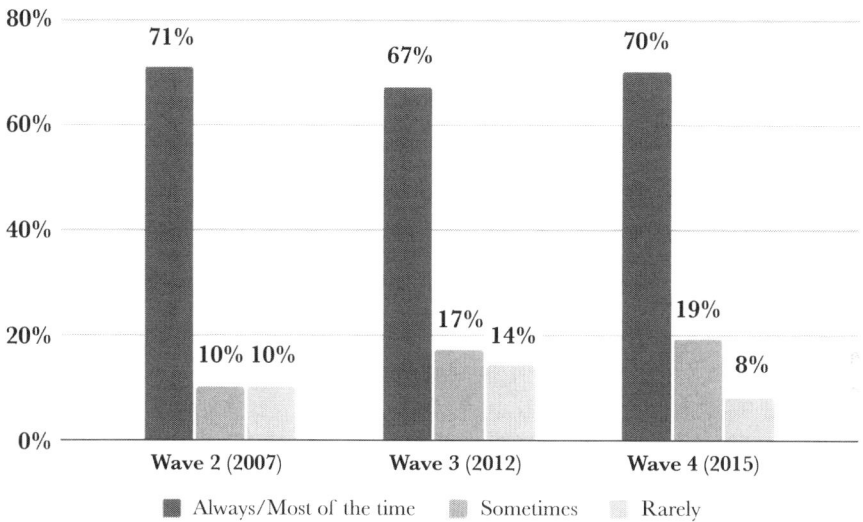

Source: ABS Cambodia Survey 2007, 2012, 2015. Author prepared.

Figure 23.3 People Can Join Any Organization They Like Without Fear

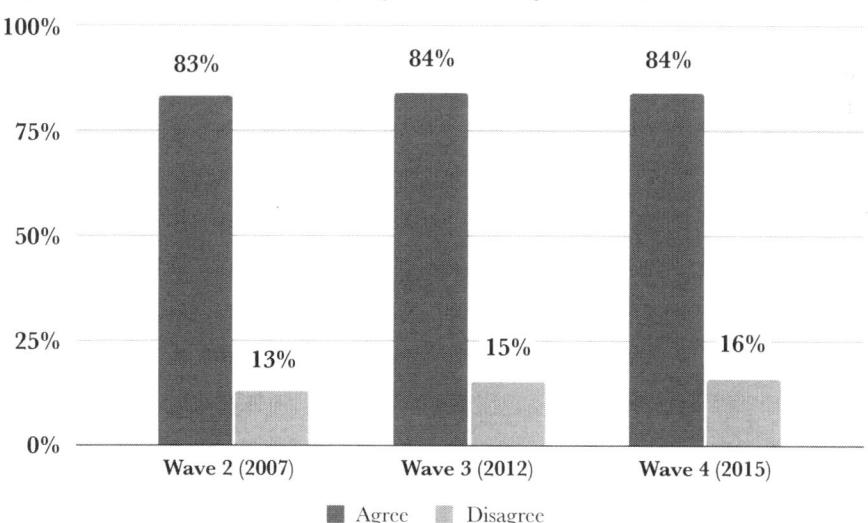

Source: ABS Cambodia Survey 2007, 2012, 2015. Author prepared.

Driving Forces Behind the Opposition Support

Citizens rallied behind the opposition despite Hun Sen's authoritarian rule for many reasons. Of these, two driving forces were significant: rampant corruption and democratic orientation. First, Cambodia has been consistently rated as one of the most corrupt countries in the world by Transparency International. Between 2012 and 2020, Cambodia's corruption perception index (CPI) score ranged from 20 to 22, ranking 160-162 out of 179 countries (from 2017 onward) and even worse than Myanmar after 2015. Similar perceptions also appear in the ABS questionnaire. As Figure 23.4 shows, the ABS asked Cambodian respondents' perceptions about corruption in the local and national governments. In all three waves, nearly half of the respondents (41 percent to 48 percent) thought that corruption among local officials was serious by choosing "almost everyone" or "most officials" are corrupt. For the national government, the evaluations were even worse than those toward the local government, with 51 percent, 49 percent, and 67 percent of respondents in the three survey waves respectively viewing officials as corrupt. The widespread perception of worsening corruption is an important reason accounting for opposition support.

Figure 23.4 Percentage of Respondents Answering "Almost Everyone/Most Officials Are Corrupt"

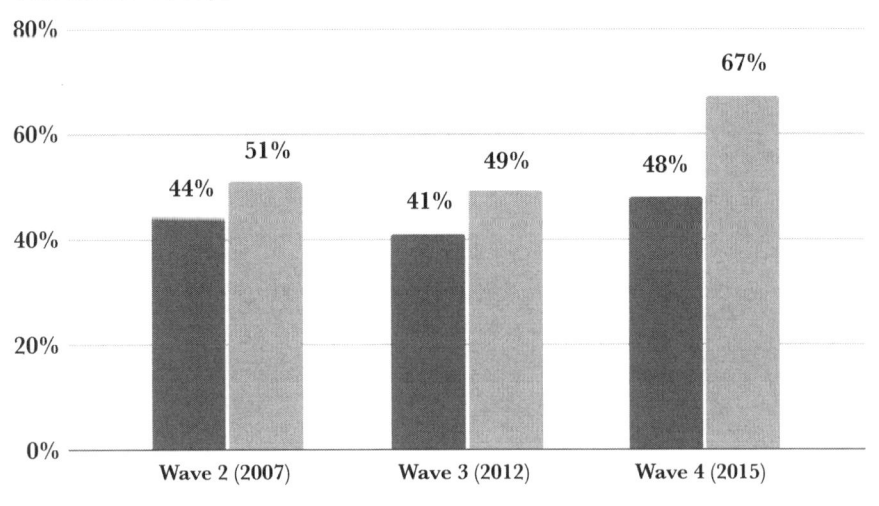

Source: ABS Cambodia Survey 2007, 2012, 2015. Author prepared.

Electoral efficacy, shown in belief in horizontal and vertical accountability, also explains strong democratic orientations in Cambodian society. As shown in Figure 23.5, Cambodians support the democratic principle of "checks and balances," with nearly 60 percent or above expressing their support for the idea of horizontal accountability where the legislature can check the administrative power of the incumbent government. Overwhelming support was also given to the idea of vertical accountability, with nearly 80 percent or above showing that they believe that "the people have the power to change a government they don't like." The result of both measures provides firm evidence that the legitimacy of competitive popular elections was rooted in people's minds, despite actions by the CPP that threatened election integrity. Therefore, instead of canceling the election, Hun Sen resorted to other seemingly legal and administrative excuses to disqualify and exclude those who could out-compete him from participating in the election but still allow weak opposition parties or his allies to run. In hindsight, what damaged the legitimacy of the 2018 election was not only the outlawing of the main opposition party and its leaders but the fact that Hun Sen's party swept all 125 seats in parliament, deviating significantly from its actual level of support. This not only demonstrates that Hun Sen's political persecution was a legal coup; it is also a message to the international community that he no longer needs competitive elections to justify his rule.

Figure 23.5 High Support for the Ideas of Horizontal and Vertical Accountability

The legislature is capable of keeping the government in check.   People have the power to change a government they don't like.

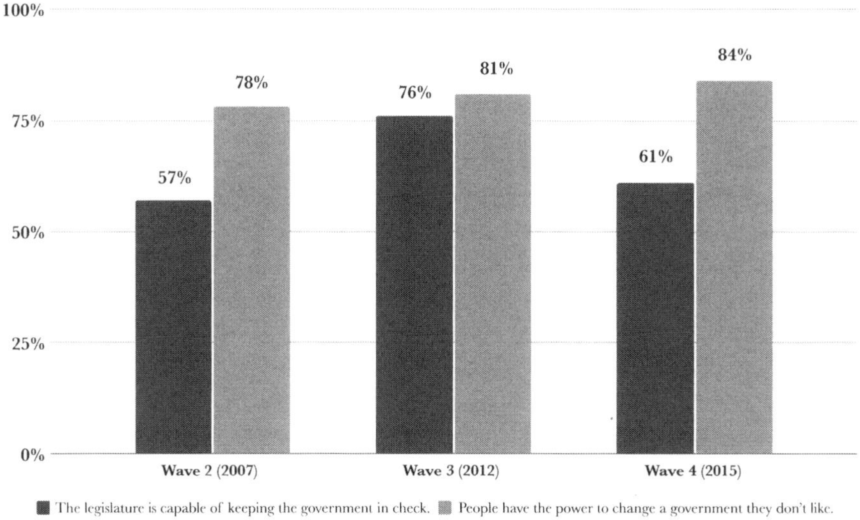

Source: ABS Cambodia Survey 2007, 2012, 2015. Author prepared.

The Chilling Effect under Constant Political Repression

Although the above finding suggests that the opposition enjoys significant support and people are willing to express this support when they cast their ballot, there was also a chilling effect under political repression enforced by the Hun Sen regime. This cannot be simply explained away by a passive culture or social traditionalism (Ollier and Winter 2007), and we can observe a decline in free political expression over time (Seewald 2020). The chilling effect on free political expression is the direct result of a fear that individuals may suffer if their opinion deviates from that of the ruling government and that people are afraid that they may be reported to the authorities, even by acquaintances. As Figure 23.6 shows, before the closely-fought 2013 election, nearly 60 percent of respondents answered that they were very or somewhat interested in politics, but that number plummeted to 10 percent in 2015, reflecting the harsher repression of the opposition that eventually culminated in the 2017 purge. A similar result was found when examining the percentage of people answering how often they discuss politics with family members or friends. As Figure 23.7 illustrates, those who answered "frequently" or "occasionally" fell from 56 percent in 2007 to 42 percent in 2012, and further to 39 percent in 2015, while those who answered "never" climbed from 44 percent in 2007 to 58 percent in 2012, and eventually to 61 percent in 2015. This shows that the comfortable victory in the 2008 election gave Hun Sen greater confidence, and therefore, greater political space was allowed by the government. But around the time of the 2013 election, a very competitive campaign with a slim margin and accusations of electoral fraud made Hun Sen realize the possibility of losing power if he failed to adopt tougher measures to restrict the opposition.

The China Factor

China is well-known as the strongest supporter of Hun Sen's regime in international society, and Hun Sen himself has explicitly acknowledged his close alliance with China (Nikkei Asia 2021). During the China Sea dispute, Cambodia was the first ASEAN country to claim neutrality (Sokhean 2020). In fact, the relationship between the countries became even closer following substantial investment in infrastructure projects, including roads, bridges, seaports, airports, railways, hydropower dams, and communication satellites, through China's "Belt and Road Initiative" (BRI) (Heng and Po 2017). Many of these projects are even donation-based or part of China's ODA (Official Development Assistance) to Cambodia in the form of grants or soft loans (Phea 2020). In return, Hun Sen's government has stood firmly with China and supported China in regional or international

Figure 23.6 Declining Explicit Expression of Political Interest

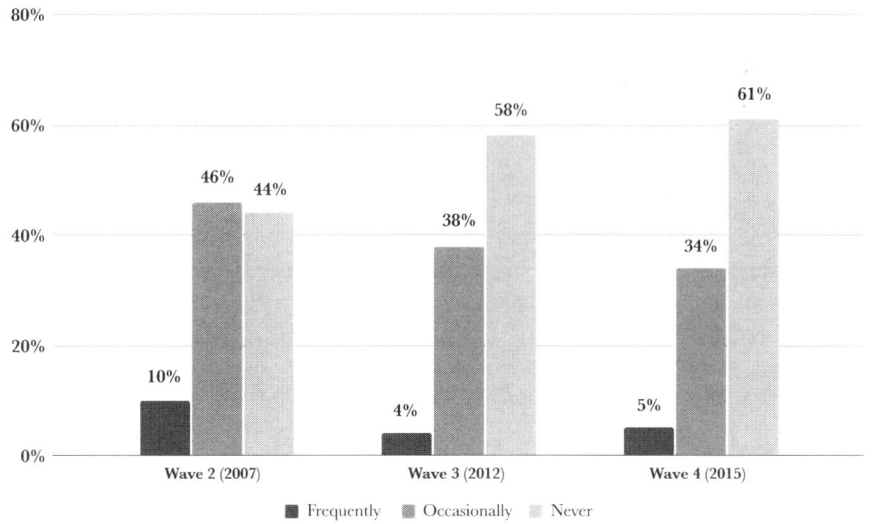

Source: ABS Cambodia Survey 2007, 2012, 2015. Author prepared.

Figure 23.7 Declining Discussion of Politics with Family Members and Friends

Source: ABS Cambodia Survey 2007, 2012, 2015. Author prepared.

organizations such as ASEAN and the United Nations on numerous occasions (Po and Primiano 2020).

China is not only Cambodia's economic patron; politically, China gives Cambodia immense support as well. Right after Hun Sen banned the main opposition party in November 2017, Beijing strongly backed the Hun Sen administration and claimed China supported Cambodia's efforts to protect political stability and hold the general election successfully (Reuters 2017). This proclamation reveals Beijing's support for Hun Sen's continuing rule, even through undemocratic means. While the European Union and the United States adopted sanctions against Hun Sen personally as well the regime as a whole (Cao 2018; Lum 2020), the actual impact on human rights improvement and democratic backsliding has been very limited. Instead, Hun Sen relied on his closest alliance with China and his authoritarian counterparts in ASEAN even more (Heng 2020). In Myanmar, both the military and the opposition (Aung San Suu Kyi) sought China's political support during the fierce competition prior to the 2015 and 2019 elections. A similar situation will also apply to Cambodia if the opposition one day regains its chance to challenge the CPP. Therefore, it is very informative to see how Cambodians view China's influence and whether it is welcomed.

As Figure 23.8 shows, a significant proportion of respondents felt that China had "a great deal of influence" (33 percent and 40 percent for 2012 and 2015, respectively), and an equally sizable proportion felt that China had "some influence" (47 percent and 42 percent, respectively). The two portions combined surpassed 80 percent, leaving only a handful believing China's influence inconsequential. Regarding assessments of favorability, as illustrated in Figure 23.9, over 60 percent of respondents perceived China's influence as positive or somewhat positive, while around 20 percent viewed it as negative or somewhat negative. Relatively few people answer with strong positive or negative options, and the eight-percentage decline in the very positive perception from 14 percent to 6 percent is likely a sign that China's BRI initiative after 2013 and its strong political support for Hun Sen might not be necessarily well-received within certain groups. Although we lack data, such unfavorable perception might have been strengthened after Hun Sen's legal coup in late 2017.

Figure 23.8 Perceived Level of China's Influence on Cambodia

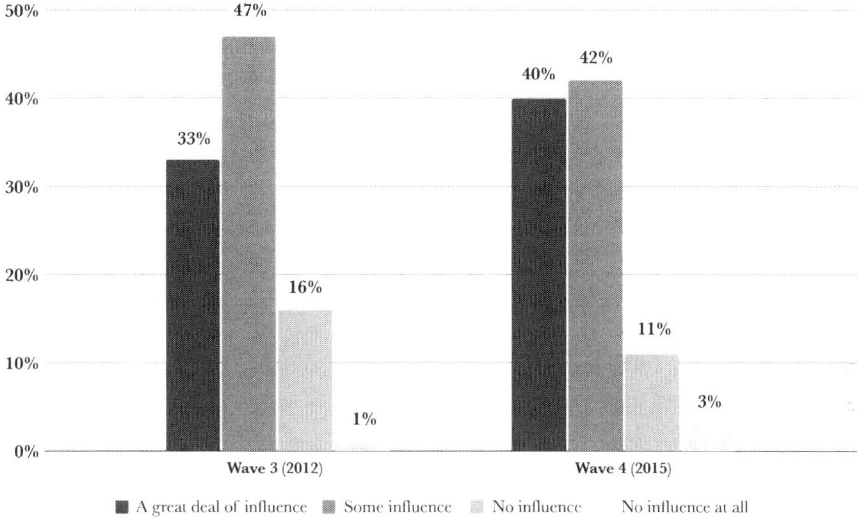

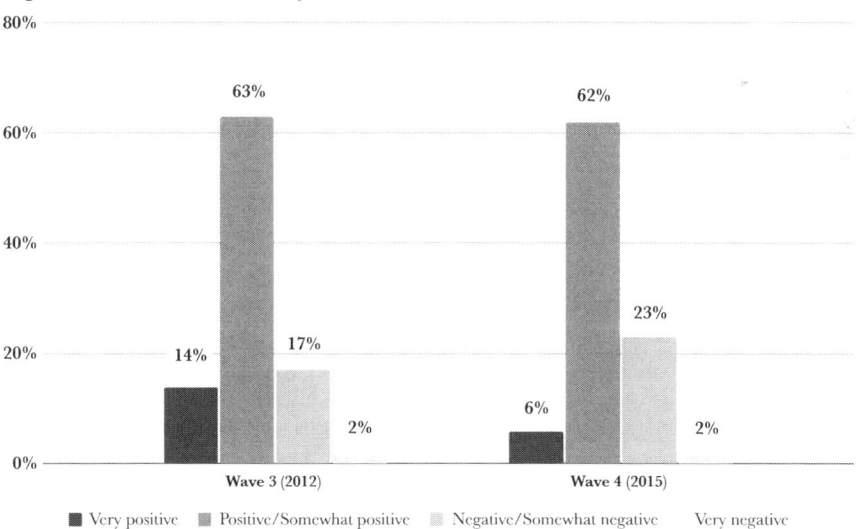

Source: ABS Cambodia Survey 2012, 2015. Author prepared.

Figure 23.9 Favorable Perception of China's Influence

Source: ABS Cambodia Survey 2012, 2015. Author prepared.

It would be helpful to interpret Cambodia's view on China through a cross-tabulation analysis by the aforementioned three groups of public opinion items, perceived corruption of the government officials (local and national), political accountability (horizontal and vertical), and psychological involvement in politics (interest and discussion). As Table 23.2 makes evident, we can conclude a consistent finding across Waves 3 and 4 for the level of China's influence that those who perceived greater government corruption at both local and national levels felt larger China's influence over Cambodia. As to the favorability question, only a marginal finding in Wave 4 that shows China's influence was rated less favorable among those who perceived greater corruption in local officials. But this finding lacks consistency in time and is not found in the similar item when national government officials are in question. Regarding political accountability, consistent findings emerge in Wave 4, where those who did not think they can hold the Cambodia government accountable in horizontal and vertical sense believe greater China's influence over Cambodia and view that influence less favorable. This indicates that growing repression on the opposition makes people even more aware of the close relation the Cambodia government established with China, which decreased China's favorability significantly and this phenomenon had not consistently appeared previously as in 2012. Finally, all the significant findings again only show up in Wave 4 for psychological involvement politics. People who have more interest in politics or discuss politics more frequently tend to perceive greater China's influence and view it more unfavorably. This finding is consistent with the accountability battery, and shows negative mobilization toward China's image has already happened cognitively as the Cambodia regime voiced out loudly its support of China during the incident like the South China Sea Dispute after 2013. Overall, the temporal coincidence of Hun Sen's repression on the main opposition party and the intending sign to strengthen the official ties with China gave rise to a strong cognitive association that Cambodia government sought to ally with China even closer when it became more authoritarian and repressive.

Table 23.2 A Cross-tabulation Analysis of China's Influence on Cambodia (Average Score of China's Influence and Its Favorability)

Items	Respondent Group	Wave	Level of Influence	Favorable Perception
Perceived Corruption				
• Corruption of local officials	Almost everyone/Most officials vs. Hardly anyone/Not much officials	w3	**3.29 vs. 3.05 (p = 0.00)**	2.89 vs. 2.96 (p = 0.12)
		w4	**3.35 vs. 3.12 (p = 0.00)**	**2.73 vs. 2.80 (p = 0.05)**
• Corruption of national officials	Almost everyone/Most officials vs. Hardly anyone/Not much officials	w3	**3.25 vs. 3.07 (p = 0.00)**	2.89 vs. 2.96 (p = 0.14)
		w4	**3.31 vs. 3.03 (p = 0.00)**	2.76 vs. 2.80 (p = 0.28)
Horizontal and Vertical Accountability				
• The legislature is capable of keeping the government in check.	Very capable/Capable vs. Not capable/Not at all capable	w3	3.13 vs. 3.22 (p = 0.19)	**2.97 vs. 2.82 (p = 0.01)**
		w4	**3.13 vs. 3.38 (p = 0.00)**	**2.80 vs. 2.68 (p = 0.00)**
• People have the power to change a government they don't like.	Strongly agree/Agree vs. Strongly disagree/Disagree	w3	3.15 vs. 3.13 (p = 0.70)	2.92 vs. 2.99 (p = 0.20)
		w4	**3.20 vs. 3.37 (p = 0.01)**	**2.80 vs. 2.61 (p = 0.00)**
Psychological Involvement in Politics				
• Interest in politics	Very interested/Interested vs. Not very interested/Not at all interested	w3	3.15 vs 3.14 (p = 0.73)	2.92 vs. 2.95 (p = 0.44)
		w4	**3.37 vs. 3.30 (p = 0.01)**	**2.61 vs. 2.71 (p = 0.01)**
• Discussion of politics with family members or friends	Frequently/Occasionally vs. Never	w3	3.19 vs. 3.12 (p = 0.15)	2.95 vs. 2.92 (p = 0.57)
		w4	**3.29 vs. 3.18 (p = 0.02)**	**2.73 vs. 2.80 (p = 0.05)**

Source: ABS Cambodia Survey 2012, 2015. Author prepared.

Conclusion

Cambodia's human rights record was bad prior to Hun Sen's ban on the opposition and became even worse afterward because of the CPP's continued crackdown on dissent, especially in the context of the ongoing COVID-19 pandemic. What is worse, international concern for the human rights issue in Cambodia has become even weaker as the political spotlight has shifted to Myanmar's military coup and the Taliban's victory in Afghanistan. So long as China keeps backing Hun Sen's regime with economic resources and political support, there are few signs that the country can return to the path of slow but steady democratization that was observed before late-2017. However, based on the public opinion data reported in this chapter, there are some reasons to be optimistic about Cambodia's democratic prospects if the opposition is allowed to return to the electoral process. In particular, the growth of civil society and the democratic orientations of ordinary citizens will be crucial if Cambodia is to return to the path of democratization in the future.

References

Cao, Cindy. 2018. "EU Trade Sanctions on Cambodia: An Ethical Debate." *EU-Asia at a Glance, European Institute for Asian Studies (EIAS)*. Oct. Accessed Sept. 14, 2021. https://www.eias.org/wp-content/uploads/2016/03/EU_Asia_at_a_Glance_Cambodia-Oct2018-V2.pdf.

Chheang, Vannarith. 2017. "Cambodian Power Shift in 2018?" *ISEAS Perspective 53*. Jul. 17. Accessed Sept. 14, 2021. https://www.iseas.edu.sg/wp-content/uploads/pdfs/ISEAS_Perspective_2017_53.pdf.

Heng, Kimkong. 2020. "Cambodia: Hard Choices." *The Interpreter*. Aug. 11. Accessed Sept. 14, 2021. https://www.lowyinstitute.org/the-interpreter/cambodia-hard-choices.

Heng, Kimkong, and Sovinda Po. 2017. "Cambodia and China's Belt and Road Initiative: Opportunities, Challenges and Future Directions." *UC Occasional Paper Series* 1(2): 1-18.

Hookway, James, and Sun Narin. 2017. "Cambodia's Supreme Court Outlaws Main Opposition Party." *The Wall Street Journal*. Nov. 16. Accessed Sept. 14, 2021. https://www.wsj.com/articles/cambodias-supreme-court-outlaws-main-opposition-party-1510834029.

Lum, Thomas. 2020. "Cambodia: Background and U.S. Relations." *Congressional Research Service Report*. Jul. 7. Accessed Sept. 14, 2021. https://www.everycrsreport.com/files/2020-07-07_R44037_3a14b710561932cabd904cad5ceecac2c9e533ee.pdf.

Morgenbesser, Lee. 2019. "Cambodia's Transition to Hegemonic Authoritarianism." *Journal of Democracy* 30 (1): 158-171. doi:10.1353/jod.2019.0012.

Nikkei Asia. 2021. "Cambodia's Hun Sen: 'If I don't rely on China, who will I rely on?'" May 20. Accessed Sept. 14, 2021. https://asia.nikkei.com/Spotlight/The-Future-of-Asia/The-Future-of-Asia-2021/Cambodia-s-Hun-Sen-If-I-don-t-rely-on-China-who-will-I-rely-on.

Norén-Nilsson, Astrid. 2019. "Kem Ley and Cambodian Citizenship Today: Grass-Roots Mobilisation, Electoral Politics and Individuals." *Journal of Current Southeast Asian Affairs* 38 (1): 77-97. doi:10.1177/1868103419846009.

Ollier, Leakthina Chau-Pech, and Tim Winter. 2007. *Expressions of Cambodia: The Politics of Tradition, Identity and Change*. London: Routledge.

Phea, Kin. 2020. "Cambodia-China Relations in the New Decade." *Konrad Adenauer Foundation*. May 26. Accessed Sept. 14, 2021. https://www.kas.de/en/web/kambodscha/single-title/-/content/cambodia-china-relations-in-the-new-decade-2.

Po, Sovinda, and Christopher B. Primiano. 2020. "An 'Ironclad Friend': Explaining Cambodia's Bandwagoning Policy towards China." *Journal of Current Southeast Asian Affairs* 39 (3): 444-464. doi:10.1177/1868103420901879.

Reuters. 2017. "China Supports Cambodia's Crackdown on Political Opposition." Nov. 21. Accessed Sept. 14, 2021. https://www.reuters.com/article/us-cambodia-politics-china-idUSKBN1DL01L.

Seewald, Kate. 2020. "Shrinking Space for Free Expression in Cambodia during Covid-19: Opportunistic Repression or Proportionate Necessity?" *Journal of Southeast Asian Human Rights* 4 (1): 140-167. doi:10.19184/jseahr.v4i1.18093.

Sochua, Mu. 2019. "The Dark Year Since Cambodia's 2018 Election." *The Diplomat*. Jul. 29. Accessed Sept. 14, 2021. https://thediplomat.com/2019/07/the-dark-year-since-cambodias-2018-election/.

Sokhean, Ben. 2020. "Cambodia Stays Neutral in South China Sea Dispute." *Khmer Times*. Jun. 26. Accessed Sept. 14, 2021. https://www.khmertimeskh.com/738181/cambodia-stays-neutral-in-south-china-sea-dispute/.

24 Burma's Failed Democratization
Kai-Ping Huang and Yun-han Chu

Burma's political development has been closely monitored, from military dictatorship to pseudo-civilian rule, then to a fully elected civilian government, and now back again to military rule. Since 2008, Burma's military junta has been drafting a new constitution to further liberalize its economy and politics. This process has reached its high point in the 2015 and 2020 general elections, in which the National League for Democracy (NLD) defeated the military-backed Union Solidarity and Development Party (USDP). Because of the mediocre performance of the NLD government, the USDP and the military expected mass public support for the NLD to decrease during the 2020 elections. The reality, however, defied their expectations, and the military intervened to end the democratic experiment. In fact, survey results indicate that Burma's chances of democracy are not all optimistic.

Burma's (short-lived) democratization has been interpreted as driven by bargaining among elites rather than public pressure and criticism (Zin and Joseph 2012; Callahan 2012; Diamond 2012; Taylor 2012; Croissant and Kamerling 2013; Pedersen 2011; Higley and Gunther 1991). However, Burma has experienced significant popular challenges to military rule, including the 1988 student protests, the 1990 elections, the 2007 Saffron Movement, and the 2015 and 2020 elections. Despite a more promising trajectory since 2007, it ended up with a military coup, repeating the events of 1988 and 1990. While the democratic regression can be explained by the breakdown of the elite pact, survey data provide some insight into the longer-term problems with democracy in Burma. What does a view from the ordinary people inform us about Burma's chances for democracy?

We answer this question by analyzing data from the Asian Barometer Survey (ABS) conducted in Burma in 2015 and 2020 ahead of the general elections. Using national population data provided by the government for sampling, the ABS surveyed approximately 1,600 people across all fifteen regions and states (including Naypyidaw). We can infer from these two waves of surveys whether Burman attitudes toward key aspects of democracy changed during the time when the NLD governed.

Figure 24.1 Preference for Democracy: Two-wave Comparison

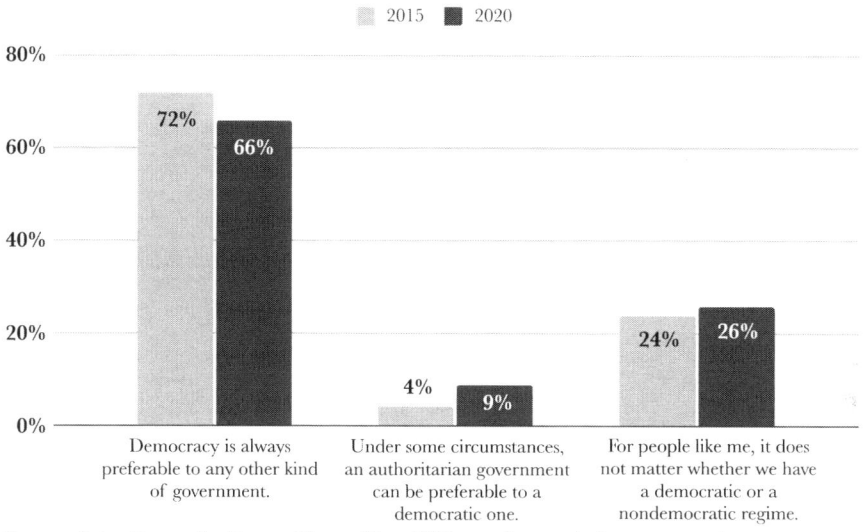

Source: Asian Barometer Survey Waves IV and V Burma Survey. Authors prepared.

In Burma, the ABS found that citizens were strong supporters of democracy, though such support was decreasing. When asked to choose between democracy and an authoritarian alternative, 72 percent of respondents said that "democracy is always preferable to any other kind of government" in 2015. Nevertheless, the support dropped to 66 percent in 2020, and 9 percent of respondents (up from 4 percent in 2015) said that "under some circumstances, an authoritarian government can be preferable to a democratic one" (Figure 24.1). A rise of 24 percent from 2015 to 26 percent in 2020 was also seen in the number of respondents who said "it doesn't matter if we have a democratic or nondemocratic regime."

Under the NLD rule, there seems to be disillusionment about democracy among a small portion of the Burman population. Although support for democracy was strong, the fact that support for authoritarian regimes was on the rise as well as those who were indifferent between regime types is alarming. In order for democracy to really take hold, improving governance and encouraging broader civic engagement will be critical. The underperformance of the NLD government could be the reason behind this. The results of the November 2015 elections were in line with the strong popular support for democracy indicated in the ABS responses, as Burma's citizens rejected continued rule by the military and its USDP government. Our data also suggest that on the eve of this breakthrough election, the people had exuberant aspirations for democracy, a phenomenon quite common to "third-wave" democracies at a comparable stage of democratization. Nevertheless, such aspirations tend to be short-lived since newly democratized countries have to overcome many challenges left by previous authoritarian regimes (Schmitter and Karl 1991). While people might be disappointed with the NLD government, they also understand that removing the military from politics will help normalize politics. A mentality like this is evident from the fact that the NLD won more parliamentary seats than expected in 2020.

In Burma, however, we found that a great majority of its citizens did not embrace liberal democracy in its substance. To assess whether people adhere to democratic values, the ABS asks a battery of questions concerning such issues as political freedom, pluralism, religion in politics, and accountability. Considering the issue of horizontal accountability, the findings from Burma indicate that despite most citizens having a high degree of democratic support, the majority still adhere to authoritarian values and beliefs. Burma's political culture retains a strong sense of authoritarianism, and the problem is compounded by a lack of understanding of how democracy should function. Figure 24.2 depicts the share of Burmese respondents who think the legislature should be a check on the government during both surveys. The principle of horizontal accountability was not supported by 73 percent of respondents in 2015. In contrast, only 64 percent of respondents disapproved in 2020. Regarding judicial independence, 65 percent of respondents disapproved of such accountability in 2015, and the number decreased to 59 percent in 2020. Burmese gradually learned that democracy should function according to the principle of checks and balances. Despite this, an overwhelming majority still believed in paternalism, in which the leaders should decide everything on behalf of the people. The percentage of respondents who regard leaders as family heads increased to 78 percent in 2020 from 70 percent in 2015.

Figure 24.2 Authoritarian Attitudes: Two-wave Comparison

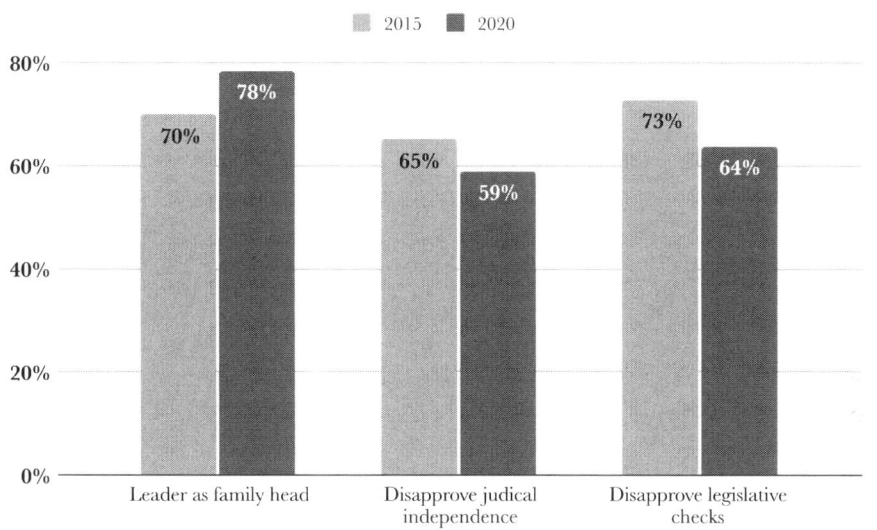

Source: Asian Barometer Survey Waves IV and V Burma Survey. Authors prepared.

The findings indicate a big gap between Burmese support for general democratic ideals and their view of how democracy actually should function. In addition, traditional values have been dominant in Burmese society, which emphasize hierarchy over equality, order over political freedom, harmony over conflict, and collective welfare over individual rights. Democracy is thought to be undermined by traditional values, as they support the centralization of power, limit pluralism, and treat citizens unequally. The ABS asks questions about hierarchy, order, harmony, and collectivism in order to measure the strength of traditional values. Of all Southeast Asian countries, Burma's respondents are most committed to traditional values. Figure 24.3 shows that more than a third (68 percent in 2015 and 61 percent in 2020) of Burma's respondents agreed that students should not question the authority of their teachers; 79 percent in 2015 and 81 percent in 2020 opposed pluralistic views; 64 percent (2015) and 51 percent (2020) said that a boy is preferred if only one child can be chosen. To have Aung San Suu Kyi succeed her father as the one who brought much-needed changes to the country certainly makes chauvinism less appealing.

Figure 24.3 Traditional Values: Two-wave Comparison

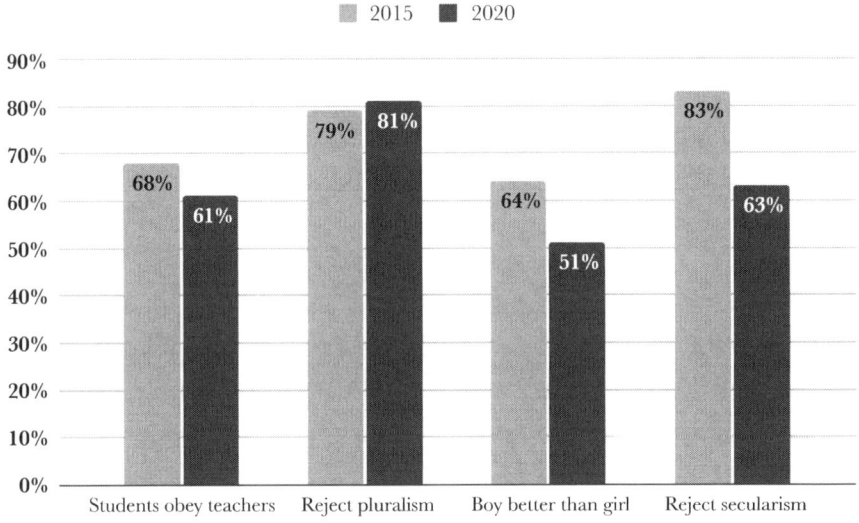

Source: Asian Barometer Survey Waves IV and V Burma Survey. Authors prepared.

As a result of their isolation, Burma's citizens have absorbed their values mainly from conservative religious and governmental institutions. It is likely that these values will change as a result of modernization, globalization, and greater regional integration. Yet, Burma's current deeply conservative political culture does not conform to the norms of equality, accountability, and pluralism, which are necessary for the functioning of a democracy. Views regarding the role of religion are most at odds with democracy. In 2015, 83 percent of respondents in Burma supported religious leaders having a consultative role in lawmaking. In 2020, the figure dropped to 63 percent, but it remains significant. These findings are concerning, given Burma's Buddhist majority and the escalation of religious conflict in recent years.

Gaps in Democratic Citizenship

Democracy can only function effectively when people are engaged in the political process. The ABS found that while the democratic space was expanding and political and social engagement was growing, cognitive capacity and social trust remained low in Burma. The proportion of respondents who expressed some level of political interest in both waves was only 46 percent. In part, this is the result of the association between the Burmese word for politics (*ninenganrayy*) and negative views of the government and of governance. Additionally, with long-term military rule and limited political inclusion and public accountability, people are wary of "politics." The lack of political knowledge among Burma's citizens, even those who claim an interest in politics, is even more concerning. Many respondents (42 percent in 2015 and 41 percent in 2020) claimed to "practically never" follow the news. Only 33 percent of those who expressed an interest in politics followed political news regularly in 2015 and 28 percent in 2020. Among those who did not express an interest in politics, only 8 percent followed (7 percent in 2020). Since the opening of the media environment in Burma, various news sources have become available to citizens in recent years. However, this has not resulted in greater political engagement. Democracy is hindered by a lack of informed citizens. While many Burmese respondents (though not a majority) show an interest in politics, they lack the knowledge necessary to be able to participate meaningfully in the democratic process.

The incongruity in the way Burmese citizens engage in political life is reflected in the way they engage in social life as well. There has long been recognition that social capital plays an important role in maintaining democracy and reducing conflict (Putnam, Leonardi, and Nonetti 1993; Varshney 2002). There is usually a correlation between the level of participation in civic organizations and the level of social trust, both of which are essential elements of social capital in most modern societies. A puzzling divergence can be observed in Burma, however. One of the many misconceptions regarding Burma's civil society is that it is small, young, and underdeveloped (Lidauer 2012). This perception is challenged by the ABS findings which reveal a pattern that is common throughout Southeast Asia: Civil society emerges in areas where political space has been allowed under authoritarian rule, such as Indonesia's religious organizations (which were allowed under the Suharto regime) or Malaysia's grassroots political parties.

The proportion of respondents who belong to organizations in Burma increases from 60 percent in 2015 to 67 percent in 2020, which is a comparatively high figure in the region. Most of the citizens belong to religious (especially Buddhist) organizations, which have deep historical roots in the country's society, as well as to community and charitable organizations, which were permitted under military rule; in order to strengthen their legitimacy, the military encouraged the formation of community organizations as a means of providing social services. According to the ABS findings, citizens also have a considerable number of social networks, with 76 percent (80 percent in 2020) having friends and family outside of their households who can offer them help if they need it. It can be said that Burma is a country with strong horizontal social ties. Burma's citizens, however, do not have a high level of social trust despite the fact that they participate actively in social organizations, as only 19 percent believe most people are trustworthy in 2015 and 17 percent in 2020. This low level of social trust is common for people living through authoritarian rules, which rely on family members and neighbors to be informers. As a result of low social trust, democracies are prone to conflict; because citizens have difficulty participating in politics and forming relationships across different groups, they are weakened and vulnerable to fragmentation in the event of conflict. The deep rifts within Burma's society are particularly relevant in view of its deeply divided society.

Does the Economy Matter?

In November 2015, the NLD won a decisive victory that was primarily interpreted as an expression of popular support for democracy. Another underlying factor suggested by the ABS is the economy. There has been a consistent breakdown in surveys showing that the economy is the most pressing concern of citizens, with a total of 50 percent in 2015 and 43 percent in 2020 identifying jobs, wages, and cost of living as the most crucial issues confronting the country (see Figure 24.4). A number of economic reforms were implemented by the Burmese government during the 1990s. Ordinary citizens, however, have not yet benefited from the improvement in the economy. In 2015, 22 percent of respondents reported that the economic situation had worsened, and the number increased to 28 percent in 2020.

Negative perceptions of Burma's economy may have played a significant role in the vote for a change of government. The majority of Burmese citizens believed that "economic development is more important than democracy" (53 percent in 2015 versus 60 percent in 2020), with citizens placing a greater emphasis on economic development in 2020. When it comes to the importance of economic equality versus political freedom, Burmese citizens were evenly split: 42 percent in 2015 and 48 percent in 2020. Despite recent reports indicating that poverty and economic development have improved, these problems remain significant. Burma's citizens feel high levels of economic vulnerability as well. A majority of citizens feared losing their main source of income (63 percent in 2015 and 79 percent in 2020). It is, therefore, not surprising that most ordinary citizens prioritize the economy over democracy.

Figure 24.4 Views toward the Economy: Two-wave Comparison

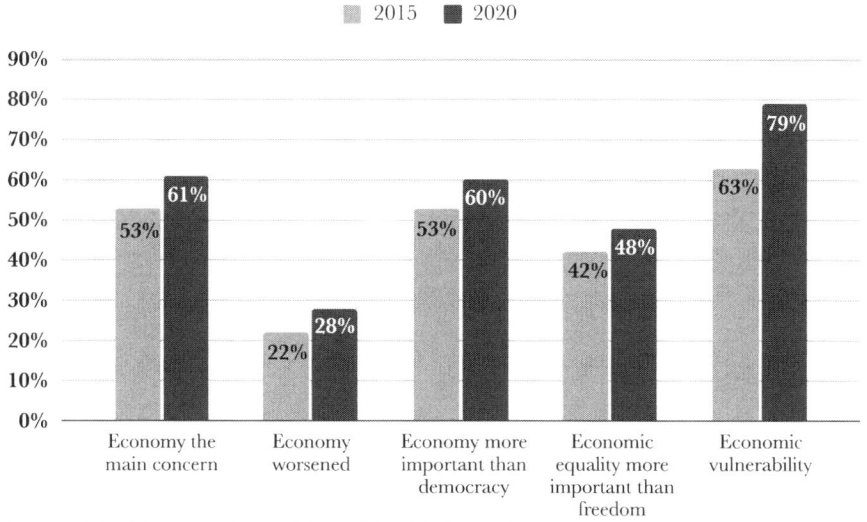

Source: Asian Barometer Survey Waves IV and V Burma Survey. Authors prepared.

As a matter of fact, this is the case throughout Asia. Burma's citizens, however, see economic improvement as being linked to democracy, whereas people in most other Asian countries believe that there is a trade-off between the two. People in Burma seem to believe that the NLD would overcome the obstacles set by the military, despite the increased demand for economic development and the reduction of economic inequality. Although the NLD failed to deliver on the economy in its first term, people still had hope in the party since there was no alternative to it; the military has an even poor record of bringing about meaningful economic development or providing the basic freedoms and opportunities that people desire. NLD, therefore, comes to represent hope. As emphatically demonstrated by the results of the 2015 and 2020 elections, a desire for greater democracy also means a great improvement in the economy.

Conclusion

The ABS findings indicate that democratization in Burma faces some significant challenges. The Burmese people welcome greater democracy, but they do not necessarily possess the underlying values that support democracy in practice, such as a belief in inclusion, secular government, and pluralism. In addition, they tend to hold illiberal and conservative values that can undermine democratic processes. While there is political engagement, there is a lack of informed citizens. The social trust is low despite the existence of robust everyday ties and an active civil society. As a final point, the election of a new government was more than just a call for democracy; it was also a call for tangible economic reform in a country where much of the population is underprivileged and vulnerable. Due to Burma's conservative political culture and politically inactive citizens, democracy is already difficult to establish even without the military coup that overthrew the NLD government in early 2021. In view of the military's decision to return to politics, Burma may not see democracy in any meaningful sense anytime soon.

Acknowledgements

This article is an abridged and updated version of "Clashing Attitudes toward Democracy," in *Journal of Democracy* 27 (2) (April, 2016), pp. 132-140, doi: 10.1353/jod.2016.0018. Bridget Welsh is credited with a previous version of this chapter and with making the Burma surveys possible through her diligent coordination.

References

Callahan, Mary. 2012. "The Opening in Burma: The Generals Loosen Their Grip." *Journal of Democracy* 23 (4): 120-131. doi:10.1353/jod.2012.0072.

Croissant, Aurel, and Jil Kamerling. 2013. "Why Do Military Regimes Institutionalize? Constitution-making and Elections as Political Survival Strategy in Myanmar." *Asian Journal of Political Science* 21 (2): 105-125. doi: 0.1080/02185377.2013.823797.

Diamond, Larry. 2012. "The Opening in Burma: The Need for a Political Pact." *Journal of Democracy* 23 (4): 138-149. doi:10.1353/jod.2012.0061.

Higley, John, and Richard Gunther, 1991. *Elites and Democratic Consolidation in Latin America and Southern Europe*. Cambridge: Cambridge University Press.

Lidauer, Michael. 2012. "Democratic Dawn? Civil Society and Elections in Myanmar 2010-2012." *Journal of Current Southeast Asian Affairs* 32 (2): 87-114. doi: 10.1177/186810341203100204.

Pedersen, Morten B. 2011. "The Politics of Burma's 'Democratic' Transition: Prospects for Change and Options for Democrats." *Critical Asian Studies* 43 (1): 49-68. doi: 0.1080/14672715.2011.537851.

Putnam, Robert D., Robert Leonardi, and Raffaella Y. Nonetti. 1993. *Making Democracy Work: Civic Traditions in Modern Italy*. Princeton: Princeton University Press.

Schmitter, Philippe C., and Terry Lynn Karl. 1991. "What Democracy Is... and Is Not." *Journal of Democracy* 2 (3): 75-88. doi:10.1353/jod.1991.0033.

Taylor, Robert H. 2012. "Myanmar: From Army Rule to Constitutional Rule?" *Asian Affairs* 43 (2): 221-236. doi: 10.1080/03068374.2012.682367.

Varshney, Ashutosh. 2002. *Ethnic Conflict and Civic Life: Hindus and Muslims in India.* New Haven: Yale University Press.

Zin, Min, and Brian Joseph. 2012. "The Opening in Burma: The Democrats' Opportunity." *Journal of Democracy* 23 (4): 104-119. doi:10.1353/jod.2012.0069.

25 Singapore: An Outlier?
Kay Key Teo, Ern Ser Tan, and Gillian Koh

Singapore has long been seen as a counterfactual to "the Modernization Theory" of political development (Lipset 1959), which in essence suggests that capitalist economic development would lead to higher support for democracy through the effect of modern higher education of citizens, and the processes of rationalization and individualization associated with that. The ruling People's Action Party (PAP) has held power for over sixty years since self-government in the transition from British colonial rule in 1959. Parliamentary elections which are called regularly adhere to democratic standards, but the electoral playing field is often argued to be uneven—conditions that fit Levitsky and Way's (2010) definition of a competitive authoritarian regime. To its credit, the PAP has delivered substantial social benefits to citizens in terms of housing, healthcare, and education—all viewed as factors essential for successful economic development, which, in turn, has provided further resources for the delivery of improved standards in those public goods over the decades. Those starting conditions were complemented by what Chan (1975) described in the 1970s as an administrative state, where the citizenry was depoliticized and the most competitive "politics" took place only within the highest levels of government. The PAP's rationale was that the nation-building and economic development project required social and political cohesion within society.

In the 1980s, there was a stirring amongst citizens for political participation, which eventually saw two opposition parties gaining a foothold in the erstwhile single-party parliament in 1991, and rising activism in civil society. Today, citizens are increasingly engaged in policy discussion and civic activism around gender rights, the environment, and social inequality. They can be persuaded by the political opposition that the governance system would benefit from more effective checks and balances on the ruling party. From the Institute of Policy Studies's 2020 post-election survey, this preference was found to be particularly salient amongst those who are young, highly educated, reside in private housing, are employed in professional or managerial occupations and are in the top income band (Institute of Policy Studies 2020). A more sceptical and even critical citizenry seems to be emerging, perhaps aided by the force of online social media as well as the demonstration effect of vociferous political and social movements that have emerged across East Asia in recent years.

On the July 10 2020 General Election held amidst the global COVID-19 pandemic, the opposition achieved the highest watermark of wresting ten seats among ninety-three seats contested and a 9 percent swing away from the PAP. This was after the PAP enjoyed an increase of 9.8 percent in voter support in the 2015 general election, taking eighty-three out of the eighty-nine seats contested (Koh, Tan, and Soon 2018). What then does this suggest about Singaporeans' orientation toward democracy in practice?

To address this question, we turn to the three waves of the Asian Barometer Survey (ABS) that have a Singapore sample—those conducted in 2010, 2014, and 2020—and look for hints of how the character of Singapore democracy will evolve over the coming decade.

Sources of Singaporeans' Perceptions of Democracy

The public in East Asia has been found to be generally supportive of democracy (Chu et al. 2008). However, Shin and Kim (2016) also found that seven out of ten East Asians[1] are "superficial democrats," or people who inflate their preferences for democracy. In fact, respondents with higher socioeconomic backgrounds express stronger preference for a system that combines democratic and nondemocratic features. Moreover, Inglehart and Welzel (2005) have suggested that the effects of modernization are likely to differ across societies due to the effect of path dependency. One might then expect to see a link between citizen experiences and their perceptions of democracy. It therefore makes sense to consider the path taken by the Singapore polity and its effect on the political orientation of Singaporeans.

Shin (2012, 223) suggests that young people who have not learned the qualities of democratic citizenship are unlikely to become "capable of expressing informed and coherent support for democracy," while Nathan (2012, 137) adds that traditional values become less of an influence when people "move to cities, experience formal education, work in modern enterprises, and engage with modern media."

Since the early years of independence, the political leadership has prioritized the development of human capital, the nation's "only resource," so that Singaporeans could contribute to the emergence of a newly and rapidly industrializing economy (Neo and Chen 2007, 97). The education system was correspondingly focused on delivering literacy and technical skills. In the 1980s, there was a shift toward promoting greater national and historical consciousness to "maintain civic awareness and responsibility" (Tan 2005, 86). History was included in the curriculum for primary and secondary education in 1984, followed by a customised and specific "National Education" curriculum in 1997, and "Social Studies" as a compulsory course in the national milestone GCE "Ordinary Level" examinations for upper secondary students in 2001. Essentially, students aged between fourteen and sixteen in 2001, or those born in 1985 or later would have experienced this version of citizenship education in the national curriculum. They would have been exposed to both local civil society and social action. In addition, as digital natives, they have access to the full experience of global media, social and political developments of the past decades.

All these milestones in the country's history will surely result in generational differences in political experience, sense of political interest and competence. Age is therefore a critical variable to explore in any analysis of political attitudes in Singapore.

Meanwhile, Shin (2012, 69) suggests that Confucianism relates to tradition in the East Asian context, emphasizing elite accountability, citizen dissent and equality, the formation of civic groups, and pluralism. It sees good government as neither democratic nor liberal, but a form of "paternalistic meritocracy" in which ordinary people, excluded from the political process, are governed by benevolent officials viewed as appropriately credentialed or trained to manage the task of governing a country (Shin 2012, 137). Since there is a combination of political participation and paternalism within Confucianism, it will also be interesting to find out how the segment of politically interested individuals, who may be influenced by these values, perceive democracy.

Hence, besides examining the overall preference for democracy and how it has evolved through the series of ABS surveys, it is also important to understand what people have in mind when they refer to the term. "Democracy" as a concept is after all highly contested, both in academic circles and in practice. Even citizens in European democracies have been found to hold different understandings of the term (Ferrin and Kriesi 2014).

Shin (2012) provides an analysis of how democracy is understood in the countries for which ABS have been conducted. He categorized the conception of democracy into two main aspects, "political-procedural," referring to characteristics like political freedom and popular elections, as well as "economic-substantive," in which economic outcomes are prioritized over political processes (Shin 2012, 264). He also notes that "in the minds of Confucian Asian people, democracy means government for the people more than it means government *by* the people" (Shin 2012, 264, emphasis by author). Given the country's experiences with a pragmatic and paternalistic government since independence, one wonders what kind of regime would Singaporeans, particularly those of the younger generation, prefer? Would younger Singaporeans be inclined toward a democracy, but one of the substantive variety, which may be mistaken for reflecting an attachment to authoritarianism? We shall now turn to analysing data comparing three waves of the ABS on Singapore to address these questions empirically.

Quantitative Analysis

We use three waves of the ABS on Singapore—the third wave in 2010, the fourth wave in 2014, and the fifth wave in 2020 to examine two hypotheses and three exploratory questions about Singaporeans' perceptions of democracy as follows:

Modernization hypothesis: Higher education is related to higher preference for democracy. [H1]

Political interest hypothesis: Higher political interest is related to higher preference for democracy. [H2]

Exploratory question 1: How will traditionalism affect preference for democracy? [E1]

Exploratory question 2: How will politically interested individuals who are influenced by traditionalist values view democracy? [E2]

Exploratory question 3: What kinds of factors influence preference for different types of democracy? [E3]

We constructed four indices: interest in politics, traditionalism, overall preference for democracy, and preference for democracy types. The first two were used as predictor variables in our analysis, while the other two were used as dependent variables.

Predictor Variables

Interest in Politics

Interest in politics is measured using three questions which ask respondents to rate general interest levels, how often they follow news about politics and government, and frequency of political discussions with family and friends. To standardise the question responses, each question was first coded into a dichotomous scale (0 = no interest, 1 = interested), before they were all summed up into an index with scores ranging from 0 to 3.

Traditionalism

This index was formulated using a summation of the questions in ABS's traditionalism section. It includes questions on filial piety and seniority, avoidance of open conflict, and group primacy. The index ranges between 0 and 56. The Cronbach's alpha for this indicator was 0.793 for the third wave, 0.852 for the fourth wave, and 0.728 for the fifth wave.

Dependent Variable

Overall Preference for Democracy
This indicator is a summation of 11 survey items examining attitudes toward democracy ranging between 0 and 41. They include questions asking how preferable democracy is compared to any other type of government, whether democracy can solve society's problems, whether it is the best form of government, as well as a series of questions determining respondents' preferences for authoritarian or democratic values. The Cronbach's alpha for this indicator was 0.778 for the third wave, 0.716 for the fourth wave, and 0.750 for the fifth wave.

Substantive versus Procedural Democracy
For the third wave and the fourth wave, this indicator was derived from four questions in the ABS asking respondents to indicate what they feel are essential characteristics of democracy. For each question, two options correspond to principles of substantive democracy, while the other two options were aligned to the principles of procedural democracy. The items were summed and recoded to form a categorical variable with three categories—a score of -1 indicated a preference for substantive democracy, a score of +1 indicated a preference for procedural democracy, while a score of 0 indicated no preference for either type.

In the fifth wave, the questions on essential democratic characteristics were condensed into one single question, with two options corresponding to procedural democracy and the other two reflecting principles of substantive democracy. While an imperfect substitute, it does allow for a comparison of trends across waves. The responses were recoded in a manner similar to that of the indicator used for the third wave and the fourth wave—a score of -1 indicated a preference for substantive democracy, while a score of +1 indicated a preference for procedural democracy. A small proportion of respondents either did not understand, could not choose an option, or declined to answer, which are relevant proxies for those who do not have clear inclinations toward a particular definition of democracy, so these responses were recoded to form the "no preference" category. However, any analyses for the "no preference" category would only be presented for reference given its small numerical size.

An alternative measure of procedural and substantive preferences was also constructed using a different set of questions which asked respondents if certain descriptions were essential characteristics of democracy. Three descriptions were related to preference for procedural democracy, while two others were related to preference for substantive democracy. The Cronbach's Alpha for these questions was 0.846. The two sets of scores were given equal weight, summed, and then recoded such that a value of -1 referred to preference for substantive democracy, a value of +1 indicated a preference for procedural democracy, while a value of 0 indicated no preference for either type.

Control Variables

We included several demographic variables—gender, age, and education—as controls. Gender was included as a dichotomous variable with the value of 1 indicating male and 2 indicating female.

Age was recoded from a continuous variable and turned into a categorical variable. Based on the earlier discussion on generational differences, we separated the survey respondents into three groups: (1) those born in 1985 or later, (2) those born between 1984 and 1965, and (3) those born in 1964 or earlier.

Education was also recoded and turned into a categorical variable with three values: (1) had technical or secondary education, or lower, (2) high school or some university education, and (3) university graduates or above.

Results

The descriptive statistics for the indicators are presented in Table 25.1.

Table 25.1 Summary of Indicators

Indicators	Third Wave (2010)		Fourth Wave (2014)		Fifth Wave (2020)	
	Mean	Median	Mean	Median	Mean	Median
Interest in politics (range = 0 to 3)	1.54	1.0	1.49	1.0	1.97	2.0
Traditionalism (range = 0 to 48)	31.11	31.0	30.79	31.0	30.68	31.0
Overall preference for democracy (range = 0 to 37)	23.36	23.0	21.69	23.0	23.79	24.0

(Continuing on the next page)

Table 25.1 Cont.

Wave	No preference	Procedural	Substantive
3	28.0%	25.2%	46.8%
4	37.7%	16.6%	45.7%
5	1.8%	43.4%	54.8%
Alternative measurement in the fifth wave	7.9%	69.6%	22.6%

Source: Asian Barometer Survey. Prepared by Authors.

Interest in politics amongst Singaporean respondents is not very high, given that the mean score was nearly right in the middle of the range. Political interest levels for the third wave and the fourth wave were similar based on the mean and median values. However, there was a marked increase in political interest levels in the fifth wave based on both mean and median scores.

Meanwhile, Singaporean respondents scored above the midpoint in the *traditionalism* indicator, with a drop in mean scores from the third wave to the fifth wave. There was a drop in mean and median scores for *overall preference for democracy* from the third wave to the fourth wave, but a rebound in the fifth wave to scores that were higher than those for the third wave.

On the overall *acceptance of democracy*, the scores remained above the midpoint.

When we compared *preferences for different democracy types*, there were some changes from the third wave to the fourth wave. The proportion of respondents under the "no preference" category increased, while there was a much lower proportion who leaned toward procedural democracy. As a result of some question changes in the fifth wave as discussed above, the proportions for this wave cannot be directly compared to those of the third wave and the fourth wave. However, there was still a larger proportion of respondents who preferred substantive democracy over procedural democracy.

For the alternative measure for procedural or substantive democratic preferences, a much larger proportion of respondents expressed some preference for procedural democracy. Both measurements of preferences for substantive and procedural democracy have high face validity on their own. However, they may likely measure different aspects of these two types of democracy, given the differences in questions. Also, the response patterns may be different given that the first measure is one question requiring a single response, while the second consists of five different questions. Furthermore, preferences for substantive and procedural democracy may not always be mutually exclusive; hence it is possible that the different question structures for the two sets of indicators produced different results.

Linear Regression: Predicting Overall Preference for Democracy

We then conducted a linear regression to examine factors influencing Singaporeans' overall attitudes toward democracy. Besides the model for main effects of the predictor variables, we also included two different interaction variables. The first was an interaction between traditionalism and education, and the second was an interaction between traditionalism and political interest. The results of the linear regression models are presented in Table 25.2. Models 1 and 2 included only the two predictor variables and demographic variables, while the rest included different interaction variables.

Table 25.2 Linear Regression Models for the Third Wave (N = 1495), Fourth Wave (N = 1039), and Fifth Wave (N = 1002)

Variables	Model 1	Model 2	Model 3	Model 4	Model 5	Model 6
Predictor Variables						
Interest in Politics	.041	.018	.021	.020	-.176	-.180
	.114***	.112**	.106**	.112***	.586***	.599***
	.212***	.135***	.145***	.133***	.798***	.686***
Traditionalism	-.124***	-.109***	-.086***	-.151**	-.182***	-.162***
	.045**	.059**	.096**	-.047	.195***	.213***
	-.206***	-.154***	-.111***	-.198***	-.019	.019
Traditionalism x Education						
Traditionalism x Technical or Secondary Education			-.152***	.092		
			-.117**	.086		
			-.279***	.339		
Traditionalism x High School or Some University Education			-.095**	.228		
			-.107**	.448*		
			-.076*	.024		
Reference group: Traditionalism x Bachelor's and Above						
Traditionalism x Interest in Politics					.223	.203
					-.517***	-.533***
					-.624***	-.585***
Demographic Variables						
Gender (Females vs. Males)	-.027			-.028		-.029
	-.063*			-.061*		-.071*
	-.099***			-.100***		-.096***
Age						
Born in 1985 or Later	.071*			.071*		.068*
	.144***			.144***		.143***
	.051			.047		.042

(Continuing on the next page)

Table 25.2 Cont.

Variables	Model 1	Model 2	Model 3	Model 4	Model 5	Model 6
Born between 1984 and 1965		.091**		.092**		.090**
		.041		-.043		-.038
		.050		*.049*		*.051*
Reference Group: Born 1964 or Earlier						
Education						
Technical or Secondary		-.104**		-.189		-.103**
Education		-.079*		-.148		-.079*
		-.249***		*-.571***		*-.246****
High School or Some University		-.099**		-.326		-.097**
Education		-.121***		-.539**		-.119***
		-.067		*-.084*		*-.057*
Reference Group: Bachelor's and Above						
Adjusted R^2	.017	.032	.026	.031	.017	.032
	.014	.043	.021	.049	.025	.055
	.086	*.147*	*.133*	*.148*	*.095*	*.156*

Note: * $p < 0.05$; ** $p < 0.01$; *** $p < 0.001$.

Logistic Regression: Predicting Preferences for Different Democracy Types

Finally, we conducted logistic regression analysis to identify predictors for the two types of democracy, using preference for substantive democracy as a base of comparison. The output of the analysis can be found in Table 25.3. When the alternative measurement in the fifth wave of the ABS survey was used as the dependent variable in the logistic regression, the output generated is reflected in Table 25.4.

Table 25.3 Multinomial Logistic Regression: Exp. (B) Reported, Third Wave (N = 1495), Fourth Wave (N = 1039), and Fifth Wave (N = 1002)

Variables	Model 1		Model 2	
Base: Substantive	No Preference	Procedural	No Preference	Procedural
Predictor Variables				
Interest in Politics	.905	.963	.915	.985
	1.058	1.166*	1.073	1.165*
	.690	*1.208***	*.761*	*1.203***
Traditionalism	.985	.972	.986	.968*
	.975**	.979	.975**	.983
	.989	*1.008*	*.959*	*1.001*

(Continuing on the next page)

Table 25.3 Cont.

Variables	Model 1		Model 2	
Base: Substantive	No Preference	Procedural	No Preference	Procedural
Demographic Variables				
Gender (Males vs. Females)			.869	.955
			1.015	1.136
			1.451	*1.547****
Age				
Born in 1985 or Later			1.333	1.455
			1.187	1.983**
			Effect size too small	*.712*
Born between 1984 and 1965			.964	1.040
			1.201	1.671*
			.928	*1.142*
Reference Group: Born 1964 or Earlier				
Education				
Technical or Secondary Education			.796	.822
			1.405	.936
			1.357	*.939*
High School or Some University Education			.832	.558***
			1.099	1.126
			.452	*1.155*
Reference Group: Bachelor's and Above				
Classification Plot	46.8%		46.7%	
	46.7%		48.1%	
	55.3%		*57.9%*	
Pseudo R-square (McFadden)	.002		.008	
	.005		.014	
	.009		*.032*	

Table 25.4 Multinomial Logistic Regression: Exp. (B) Reported, Fifth Wave (N = 1002) Alternative Measurement of Procedural and Substantive Democracy Preferences

Variables	Model 1		Model 2	
Base: Substantive	No Preference	Procedural	No Preference	Procedural
Predictor Variables				
Interest in Politics	.709**	1.264***	.664***	1.130
Traditionalism	1.003	.975	1.017	.995

(Continuing on the next page)

Table 25.4 Cont.

Variables	Model 1		Model 2	
Base: Substantive	No Preference	Procedural	No Preference	Procedural
Demographic Variables				
Gender (Males vs. Females)			.994	1.058
Age				
Born in 1985 or Later			1.816	1.649*
Born between 1984 and 1965			1.175	1.262
Reference Group: Born 1964 or Earlier				
Education				
Technical or Secondary Education			.689	.464***
High School or Some University Education			1.000	.718
Reference Group: Bachelor's and Above				
Classification Plot	69.6%		69.6%	
Pseudo R-square (McFadden)	.023		.042	

Conclusion

What then have we found about the predictors and trends for political development over the decade? Here, we report only the statistically significant findings from the regression analyses.

First, H1 is supported because higher education is positively related to a preference for democracy. The modernization thesis is working its way through the Singapore body politic—with each generation and its exposure to education. Lipset (1959) had suggested that the link between democratic preference and education lies in the development of civic engagement and freedom of discussion in interpersonal interactions. However, Singapore's education curriculum is focused mostly on technical skills like science and mathematics, and its civic education is geared toward strengthening social stability and nation-building, which would be more beneficial to developing analytical skills and technical knowledge rather than the skills identified by Lipset. Hence, it seems more possible that the education effect is a result of skills like analysis and comprehension developed at secondary and tertiary levels of education (Campante and Chor 2012), rather than a preference for civic engagement or freedom of discussion.

Second, in relation to H2, we found that political interest has no consistent effect on the preference for democracy.

Third, on E1, traditionalism is not a clear predictor for democratic preference, switching from having a negative, then positive, and again negative effect through the three waves of surveys.

Fourth, on E2, the combined effect of political interest and traditionalism do not provide much explanatory power for the preference for democracy. In particular, respondents with high traditionalism and high political interest in Waves 4 and 5 have lower democratic preference, indicating that political interest may not always lead to support for democracy. These findings correspond to Shin's (2012) observation that young people are not well-versed in democratic citizenship. This indicates that political attitudes developed while living in a regime that is more of a "paternalistic meritocracy" may differ from conventional expectations. Taken together, the results of H2, E1, and E3 suggest the need to further examine the effect of lived political experiences on political attitudes.

Fifth, on E3, the data suggests that higher political interest and being younger make it more likely that support for procedural democracy prevails over substantive democracy. This final set of findings suggests that political development in Singapore is indeed on a modernization trajectory. In particular, if views of younger Singaporeans continue on this trajectory and do not change as they grow older, this trend will likely render Singapore less of an outlier. Overall, this set of findings suggest that the PAP's decision after the July 2020 general election to institutionalize and recognize the need for a more "normal" competitive political system by appointing the Secretary-General of the opposition Worker's Party the Leader of the Opposition, was an appropriate one, even if seemed paradoxical in relation to its own long-term dominance.

Note

1. Includes Japan, Korea, Mongolia, the Philippines, Taiwan, Indonesia, China, Thailand, Singapore, Vietnam, Cambodia, Malaysia, and Myanmar.

References

Campante, Filipe R., and Davin Chor. 2012. "Schooling, Political Participation and the Economy." *The Review of Economics and Statistics* 94 (4): 841-859. doi: 0.1162/REST_a_00206.

Chan, Heng Chee. 1975. *Politics in an Administrative State: Where Has the Politics Gone?* Singapore: Department of Political Science, University of Singapore.

Chu, Yun-han, Larry Diamond, Andrew Nathan, and Doh Chull Shin. 2008. *How East Asians View Democracy*. New York: Columbia University Press.

Ferrin, Monica, and Hanspeter Kriesi. 2014. "European's Understanding and Evaluations of Democracy: Topline Results from Round 6 of the European Social Survey." *ESS Topline Result Series*. Vol. 4. September. Accessed Jan. 13, 2021. https://www.europeansocialsurvey.org/permalink/800ea36f-3a8d-11e4-95d4-005056b8065f.pdf.

Inglehart, Ronald, and Christian Welzel. 2005. *Modernization, Cultural Change, and Democracy*. New York: Cambridge University Press.

Institute of Policy Studies. 2020. *POPS (10) - IPS Post-Election Survey 2020*. Institute of Policy Studies. Accessed March 11, 2021. https://lkyspp.nus.edu.sg/docs/default-source/ips/pops10_ge2020-survey_061020.pdf.

Koh, Gillian, Ern Ser Tan, and Debbie Soon. 2018. *Asian Barometer Country Report-Singapore*. Asian Barometer Working Paper Series No. 147. Taipei: Asian Barometer Survey.

Levitsky, Steven, and Lucan A. Way. 2010. *Competitive Authoritarianism: Hybrid Regimes After the Cold War*. Cambridge: Cambridge University Press.

Lipset, Seymour Martin. 1959. "Some Social Requisites of Democracy." *American Political Science Review* 53 (1): 69-105. doi:10.2307/1951731.

Nathan, Andrew. 2012. "Confucianism and the Ballot Box: Why 'Asian Values' Do Not Stymie Democracy." *Foreign Affairs* 91: 134-139.

Neo, Boon Siong, and Geraldine Chen. 2007. *Dynamic Governance: Embedding Culture, Capabilities, and Change in Singapore*. Singapore: World Scientific.

Shin, Doh Chull. 2012. *Confucianism and Democratization in East Asia*. Cambridge: Cambridge University Press.

Shin, Doh Chull, and Hannah June Kim. 2016. "Do People in East Asia Truly Prefer Democracy to Its Alternatives? Western Theories versus East Asian Realities." Paper presented at the Asian Barometer Conference, August 9-11, 2016, Taipei: National Taiwan University.

Tan, Jason. 2005. "National Education." In *Shaping Singapore's Future: Thinking Schools, Learning Nation*, edited by Jason Tan and Pak Tee Ng, 82-94. Singapore: Pearson/Prentice Hall.

26 The Impact of Power Transition in Malaysia's Changing Democracy

Min-hua Huang

The unprecedented power transition in May 2018 is undoubtedly the most critical political event in post-independence Malaysia (Welsh 2018). The long-time one-party dominant system, governed by the United Malays National Organization (UMNO), and its coalition, Barisan Nasional, was overturned democratically by the opposition alliance, Pakatan Harapan (PH), in an unexpected and unforeseen way (Ostwald and Oliver 2020). Ironically, the two leaders who together achieved this political victory, Mahathir Mohamad and Anwar Ibrahim, were formerly political foes after Mahathir removed all of Anwar's posts in September 1998 following a political struggle within the UMNO leadership (Abbott 2000). The drama was repeated again in February 2020 when Mahathir refused to hand over power despite being the world's oldest prime minister at the age of 94 (Welikala 2020). Following Mahathir's eventual resignation and the ensuing political turmoil, the designated "prime minister in waiting" was once again blocked from the top post and Muhyiddin Yassin, who had defected from the PH and reformed his alliance with UMNO, took the top job (Tayeb 2021). Muhyiddin was appointed prime minister by the King of Malaysia (Yang di-Pertuan Agong) despite lacking majority support in parliament (Regencia 2020). Before UMNO withdrew its political support in July 2021, Muhyiddin ran a minority government using executive orders to fight against the COVID-19 pandemic and the country under a state of emergency due to the worsening pandemic (Sarifin and Yusoff 2020). Muhyiddin was ultimately forced to resign after the state of emergency expired on August 1, 2021, and he failed to retain sufficient support from UMNO lawmakers (Chu, Latiff, and Lee 2021).

This chapter will focus on the political impact of the first power transition in decades in post-independence Malaysia, particularly highlighting significant changes that depart from the previous trends, with relevant data from four waves of the Asian Barometer Survey (ABS) in 2007, 2010, 2014, and 2019. In our analysis, we distinguish between supporters of the losing and winning camps to evaluate the impact of the first power transition on political attitudes. Notice that

Barisan Nasional was the winning camp prior to 2018, and Pakatan Harapan only became the winning camp in the most recent fourth wave survey in 2019. The main conclusion shows that the impact of the first power transition was mostly positive, bridging gaps between the supporters of the two camps in political trust, democratic evaluation, liberal orientation, and regime support, despite some negative effects on political efficacy among supporters of Pakatan Harapan, which are likely associated with the coalition's internal power struggle.

Converging Trust in Political Institutions

Successful democratization requires the right institutional and behavioral conditions to achieve. Institutional conditions refer to a free and fair electoral process that allows the opposition to challenge the incumbent and achieve power alternation and also includes a political environment that protects civil liberties and political rights while upholding the rule of law. However, less attention has been given to the behavioral conditions by which the incumbent and the opposition at both elite and mass levels know how to interact in a democratic system, even though they are competing with each other or serving different roles. Malaysian politics has long been characterized as a "one-party dominant system," in which political negotiation, competition, alignment, and many other behaviors proceeded within the ruling coalition, Barisan Nasional, which had governed Malaysia ever since its independence. It is, therefore, little surprise that elite politics become so fragile after May 2018 when Pakatan Harapan defeated Barisan Nasional and took over power, for the reason that all parties had to learn how to align or compete with each other, not just for forming a government with majority support, but also for intra- or inter-party competition to advance their political interests. This can explain Mahathir's sudden resignation as prime minister and his subsequent attempt to rebuild political support to reclaim the post, as well as the responses of other members of the political elite, including Anwar, Muhyiddin, and even the Agong. In hindsight, the so-called 2020-2021 political crisis was the result of an unresolved elite power struggle within Barisan Nasional between Mahathir and Anwar that continued even after the power transition, giving Muhyiddin the opportunity to unexpectedly win the top post.

Then how did the mass public perceive and adapt to the first power transition of the government? This question is very important because people will vote in the next general election on the basis of their cognitive judgment and evaluation after they experienced these political events. More importantly, those who originally perceived themselves as the long-term supporters of the opposition have now become supporters of the incumbent government and vice versa. Such cognitive change occurred suddenly when Mahathir and Muhyiddin resigned in February 2020 and August 2021, respectively, but through government reformation and party realignment under Malaysia's parliamentary system rather than fresh elections. To a certain extent, the 2018 transition of power triggered a series of learning processes for both elites and the masses as they try to adapt to the new political reality. This chapter will illuminate the impact on political attitudes after Pakatan Harapan replaced Barisan Nasional as the ruling party, ending the one-party system for the first time in six decades. Due to the timing of the latest wave of the ABS survey in Malaysia (April to May 2019), the analysis only covers the period before the 2020-2021 political crisis. In view of the above limitations, the analytical purpose is confined to assessing the impact on the political attitudes of winners and losers (Anderson et al. 2005) between 2007 and 2019, with particular focus on the different results before and after 2018.

An immediate impact is how the vantage point of election winner or election loser affects people's trust in political institutions. As Figure 26.1 makes evident, the institutions most directly associated with the power transition are the prime minister [Figure 26.1 (a)] and the national government [Figure 26.1 (b)]. Political trust toward the prime minister hovered around 90 percent among the winning camp and gradually declined from the mid-50s percent to the mid-40 percent among the losing camp prior to 2018. The gap narrowed to only 28 percent in 2019, compared to 34 percent in 2007, 42 percent in 2010, and 46 percent in 2014. This suggests that while the winning camp was far more supportive of the prime minister than the losing camp, the level of polarization actually declined. A similar pattern also appears in trust toward the national government, with a narrower 24 percent gap between the winning and losing camp in 2019 compared with previous larger gaps, specifically 39 percent in 2007, 38 percent in 2010, and 34 percent in 2014. Overall, people largely trusted the prime minister and the national government, with levels of trust of nearly 50 percent even in the opposition supporters. For those who voted for the winning camp, levels of trust were in the mid-80s percent and above. However, the lower levels of polarization suggest that citizens still support the political system even when their preferred party does not win the election.

Figure 26.1 Trust in Political Institutions

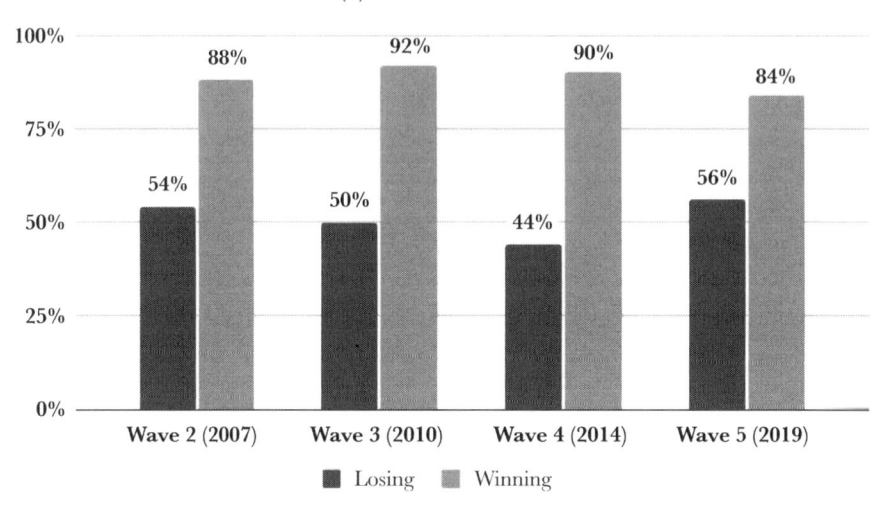

(a) **Prime Minister**

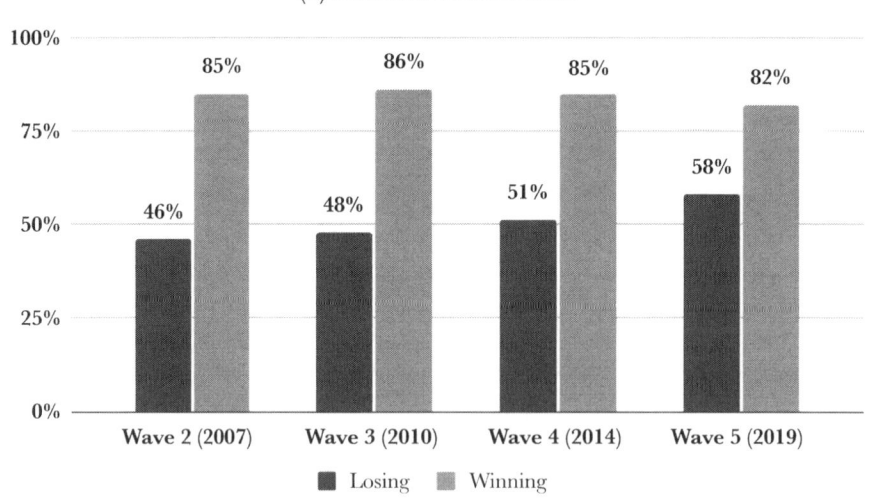

(b) **National Government**

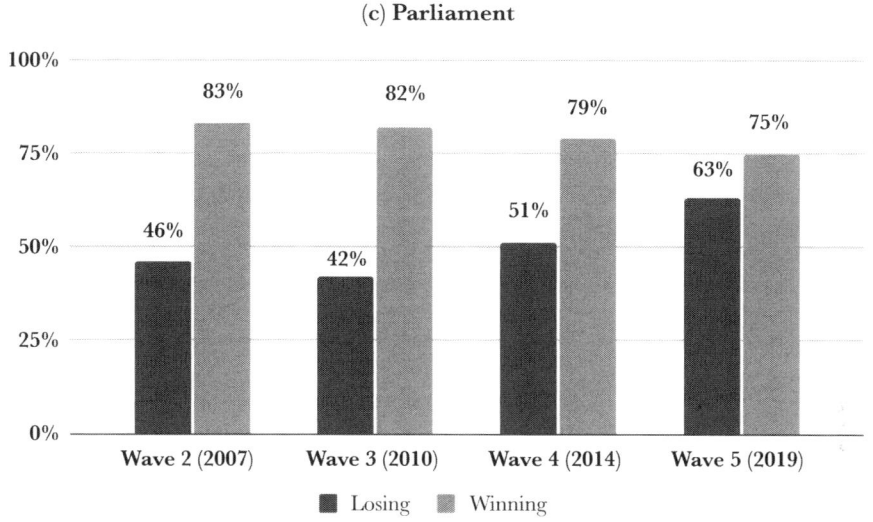

(c) Parliament

Source: Asian Barometer Malaysia Surveys. Author prepared.

A further intriguing result is presented in Figure 26.1 (c), which shows people's trust toward the parliament as a political institution. As can be seen, the gap between the winning and losing camps was even narrower (12 percent) in 2019. This contrasts with much larger gaps of 37 percent (2007), 40 percent (2010), and 28 percent (2014) in previous waves. The genuine power alternation through a democratic election actually increased trust in parliament and reduced polarization between the winning and losing camps because people realized the parliament was not just serving a rubber stamp for the ruling government, and that both the ruling and opposition parties can debate, compete, and cooperate in the parliament and thereby influence policy.

Emerging Consensus on Democratic Evaluation

While Malaysia's party realignment is still ongoing, the power alternation has already had a huge impact on political attitudes. Psychologically, people are faced with a new reality that no party can remain in office indefinitely, and they must think about politics from a different angle once the party they support loses an election or fails to enter the governing coalition. However, although no party is guaranteed to win the election, people are likely to perceive a more impartial democratic system when all parties have a chance to win the election or form the government. As Figure 26.2 shows, prior to 2018, when respondents were asked to evaluate how satisfied they are with the way democracy works in Malaysia, the gaps were consistently above 0.7 on a one to four scale (0.78, 0.77, 0.74 in 2007, 2010, and 2014 respectively). However, the figure fell to 0.15 in 2019, indicating a more balanced evaluation between the winning and losing camp. In other words, neither the winners nor the losers evaluate their satisfaction simply because of the result of the election. The emerging consensus about the democratic system signifies the emergence of more impartial and less partisan evaluations among citizens.

Figure 26.2 "How Satisfied Are You with the Way Democracy Works in Our Country?" (1-4 scale, 1 for not at all satisfied, 4 for very satisfied)

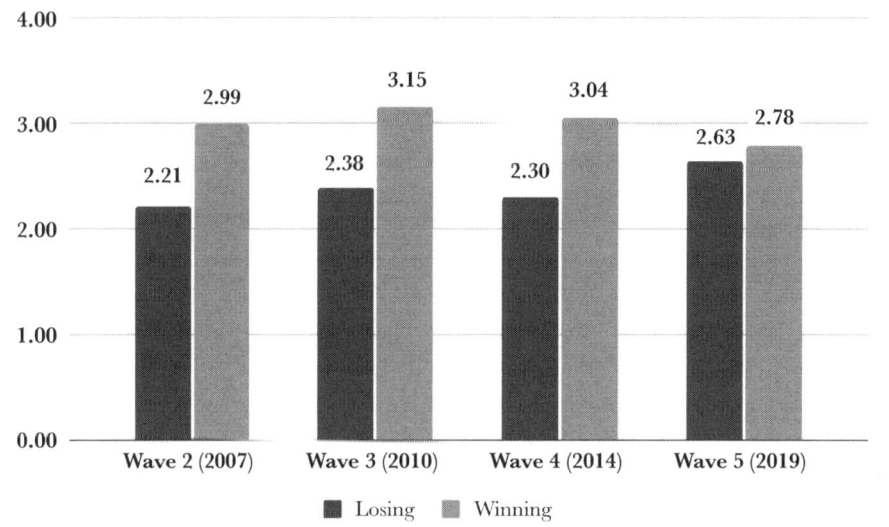

Source: Asian Barometer Malaysia Surveys. Author prepared.

A similar but different measure was administered to ask respondents how they perceived the level of democracy in their country. The result shows the same pattern of emerging consensus after the 2018 power alternation. As Figure 26.3 makes evident, those who voted from the winning camp rated Malaysia as more democratic than those who voted for the losing camp before 2018. The gap is at least above 0.6 (0.72, 0.61, and 0.66 for Waves 2-4), but this difference vanished completely in the 2019 survey, with only a trivial 0.01 difference between the assessments of the winning and losing camps. Again, this means an emerging consensus between winners and losers because now the democratic system allows a fair chance for all parties to compete for victory as well as to participate in the process of government formation. The sense of relative deprivation from being excluded from power was largely abated, and hence, the democratic evaluations converged, becoming more impartial and less partisan. In other words, the long-term perception about the unfairness of the democratic system was eliminated as people witnessed the end of the one-party system. That generated a more honest and balanced view toward the democratic system, rather than biased opinions incentivized by partisan interest.

Figure 26.3 "In Your Opinion How Much of a Democracy is Our Country?" (1-4 scale, 1 for not a democracy, 4 for a full democracy)

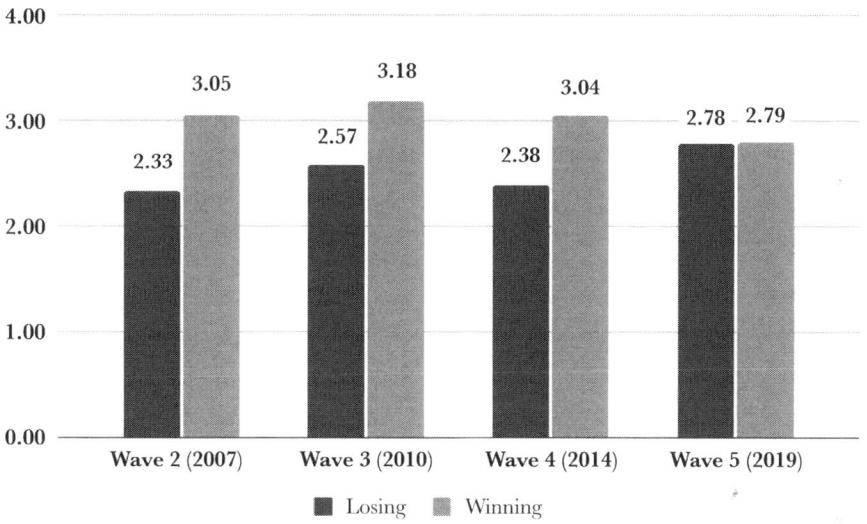

Source: Asian Barometer Malaysia Surveys. Author prepared.

Diminishing Political Efficacy Among Supporters of Pakatan Harapan

After Pakatan Harapan took over the governing power, the internal tension between Mahathir and Anwar ran high, particularly with regards to the controversy surrounding the under-the-table deal where Mahathir agreed to hand over power to Anwar in two years. In fact, even the supporters of Pakatan Harapan had little influence over how this political fissure would evolve. It is not surprising that political apathy and inefficacy gradually increased as the power struggle inside Pakatan Harapan intensified. As shown in Figure 26.4, prior to 2018, there was little difference in the level of political interest between supporters of the winning and losing camps. However, in the 2019 survey, the measure of political interest in the winning camp declined steeply to 2.28. Furthermore, the difference in political interest between the winning and losing camp was 0.36, which was significant at the $p = 0.05$ level. Furthermore, the score of 2.28 in 2018 for supporters of Pakatan Harapan was lower than the three previous waves when the coalition was in opposition.

Figure 26.4 "How Interested Would You Say You Are in Politics?" (1-4 scale, 1 for not at all interested, 4 for very interested)

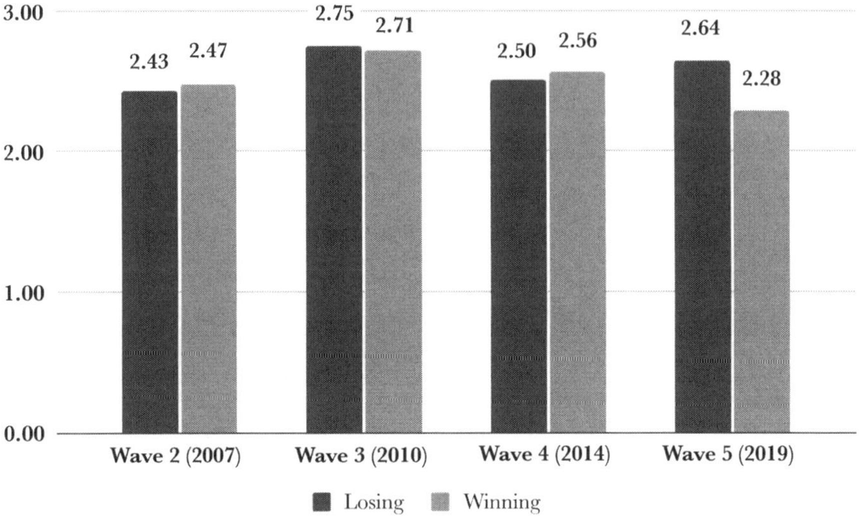

Source: Asian Barometer Malaysia Surveys. Author prepared.

This phenomenon can be vindicated by examining the evolving level of political efficacy for the winning and losing camp before and after 2018. As illustrated in Figure 26.5, while the general level of internal political efficacy was not high (mostly below the 2.5 mid-point) and fluctuated over time, the difference between the winning and losing camps was low and not statistically significant (-0.03, -0.16, 0.01 for the second wave to the fourth wave). Nevertheless, the measure dropped to 1.94 for the winning camp in 2019 (supporters of Pakatan Harapan), which was an all-time low for both of the winning and losing camps for all waves, while the efficacy score still remained at a similar level (2.3) for the losing camp. This finding clearly suggests that supporters of Pakatan Harapan were showing more apathy and less political efficacy, which likely reflects their disappointment and frustration toward the PH political leadership. Given these results, it is not difficult to see why the 2020-2021 Malaysian political crisis happened. Even before the crisis, Pakatan Harapan supporters already felt frustrated and powerless about the deep fissure inside the governing coalition.

Figure 26.5 "I Think I Have the Ability to Participate in Politics" (1-4 scale, 1 for strongly disagree, 4 for strongly agree)

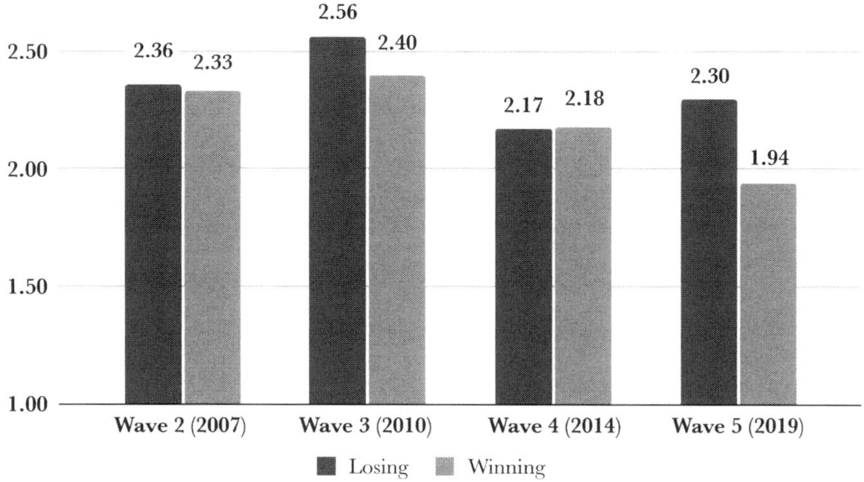

Source: Asian Barometer Malaysia Surveys. Author prepared.

Reducing the Gap in Liberal Democratic Values

Political values, in theory, are the results of a long-term sociological process. Nonetheless, a critical political event such as experiencing the first power rotation of government might cause significant changes to people's value orientation. In particular, citizens who always supported the opposition but now become supporters of the winning camp might actually become more dissatisfied with democracy because the government constantly needs to make tough decisions, some of which are bound to be unwelcome and viewed as authoritarian by those who disagree. It would be very interesting to see whether value change was triggered by the power alternation and in what fashion.

In the ABS, the liberal-democratic values battery is designed to capture how strongly respondents reject authoritarian values. It is composed of seven negatively worded questions associated with authoritarian orientations. Rejection of these orientations indicates adherence to liberal-democratic values, including political equality, popular accountability, political liberalism, political pluralism, and separation of power. Due to a greater inclination of social conformity in Asian cultures, it requires a greater cognitive threshold to express genuine liberal-democratic values by negation. That explains why this battery is all negatively phrased to the underlying attitudinal measure. All seven items apply a 4-point Likert scale, and a composite score for the liberal-democratic value is formulated by taking the average of the seven items.

Figure 26.6 Composite Scores of the Liberal Democratic Value (1-4 scale)

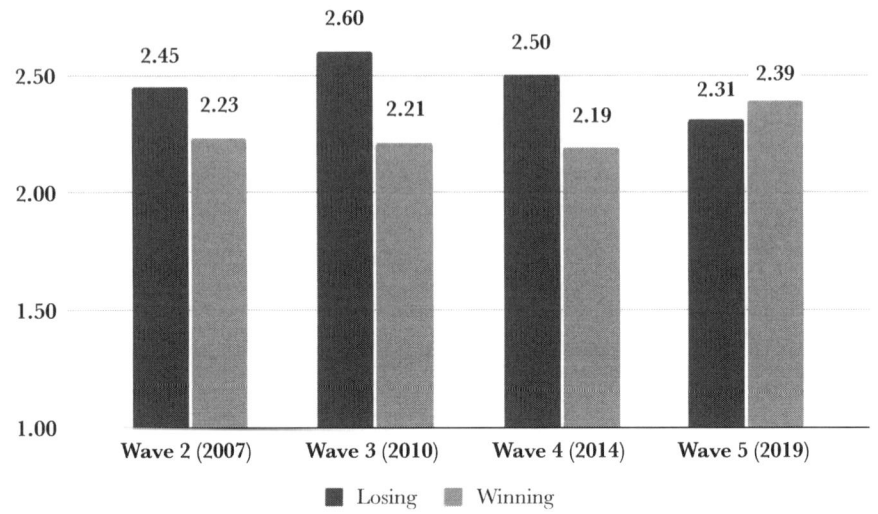

Source: Asian Barometer Malaysia Surveys. Author prepared.

As Figure 26.6 shows, the composite scores for the winning and losing camps remained quite stable over time before 2018. The winning camp scored between 2.19 and 2.23, significantly lower than the losing camp, which ranged from 2.45 and 2.6. However, in the latest 2019 survey, the composite score for the winning camp increased to 2.39 while the losing camp dropped to 2.31, showing a non-significant margin of the 0.08 difference. While we can argue that the winning camp in 2019 was, in fact, the losing camp in three previous surveys and vice versa, the narrower gap has shown the fact that the power alternation profoundly does impact citizens' liberal democratic values by changing their vantage point.

Another related attitudinal measure is related to diffuse regime support. In a one-party dominant system, supporters of the opposition may distrust political leaders because the party they support never has the chance to win the elections and become the ruling party. In the ABS, there is an item designed to tap into such orientation, specifically asking respondents to what extent they agree with the statement "you can generally trust the people who run our government to do what is right." For the Malaysian case, the referent of this item was the leadership of Barisan Nasional prior to 2018, and the leadership of Pakatan Harapan in 2019. The findings are shown in Figure 26.7. As can be seen, the winning camp consistently showed greater trust toward the political leadership than the losing camp, but the margin reduced from 0.5, 0.81, and 0.66 in the first three waves to only 0.31 in 2019. Again, this shows a narrowing gap in diffuse regime support following the power alternation in 2018.

Figure 26.7 "You Can Generally Trust the People Who Run Our Government to Do What Is Right." (1-4 scale, 1 for strongly disagree, 4 for strongly agree)

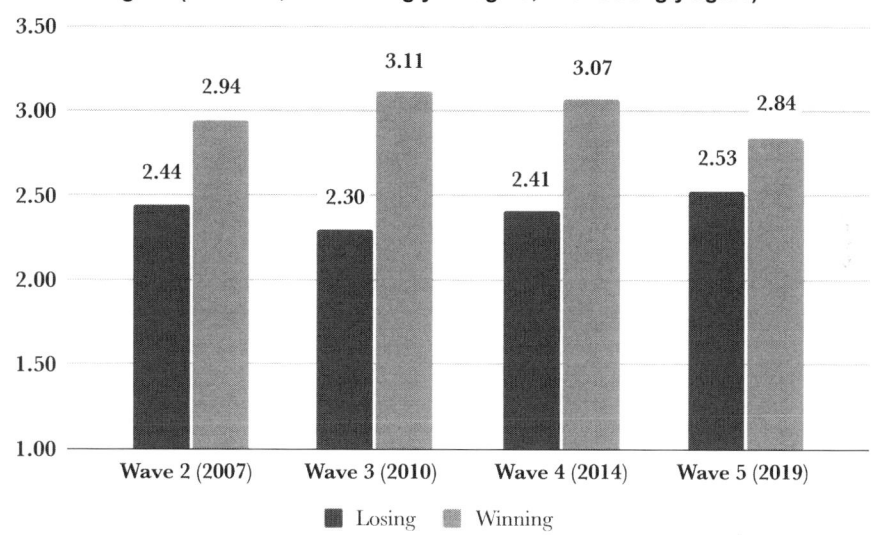

Source: Asian Barometer Malaysia Surveys. Author prepared.

Robust Regime Legitimacy

The overall impact of the power alternation eventually boils down to whether people reach a consensus about regime legitimacy, regardless of whether they support the winning or losing camps. In the ABS, two of the measures in this conceptual category tap into this attitude by providing negative and positive qualifications. The first item asks respondents whether they agree with the statement: "A system like ours, even if it runs into problems, deserves the people's support." Here, "even if it runs into problems" specifically highlights a negative qualification. The statement of the second item is "I would rather live under our system of government than any other that I can think of" and the implicit positive connotation suggests that the system works well and deserves the people's support. If the respondents from different camps both converge on a similar level of regime support, that means the winner/loser factor no longer biases responses upward or downward due to partisan interest. This would be a strong indication of robust regime legitimacy, helping ensure long-term democratic consolidation.

Figure 26.8 "A System Like Ours, Even If It Runs into Problems, Deserves the People's Support."

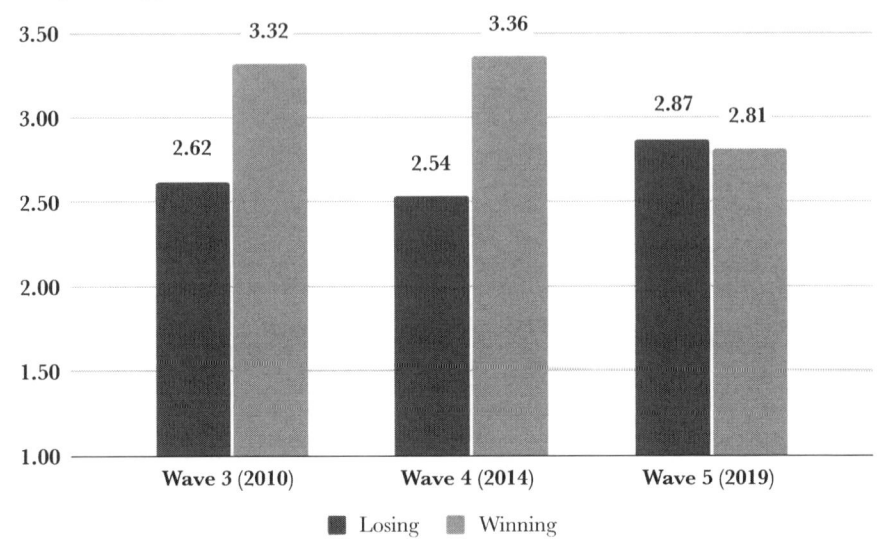

Source: Asian Barometer Malaysia Surveys. Author prepared.

Figure 26.9 "I Would Rather Live Under Our System of Government Than Any Other That I Can Think of."

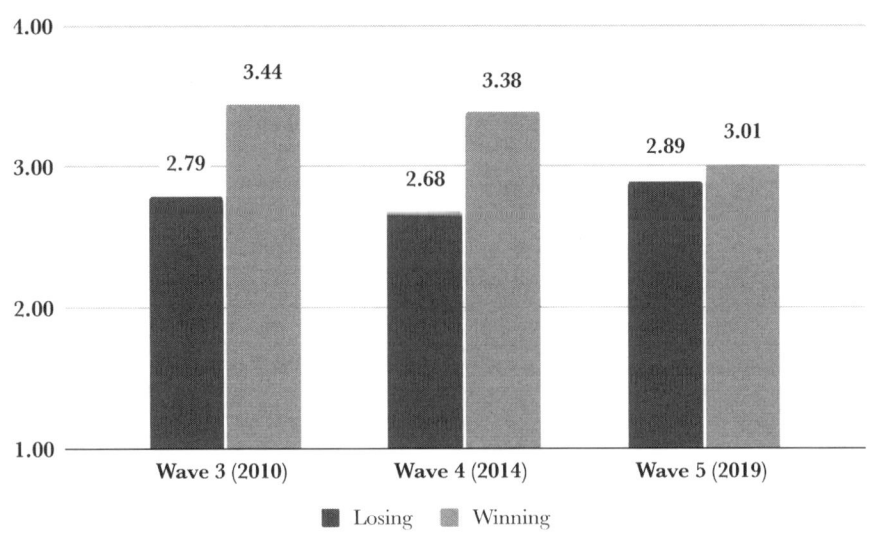

Source: Asian Barometer Malaysia Surveys. Author prepared.

As Figure 26.8 and Figure 26.9 show, supporters of the winning camp had consistently higher levels of regime support, scoring between 3.32 and 3.44, compared to between 2.54 and 2.79 for supporters of the losing camp. However, such gaps no longer existed by the time of the 2019 survey, and the margins of difference for both items (-0.06 and 0.12) were non-significant at the $p = 0.05$ level. This conveys an important conclusion: No matter which party people vote for, they support their political system at the same level. Given there is a high probability of more power alterations and changes of government in future elections, the above findings provide a relatively optimistic outlook for future democratic development in Malaysia because people responded to the first power alternation by reaching a consensus in support of their democratic system, even though the election created losers as well as winners.

Conclusion

Achieving the first power alternation is usually a milestone for democratization. This is certainly the case for Malaysia, particularly given the country's one-party dominance in the past six decades following independence in 1957. This chapter analyzed the impact of Malaysia's first power alternation on the political attitudes of its citizens. The result reveals much brighter prospects for Malaysia's future democracy because the general public responded to the power alternation by reaching a cross-partisan consensus on institutional trust, democratic evaluation, liberal-democratic values, and, most importantly, regime legitimacy. This consensus should not be taken for granted but rather viewed as a prudent response of supporters of both the winning and losing camps who are willing to accept the integrity of the democratic system and participate in the system. Although the ongoing political crisis has created political uncertainty in elite politics, this uncertainty should eventually be resolved through the ballot box, ensuring that the democratic voice of the people is heard.

References

Abbott, Jason P. 2000. "Bittersweet Victory: The 1999 Malaysian General Election and the Anwar Ibrahim Affair." *The Round Table* 89 (354): 245-258. doi:10.1080/750459438.

Anderson, Christopher J., André Blais, Shaun Bowler, Todd Donovan, and Ola Listhaug. 2005. *Losers' Consent: Elections and Democratic Legitimacy*. New York: Oxford University Press. doi:10.1093/0199276382.001.0001.

Chu, Mei Mei, Rozanna Latiff, and Liz Lee. 2021. "Malaysian PM Muhyiddin Resigns as Political Crisis Escalates." *Reuters*. Aug. 16. Accessed Sept. 13, 2021. https://www.reuters.com/world/asia-pacific/malaysian-pm-expected-resign-after-months-political-turmoil-2021-08-16/.

Ostwald, Kai, and Steven Oliver. 2020. "Four Arenas: Malaysia's 2018 Election, Reform, and Democratization." *Democratization* 27 (4): 662-680. doi:10.1080/13 510347.2020.1713757.

Regencia, Ted. 2020. "Malaysia's King Appoints Muhyiddin Yassin as Prime Minister." *Aljazeera*. Feb. 29. Accessed Sept. 13, 2021. https://www.aljazeera.com/news/2020/2/29/malaysias-king-appoints-muhyiddin-yassin-as-prime-minister.

Sarifin, Muhammad R., and Nur H. Yusoff. 2020. "Reactions of Malaysian Citizens towards Movement Control Order (MCO) during the Transmission of COVID-19 Pandemic." *EurAsian Journal of BioSciences* 14: 4101-4108.

Tayeb, Azmil. 2021. "Malaysia in 2020: Fragile Coalitional Politics and Democratic Regression." *Asian Survey* 61 (1): 99-105. doi:10.1525/as.2021.61.1.99.

Welikala, Asanga. 2020. "The Dismissal of Prime Ministers in the Asian Commonwealth: Comparing Democratic Deconsolidation in Malaysia and Sri Lanka." *The Political Quarterly* 91 (4): 786-794. doi:10.1111/1467-923x.12916.

Welsh, Bridget. 2018. "'Saviour' Politics and Malaysia's 2018 Electoral Democratic Breakthrough: Rethinking Explanatory Narratives and Implications." *Journal of Current Southeast Asian Affairs* 37 (3): 85-108. doi:10.1177/186810341803700305.

27 Evolving Social Norms and Political Ideology in Mainland China, 1993-2019

Jie Lu, Xuchuan Lei, and Yang Zhang

Since the late 1980s, survey research has become an increasingly important and accessible tool for China scholars to examine various socioeconomic and political phenomena. As one of the most renowned survey researchers in the China field, the late Dr. Tianjian Shi (who was known to his colleagues worldwide as "TJ") directed and contributed to numerous survey projects in mainland China before his very unfortunate passing away in late 2010. As a key component of his lasting and invaluable academic legacy, six waves of national surveys in mainland China have collected precious micro-level longitudinal evidence to shed light on the Chinese people's critical political attitudes and behaviors, as well as their evolution over the past decades. Since the early 2000s, this ongoing research project initiated by "TJ" has been effectively integrated into a much larger and more ambitious comparative survey research project on political attitudes and behaviors in Asia, that is, the Asian Barometer Survey (ABS).

This chapter will briefly review the history of the survey project initiated by "TJ," as well as key theoretical themes identified by him (which still guide related data collection, empirical tests, and theoretical development). Then the chapter will examine the change and continuity in a few critical components of the social norms and political ideology in mainland China over the past decades, relying on six waves of rolling cross-sectional national surveys. The last section concludes and offers suggestions for future work.

Tianjian Shi and the ABS Mainland China Survey

Tianjian Shi's contribution to the development of survey research in mainland China cannot be over-emphasized. In the late 1980s, "TJ" worked with his friends in Beijing for a first city-wide survey to examine people's political attitudes and behaviors. This is one of the very first academic political surveys in mainland China, using probability sampling, face-to-face interviews, and a standardized questionnaire. As a then Ph.D. candidate at Columbia University, "TJ" modeled this survey based on the seminal and classic works of *The Civic Culture* (Almond and Verba 1963) and *The American Voter* (Campbell et al. 1964). He tried to uncover the dynamics of political participation in a socialist society embarking on an unprecedented socioeconomic and political transition by taking its unique and evolving institutional settings into consideration. His dissertation, later published by Harvard University Press and entitled *Political Participation in Beijing* (Shi 1997), has become a piece of landmark research in comparative political participation.

Building upon the experience of this city-wide survey, "TJ" initiated his more ambitious national survey research project on political culture and political participation in mainland China. To ensure the quality of collected data and minimize unnecessary interference from the Chinese government (which might compromise the academic integrity of the surveys), he collaborated closely with Chinese scholars of political science, sociology, economics, and anthropology (Shi 1996). In the early 1990s, "TJ" expanded his mainland-centered survey research into a broader comparative project, in collaboration with Professors Fu Hu and Yun-han Chu from Taiwan and Professor Hsin-chi Kuan from Hong Kong, on political culture and political participation in the Greater China region. This comparative survey project covering Greater China provided the breeding ground for the later ABS project. Since the early 2000s, "TJ" had personally directed two rounds of the national survey in mainland China in collaboration with the Institute of Sociology at the Chinese Academy of Social Sciences (in 2002) and the Research Center for Contemporary China at Peking University (in 2008) respectively, as part of the ABS project. These surveys have provided the key empirical evidence for his widely-cited journal articles (Lu and Shi 2009; Shi 1999a, 1999b, 2001; Shi and Lu 2010), as well as his posthumous and highly-regarded book published by Cambridge University Press and entitled *The Cultural Logic of Politics in Mainland China and Taiwan* (Shi 2015).

Before his unfortunate passing away in late 2010, "TJ" was still planning for the third wave of ABS mainland China Survey and refining the questionnaire. Although he could no longer personally supervise the administration of ABS mainland China survey in 2011, 2015, and 2019, the theoretical framework proposed by "TJ" has still guided related survey administration, data collection, empirical tests, and theoretical development. Nowadays, the ABS mainland China survey is based on and supported by an extensive research network with dozens of researchers of political science, economics, sociology, and legal studies from a number of research institutes in mainland China. Besides the ABS core modules, the mainland China survey also features its own survey instruments focusing on the evolution of political culture and political participation in today's largest socialist society, as well as the interactions between the two in shaping mainland China's trajectory of development. It should be fair to argue that Tianjian Shi's deep-ingrained impact on the ABS mainland China survey (i.e., the focus on political norms and ideology) has become its key and prominent characteristic and helped establish the unique status of this survey project for China studies and comparative politics.

Evolution of Social Norms and Political Ideology in Mainland China

Numerous studies have effectively established the lasting and significant impact of Confucian cultural traditions on some Asian societies' political dynamics, with mainland China as the most prominent case (Bell 2015; Dickson 2016; Lu and Shi 2015; Shin et al. 2012). Among related Confucian social legacies, students of Chinese politics have highlighted, inter alia, hierarchical orientation toward authorities, collectivism, conflict avoidance, and general social trust for examination. Among related Confucian political legacies, paternalistic meritocracy as an ideal way of governance has been widely discussed in the scholarship of Chinese politics. Thanks to the initial design of Tianjian Shi, the ABS mainland China survey has incorporated some key survey instruments to capture the aforementioned features of Confucian social and political legacies since the early 1990s. These signature instruments of the ABS mainland China survey can provide critical micro-level information for us to assess the evolution of social norms and political ideology in today's largest socialist society, against its turbulent socioeconomic and political transitions over the past decades. In this chapter, we focus on the following seven instruments with longitudinal information collected in six waves of representative surveys from mainland China between 1993 and 2019.

There are three instruments tapping some key features of Confucian social legacies: (1) "Generally speaking, would you say that 'Most people can be trusted,' or that 'You must be very careful in dealing with people'?" (2) "Even if parents' demands are unreasonable, children still should do what they ask." (3) "When a mother-in-law and a daughter-in-law come into conflict, even if the mother-in-law is in the wrong, the husband should still persuade his wife to obey his mother." The first is a widely used instrument for general social trust and the second and third are two different instruments for the hierarchical orientation toward authorities (e.g., using parents and in-laws as particular symbols of authorities). Respondents were offered a 4-point Likert scale of agreement/disagreement to record their responses to the two statements on possible orientations toward authority. Theoretically, Confucian social legacies are expected to feature a relatively high level of general social trust and widespread hierarchical orientation toward authorities.

There are four instruments tapping some key aspects of Confucian political legacies: (1) "When judges decide important cases, they should accept the view of the executive branch." (2) "Government leaders are like the head of a family; we should all follow their decisions." (3) "People with little or no education should have as much say in politics as highly-educated people." (4) "If the government is constantly checked by the legislature, it cannot possibly accomplish great things." The first is an instrument for rule of law. The second is an instrument for paternalistic leadership. The third is an instrument for elitism. And the last is an instrument for political checks and balances. Respondents were offered a 4-point Likert scale of agreement/disagreement to record their responses to the four statements. Theoretically, paternalistic meritocracy (as an ideal way of governance promoted by Confucian political legacies) is expected to highlight the value of paternalistic leadership, justify more political inputs from those with merit (e.g., better education), ensure sufficient discretionary power for virtuous and competent leaders, and prioritize substantive justice over procedural justice.

To maximize the validity of longitudinal comparison, we dichotomized all instruments to highlight the average endorsement of Confucian social and political legacies among the Chinese people. All calculations incorporated appropriate sampling weights to ensure the representativeness of descriptive statistics. Furthermore, to get conservative estimates, all non-responses were coded as zeroes (i.e., indicating rejection of Confucian social and political legacies). Figures 27.1 and 27.2 display the changes in the Chinese people's responses to the seven instruments between 1993 and 2019.

Figure 27.1 (a) illustrates the weighted percentages of the Chinese people believing that "most people can be trusted" in general. As shown in Figure 27.1 (a), between 41 percent and 58 percent of Chinese citizens did report somewhat trust in most people. The gradual decrease from around 58 percent in 2008 to 41 percent in 2015 also witnessed some bounce-back in 2019 at around 52 percent. Thus, despite the ups and downs, it should be fair to argue that there is some longitudinal stability in mainland China's general social trust. In the late 2010s, about half of Chinese citizens believed that "most people can be trusted." This was about the same size as that in the early 1990s. Figures 27.1 (b) and 27.1 (c), on the other hand, suggest a different pattern when the hierarchical orientation toward authority is under examination. As displayed in Figure 27.1 (b), the percentage of Chinese citizens believing in unconditional obedience to parents' demands gradually decreased from around 36 percent in 1993 to around 25 percent in 2019, despite the bump in 2008 at around 48 percent. Similarly, as shown in Figure

27.1 (c), the percentage of Chinese citizens believing in unconditional respect for in-laws also dropped from around 57 percent in 1993 to around 25 percent in 2009, despite the bumps in 2008 and 2011 at around 58 percent. Overall, it should be fair to argue that the Chinese people's endorsement of the hierarchical orientation toward authorities (e.g., parents and in-laws, in particular) has witnessed some significant erosion over the past decades. In the late 2010s, about a quarter of Chinese citizens still endorsed the hierarchical orientation toward authorities. This was about half as much as that in the early 1990s. It seems that Confucian social legacies in mainland China, on average, have witnessed some pushbacks over the past decades. Although general social trust has been maintained at a relatively high level, popular endorsement of the hierarchical orientation toward authority has been seriously challenged and witnessed serious erosion.

Figure 27.1 Evolving Social Norms in Mainland China (1993-2019)

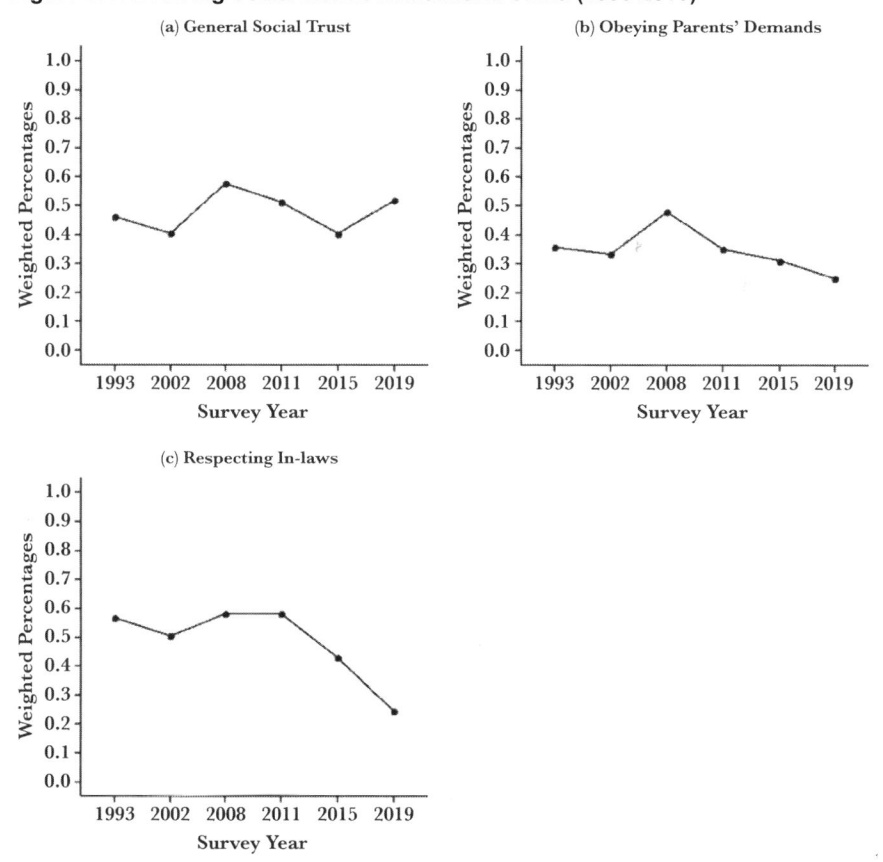

Source: Asian Barometer Survey. Authors prepared.

As discussed in the literature, Confucian political legacies feature the promotion of paternalistic meritocracy as an ideal way of governance. This differs from the liberal democracy model which emphasizes political checks and balances, division of power, election-based political accountability, and procedurally ensured political rights for all citizens. Figure 27.2 shows how Chinese citizens responded to the four instruments tapping related Confucian political legacies. As shown in Figure 27.2 (a), the percentage of the Chinese people believing that judges should consult the executive branch's views when deciding important cases dropped from around 64 percent in 1993 to about 39 percent in 2008; nevertheless, this percentage bounced back afterward and stabilized around 47 percent between 2011 and 2019. As displayed in Figure 27.2 (b), a larger percentage of the Chinese people have embraced paternalistic leadership, despite the ups and downs between 1993 and 2019. In the early 1990s, close to 73 percent believed that paternalistic leaders' decisions should be followed. After a big drop in 2002, this percentage also bounced back and stabilized around 63 percent between 2008 and 2019. Figure 27.2 (c) shows a similar but more dramatic U-curve pattern regarding the Chinese people's endorsement of merit-based political rights. In 1993, close to 67 percent believed that people with better education should have more say in politics. This percentage plummeted to around 7 percent in 2002.[1] Afterward, however, it gradually climbed back to around 19 percent in 2019. Figure 27.2 (d) is the only figure showing a somewhat reversed image, that is, an inverted U-shaped curve. In 1993, around 34 percent of the Chinese people believed that legislative checks could be harmful for the government's operation. After a small drop in 2002 (to around 27 percent), this percentage grew to about 45 percent in 2011 and then dropped back to around 34 percent in 2019. Overall, it should be fair to argue that different from the declining popularity of Confucian social legacies in contemporary China, Confucian political legacies still have a noteworthy popular base in today's China. This is particularly salient, when paternalistic leadership, executive-judiciary relationship, and legislative checks are under examination. Although a much smaller percentage of the Chinese people are willing to allow more say in politics for those with better education, this percentage has witnessed steady growth since the early 2000s. If economic growth indeed has the transformative power of changing societies as suggested by the advocates of modernization theories (Inglehart 2018; Welzel 2013), at least in mainland China, its impact is primarily felt in the social rather than political domains.

Figure 27.2 Evolving Political Ideology in Mainland China (1993-2019)

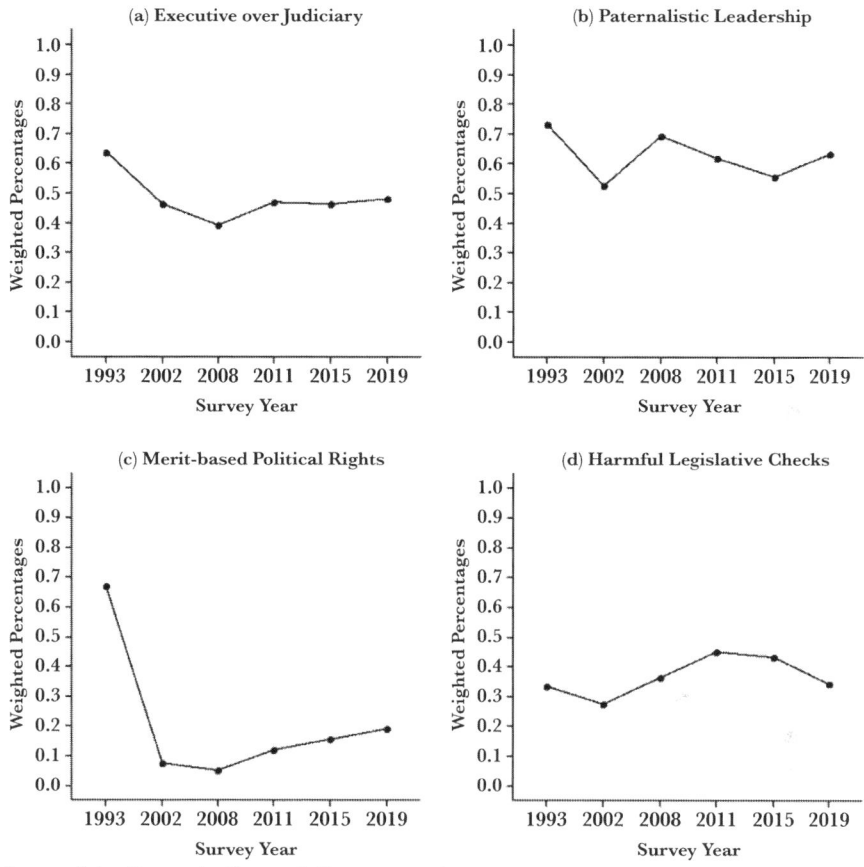

Source: Asian Barometer Survey. Authors prepared.

Conclusion and Suggestions

Thanks to survey researchers' collective and continuous efforts over the past decades, students of Chinese politics have much richer micro-level information to examine various aspects of China's political dynamics. As a pioneer of China's academic survey research, Tianjian Shi initiated the research project focusing on political culture and participation in contemporary China. This research project later joined similar research projects in other Asian societies and has become part of today's Asian Barometer Survey program. Although "TJ" very unfortunately passed away in late 2010, the framework developed by him has guided subsequent ABS mainland China surveys' administration, data collection, empirical tests, and theoretical development.

Using longitudinal information collected via six waves of representative surveys in mainland China, we have reviewed the changes in how Chinese citizens respond to some key Confucian social and political legacies. Overall, significant socioeconomic transformations over the past decades have eroded the population base of Confucian social legacies in mainland China. A clear trend of decreasing embracement of the hierarchical orientation toward authorities (i.e., parents and in-laws in particular) has been documented in the survey data, despite a relatively stable and moderately high level of general social trust. This pattern is compatible with what has been predicted by modernization theories. Nevertheless, a similar trend is not found among the Chinese people's response to Confucian political legacies. Still, a significant percentage of Chinese citizens appreciate paternalistic leadership, believe in the necessity of consulting the executive branch in judicial practice, and see legislative checks as harmful for government operation. Although a much smaller percentage of Chinese citizens are willing to grant more say in politics to better-educated citizens, this percentage has indeed observed dramatic growth since the early 2000s. Without further analysis, it is premature to tell why distinct trends are documented in the respective evolution of Confucian social and political legacies in today's China, despite the transformative forces unleashed by its ongoing economic development over the past decades. Nevertheless, how the Chinese government has been, on the one hand, gradually limiting its presence in socioeconomic domains (especially those closely related to the Chinese people's private concerns) and, on the other hand, reinforcing its dominant role in shaping critical political discourse by mixing beneficial components from both Marxist and Confucian traditions might offer some useful clues here.

Clearly, distinct dynamics might be working in shaping contemporary China's social norms and political ideology. Existing scholarship has highlighted some positive correlations between Confucian social and political legacies in China. However, it seems that, given the pressure from continuous economic modernization as well as the Chinese government increasing emphasis on political propaganda and ideological indoctrination, scholars may have to resort to different theoretical frameworks to effectively understand how the two domains may change, despite some positive feedback in-between. For such tasks, the ABS project has much more to contribute, given the longitudinal and comparative data it has compiled. For us, the best way to honor scholars like "TJ" might be to build a more dynamic theory of political culture and related changes via systematic and industrious empirical exercise.

Note

1. This dramatic drop between 1993 and 2002 might have be driven by the change in the wording of the instrument. The 1993 instrument asked whether agree or disagree that "Highly-educated people should have more say in politics." Since 2002, the wording has been changed to "People with little or no education should have as much say in politics as highly-educated people."

References

Almond, G. A., and S. Verba. 1963. *The Civic Culture: Political Attitudes and Democracy in Five Nations*. NJ: Princeton University Press.

Bell, Daniel A. 2015. *China Model*. Princeton: Princeton University Press.

Campbell, Angus. 1964. *The American Voter: An Abridgement*. New York: Wiley.

Dickson, Bruce. 2016. *The Dictator's Dilemma: The Chinese Communist Party's Strategy for Survival*. Oxford University Press.

Inglehart, Ronald. 2018. *Cultural Evolution: People's Motivations Are Changing, and Reshaping the World*. New York: Cambridge University Press.

Lu, Jie, and Tianjian Shi. 2009. "Political Experience: A Missing Variable in the Study of Political Transformation." *Comparative Politics* 42 (1): 103-120. doi: 10.5 129/001041509X12911362972917.

—. 2015. "The Battle of Ideas and Discourses Before Democratic Transition: Different Democratic Conceptions in Authoritarian China." *International Political Science Review* 36 (1): 20-41. doi: 10.1177/019251211455130.

Shi, Tianjian. 1996. "Survey Research in China." In *Rethinking Rationality*, edited by Michael X. Delli Carpini, Leonie Huddy, and Robert Y Shapiro, 213-250. Greenwich, Conn: JAI Press.

—. 1997. *Political Participation in Beijing*. Cambridge, Mass: Harvard University Press.

—. 1999a. "Village Committee Elections in China: Institutionalist Tactics for Democracy." *World Politics* (JSTOR): 385-412.

—. 1999b. "Voting and Nonvoting in China: Voting Behavior in Plebiscitary and Limited-Choice Elections." *The Journal of Politics* 61 (4): 1115-1139. doi:10.2307/2647556.

—. 2001. "Cultural Values and Political Trust: A Comparison of the People's Republic of China and Taiwan." *Comparative Politics* (JSTOR): 401-419.

—. 2015. *The Cultural Logic of Politics in Mainland China and Taiwan*. New York: Cambridge University Press. doi:10.1017/cbo9780511996474.

Shi, Tianjian, and Jie Lu. 2010. "The Meanings of Democracy: The Shadow of Confucianism." *Journal of Democracy* 21 (4): 123-130. doi:10.1353/jod.2010.0012.

Shin, Doh Chull, To-ch'ŏl Sin, and others. 2012. *Confucianism and democratization in East Asia*. New York: Cambridge University Press.

Welzel, Christian. 2013. *Freedom Rising*. New York: Cambridge University Press.

28 Ideology in Vietnam: Evidence from Asian Barometer Survey Data

Paul Schuler, Mai Truong, and Chris Weber

In this chapter, we explore the structure of ideology in Vietnam. We also explore the explanatory antecedents of ideology in Vietnam. Ideology—the latent structure underlying social and political belief—is primarily studied in democracies to determine political preferences and polarization. Using new Asian Barometer Survey data, we extend this analysis to explore the structure of ideology in Vietnam, a country with a single-party system. Our results show that there are systematic groupings of preferences in Vietnam. The configuration of preferences is multidimensional, and the latent traits of these dimensions are positively correlated. We also find that party closeness consistently predicts support for authoritarian policies, nationalism, and redistribution. Perhaps counterintuitively, we find little difference between north and south Vietnam, with actually a slight preference for authoritarian policies in the south.

Ideology—the mechanism by which political and social beliefs are often constructed—has been heavily studied in western democracies. Comparatively less is known about ideology in single-party systems, such as Vietnam. How is ideology configured in Vietnam? What explains variation in ideological belief in Vietnam? How do party membership, gender, ethnicity, and regional identity affect the structure of political ideology in Vietnam? Students of democracies have long focused on how ideology structures vote choice (Campbell et al. 1960; Ansolabehere, Rodden, and Snyder Jr. 2008), and conversely, how party elites may structure ideology (Nicholson 2012; Carmines and Stimson 2020). The attention on ideology, by which we mean a system or structure of beliefs, is warranted as it plays an important role in shaping political policy decisions and the ability of elites to shape public opinion.

While ideology and its consequences are well documented in western democracies, there is comparatively less empirical research on ideology in autocracies. Emerging research suggests that the ideological configuration of the autocracy may have lasting effects on electoral politics long after any democratic transition (Pop-Eleches and Tucker 2019; Dinas and Northmore-Ball 2019).

Perhaps more importantly, ideology may play a role in the ability of democracy advocates to build a coalition capable of challenging autocracies.

For these reasons, it is important to understand the structure of ideological belief in Vietnam. The country is also unique and important to understand for a variety of additional reasons. The country has a unique history, considering several hundred years of French colonialism, Chinese expansionism, and a historic division emerging in the North and South. Due to the different historical trajectories from pre-colonial Vietnamese through the division between North and South Vietnam from 1954-1975, scholars have suggested the south has a more market-based, trade-based economy (Gainsborough 2003; Sanders 2014). They also have different experiences with Confucian norms and authoritarian institutions, which may lead to greater resistance to autocracy in the south and greater acceptance of autocracy in the north (Taylor 2013, 964). Attitudes toward China may also vary across the country, with the north seen as more open to Chinese influence and the south more resistant (Taylor 2013).

If this is the case, this has important implications for patterns of resistance to the Communist Party in Vietnam. The Communist Party did have difficulty imposing central planning in the south from 1975 after unification until it largely abandoned central planning in 1986 (Fforde and de Vylder 1996). To what extent was this difficulty a function of entrenched ideological differences in the south? To what extent do those ideological differences—if ever present—persist? In addition to the north-south identity, another potential cleavage within Vietnam, which likely affects ideology is between the lowland regions and the highland regions, where most of Vietnam's contemporary ethnic minorities live (Goscha 2016). The differences between the lowland Viets or Kinh and the highland minority groups have received substantial attention by a wide range of scholars [e.g. Hickey (1982); Turner, Bonnin, and Michaud (2015)]. Thus, it is important to see if ideology varies between Kinh and minority groups.

While these characterizations are widely asserted in research on Vietnam, they are seldom assessed with empirical data. Furthermore, existing research on ideology from authoritarian rule suggests that ideology is weakly constrained. For example, Pan and Xu (2018) in China find that while ideology exists in China, it is much more weakly constrained than in democracies. Others find similar dynamics (Wu and Meng 2017). One important reason why ideology may be less constrained under authoritarian rule is that the lack of an opposition party means that elites provide less structure for citizen beliefs. This may be particularly true as authoritarian parties themselves become less ideological, as has been the case in China and Vietnam as they shed their extreme left-wing, centrally planned economies.

Using the Asian Barometer Survey data, we examine the structure of ideology in Vietnam. We analyze seventeen items by exploring the latent structure of ideology. We rely heavily on two techniques—exploratory factor analysis (EFA) and confirmatory factor analysis (CFA). EFA is used to examine how many dimensions are contained in the data, while CFA is used to determine how well certain factors explain the data. Thus, our primary interest is that of measurement: How effectively can variation on these items be explained by one or several underlying factors? We find that the structure of ideology in Vietnam is aligned across three conceptual dimensions—authoritarian policy, nationalism, and redistribution. After we elaborate on these dimensions, we then examine the variables that explain variation on these factors.

Asian Barometer Survey Data

The Asian Barometer provides a unique opportunity to explore the structure of ideology in Vietnam. In particular, we are able to explore the dimensionality underlying Vietnamese ideology. Perhaps beliefs can be arrayed on a single left-right continuum, a characteristic of ideology in western democracies. Or, perhaps ideology is multifaceted, with separate correlated components.

To assess the existence of possible ideological cleavages, we collect a range of questions from the ABS survey that align on possible ideological dimensions found in China. These include respondents' beliefs and attitudes about: (1) redistribution; (2) nationalism; (3) globalization; (4) authoritarian policies. We choose these issue areas because they have been examined in other authoritarian regimes, such as China (Pan and Xu 2018).

Redistribution was measured with four items. Respondents were asked beliefs about income equality, universal access to housing, medicine and food. Nationalism was also assessed with four questions: feelings toward the national anthem, how proud they feel being Vietnamese, how important it is to be Vietnamese, and how well the word Vietnamese describes them. Globalization was measured based on the extent to which they agree that "Vietnam should defend our way of life and should limit the imports of foreign goods to protect our farmers and workers."

Finally, authoritarian policy preferences were approximated using seven questions: (1) whether government should consult religious authorities when interpreting the laws; (2) whether people with little or no education should have as much say in politics as highly-educated people; (3) whether we should all follow the decisions of government officials who are like the head of a family; (4) whether the government should decide whether certain ideas should be allowed to be discussed in society; (5) whether harmony of the community will be disrupted if people organize lots of groups; (6) whether when judges should accept the view of the executive branch when deciding important cases; (7) whether the government can possibly accomplish great things if it is constantly checked (i.e. monitored and supervised) by the legislature. Table 28.1 provides descriptive statistics of all these items.

Table 28.1 Descriptive Statistics of Items Used to Construct Latent Traits of Ideology in Vietnam

Variables/Items	N	Mean	SD	Min	Max
Redistribution					
Income	1157	2.80	0.82	1	4
Housing	1167	2.92	0.82	1	4
Medicine	1187	3.19	0.81	1	4
Food	1179	3.11	0.80	1	4
Nationalism					
Anthem	1183	3.55	0.60	1	4
Pride	1179	3.48	0.55	1	4
Identity	1179	3.42	0.62		
Descriptive	1193	3.63	0.59	1	4
Globalization					
Our Way	1155	1.76	0.43	1	2
Protect Farmers	1141	1.63	0.48	1	2
Authoritarian Policy					
Consult Authority	1098	2.68	0.82	1	4
Elitism	1129	3.10	0.78	1	4
Family	1132	2.54	0.87	1	4
Speech	1104	2.98	0.73	1	4
Harmony	1120	2.99	0.83	1	4
Executive	1053	2.98	0.66	1	4
Oversight	1046	2.67	0.82	1	4

Source: Asian Barometer Survey. Authors prepared.

The Structure of Political Ideology in Vietnam

We start by exploring the dimensional structure underlying these data. We do this by using exploratory factor analysis, which does not require the researcher to define the number of dimensions or how the questions load onto a particular dimension. In particular, we present the "scree plot" in Figure 28.1. The plot shows the eigenvalues of the true data, which is a measure of how much variation of the data is explained by a given factor, as well as the eigenvalues of synthetic data. One generally prefers a dimensional structure with eigenvalues greater than one and where the true eigenvalues exceed the synthetic eigenvalues; in this case, a rough approximation is that four factors should provide a reasonably good fit-to-data. Inspection of the data revealed a dimension reasonably labeled "preference for economic redistribution." A second dimension could be approximated as a nationalist orientation, a third a preference for authoritarian governing arrangements, and a fourth represented by one's globalist orientation. This suggests that a four-dimensional structure fits the data.

While useful, the EFA does not allow us to estimate the relationship between latent factors and independent variables. Therefore, the CFA is an important extension. First, we can impose restrictions on the factor structure and explore how well such a model does replicating the original dataset. Second, CFA has a natural extension to Structural Equation Modeling (SEM), which we use here to explore the relationship between a set of latent factors and a set of respondent level independent variables, such as age or region (Kaplan 2008).

Figure 28.1 Parallel Factor Analysis

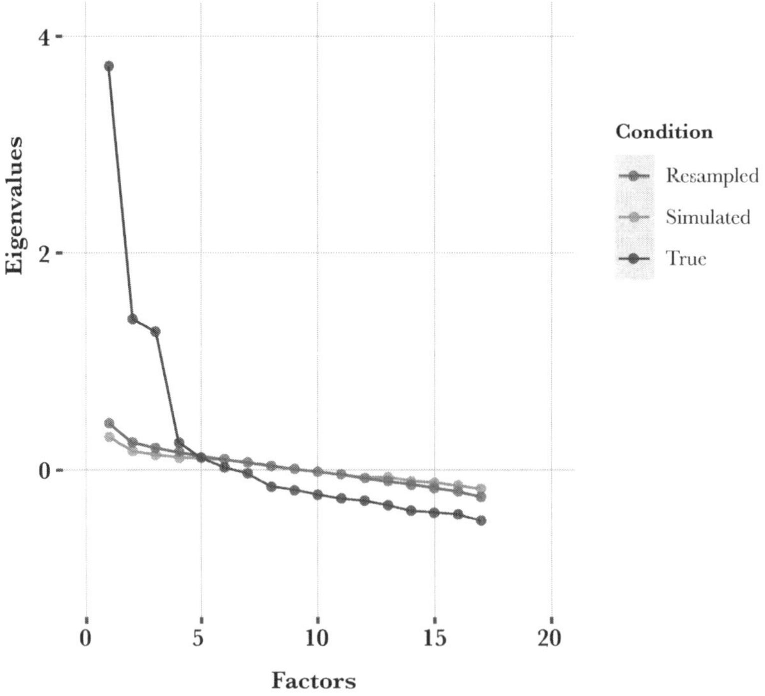

Source: Authors prepared.

Unfortunately, the globalization factor poses an insurmountable problem for the CFA: Barring several strong assumptions, we cannot reasonably estimate factor models when a factor is defined by only two items. However, as Figure 28.1 shows, the globalization factor explains the least variation. Thus, in subsequent CFA we incorporate the globalization questions into the nationalism factor.

Estimating a three-factor model using Lavaan in R (Rosseel 2012), the three-factor model provided an excellent fit-to-data (CFI = 0.98, TLI = 0.98, RMSEA = 0.04). We present this model in Table 28.2. What is also noteworthy in this model is that the factors are somewhat strongly correlated. For instance, the redistribution and nationalism factors are correlated ($r = 0.38$). The redistribution and authoritarian policy factors are also strongly correlated ($r = 0.31$) as are the nationalism and authoritarian policy factors ($r = 0.29$). While these factors are empirically unique, they are not unrelated.

Table 28.2 Confirmatory Factor Analysis of ABS Data

	Redistribution	Nationalism	Authoritarian Policy
Income	1.00	--	--
Housing	1.24	--	--
Medicine	1.21	--	--
Food	1.16	--	--
Anthem	--	1.00	--
Pride	--	1.05	--
Identity	--	1.07	--
Descriptive	--	0.97	--
Our Way	--	0.58	--
Protect Farmers	--	0.30	--
Consult Authority	--		1.00
Elitism	--		0.93
Family	--		1.22
Speech	--		1.19
Harmony	--		1.00
Executive	--		1.34
Oversight	--		1.11
Model Fit			
CFI	0.98		
TLI	0.98		
RMSEA	0.04		
N	1200		

Source: Authors prepared.

The high positive correlation among these latent factors reveals an interesting pattern about the structure of ideology in Vietnam. Specifically, respondents who support redistribution are more likely to support authoritarian policies and more likely to be nationalistic. Those who support authoritarian policies are more likely to score high on nationalism. Given that Vietnam is a single-party regime where the CPV has the power to impose its preferred policies and its definition of nationalism, the relationships among these latent factors make sense. In sum, through CFA, we find systematic groupings of preferences in Vietnam and these latent factors are significantly correlated.

What Explains Variation in Ideology in Vietnam?

Next, we examine whether demographic characteristics affect ideology in Vietnam. In other words, does ideology vary across some demographic variables? We focus on five covariates which may affect ideology in the context of Vietnam, including party membership, gender, age, ethnicity, and whether a respondent lives in the north or the south.

We use these variables for several reasons. In a single-party regime, one's relationship with and attitudes toward the party should impact one's views toward policies and political issues. Party is a three-category variable where high scores denote closeness to the Communist Party. Age may be an important characteristic as well. It is plausible that older generations who had more experiences with the command economy may have different beliefs, compared to those born and raised after Vietnam liberalized its economy. Age is a continuous variable.

As discussed earlier, while Vietnam is a relatively homogenous country, scholars have theorized differences between Kinh people and other ethnic minority groups. Regarding the impact of ethnicity, we create a dummy variable in which "1" is coded when a respondent comes from an ethnic minority group and "0" otherwise. The final demographic characteristic of interest is region. We focus on whether a respondent comes from the north or the south. As we mentioned earlier, given the past divides between the two regions throughout the history of Vietnam, this regional characteristic may influence respondents' beliefs and attitudes. Gender is also a binary variable with female respondents coded as "1," and male as "0."

We proceed by regressing each of the latent factors on the aforementioned demographic characteristics. High scores on the latent variable mean higher preference for authoritarian policies and redistribution, and higher nationalistic attitude.

Table 28.3 Regression of Factors on Covariates

	Authoritarian Policy	Nationalism	Redistribution
Party	**0.134**	**0.48**	**0.21**
	(0.03)	**(0.04)**	**(0.03)**
Sex	0.001	**0.12**	-0.02
	(0.04)	**(0.06)**	(0.05)
Age	0.003	**-0.006**	-0.00
	(0.002)	**(0.003)**	(0.002)
Minority	0.05	-0.15	-0.19
	(0.09)	(0.16)	(0.13)
South	**0.14**	**0.23**	0.001
	(0.04)	**(0.06)**	(0.005)

Note: High scores denote agreement with these items. Entries in bold are two times the standard error and statistically significant at the $p<0.05$ level.

Table 28.3 shows the results. It reveals a very interesting pattern regarding closeness to the party. Party closeness consistently predicts beliefs and attitudes toward authoritarian policies, nationalism, and redistribution. Compared to those who do not report closeness to the Communist Party, respondents who do are more likely to support authoritarian policies and redistribution and are more likely to feel nationalistic. Although the survey does not directly ask about party membership, those who say they are close to the party may think positively of or be directly co-opted by the party. Thus, those respondents may generally agree with the party's policies and guidance.

Regarding the other covariates, there is not a consistent relationship between respondents' gender and their ideology. Gender is not significantly correlated with nationalism and preference for redistribution. However, we find there are differences in terms of preference for authoritarian policies between men and women. Compared to male respondents, female respondents are more likely to support authoritarian policies.

Surprisingly, given the supposed differences between ethnic Kinh people and ethnic minority groups, the results show no differences in terms of attitudes toward redistribution, nationalism, and authoritarian policies. Compared to the Kinh, those coming from an ethnic minority group do not feel more or less supportive of redistribution and authoritarian policies. They are also not more or less proud of being Vietnamese.

With regard to region, residence in the north or the south does not significantly correlate with ideology. Contrary to existing theories, southern attitudes toward redistribution are not significantly different from that of northern respondents.

Additionally, and more surprisingly, respondents in the south are more supportive of authoritarian policies. Finally, perhaps more consistent with existing work on anti-Chinese sentiment, southern respondents seem to express higher nationalism than their counterparts in the north. However, here it is worth noting that respondents generally express high nationalism across the country; it is just relatively higher in the south. As Table 28.1 shows, the means for each of the four items that construct the nationalism latent factor are all above 3.0. On a scale of 4, this suggests that respondents are generally nationalistic. Thus, this finding does not mean that northern respondents are not nationalistic, while their southern counterparts are.

Finally, age does not have a consistent relationship with these four latent factors. There are no differences in terms of preference for authoritarian policy and redistribution between respondents of different ages. However, it seems that older respondents are less nationalistic. One-year increase in age leads to a 0.006-point decrease in nationalism score.

In sum, this section finds that party closeness consistently predicts respondents' preference for authoritarian policy, nationalism, and redistribution. Because other demographic variables do not have any significant relationship with any of the latent factors or only are correlated with one of the factors, it is hard to conclude whether ideology varies across these variables.

Conclusion

This chapter suggests that despite being a single-party regime, there exists systematic groupings of preferences in Vietnam, revolving around attitudes toward authoritarian policy, redistribution, and nationalism. The configuration of preferences is multidimensional, and the latent traits of these dimensions are positively correlated. Those who prefer redistribution are more likely to support authoritarian policy and are more nationalistic. We also find that party closeness consistently predicts authoritarian policy, redistribution, and nationalism. Very interestingly, despite the long debate on the differences between the north and the south, and between ethnic minority groups and the ethnic Kinh people, these factors do not have consistently significant relationships with the four latent traits.

References

Ansolabehere, Stephen, Jonathan Rodden, and James M. Snyder Jr. 2008. "The Strength of Issues: Using Multiple Measures to Gauge Preference Stability, Ideological Constraint, and Issue Voting." *American Political Science Review* 102 (2): 215-232. doi:10.2307/27644512.

Campbell, Angus, Philip E. Converse, Warren E. Miller, and Donald E. Stokes. 1960. *The American Voter*. New York: John Wiley.

Carmines, Edward G., and James A. Stimson. 2020. *Issue Evolution: Race and the Transformation of American Politics*. Princeton: Princeton University Press.

Dinas, Elias, and Ksenia Northmore-Ball. 2019. "The Ideological Shadow of Authoritarianism." *Comparative Political Studies* 53 (12): 1957-1991. doi:10.1177/0010414019852699.

Fforde, Adam, and Stefan de Vylder. 1996. *From Plan to Market: The Economic Transition in Vietnam*. New York: Westview Press.

Gainsborough, Martin. 2003. *Changing Political Economy of Vietnam: The Case of Ho Chi Minh City*. London: Routledge.

Goscha, Christopher. 2016. *Vietnam: A New History*. New York: Basic Books.

Hickey, Gerald. 1982. *Free in the Forest: Ethnohistory of the Vietnamese Central Highlands, 1954-1976*. New Haven: Yale University Press.

Kaplan, David. 2008. *Structural Equation Modelling: Foundations and Extensions*. London: Sage.

Nicholson, Stephen P. 2012. "Polarizing Cues." *American Journal of Political Science* 56 (1): 52-66. doi:10.1111/j.1540-5907.2011.00541.x.

Pan, Jennifer, and Yiqing Xu. 2018. "China's Ideological Spectrum." *The Journal of Politics* 80 (1): 254-273. doi:10.1086/694255.

Pop-Eleches, Grigore, and Joshua A. Tucker. 2019. "Communist Legacies and Left-Authoritarianism." *Comparative Political Studies* 53 (12): 1861-1889. doi:10.1177/0010414019879954.

Rosseel, Yves. 2012. "Lavaan: An R Package for Structural Equation Modeling and More. Version 0.5-12 (BETA)." *Journal of Statistical Software* 48 (2): 1-36. doi: 10.18637/jss.v048.i02.

Sanders, Scott R. 2014. "North Versus South: The Effects of Foreign Direct Investment and Historical Legacies on Poverty Reduction in Post-Đổi Mới Vietnam." *Journal of Vietnamese Studies* 9 (2): 46-67. doi:10.1525/vs.2014.9.2.46.

Taylor, K. W. 2013. *A History of the Vietnamese*. New York: Cambridge University Press. doi:10.1017/cbo9781139021210.

Turner, Sarah, Christine Bonnin, and Jean Michaud. 2015. *Frontier Livelihoods: Hmong in the Sino-Vietnamese Borderlands*. Seattle: University of Washington Press.

Wu, Jason Yuyan, and Tianguang Meng. 2017. "The Nature of Ideology in Urban China." *21st Century China Center Research Paper No. 2017-08*. doi:10.2139/ssrn.3038790.

Index